SIXTY VOICES

CHELTENHAM

Jill Esmond

Sixty Voices

CELEBRITIES RECALL THE GOLDEN AGE OF BRITISH CINEMA

Edited by
BRIAN McFARLANE

BFI PUBLISHING
with the assistance of
MONASH UNIVERSITY, MELBOURNE

First published in 1992 by the
British Film Institute
21 Stephen Street
London W1P 1PL

British Library Cataloguing in Publication Data

McFarlane, Brian
  Sixty Voices
  I. Title
  791.43092

ISBN 0-85170-353-4
      0-85170-349-6 pbk

Designed by Geoff Wiggins

Set in Bodoni by Fakenham Photosetting Ltd, Norfolk
Printed in Great Britain by
St Edmundsbury Press, Bury St Edmunds

*This book is dedicated to the interviewees
and to the memory of Jill Esmond*

Contents

Foreword

It is a long time since *The Lady Vanishes* was made at Islington Studios in north London – and Bundaberg, a town two-hundred miles north of Brisbane on the Queensland coast, where I am at the moment touring in a play with my husband, John McCallum, is a long way from Islington. In fact, thirteen thousand miles away – and *The Lady Vanishes* was made fifty-three years ago. But such is the long arm of television that the making of the film was all brought back to me a few nights ago when it was shown on local television. And such are the tricks of memory that many incidents, which happened during the shooting of the film, came back clearer to me than events of a few months ago.

Alfred Hitchcock – not an easy director to work with – was considered a very *avant-garde* film-maker at that time, but I don't think even he visualised the twenty-year golden period of British films which lay ahead, and of which *The Lady Vanishes* was a forerunner, or that it would still be shown in fifty-three years time and to such a wide public – one of television's few pluses against its many minuses vis-a-vis the film industry.

I count myself very lucky to have been part of this golden period of British films, 1940-60, which Dr McFarlane has brought to life in this book through his diligent and caring research and perceptive interviewing. How extraordinary it was that when Britain was fighting desperately for existence, a film industry was being forged which very nearly overtook Hollywood for world supremacy. But, of course, it was because of the war that creative people in Britain made films which were truer to life and with a new realism to which people all over the world could respond, and which they found preferable to the chocolate-box confections of Hollywood.

It is a sad sequence, really, that Hollywood, since the 60s, with its resources and expertise, has been better able to combat televison and has easily regained supremacy. Is it too much to hope that British cinema may even yet find its voice again?

Googie Withers

Introduction

Growing up in rural Victoria, Australia, in the late 1940s, I came to think of British films as exotic. While American films would all turn up in time, the number of British films was small indeed. This was surprising in view of the then close ties between Britain and Australia. However, the films that did filter through (usually several years later) made indelible impressions. Very early recollections include Rosamund John ministering in the garden to the dying Leslie Howard at the end of *The First of the Few*; Alfred Drayton's bullet head in Jeffrey Dell's charming comedy, *Don't Take it to Heart*; Lance Comfort's *Great Day*, which still seems an unusually abrasive picture of village life; and a few obvious box-office hits like *The Third Man* and *The Red Shoes*.

There was not much else, except what one saw on visits to Melbourne, where two (and later three) city cinemas showed nothing *but* British films to substantial minority audiences. There was always a sense of a cinema, other than Hollywood's, which, frustratingly, suggested riches beyond one's grasp. With the hindsight of forty years, one realises that this was, indeed, the key period of British cinema and that one was right to be frustrated at not seeing more of it.

Those audiences – perhaps largely middle-class – who flocked to the cinemas that were screening British films saw, or believed they saw, representations of life more like their own. At this time, there was no educated awareness of the excellence of Hollywood cinema with its virtues of energy, skilful manipulation of melodramatic narrative models, and its classlessness. Hollywood was all too often equated with vulgarity and artificiality, whereas British films were thought of as 'restrained', 'natural', 'realistic'.

The audiences that patronised British films no doubt appreciated their literary qualities (they were often, of course, based on literary classics, which they tended to treat with more respect than was the case in Hollywood); their low key depiction of wartime exploits (reflecting often the influence of the British documentary movement) chimed with the Australian regard for Britain's conduct of and during the war; the comedies, especially the Ealing products and such hits as *Genevieve* and *Doctor in the House*, had instant appeal, sometimes well beyond the exclusively 'British' cinemas.

This book really grew out of another in which I was exploring the parallels that existed between the new Australian cinema of the 1970s and 80s and British cinema of the 1940s and 50s, as two examples of English-speaking countries seeking to establish an identity of their own in the face of American dominance of their screens. As part of my research for this earlier project, I interviewed about thirty practitioners of British cinema in what seemed to me its key period - that is, its period of greatest prestige and productivity. The aim was to find out how those involved in the period perceived it.

In the process, I found I was being given much more information than I could use in that project, information which I felt should have a wider currency. It seemed to me that, with the unfailingly helpful and courteous co-operation of the interviewees, I was piecing together a kind of history of British cinema in those decades. And so the present book took shape and the number of interviews doubled.

History of the cinema is not simply a matter of legislation, or studios, or box-office performance, or of any other factually ascertainable set of statistics. The reminiscences and personal experiences of individual participants in creating the body of work we think of as British cinema in the 40s and 50s very often throw a new light on it. Succeeding critical waves enshrine this or that film-maker, but the essentially collaborative aspect of film production suggests that there may also be more to find out about how certain films came to be as they are. We are not talking about hard evidence here, but about the perceptions of those involved. These can provide a history at least as revealing as the standard reference works. One speaks, for instance, with careless *auteur-ism* of David Lean's *Great Expectations*; as one listens to/reads Ronald Neame, Valerie Hobson, Anthony Havelock-Allan, John Mills, Alec Guinness, Kay Walsh and Bernard Miles, it becomes clear just how complexly collaborative screen art is. Further, different people involved in the same enterprise frequently have, if not contradictory at least non-parallel, sometimes complementary views on the making of a famous film.

More than half the interviews in this book are with actors. If this seems disproportionate, it should be borne in mind that, first, they are much more numerous than the other collaborators; second, they have been largely responsible for attracting public attention to what is essentially a popular art; and, third, they throw some very interesting light on why British cinema was as it was – in relation, for instance, to such key matters as the British stage-screen connection. Unsurprisingly, one tends to get a more 'global' view of the process of film-making and of the British film industry from producers and directors, their perceptions sometimes meshing revealingly with those of the actors.

This particular period – from, roughly, 1940-60,

reaching a peak of prestige perhaps in the mid-to-late 40s – has been chosen because it exemplifies so many of the preoccupations and strengths of British cinema. During this period British cinema came nearer to asserting a national identity than at any other, an identity that mixes the literary with the realist, the whimsical with the more broadly comic, the stylish with the (often undervalued) melodramatic. No other period seems as richly varied, as productive, or as intensely British. The latter, it must be said, embraces weaknesses as well as strengths: the inherently class-bound attitudes, the sometimes over-decorous treatment of literary and theatrical sources, an inhibiting gentility, *as well as* clear, unmannered story-telling, an often moving restraint in emotional matters, and a capacity for finding comedy in many unlikely aspects of the national life.

The following interviews represent the tip of an iceberg: they are the result of editing over 120 hours of tape. The interviewees have given their approval of what is published – and, indeed, of a good deal for which, sadly, there was not room on this occasion. Each was sent a transcript of the interview and made whatever additions or deletions were felt to be necessary. One interviewee worked on the principle of 'I'll cut out anything nasty I've said about other people – unless it's true!'

Thanks are due to many people. Above all, of course, I am grateful to the owners of the 'voices' who gave so generously of their time and recollections, either in person or, in a few cases, by telephone or letter.

I also want to thank Lindsay Anderson, one of the most discerning critics of the 1940s and 50s and a key film-maker of the following decade. He not only shared his often trenchant, always stimulating, views of the period's films, but also helped me to make contact with several of the interviewees and even conducted one of the interviews for me, using my questions, when I had had to leave England before being able to meet the actor concerned.

I also thank documentary film-maker Stephen Peet for putting me in touch with several interviewees, and the producer-agent-writer Richard Gregson, who gave me much valuable information as did the following: film critics Phillip French (of *The Observer*), Geoff Brown (of *The Times*), Tim Pulleine (of *The Guardian*); author and critic Charles Barr; and Clyde Jeavons, Curator of the National Film Archive, and David Meeker, Feature Films Acquisitions Officer, both of the British Film Institute, London. As an Australian, I found the overview of British cinema that these people gave me enormously helpful. I am very grateful, too, for the editorial assistance of Christine Gledhill and Edward Buscombe of the British Film Institute.

The daunting work of typing up the interviews from the tapes was done by Sam Oliphant, Sophie McFarlane, Toula Zarris, Jennifer Trigger and Cheryl Yewers, and I thank them for their patience and efficiency.

This whole project has been an enormous pleasure to me. Indeed, it has become a labour of love, but it might not have seen the light of day in its present form without the support of two institutions. First, the British Film Institute has been an enthusiastic and helpful publisher; and, second, funds made available by Monash University, Melbourne, Australia, not only assisted with the expenses of research but also contributed to the publication. This enabled a substantially fuller record of the interviews than would otherwise have been possible. To both these institutions I gratefully acknowledge my indebtedness and thanks.

Finally, I thank my wife Geraldine for her patience, support and help throughout all stages of this project.

Brian McFarlane
Melbourne, August 1992

The Mark of Cain* (1947), The Romantic Age, Elizabeth of Ladymead (1940), The Franchise Affair (1950), Out of True, Life in Her Hands, White Corridors (1951), The Brave Don't Cry (1952), The Kidnappers, Johnny on the Run (1953), The Dark Stairway, Lease of Life (1954), The Secret Tent, A Town Like Alice (1956), Heart of a Child, Robbery Under Arms, Lucky Jim, The Barretts of Wimpole Street (1957), Solomon and Sheba, SOS Pacific (1959), Spare the Rod (1961), The Inspector, The Waltz of the Toreadors (1962), The Silent Playground, The Three Lives of Thomasina (1963), Half a Sixpence (1967), Country Dance, Run a Crooked Mile (1969), The Night Digger (1971), The Lady Vanishes (1979).
* Scenes deleted from final print.

One of the incontestable strengths of British cinema in the 1940s and 50s was the range of character players who could be counted on to stamp their scenes with authority in even the most anodyne enterprises. Jean Anderson, tall, eloquent of face and voice, has an honourable place among their ranks. She is in fact such a striking presence, especially in the films she made for Philip Leacock and Jack Lee, that it comes as a surprise to find she has not made as many films as one had supposed. Usually cast in austerely kindly roles, most notably in *The Kidnappers*, her own favourite, Jean Anderson has a quality of stillness that compels attention. Very adept at sympathetic professionals, she could nevertheless be convincingly sinister (as in the dire remake of *The Lady Vanishes*), or bossy (as the parishioner in *Lease of Life*), and, at least once, in *Lucky Jim*, she showed a fine flair for comedy.

Interview date: June 1990.

When you came to feature films in the late 40s, after being on the stage since 1929, did you have to make many adjustments in technique?

I learnt technique through working in documentaries for the Ministry of Information during the war, under excellent directors like Phil Leacock. It's a matter of learning not to project to an audience, and of being more relaxed, with less facial expression. You learn that in close-up your *eyes* can tell it.

That work later led to my being in four films for Phil, one of which was *Out of True*, England's answer to *The Snake Pit*. I enjoyed that film enormously. Then there was *Life in Her Hands*, in which I had to go through the entire process of teaching Kathleen Byron what a nurse did when a baby was being born! Then I had a small part in *The Brave Don't Cry*, about a Scottish mining disaster; the actors were almost all Glasgow citizens and, of course, I have a Scottish background. It was through that small part that I got *The Kidnappers* which was the most marvellous part for me, without a surplus word of dialogue. I can still watch that film and *A Town Like Alice* and forget it's me up there.

Those films established a certain image of you as the wise, understanding, if somewhat astringent type. Is it good for an actress to have an image?

I think so; I've been very lucky in that way. Some producers see me as a warm sympathetic character and some see me as very dominating. Probably my biggest success, as far as the public goes, was a television series called *The Brothers* in which I played a pretty dominating matriarch. My mail at the time was pretty equally divided between those who thought she was a wonderful woman whose wretched boys didn't understand her, and others who thought she was 'just like my mother-in-law'!

You worked with several veteran Hollywood directors . . .

Yes, I liked King Vidor enormously, but he couldn't cope with [Gina] Lollobrigida in *Solomon and Sheba*; he would argue very nicely with her, but she made her own rules and he had no luck at all. If you were taller than she, you must not be level with her; and she always liked walking into close-up at the end of a scene so that I, even as her friend, must never have an arm left in frame for her close-up! It was a very unhappy film; there was a dreadful hiatus after Tyrone Power died and before we got Yul Brynner. Tyrone was so loved by everyone. King Vidor was a great director.

George Sidney, was really the wrong director for Tommy Steele, who had been playing his *Half A Sixpence* role in the theatre for quite a few years. It was difficult for him to cut it down for film, and he got no help at all from George Sidney who was really only interested in building up the dance routines.

Then there was Sidney Franklin, who made both the original and the remake of *The Barretts of Wimpole Street*. I never thought I would get that part. It was played originally by tiny Una O'Connor, who used to go about as if she was on roller skates, which got big laughs. I went to the interview expecting so much *not* to get the part that I was completely relaxed and laughing. I even said, 'I'm not going to do that business of pretending I'm on roller skates!' and Sidney Franklin assured me that was all right. But it was not a happy film. I had always thought of Jennifer Jones as being what I call an '*actress* star'; but when we came to work, however, she

Vincent Winter, Adrienne Corri, Jon Whiteley and Jean Anderson in *The Kidnappers*, 1953

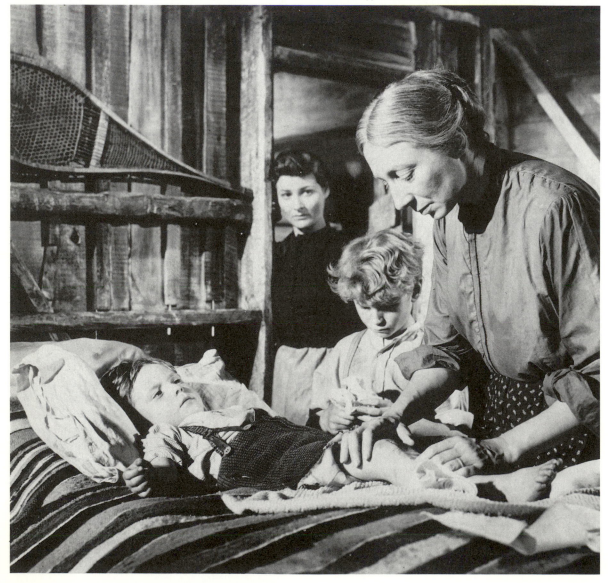

needed to be told every thought that went through her head. She was terribly 'starry' and nervous. I played Wilson, her companion, and to her I was just a piece of furniture. She never spoke to me, but Virginia McKenna [Henrietta] was lovely. I made two films with Virginia and she is a wonderful actress.

How did you feel about the wholesale importation of American actors into British films in the 50s?

I was always rather thrilled to play with them because, in those days, we thought Hollywood was 'it'. When we were making *The Kidnappers* at Pinewood, there was a big American-financed film also being made, called *The Million Pound Note* with Gregory Peck. That was one of my high spots because I had the dressing room next to him and used to see him lying on his chaise longue with his guitar. There we were on *The Kidnappers*, a tiny budget film with that wonderful Scottish actor Duncan McCrae, the two children, Adrienne Corri and myself, and *The Million Pound Note* had every star in London playing small parts. The irony was that our film was a big success and *The Million Pound Note* wasn't.

Did you enjoy working at Ealing on *Lease of Life* with Robert Donat?

I was thrilled to be in one of the last Ealing films. I had worked with Robert in the theatre in the 30s, at the famous Festival Theatre, Cambridge, but I hadn't seen much of him since then. When we were working on *Lease of Life*, he was a very sick man. You would be asked be asked to rehearse a scene with him in his car, and we would do a few lines and then he would have a coughing fit. He would apologise and we would try again later. The funny thing about that film was that, as a very 'county' lady, I had a dog; then they said, 'We've decided you're not going to have the dog but we're giving you Edie Martin instead'. She was about five-feet-nothing and we did look very funny with her always sort of peering up at me!

Do you remember *The Mark of Cain*, your very first film?

I can remember having to take Sally Gray in charge as a wardress and going through her bag. She was supposed to have murdered her husband. I was excited at my first film coming on in the West End and the posters going up; there was my photograph, even for this tiny part, so I went to see the film and my scene had been cut! But I do remember Brian Desmond Hurst who directed it; he was a great character.

Do you remember working with Herbert Wilcox and Anna Neagle?

Yes, they were extremely nice and courteous to work with. That was the first time I ever had a stand-in. I was playing a very 'refeened' lady help. My very first line, when I was handing out the plates and things, was after Anna asked what time would I be going. I had to reply, 'I have a slow puncture in my front' – it brought the house down.

And do you recall working with Pat Jackson in *White Corridors*?

Yes, I loved it. I think I had worked with him earlier in documentaries. I played the casualty sister in that, a good little part. I saw the film again recently and thought how good it was; it has such reality about it. Pat was a very good director and such a nice man.

Unlike most British war films, *A Town Like Alice* concentrates more on women than men. Was it a happy experience?

Oh, yes, very Renee Houston hated being made to look awful in it, but I thought she was wonderful. For three days we were wading in a stagnant lake in Burnham Beeches, carrying heavy stretchers with babies and about six heavy rifles on them. We were in bare feet in water. They did long tracking shots with the camera, very difficult shots to get, and it took ages to do them. It was very cold and they had a bottle of rum for us, to bring the circulation back occasionally. Marie Lohr fell, poor thing. She was very old and so was Nora Nicholson; I was the youngest of that lot.

Once, there was a very heavy white frost and Nora had to kneel down in this frost and say the Lord's Prayer, even though she was an old lady then. Of course, we were in rags, with bare arms, legs and feet. Another night the cold was so awful, and all the extras playing Australian soldiers were lined up to watch the scene in which Peter Finch gets crucified. (I loved working with him by the way.) As we women walked past this line of extras you could hear their teeth rattling. They had to stand close together to prop each other up, so as not to show how much they were shaking. But we all survived it, and I maintain that all that discomfort helped the film. Once, I recall, they sprayed us, in freezing weather, with ice-cold glycerine for sweat!

At about this time you were also in *Lucky Jim*. It seems to have been a troubled production.

Yes, it was. Charles Crichton started directing it for the

Boultings, and he had a great reputation. He had engaged me in a great comic part and he wanted to be very true to the book. We all knew exactly what we wanted – a sophisticated light comedy. We started shooting, with Hugh Griffiths playing my husband, and we turned up at the end of the first week's shooting to find that the Boultings had taken over the production and they wanted it as a *tour de force* for Ian Carmichael. It was made broader than had originally been envisaged. It has some very funny things in it, all the same, including a scene where I had to ride one of those motorised bicycles and Terry-Thomas had to ride a Vespa scooter.

You finished the 50s with what sounds like a rather hectic melodrama, called *SOS Pacific* . . .
That was my first really international film. It had French, German, British and American stars, lovely Pier Angeli and an excellent director in Guy Green. We made that in the Canary Islands. Dickie Attenborough nearly died on it. We had a seaplane in the film, from which we had to be rescued in rafts. There was a question of whether they could shoot this stunt because there was a very rough sea that day. They waited and waited and then decided to have a go. I think Dickie was in the small boat that the camera was on. I can't quite remember what happened, but he came ashore absolutely unconscious. He was shot off to hospital to be revived. His character actually was killed by a shark in the film, which went over the top in the end, unfortunately, because a lot of the drama was quite exciting. Everybody adored Pier Angeli who was so beautiful; and Dickie brought her back to England for *The Angry Silence*.

What is your favourite amongst your films?
Oh, *The Kidnappers* still, and *A Town Like Alice*.

Ken Annakin

The Sixteen Tasks of Maintaining Vehicles*, We Serve* (1941), Cooks*, London* (1942), A Ride with Uncle Joe* (1943), Black Diamonds, The New Crop, Combined Cadets* (1944), A Farm in the Fens*, Crop Rotation*, Make Fruitful the Land*, Pacific Thrust*, Three Cadets* (1945), We of the West Riding*, It Began on the Clyde*, British Criminal Justice* (1946), Turn It Out*, Holiday Camp, Broken Journey (1947), Here Come the Huggetts, Miranda, Quartet ('The Colonel's Lady') (1948), Vote for Huggett, Landfall, The Huggetts Abroad (1949), Trio ('The Verger'), Double Confession (1950), Hotel Sahara (1951), The Planter's Wife, The Story of Robin Hood and His Merrie Men (1952), The Sword and the Rose (1953), The Seekers, You Know What Sailors Are (1954), Value for Money (1955), Loser Takes All, Three Men in a Boat (1956), Across the Bridge (1957), Nor the Moon by Night (1958), Third Man on the Mountain (1959), Swiss Family Robinson (1960), A Very Important Person, The Hellions (1961), Crooks Anonymous, The Fast Lady, The Longest Day (co-dir.) (1962), The Informers (1963), Those Magnificent Men in Their Flying Machines, The Battle of the Bulge (1965), The Long Duel (1966), The Biggest Bundle of Them All (1967), Those Daring Young Men in Their Jaunty Jalopies (1969), Call of the Wild (1972), Paper Tiger (1974), The Fifth Musketeer (1977), Cheaper to Keep Her (1980), The Pirate Movie (1982), Pippi Longstocking (1986).
* Documentary short films.

In many ways Ken Annakin's busy, nearly fifty-year-long career follows a classic pattern for British directors. Invalided out of the RAF, he quickly became involved with documentary film-making, like so many of his contemporaries, before embarking on feature films. His first batch of features was made for Gainsborough Studios, under the regime of Sydney Box, and included such typical Gainsborough products as the 'Huggett' films and the Somerset Maugham compendia. To *Holiday Camp*, which introduced the Huggetts, he brought some of the feeling for ordinary lives he had acquired in the documentary field. In the 1950s he began a very successful association with Walt Disney for whom he made four popular films. His 50s output also features outpost-of-empire films (*The Planter's Wife, The Seekers, Nor the Moon by Night*) and several light comedies (including the inventive *Hotel Sahara*), before moving on to the international phase of his prolific career. In spite of the big box-office successes of such large-scale enterprises as *Those Magnificent Men and Their Flying Machines*, which he handled with assurance, it is nice to know that he would like best to be remembered for 'The Colonel's Lady', one of the *Quartet* stories and *Across the Bridge*, a taut adaptation from Graham Greene, two very accomplished pieces about which he feels strongly.

Interview date: June 1990.

One source claims that you began in films as an assistant cameraman and that you were also assistant director to Carol Reed.
That's true. After I was injured in the Liverpool blitz, the RAF switched me from being a flight mechanic into the Film Unit. I worked on films for the Ministry of Information and the British Council, and on Army and RAF training films. The switch to being an assistant director came about when I was working as Camera Operator on *We Serve*. This was a recruiting film for women in the army that was being directed by Carol Reed, with important actresses like Flora Robson working for £5 per day. Finally, one day, Carol said, 'I think you should switch over to our side', meaning into directing. Maybe he thought I wasn't very good with a Mitchell Camera! At any rate, I switched to being his assistant and, after that, I directed quite a lot of documentary and training films.

You were very busy between 1942-6, making documentaries and shorts. How did you get in to feature films?
I became attached to Verity Films run by Sydney Box, who opened many doors for me. Just before the war

finished, Sydney had made the very successful picture, *The Seventh Veil* and was given the job of running Gainsborough Pictures. He said to me, 'You ought to be making features, Ken, because you've got a good story mind and visual sense. Try and get one picture to make which shows that you can handle actors as well as documentary people'. I was lucky in that I got a picture called *British Criminal Justice*, which really explained the British system of law and gave me a wonderful break. Sydney kept his promise and gave me *Holiday Camp* to direct. I was dying to get into feature films, but I was a typical documentary guy and *Holiday Camp* taught me a lot about fictional movies – like the need for humour and good women's roles.

Whose brainchild was *Holiday Camp*? There are no fewer than six writers credited to it.

Godfrey Winn was the first writer engaged for it. He was a popular magazine writer, and he and I went to Butlin's Holiday Camp at Filey to see what really happened and to devise a story. I think he put together a very good story but then Sydney and Muriel Box, who were both writers, decided we should add certain elements like the Heath Murder character played by Dennis Price; that was news then, so Muriel worked it into the story.

I remember a round-table conference when Ted Willis (a working-class writer from the Unity Theatre), Peter Rogers (who later wrote the 'Carry On' pictures), Mabel Constanduros (who was a popular writer of very funny, working-class plays) all came together to add their ideas. Godfrey wasn't terribly happy about this because he thought he was going to have a single screen credit, but it was a great popular success, partly perhaps because I had come from documentary films and British cinema at that time was very artificial.

The Huggetts absolutely caught the spirit and feeling that existed after the war. Whilst waiting for the invasion, troops were always being lectured on equality and how, when they came home, England would be the country where everybody had equal opportunities. People didn't want more fairy stories; they wanted something in which they could recognise themselves. Being of lower middle-class origins myself, I felt at home with these people who were having a fine holiday in a very cheap place which provided wonderful entertainment. I think I caught the spirit of the holiday camps and we had a very warm, natural cast. Kathleen Harrison was a wonderful, working-class actress; Jack Warner was a very amiable type whom people loved to watch; Flora Robson was a great theatre actress with a gift for pathos,

and her story with Esmond Knight, as the blind radio commentator, was very touching; and Hazel Court, my first 'star', is still a friend here in LA.

I'm not embarrassed about *Holiday Camp* today, although the later Huggett films don't hold up so well. I must say, too, that *Miranda*, my third feature, also holds up well today. My favourite scene in *Miranda* is the one where Glynis [Johns] gives Margaret Rutherford the pearls. Maggie was wonderful when we were shooting that scene. She was a complete original, she had no technique at all that she admitted to. I recall telling her to do that funny little flutter of her lips as she came into close-up, and she said, 'I don't do any fluttering of my lips'! You had to shoot until you caught what you wanted from her. What she did have was an original zany quality and you felt that she was a very strong, loving person you'd like around.

What do you remember about filming *Broken Journey*?

When we finished *Holiday Camp*, Sydney Box came up with a fascinating story of a plane crash in the Alps. He had engaged Bob Westerby to write it and he told me to go to France, find a crashed aeroplane and a location to shoot it! So I went to France and was lucky to find an old Dakota that had crashed. I then found a plateau just under Mont Blanc, at Les Huches, and discussed with the man who owned the *télérifique* how we could cut up this plane and get it up the mountain. I went home, polished the script with Bob Westerby, cast it with Sydney and was back in France four weeks later for location shooting, using doubles.

I found a wonderful climber and stills photographer in Chamonix; he was able to go up and photograph on glaciers, where normal cameramen couldn't work, and he made a second unit for me. When I came back to England we shot for forty-odd days in the studio – in summer, using a lot of back projection. We had Phyllis Calvert, a natural screen actress, Margot Grahame, a bit stagey but a very funny woman all the same, and also Francis L. Sullivan, Guy Rolfe and Mary Hinton in the cast.

Gainsborough was a very important studio making twenty-eight pictures a year under Sydney, so he could get almost anyone he wanted. It was a happy experience working for the Box family. Sydney was an inspiring boss, and Betty [Box] supervised all the production at Islington where I made *Miranda*.

The films from the Somerset Maugham stories

hold up very well. Was it difficult to get big-name stars to play in a third or a quarter of a film?
Not really; they all loved the idea of working on a Maugham story because he was recognised as one of the best story-tellers of that era. 'The Colonel's Lady' [from *Quartet*] is one of the best pictures I ever made, and is touching though sentimental. Nora Swinburne was great as the writer of 'a secret love' and Cecil Parker was superb as her county-squire husband. 'Mr Knowall', in *Trio*, was also a very good story. That's the one with Nigel Patrick. 'The Verger' was a good character study, with Kathleen Harrison and James Hayter. But, of all my British films, I would like to be remembered for 'The Colonel's Lady' and for *Across the Bridge* which I made in 1957.

The importation of American stars was common in the 50s; you had Yvonne De Carlo in *Hotel Sahara*, one of my favourites among your films.
I like it, too. It ran for years in Germany because it was the first film to show that many Germans were human beings serving just like other soldiers. The idea for *Hotel Sahara* came from George Brown, the producer, and it was one of the best pictures he ever made. The screenplay was written by George himself and Patrick Kirwan. The witty stuff came from Kirwan, but George had a great feel for it because he had been with the Desert Rats.

Yvonne was charming to work with even though she wasn't the greatest of actresses. Getting a scene in the can was terribly difficult with the cast I had. All Ustinov needed was *one* rehearsal; you knew you had to shoot by the third rehearsal, otherwise he would start playing the scene like ten other actors, mimicking them because he was bored. But Yvonne was a girl who had been taught to do things step by step, so I had to do private rehearsals with her and keep Peter out of the way, in order to get her performing equally well. Despite its desert exteriors, the film was made entirely at Pinewood.

Starting in 1952, you made the first of four films for Disney. How developed was the Disney set-up in England at that time?
It was not developed at all; he just had Carmen Dillon designing everything and Guy Green working for him as a cameraman. Apart from that, there was no real set-up. *Robin Hood* was a great lesson to me because Guy had been on the picture a long time before I came on, and he and Carmen had designed practically every set-up and they'd all been approved by Walt in Hollywood! With

the second movie I directed, *The Sword and the Rose*, I was in from the beginning and every set up was *my* design.

I learnt a tremendous amount on these two productions so that, by the time I made *Swiss Family Robinson*, Walt and I were on a completely friendly, equal basis and it was a joy creating with him. By that time, too, there was a true Disney Organisation in England.

We made *Robin Hood* and *The Sword and the Rose* at Denham; *Third Man on the Mountain* mainly in Switzerland, with the small amount of studio work done at Pinewood. *Swiss Family Robinson* was made entirely on location in Tobago and in a studio that I built there out of corrugated iron sheets. We had terrible sound because torrential storms battered on the tin roof, so I had to spend twenty-eight days at Pinewood post-synching the entire film.

You made three 'outpost-of-Empire' films in the 50s: *The Planter's Wife*, *The Seekers* and *Nor the Moon by Night*. Why do you think there were suddenly so many of these films?

Rod Steiger in *Across the Bridge*, 1957

Because a few of us wanted to go on location in interesting places, I guess! I know I did *The Seekers* because I wanted to go back to New Zealand. It wasn't a great script; it was George Brown again, and he had a playwright called Bill Fairchild write the script, which was only so-so from the first. We did our best with it during shooting, but the premise and the casting were ridiculous. The part in the opening reel about the creation of the Maori world was all right; the rest was junk. We took only Jack Hawkins, Laya Raki and Noel Purcell to New Zealand because George was very tight with the money. It was a fourteen-day continuous shoot and the shop steward caused us to miss the geyser blowing because the tea wagon hadn't arrived for the morning break! I stayed behind with the cameraman and we did a lot of "doubling" ourselves.

Of the three films you mentioned, I am quite proud of *The Planter's Wife*. For that I went to Malaya, but it was too dangerous to take actors there so most of it was shot in Ceylon, the rest in Pinewood. I shouldn't really have accepted *Nor the Moon by Night*, but I wanted to see South Africa! The film I really wanted to do was *The Singer Not the Song* which was eventually made by Roy Baker, with Dirk Bogarde.

In Natal we had all kinds of disasters: Belinda Lee tried to commit suicide by cutting her wrists; [Patrick] McGoohan turned his car over three times and had concussion; one day there was only me and a snake available to work! We were filming in the 'Valley of a Thousand Hills', where all the trouble is now between the Zulus and Mandela's ANC. In 1958 it was a marvellous place to work and I met my wife, Pauline, there. That was a plus, but the picture was a mediocre hotch-potch.

You were associated with some well-known British producers throughout the 50s — Peter Rogers, John Stafford, and Jack Clayton. What sort of relationship did you have with your producers?
With John Stafford I had a marvellous relationship; with George Brown a good relationship until he became very mean in New Zealand. Clayton wasn't really a producer but the production controller on *Three Men in a Boat*. He was very envious of me because he wanted to direct! You expect a producer to back you through thick and thin, and to try to help you obtain the best picture possible. I hate a weak producer who allows stars to behave in a way which is against the interests of the picture, or who doesn't fight for the extra finance you need to achieve what you and he set out to do. I have done several pictures, as we all have, during which you get fed up with the producer and decide to produce yourself. It doesn't work, though, because you are wearing two different hats. The way I have solved the dilemma on the last few pictures is to have my wife as either associate producer or, if possible, producer. She can be quite tough on running the picture, but her interests are *identical* with mine.

You made two films based on novels by Graham Greene — *Loser Takes All* and *Across the Bridge*. What attracted you to these projects?
Across the Bridge was a very classy picture, and very non-British! I took stills of locations in Texas and Mexico, then we staged the whole movie in Spain. I'm very proud of that picture. John Stafford found the short story and engaged a young writer, Guy Elmes, to expand it. The movie is really half a Graham Greene story (the part from when he has crossed the bridge) and Guy 'manufactured' the story that leads to the bridge. So it was based on Greene's moral attitude and Schaffer's [Rod Steiger] new character, and it worked marvellously.

I wanted to make *Loser Takes All* because, in its moral attitude to wealth, it was different. It was a satirical comedy which Graham Greene wrote to work off his spleen against Sir Alexander Korda for having messed up his life over a period of years. Robert Morley played the "Korda" role brilliantly. Unfortunately, the head of British Lion insisted that Rossano Brazzi play the role of Bertrand. Brazzi had made a hit in David Lean's *Summertime* but he was completely wrong casting for *Loser Takes All* because Bertrand was a very English chap. The basic concept of Graham Greene's story is the opposite of what normal people want; everyone wants to win money and everyone admires someone who has a system that wins in a casino. Nobody could understand it when Glynis Johns said she would prefer an honest student's love, rather than her husband's now he is rich! I spent a lot of time with Graham Greene, and now that I write screenplays myself I still think very much of Graham and his credo.

Renee Asherson

The Way Ahead (1944), *Henry V*, *The Way to the Stars* (1945), *Caesar and Cleopatra* (1946), *Once a Jolly Swagman* (1948), *The Small Back Room* (1949), *The Cure for Love* (1950), *Pool of London*, *The Magic Box* (1951), *Malta Story* (1953), *Time is My Enemy* (1954), *The Day the Earth Caught Fire* (1961), *Rasputin the Mad Monk* (1965), *Smashing Bird I Used to Know* (1969), *Theatre of Blood* (1973), *A Man Called Intrepid* (1979).

To be directed in your first three films by Carol Reed, Laurence Olivier and Anthony Asquith was as good a start as a British actress could expect in the 1940s. Even if the roles were small, Renee Asherson began in good company, and as Olivier's Princess Katherine in *Henry V* she is entirely charming, securing her niche in 1940s British cinema. Her English lesson scene with Ivy St Helier as her lady-in-waiting is one of the film's most perfectly judged. She was a convincing working-girl heroine in *Once a Jolly Swagman* and in Ealing's *Pool of London*, and she held her own in the broad comedy of *The Cure for Love* in which she was directed by, and co-starred with, her husband, Robert Donat. It says something for the quiet authority of her playing in the latter that one remembers her against the stiff competition of such noted comic players as Dora Bryan and Gladys Henson, as well as the dominant star presence of Donat himself. After the 40s, she rarely had another worthwhile film role, though, from 1955 onwards, television offered many better opportunities. And, as she says, the stage remained her first allegiance.

Interview date: June 1990.

Was your stage training valuable to you when you went into films?

There were things that you had to unlearn, but the first film I did was *Henry V* and I was with an actor directing, so I was lucky. Larry [Olivier] saw me when I was at the Mercury, doing a revival of *The Mask of Virtue*, the play in which Vivien Leigh had made her name. Apparently they came to see the play and then asked me to do a test for *Henry V* – I didn't even know Larry was filming it. Larry also asked Janet Burnell who was playing my mother to test for the Queen, and we both got the parts. It had been intended that Vivien should play the Princess but, after *Gone With the Wind*, her agents didn't think it was a big enough part for her.

Those scenes you have with Ivy St Helier are charming.

Yes, and she was lovely to be with. She was as nervous as me. I had not done any filming, and she had only done *Bitter Sweet* in the 30s because she was a Coward actress.

Did you have a lot of rehearsal for those court scenes?

I went through the wooing scene with Larry on that extraordinary set and he told me to go to a teacher called Alice Gachet who taught French drama at RADA and go through the scenes with her. So I did, and I then got hold of a Frenchman who had a beautiful Parisian accent. I would go through my scene with him, working on the French accent and listening to every intonation. When he saw the film he said that I sounded like a Russian speaking French!

I did *The Way Ahead* whilst I was waiting to retake the wooing scene. Larry wanted to retake the wooing scene, not, he said, because of me, but because he didn't like himself in it. It was an immensely demanding thing to direct and play at the same time. He had never directed a film and everyone was slightly sceptical, especially that marvellous cameraman, Bob Krasker, who used to look through his viewfinder, shake his head and say, 'No, no, no!' But Larry fought all the way and, as a result, he didn't altogether like himself when he saw the wooing scene. When he showed me the black and-white rushes I absolutely hated seeing myself, it was such a shock! The film was made in colour, with the only colour camera in the country at that time, but the rushes were in black-and-white. It was done in a very stylised way, with sloping floors and strange perspective, taken from a medieval Book of Hours – the Duc de Berri's, I think – which makes it much less dated than it would otherwise be. The French court scenes are done with a comic edge which gives them a weird charm, whereas in Kenneth Branagh's *Henry V* these scenes are totally realistic like the whole film.

You had a small part in *The Way Ahead* [released before *Henry V*].
My part *was* tiny but, as you say, I really started at the top with my first two films being for Laurence Olivier and Carol Reed! I played Mary Jerrold's daughter and I remember she was an enchanting person. I can't remember much about Carol Reed as a director because I was so scared; I just did what he told me as far as I could.

Following your trend of working with top directors, you next made *The Way to the Stars* for Anthony Asquith. Did you have a good agent getting you these roles?
I got an agent for the first time just before I did *Henry V*. Perhaps because of *Henry V* my name got around a bit. I didn't know Anthony Asquith at all, so I don't know how I came to get that part. I was very scared in that film, too, because I was up against the real 'film thing' and Asquith, like Carol Reed, was a complete film man. I suddenly became aware of the cameras and all the technicalities and I was rather at sea, whereas in *Henry V* I was in a sort of dream and it didn't matter whether there were cameras or not.

I understand Anthony Asquith was a very gentle director of actors.
Oh, yes, a very charming man. I wasn't scared of him, it was just that the medium suddenly became unfamiliar. After a few more films, I came to understand more about filming, but I never, except at the beginning, did any films on end, and with long enough parts, to get really used to the medium. So it has always eluded me. I would

love to get a grasp of it and really feel at home. I would like to have grasped more the very naturalistic level at which you must play; I *did* do it, but I never *knew* whether I did! I never had a part long enough to get totally relaxed in it.

What do you remember of making *Caesar and Cleopatra*?
Just before *Henry V* came out, this extraordinary man Gabriel Pascal asked to see the rushes and he then wanted me to be in *Caesar and Cleopatra*. Meanwhile, Larry had asked me to go with him to the Old Vic and I had, of course, said yes. Because I was so ignorant of theatre matters, this American agent [Al Parker] had unbeknown to me tied me up to Pascal for first call for half a year, in anticipation of doing *Caesar and Cleopatra*. Had I been less frightened of everybody, I would have gone straight to Larry who probably would have got me out of it. But I didn't dare approach him, so I found myself trapped. When I finally came to my scene I was so furious with Pascal that I burst into tears and wasted feet of Technicolour before I could do the scene! It was a very tense, emotional affair and they had a lot of high-powered personalities together in it.

Pascal was an extraordinary character – half-genius, half-conman I think. He had the most marvellous cast of course: Claude Rains was wonderful as Caesar. I only had one scene with Vivien and was with her very little. I was staggered at the sets and Oliver Messel's costumes – they were beautiful. Still, in spite of the outstanding cast and everything, it looks like a sort of stage thing. I think it is because Pascal was no film director. He was heavy-handed and there were tensions, and many frustrations because of him, and people weren't pulling together.

Did you enjoy playing the nice, ordinary girl who saved Dirk Bogarde from himself in *Once a Jolly Swagman*?
Yes, I liked the film, because there were very nice people in it. Dirk was very tense as far as I can remember and I'm tense, too. But I can't honestly remember much of it. All my stuff was done on the set, although some of the rest was done in London on the dirt-track race circuit.

After playing important roles, it was surprising to see you in the small role of the ATS corporal at the end of *The Small Back Room*.
I think I just hadn't been offered much else at the time. And Powell and Pressburger had such a name that my agent probably felt I should take the part. It was shot on

Ivy St Helier and Renee Asherson in *Henry V*, 1945

a beach somewhere in Dorset. Powell had a reputation for being slightly alarming to actors, but I don't think my part was big enough for that to worry me. He was more concerned with the leading lady, Kathleen Byron, an unusual person, with a very interesting face. I found David Farrar very nice, too. He and Kathleen were very good in the film.

Having already played Millie in *The Cure for Love* on stage, did you have to make many adjustments for your screen performance?
It was rather nice to do a film of something you knew a lot about, but, of course, there were some scenes which hadn't existed in the play. It was co-scripted by Walter Greenwood and my husband Robert Donat, who were great friends. I played a Cockney evacuee, billeted on Marjorie Rhodes. It was very broad comedy at times, but also very warm and human, I think. Walter really seemed to understand about working-class lives, par-

ticularly in the North. Marjorie had also been in the play, as had Thora Hird who played Mrs Dorbell. I enjoyed playing that sort of comedy: I wasn't actually dispensing the broad comedy but was in humorous situations.

You made your only film at Ealing, *Pool of London*, in 1951. How did you find Ealing as a place to work?
It had rather a nice atmosphere, as I remember. Its people seemed to stay there forever which helped with this, and it seemed much less formal and claustrophobic than places like Denham, where you tended to feel trapped.

I haven't seen *Pool of London* for ages, can't even remember what it was about. I did a lot of my work on location near the docks; I remember Michael Relph and Basil Dearden, who made it, but not vividly. I have just worked again with Leslie Phillips, my boyfriend in it, for the first time since then, in a TV pilot for a series, *Life After Death*.

Why did you make so few films after that? Were the 50s not a good decade for women in British films?

Perhaps that was it. I just seemed to do almost no films, I seemed to drop out of it. It wasn't a conscious decision to turn films down, just that I wasn't offered many. I did *The Malta Story* in 1954, directed by Brian Desmond Hurst, and spent a hard-working week on location in Malta. Alec Guinness was there, but I never actually met him; my part was totally separate from his. Most of my work was with Anthony Steel.

Were you under contract?

I was offered a contract soon after *Henry V* by the Rank Organisation, but Larry said I shouldn't tie myself up. In England, they used their contract players most of the time. I could have gone to Rank and would probably have been sent to the Charm School. I was once asked to go to Hollywood but didn't because I was doing something on stage with my husband, Robert Donat, and it would have been too difficult to dash off to Hollywood then.

In Which We Serve (1942), *Schweik's New Adventures*, *The Hundred Pound Window* (1943), *Journey Together* (1945), *A Matter of Life and Death*, *School for Secrets* (1946), *The Man Within*, *Dancing with Crime*, *Brighton Rock* (1947), *London Belongs to Me*, *The Guinea Pig* (1948), *The Lost People*, *Boys in Brown* (1949), *Morning Departure* (1950), *Hell is Sold Out*, *The Magic Box* (1951), *The Gift Horse*, *Father's Doing Fine* (1952), *8 O'Clock Walk* (1954), *The Ship That Died of Shame* (1955), *Private's Progress*, *The Baby and the Battleship* (1956), *Brothers-in-Law*, *The Scamp* (1957), *Dunkirk*, *The Man Upstairs*, *The Sea of Sand* (1958), *Danger Within*, *I'm All Right Jack*, *Jet Storm*, *SOS Pacific* (1959), *The Angry Silence*, *League of Gentlemen* (1960), **Whistle Down the Wind* (1961), *Only Two Can Play*, *All Night Long*, *The Dock Brief*, **The L-Shaped Room* (1962), *The Great Escape* (1963), *Seance on a Wet Afternoon*, *The Third Secret*, *Guns at Batasi* (1964), *The Flight of the Phoenix* (1965), *The Sand Pebbles* (1966), *Dr. Dolittle* (1967), *The Bliss of Mrs Blossom*, *Only When I Larf* (1968), **Oh! What a Lovely War*, *David Copperfield*, *The Magic Christian* (1969), *The Last Grenade*, *Loot*, *10 Rillington Place*, *A Severed Head* (1970), *Young Winston (1972), *And Then There Were None* (1974), *Conduct Unbecoming*, *Rosebud*, *Brannigan* (1975), *A Bridge Too Far (1977), *Magic (1978), *The Human Factor* (1979), *Gandhi (1982), *A Chorus Line (1985), *Cry Freedom (1987), *Chaplin (1992).

* No acting role – producer and/or director.

Few names have been so tenaciously associated with the survival of British cinema as that of Richard Attenborough. In the last two decades he has concentrated on making a series of large-scale films, among which *Gandhi* was a multi-award-winning commercial and critical success. His other films as director (or producer-director) have been similarly ambitious, often showing that sense of social concern which he sees as so important a responsibility of the film-maker. During the 1940s and 50s, he appeared in over thirty films but expresses dissatisfaction with many of his film roles, in which he began to feel himself typed. Nevertheless, there are some remarkable performances in this period, dating from his memorable bit role as the frightened seaman in *In Which We Serve*. His cold-eyed killer in *Brighton Rock* is one of the most chilling performances in British cinema of the 40s and accounts for much of the film's power to disturb some forty years later. As the weak, flashy Percy Boone in *London Belongs to Me*, the schoolboy used for social experiment in *The Guinea Pig*, the profiteering ex-serviceman in *The Ship That Died of Shame*, and the workman sent to Coventry in *The Angry Silence*, he created a gallery of sharply drawn characters that suggest a wider range than he may himself allow. He was willing to take risks as an actor and he became one of that rare species, the character star.

Interview date: October 1959.

How did you come to make your film debut in *In Which We Serve*?

I went to RADA in 1941 on a scholarship. During that year I acted in Eugene O'Neill's *Ah Wilderness!*, in a little repertory on the periphery of London, where I was seen by the American agent, Al Parker. He heard that Noel Coward was looking for new faces for his ship's crew in *In Which We Serve*, a film about the Mountbatten story of the war in the Mediterranean, and he got me an audition. I had a screen test as well, and, as a result, Coward cast me as the young stoker. I might say that if you coughed you missed me, but getting to know Noel was the great thing. He was the most influential and supportive figure in my early life.

Your association with the Boultings seems crucial, too . . .

Yes. When I was in Flying Training Command, I was seconded to the Royal Air Force Film Unit under the direct command of John Boulting, and played in a film called *Journey Together*, which Terry Rattigan wrote and John directed. It was his first film and people like

Bernard Lee, Pier Angeli and Richard Attenborough in Guy Green's *The Angry Silence*, 1960

George Cole, David Tomlinson and Bessie Love were in it. But a miracle occurred for me in that the Royal Air Force flew Edward G Robinson over from Los Angeles. I came to know him very well and he granted me a vision of *film* acting which I had never encountered before.

Throughout the 40s you had a series of interesting parts. Was someone guiding your career at this time?

Nobody was *guiding*. I was still under contract to Al Parker who was a mentor in some measure, but the person who really took me under his wing was John Boulting – John *and* Roy. Roy was in the Army and John was in the Royal Air Force as I was, so my association with John was closer. John became not only my instructor in many ways (he had a wonderful, wonderful gift for dealing with actors), but also my closest friend. He lent me the money to get married, and he was a most extra-

ordinary, courageous, remarkable man. He served in the International Brigade in Spain.

It was John who first talked to me about Thomas Paine, about whom I want to make my next movie. I shall dedicate it to John as it belongs to him, really. After *Journey Together*, John and Roy said, 'If we come out of the war, and go into production, we'd like you to be under contract to us'. This was during 1944 or 1945.

In *A Matter of Life and Death*, I only say two words. This film happened because I was engaged to Sheila [Sim], and she had done *A Canterbury Tale* for Micky Powell. I came home on forty-eight hours leave and Sheila had to go down to see Micky, so I went down with her in my uniform. Micky said, 'How long are you here for?', and I said, 'Forty-eight hours'. He said, 'Just enough time to do a part for me', and that's how I played in *A Matter of Life and Death*.

I came out of the Air Force in 1946 and played in *The*

Man Within by virtue of Sydney Box seeing *Journey Together*. It was the first colour movie at Shepherd's Bush. I remember we constantly had to stop. The heat required for colour in those days was so intense that we would be in the middle of a scene and the sprinklers would go off. We all wore bright orange make-up. It seems like another world now. It was a very bad film, I think, but it was marvellous to play with Michael Redgrave, who was a sweet man and a lovely actor.

Your Pinky in Graham Greene's *Brighton Rock* is one of the most vivid performances in 40s British cinema. How do you regard it now?
I haven't seen it for a very long time. Whatever quality it does have, I don't think it would have been anything like as good, if it had not been for John. Having played it in the theatre was both an advantage and a disadvantage. I already had quite firm characterisation concepts, and, although this meant that I was familiar with the character and didn't therefore have to do a great deal of additional thought and research, nevertheless it was conceived in theatrical terms. John forced me into transferring it into the cinema. It was a very bold film and, when you think of that sort of sociological subject matter and the truth of its settings, it was a very remarkable film for 1946.

How difficult was the filming in Brighton? I gather a lot of it was done on location.
Very difficult. There was a lot of opposition because it was felt that the story had cast shame upon the comfortable seaside town of Brighton and so on. But that was all dealt with. We had to use a caption saying, 'Of course Brighton is not like this today'.

Brighton Rock had a joint writing credit for Terence Rattigan and Graham Greene. They seem improbable collaborators.
Absolutely. What happened was that John [Boulting], who worked with Terry on *Journey Together*, asked him to do the screenplay. When it was finished John took it to Graham, who had major reservations about it, so he did a rewrite of Terry's version. Graham had had very little film-writing experience at that time, so the credit became a joint one. They never worked together; it wasn't a co-operative effort. But Graham was very complimentary about the film. He sent me a copy of *Brighton Rock* in which he wrote, 'For my perfect Pinky'. I treasure it almost as much as anything I've ever had.

What differences did you find between the stage
and screen versions of your performance as Pinky?
Oh, inevitably in the theatre the degree of subtlety of characterisation, of ambivalence of attitude, is just not possible, particularly when the piece has to move at such a great pace. When we were filming, John used to make me go through and work out every reaction and thought that would occur to that person in a particular situation. He would then say, 'Now Dick, we've got all this worked out, in terms of this reaction to what Rose said [or whatever]. Now, those thoughts will go through your mind *infinitely* faster than you can possibly *consciously* convey them. But they have to *be* there and if I shoot it right, I will find those on the screen for you'. He taught me that there was no such thing in cinema acting as a short-cut.

Some critics greeted *Brighton Rock* as a splendid example of realism; others talked about a dilution of Greene's novel. What do you think?
There *is* a dilution, firstly, from containing a very complex and sophisticated novel within an accepted screen length of one-hour thirty, or forty minutes. Again, the question of sophisticated thought and argument was difficult to spend sufficient time on. So we did dilute in a way: we simplified. And there were moments, particularly at the end – Graham still didn't like the end of the movie, but I thought it was a very skilful end – that was Terry [Rattigan]. What people don't remember – and I don't know whether they were contemporary views or not – is how much courage there was in making that movie at all in 1946.

You followed *Brighton Rock* with several films that now look as if they're addressing themselves to a range of social problems: *The Guinea Pig*, *The Lost People*, and *Boys in Brown*. Did they seem to you significant at the time?
The Guinea Pig seemed very significant, but, again, that was John and Roy. Roy directed and John produced for Charter Films. Both were highly socially conscious and aware. Therefore the statement made in Warren Chetham-Strode's play was the thing that excited them in moving it on to the screen. For the other films I cannot claim any motivation of social awareness, although I come from parents who were constantly consciously aware of social problems and the environment in general, and our place in it. And so, throughout my life, things which had that particular feeling, in any sense, appealed to me. But for *Boys in Brown*, *Lost People* and

so on, I cannot claim that those were the reasons; unlike *10 Rillington Place*, for instance, which I did for very specific reasons.

Did you feel *The Guinea Pig* was consciously directed against the class system as such?
Without question. I'm not sure how passionate Warren was, but the reason John and Roy wanted to do the picture was their active opposition to the class system. It was an *attack* on the class system; if they had thought it was merely a palliative, they wouldn't have made the film. There was a condescension towards the 'lower classes' that manifested itself, in some measure, in the sort of work we did. I mean you've only to look at some of the wartime pictures to appreciate that.

You were extremely busy throughout the 50s, over twenty films by my count. How satisfied were you with the kinds of films being made?
I don't think many people were satisfied, and I certainly was not satisfied with my own participation. The industry seemed indigenously immensely secure and, with the Rank Organisation, what was the old ABPC Corporation and eventually British Lion, the great Two Cities (the prestige company under Filippo Del Giudice), the Korda pictures, it seemed that we were on a bandwagon which was really rolling quite happily. A number of us who placed aesthetic considerations high on our agenda were concerned that the fundamental quality of much of what we were doing was in question and that the wrong priorities were being addressed. Commercial success, presentation, and promotion were everything, while the actual kernel of the thing was very often not what it ought to be. This resulted, as far as I was concerned, in a dissatisfaction with the degree to which I was typecast. It seemed to us that the same old movies, in some form redressed, re-shaped, were being churned out. There were very few people challenging the subject matter or the form in which pictures were made, so that, rather like typecasting, you went on making the kind of movie which had a history of success.

You did at least three films in the 50s that, in one way or the other, break out of that mould: *The Ship That Died of Shame*, *I'm All Right Jack* and *The Angry Silence*. What do you think of these in retrospect?
The Ship That Died of Shame came from Ealing and I think Mickey [Balcon], withal conforming to the Ealing comedies which, God knows, were very remarkable in

the history of British cinema, nevertheless ventured every now and again into other territory. Mickey had an urge to move out of the genre which he had been largely responsible for creating. It was this urge that led to *The Ship That Died of Shame*. *I'm All Right Jack*, was very much an expression of the Boultings' disillusioned, radical views. That, and *Private's Progress* and *Carlton-Browne of the F.O.* were very much John and Roy's style. These were attacks on institutions, whether of the left or right, with a satirical capability which was unique, in many ways, to them.

The Angry Silence was a different matter. That arose for the reasons I was just talking about, not only as far as I was personally concerned, but I was desperately distressed at the direction in which British cinema was starting to go in the mid-to-late 50s. It was down a blind alley. It was, in fact, becoming dominated in large measure by the requirement of Eagle-Lion and others to find markets in the US. This involved making concessions and bringing over usually (I am afraid) fading American stars to supposedly bolster a marquee value in the United States. And, as I said before, playing the same old stuff over and over again.

I decided quite consciously, at this stage, to give up acting for a time. I went to Al Parker, my agent, and talked with my wife: I would eventually persuade somebody to allow me to play not only parts of my own age but to venture outside. Whatever I did, I would not go on playing these baby-faced young ingenues.

After that decision, I found the story which had been written by Michael Craig and his brother Richard Gregson, and persuaded Bryan Forbes to write the screenplay. I then set about trying to make it. I went to everybody except the Boultings. I was determined not to go back into the nest, as it were, but nobody would give me a penny. 'Dealing with a social subject in this way will empty the cinemas. Nobody would be interested. Anyway, who the hell are you? You're an actor, actors have no brains, etc, etc . . .'. Finally, in absolute despair, I had to go to British Lion – to the Boultings, Launder and Gilliat, and two remarkable people, Lord Arnold Goodman and Sir Max Rayne (now Lord Rayne).

They had a board meeting and said they thought the script was marvellous, the subject courageous, but that the budget, which was £142,000, was out of the question. However, if I could make it for £100,000 they would back it. So Bryan went back and started to cut out this and reduce that, and I remember very clearly ringing him and saying, 'Forbsie, this is a bleeding disaster. If we cut the picture now – it's a small picture anyway –

we are going to reduce the whole drama, the whole concept, the set-up. We cannot do this. What we have to do, is do it for nothing! We've got to persuade everybody – the costumiers, the lawyers, the accountants, the musicians, the actors, the cameraman – to come in for absolute scale salary; I'll get 70 to 80 per cent of the picture in profit terms and we'll divide it proportionately to their true salaries'. Anyway, the concept was accepted and I set about persuading everybody.

Two-and-a-half weeks before the picture started shooting, I still couldn't persuade any actor to play the part of Tom for nothing. After keeping us waiting for weeks, Kenny More eventually said no. So I played in *The Angry Silence* because I couldn't get anybody else to do it. It was lucky for me, because it permitted me to do something that had the contemporary social awareness I wanted so desperately. I mean *The Angry Silence* changed, for what it's worth, my acting career. It was perhaps the best thing Guy Green ever did, I think, and it had wonderful performances. Pier Angeli gives a devastating performance in it, and Bernard Lee . . . what a wonderful actor that man was. It really was, I think, a beautifully made movie.

What is your attitude to the way in which the Government has intervened in the British film industry?

There has been, in my opinion, only one minister who – no, two in fact, but one very evidently so – who has ever actually taken on board the artistic, social, commercial value of British cinema and that is Harold Wilson. Harold set up the Eady Fund and created a possible banking situation for British cinema.

British cinema has, in large measure, moved from what was called the Board of Trade; it's now called the DTI (Department of Trade and Industry). Now it wobbles between the DTI, the Home Office, the Foreign Office and, indeed, the Arts and Libraries and Education Offices. In other words, there are about five different ministries which, in some way or another, deal with the cinema in the UK. The result is that on each of those individual agendas, cinema – if it can be seen at all – is likely to be far down at the bottom. We are in this ridiculous position of being spread so thin over so many ministries that we have no muscle whatsoever.

The only other person who ever did anything was Geoffrey Howe at the time of *Chariots of Fire* and *Gandhi*, when we were doing quite well in investment terms of capital allowances. 'Capital allowances' means that you may set your production costs against your overall company accounts long before you know precisely when the film is going to be shown, what the returns will be, etc. You may claim immediately on that investment in fiscal terms. I remember going to Geoffrey when he was Chancellor, and his very clearly saying, 'Look, I don't favour capital allowances for everything but I do see that it would cripple the film industry to lose them at a stroke and I will reduce them slowly over a period of five, six or seven years'.

When Geoffrey left, Nigel Lawson came in and said, as he was perfectly entitled to, 'I'm not having any exceptions, capital allowances are out'. Within three months the whole of the funding of British cinema from the City disappeared. It was the most heart-breaking blow. Now it's a one-off deal every time, and the really cruel thing is that we are not going out with begging bowls. What we are asking is that the country values its film industry. We are still thought of as a crude imitation of the theatre here.

Roy Ward Baker

The October Man (1947), *The Weaker Sex* (1948), *Paper Orchid, Morning Departure* (1949), *Highly Dangerous* (1950), *The House in the Square* (1951), *Night Without Sleep, Don't Bother to Knock* (1952), *Inferno* (1953), *Passage Home* (1955), *Jacqueline, Tiger in the Smoke* (1956), *The One That Got Away* (1957), *A Night to Remember* (1958), *The Singer Not the Song* (1960), *Flame in the Streets, The Valiant* (1961), *Two Left Feet* (1963), *Quatermass and the Pit, The Anniversary* (1967), *Moon Zero Two* (1969), *Vampire Lovers* (1970), *Dr. Jekyll and Sister Hyde* (1971), *Asylum* (1972), *And Now the Screaming Starts, Vault of Horror* (1973), *The Legend of the Seven Gold Vampires* (1974), *The Monster Club* (1980).

A man who has made two striking *films noirs* and one of the best 3-D films (*Inferno*), sunk the *Titanic*, grappled with 'Quatermass', and presented Bette Davis as a one-eyed monster would seem to have had a richly varied career. Roy Ward Baker is not in any doubt about the obligation of films, in whatever genre, to be enjoyable; and casting one's eyes over his 1940s and 50s credits, one finds that he has made several of the most enjoyable films of the period, though 'enjoyable' seems too bland a word for the tensions of, say, *The October Man*, or the genuinely chilling first two-thirds of *Tiger in the Smoke*, or the impressive staging of the *Titanic* disaster in *A Night to Remember*, or the very lively war escape thriller, *The One That Got Away*, or the submarine drama, *Morning Departure*, which brought him to the attention of Hollywood. Roy Ward Baker's British films are characterised by well-chosen casts performing with clarity and conviction, by a no-nonsense approach to story-telling, and by their propensity to be oddly unnerving, possibly partly the result of the camera techniques he speaks of.

Interview date: June 1991.

You made some of the most enjoyable British films of the 40s and 50s. Do you regard viewer-pleasure as a top priority?

I don't think there's any other reason for making a film. There's no point in making films in a vacuum, or for your twelve friends in Hampstead or wherever. I am not saying I would do anything to please an audience; indeed, I try to provoke them, and poke them in the eye occasionally. Of course, the ordinary working director's life is such that we do a lot of pictures simply because they are on offer. We never have perfect freedom of choice.

Were you occupied with film-making during the war?

Yes, I was in the Infantry for three years, then a message was sent around that anyone who had experience in making films should send their names into the War Office, which I did. I was taken on as a production manager with the Army Kinematograph Service. After about six weeks a film came up that had nobody to direct it, so I proposed myself. It was eight reels of what we would now call 'urban guerilla warfare' – how to clear a street. I shot it in Battersea which had been very heavily bombed by that time, so I had the most magnificent set – all absolutely genuine! I went on to make straightforward instructional films, like 'how to handle a twenty-five-pounder gun', and so on.

One day I met Eric Ambler at an army church parade. Later he became the executive producer for the Army film unit, so I came to work with him quite a lot. We became very close friends and, when we could see that the war was going to be over very soon, we began to think about what we would do afterwards. Eric had already had several of his books filmed and Del Giudice from Two Cities (really part of the Rank Organisation) wanted him to write a script and produce it as soon as the war was over, and Eric asked me to direct it. That's how *The October Man* came about.

The character, played by John Mills, in *The October Man* is a typical Roy Ward Baker protagonist — a man pushed to the edge to see how he might react.

That has always intrigued me, because most people lead comparatively ordinary lives and don't come up against enormous crises. To me, one of the most interesting things about *Morning Departure* is when they all get bottled up in that submarine and the question is how will they react to facing death. We had a very fine cast in *The October Man*, most of whom were not under contract. It was only later, when the Rank Organisation moved into production properly instead of doing it through Two Cities, that they started to build up a catalogue of star names. Catherine Lacey was superb as the landlady. She is one of those actresses who never gave a bad performance. It just wasn't in her to do so.

***Morning Departure* is an adaptation of a play, by Kenneth Woollard. Did William Fairchild's adaptation alter it very much?**

In general, he kept very close to the original but, of course, in the play the rescue operation all had to be done with frantic telephone calls, whereas we could actually show it. The story was really more suited to the cinema than the theatre. The downbeat ending of the four men dying was in the play also.

I was very proud of that film and still am. It was an immense success in its day and that's how I came to go to Hollywood in 1952, because the Americans had seen that film. It's probably a bit dated now, but, even now, in any service, there is still a pretty rigid distinction between the officers and the other ranks. Under stress this does break down in a sense, but, even at the end of the film, the two officers are still officers and the other two are still the other ranks. They are never on a class-less level, even though they are on an equal level in that they know they are all going to die at any moment.

You worked again with Eric Ambler on *Highly Dangerous* (1950) and *A Night to Remember* (1958). Did you find him a particularly sympathetic collaborator?

Oh, yes, we developed a long-lasting friendship. One thing about Eric is that he always presents you with a script which is beautifully finished in every detail. *Highly Dangerous* wasn't a very successful picture. I think Margaret Lockwood wanted to play a modern woman and this character was a scientist, to do with germ warfare. It was Eric Ambler's first or second book,

although the book had a different title and the main character was originally a man. Eric changed the character to a woman to make it more interesting. It was a good idea, but I don't think I did it very well.

Dane Clark, your leading man, seemed a poor man's John Garfield. What do you think of the practice of importing American stars throughout the 1950s?

It was all part of the fatal delusion, started in the 1920s, that we could distribute our pictures in America. But there is no *need* for British pictures there. Most of the successful British pictures, like *Chariots of Fire*, have not been directed at America anyway. In making that film, I don't think anyone, for one moment, considered the American distribution. But David Puttnam, being the brilliant salesman he is, did it anyway and they loved it.

What was your experience of working with Tyrone Power and Ann Blyth in *The House in the Square*?

They were both absolutely marvellous. Tyrone Power was one of the nicest men I've ever met, and really super-professional. I learned quite a lot from him. He was amenable, a perfect gent. Ann Blyth was fine; she was actually more of a singer. She played rather a misty character, not entirely real, and I thought she did it very well. That was an American picture made here for 20th Century-Fox.

You worked with the great cameraman, Georges Périnal on that film, and with Geoffrey Unsworth. What have you, as a director, looked for and valued in a cameraman?

A top cameraman, is vital. It even affects the editing. If you have a slipshod cameraman you will find when cutting some of the sequences that they don't seem to fit properly, because the lighting has gone awry, or he has changed his mind in the middle of a scene. I've been very fortunate in that respect. Geoff Unsworth was a bosom friend, a really charming man. He developed his reputation because he was extraordinarily good at photographing women. Very few British cameramen had bothered to do that well. The quality I value most in a cameraman is being *simpatico* with the story, the characters and the atmosphere. There is also a great deal in being a good lighting man.

When you returned from Hollywood in the mid-

50s, did you work for the Rank Organisation for four to five years on films like *Jacqueline*, *Passage Home* and *Tiger in the Smoke*?

Yes, those were all Rank films made at Pinewood. It was actually about seven years, from 1954 to about 1961.

What recollections have you of working with Peter Finch in *Passage Home*?

Oh, very good. He was a genuine actor. Even though he was very successful in films and did some wonderful things, particularly later in America, he was probably more of a theatre actor than a cinema actor. I liked him. He was a wonderful sort of con-man – he had about three different life stories he would tell you, all completely different and hilariously funny. I really don't know what the truth was and I didn't care. He was such great fun and a very, very good actor. *Passage Home* had a marvellous cast. I remember Diane Cilento was in it and Pat McGoohan; I think Tony Steel was under contract to Rank and Michael Craig may have been, but the others weren't.

Would you agree that *Tiger in the Smoke*, from Margery Allingham's novel, is a genuinely scary thriller?

It never really worked because its dénouement depends on the revelation of a wonderful treasure in Brittany. The writing and description, incidentally, was very detailed about what the place should be like and, of course, I never could find a place that remotely resembled it. So when they open the box and the treasure is just a plaster statue of the Madonna, it just wasn't good enough, not striking or thrilling enough.

Anthony Pelissier did the basic screenplay adaptation and about half the script, then he went off to direct some television thing and Leslie Parkyn, the producer, and I more or less had to complete the script ourselves. I'm not sure we did a very good job. We had a marvellous cast, the atmosphere was all there, with Geoffrey Unsworth on camera, and, strangely enough, this was the first film when some of the critics began to take me seriously. Suddenly I found myself getting a slightly fancy reputation, which I thought was rather nice. I don't know why that film did it, though. The major flaw was Tony Wright – he was wrongly cast; it should have been Stanley Baker or Jack Hawkins, someone you could really be frightened of.

The trick I used in *Tiger in the Smoke* was to shoot the whole picture on a baby crane and the camera is, in fact,

always moving, never absolutely still. I did this to produce a feeling of unrest; nobody ever commented on it and I think I should have been bolder. Or perhaps it was one of those subliminal effects. It was all shot at Pinewood, except for some location work at Liverpool Street station and in Brittany. I got a certain amount of criticism about Donald Sinden and Muriel Pavlow because they were so immaculate and middle-class. I wouldn't play them like that now, but I think it was right at that time.

Among the many British war films of the 1950s *The One That Got Away* suddenly stands out. Where did you find the story?

I had a friend who ran a bookshop in Piccadilly and one day he said he had two books for me – *The One That Got Away* and *A Night to Remember*. I read them both over the weekend. *The One That Got Away* was an essay in total realism. There was a lot of opposition to my making the film, and I was heavily criticised for making a German into a hero. I was determined to make it, for two reasons. Firstly, it was a marvellous chase story, like a Western in some ways. Secondly, I'd got sick to death of the propaganda pictures during the war, and after the war they went on making the Nazis either beer-swilling Krauts or homosexual Prussians. So I thought something should be said to show the Germans for the very resourceful and determined people they can be.

I decided that the main character was in a way a villain/hero, and, since everyone in Europe reads from left to right, throughout the movie I always had him going from right to left and everyone else going from left to right. That was another thing that nobody noticed; but I hoped it worked unconsciously to differentiate him from the others. Then there was a tremendous fuss about who would play the main part. Originally the studio refused to have a German, but I insisted. Luckily, just at that time there was a luncheon at Pinewood to entertain a lot of the Rank's European representatives, including our man in Hamburg. I asked him if he could help me. He phoned me as soon as he got back to Germany and I went over there. As soon as I clapped eyes on Hardy Kruger I knew he was it. We got on very well and it was one of the best experiences I've ever had with an actor.

The Canadian sequences were mostly shot in Sweden and partly on the stage we built. It was very arduous; it went over schedule; everyone was worried. I had another marvellous cameraman called Eric Cross, the only time I worked with him. He was a documentary and exterior man – Julian Wintle brought him into the film, and he was absolutely right. Eric was a rock; he simply wouldn't shoot unless it was right and, of course, the end result was superb.

You next filmed *A Night to Remember*. Did you have a special feeling about the *Titanic* as a subject?

Oh, yes. The whole purpose of making the film was to show a society which had persuaded itself that you could make a ship which could never be sunk. It turned out that William MacQuitty was going to produce and you couldn't have a better man than that. He was emotionally involved because he is an Ulsterman and the ship was built at the Ulster shipyards. He remembers, as a very small child, being held in his father's arms to see the *Titanic* as it went down the river. We built half the deck on the back lot of Pinewood. It needed a lot of organising and planning, but luckily Vetchinsky was the art director – I'd known him since I first went to work at Gainsborough and had worked with him many times.

You could say that the people who believed the ship to be invulnerable were a bunch of arrogant fools, but it's no good caricaturing them. There *are* one or two people caricatured in the picture – like the aristocrats played by Patrick Waddington and Harriette Johns – but those sort of people *were* caricatures even in their own lives.

Michael Goodliffe was in *The One That Got Away* and several of my pictures after that; he was a great favourite of mine. Laurence Naismith was also in several things I did, as were Sam Kydd, Victor Maddern and quite a few others. They were reliable people and they fitted in so easily and so well.

I have not seen your film *The Singer Not the Song*, which has acquired an extraordinary cult reputation. Why, do you think?

I hated it. It broke my heart, and put me completely out of kilter for years afterwards. It was a disaster. I'm told it's a cult picture and quite probably in countries with large Catholic communities it has some special reference. I should never have made it. I actually turned it down once and said if they really wanted to make the picture they should get the great Spanish/Mexican director Luis Bunuel to do it.

I fought it off for over twelve months, but the Rank Organisation pressured me to make it. I can't think why they wanted the damned thing. It wasn't a good book. It was the old phoney story of a little girl falling in love with a priest, and it's been done so many times. It has not been financially unsuccessful, and if I go to France I have a much bigger reputation there than I do here – principally for that film and for *Quatermass and the Pit* which they loved. But, as far as I'm concerned, that film just gives me the horrors. Anyway, it's all a long time ago and many much pleasanter things have happened to me since.

John Mills, Joan Greenwood and Catherine Lacey in *The October Man*, 1947

The Blue Lagoon (as stunt double), *A Warning to Wantons*, *The Interrupted Journey*, *Stop Press Girl* (1949), *Come Dance with Me* (1950), *Talk of a Million*, *London Entertains*, *Encore* (1951), *The Drayton Case* (1953), *The Dark Stairway*, *Dangerous Voyage*, *Devil's Harbour*, *The Black Rider* (1954), *John and Julie*, *The Blue Peter*, *The Big Fish*, *Stolen Time* (1955), *The Baby and the Battleship*, *A Town Like Alice*, *Secret of the Forest*, *Reach for the Sky* (1956), *Face in the Night*, *Robbery Under Arms* (1957), *Blood of the Vampire*, *Sea of Sand* (1958), *Danger Within*, *Summer of the 17th Doll* (1959), *Dentist in the Chair*, *Identity Unknown*, *Feet of Clay*, *Dead Lucky* (1960), *Nearly a Nasty Accident*, *Very Important Person*, *Highway to Battle*, *The Middle Course*, *A Matter of WHO* (1961), *Carry on Cruising* (1962), *Echo of Diana*, *Mouse on the Moon* (1963), *Follow that Camel* (1967), *Where Eagles Dare* (1968), *Oh! What a Lovely War* (1969), *Not Tonight Darling* (1971), *Clinic Xclusive* (1972), *Deathcheaters* (1976), *The Irishman* (1978), *Alison's Birthday* (1979), *Time Lapse*, *Breaker Morant* (1980), *Deadline* (1981), *Phar Lap* (1983), *Flight into Hell*, *Butterfly Island* (1985), *The Year My Voice Broke* (1987), *Turtle Beach* (1990).

Vincent Ball's career in 1950s British cinema is instructive about what was available to a working actor at the time. As a man with family responsibilities, he took what work came along, including a television series which was more lucrative than most film work. He had ample experience of the 'B' films of British cinema of the period, films of a kind that virtually disappeared in the 60s, as the nature of exhibition altered and as television took up some of the 'B' film genres. Ball worked with the legendary Danzigers who regularly made films in three weeks and less, and with prolific directors such as Montgomery Tully and Wolf Rilla. Threading their way through these films was a steady line of 'A' films, such as two films he made with director Jack Lee, *A Town Like Alice* and *Robbery Under Arms*, two war films, Guy Green's *Sea of Sand* and Don Chaffey's *Danger Within*, and Richard Attenborough's *Oh! What a Lovely War*. A likeable, convincing actor always, his work has gained authority in recent years when he has appeared in Australian films and television.

Interview date: October 1991.

Did you really begin as a stunt double?
Yes. One day I read in a Sydney paper that they were looking for someone for the original *Blue Lagoon* [1948], with Jean Simmons. So I sent some photographs showing off my muscles to the Rank Organisation at Pinewood. About three weeks later I got a reply saying I would be considered for the part if I should ever be over that way.

Six months later, via a Swedish cargo boat, I arrived in England and took my very tatty letter to Pinewood, where the man who had written it, Dennis Van Thal, apologised for the fact that they had already been to Fiji and back and finished the film. Then he asked if I could swim and explained that Donald Houston couldn't; so they offered me £10 a day to do the underwater swimming sequences in the big studio tank. My first job was wrestling rubber octopuses in the tank at Pinewood. That's my body you see in *Blue Lagoon*. I remember Frank Launder saying, 'Vince old boy, try to keep your face away from the camera, there's a good chap'.

After about eighteen months I won a scholarship to RADA where I spent about two terms. Then I had a day off and went to audition for the film, *Talk of a Million* with Jack Warner and Barbara Mullen, directed by John Paddy Carstairs. I did the test playing an Irishman with a couple of chaps from the Abbey Theatre and eventually got the part. RADA gave me a term off to do it. I also had bit-parts in *Stop Press Girl*, and *Interrupted Journey* which starred Valerie Hobson.

You made a number of supporting or 'B' pictures during the 50s.
Yes, do you remember the Danziger brothers? They used to make films every ten days and I'd go from one film set to another; we made most of them at Elstree. If I finished one film at Friday lunchtime, I'd walk to another set and start the next one that afternoon, changing my jacket or

whatever for the new character. I made about ten of these films and can't even remember their names. It was good experience, but you got the tag of 'B' picture actor.

I remember Danziger used to do four-minute takes, which was very demanding on the actors. Mostly, you didn't have time to learn the dialogue. Doing a Danziger was really the end of the line, but I had a wife and kids and a mortgage to pay. I would play a lead for ten days and get my money – in cash, which was most unusual. The films were made on a shoestring, with minimum crews.

I remember finishing a film for Montgomery Tully and he pulled out another script, saying, 'What about this one? I haven't read it yet'! While we were chatting, some new wallpaper was being slapped up on the set and the furniture was moved around, then we started again! It was the time when cinemas showed double features, so at least they knew then they had an assured outlet for their films.

Around this time, there was *Dangerous Voyage*, directed by Vernon Sewell, for whom I did at least two films. He had a yacht called the *Gelert* and we sailed on it to France to shoot part of the film. Vernon didn't have permission to shoot there so he'd conceal the camera under his mac and film me walking into a police station or whatever. We lived on the yacht, supposedly on holiday but sneakily making a film. We also shot from the back of a van or through windows.

I remember, doing a couple of films for Wolf Rilla – *The Black Rider* in 1954, and *The Blue Peter*, in Wales, with Kieron Moore and Greta Gynt. The latter was quite a big deal, we were in Wales for six or seven weeks filming.

You were also on television a lot, weren't you?
Yes, I had my own programme, junior television on ATV, which I did for four years, telling stories about the Australian bush hospital at Wee Waa in NSW, reading Banjo Patterson and talking about the brumbies and so on. When Lew Grade offered me a contract at £100 a week, I took it. Later I wanted to get out of the ATV job and when Bob Baker rang me up to ask if I'd like to go to North Africa to make *Sea of Sand*, I said, 'Yes, please!' I made *Sea of Sand* with Michael Craig, John Gregson and Dickie Attenborough, and Dickie asked me what I planned to do next. He was going to do a film called *Danger Within* for Don Chaffey. When I got back to London I was called to see Don and found I had a part in the film, which was very nice of Dickie.

Those were superior examples of the 50s war films. Where were they made?
Sea of Sand was made in Tripoli in North Africa. We had six of the worst old army trucks in North Africa; half the time they didn't work and were being towed past the cameras, even though they'd had new engines fitted. But it was probably one of the best locations I've ever been on – we stayed at the Imperial Hotel by the sea. It was pretty rough filming in the desert but we played poker, drank a lot of beer, and swam.

Danger Within was set in Italy, but made in England; a camp was built out near Gerrards Cross and we shot it there. I've made six or seven films for Don Chaffey, particularly here in Australia where he now lives. We became mates and he just finds parts for me. I'm sure he wouldn't, though, if he didn't think I could do the job.

What was your experience of working with Donald Wolfit in *Blood of the Vampire*?
Oh, marvellous. He would drag Victor Maddern and me into his room, lie on the bed and talk about the theatre for hours. It was fascinating. He was very grand, very much *Sir* Donald, but he treated us well. Henry Cass was called in at the last moment to direct the film; I don't think he'd even read the script when he arrived on the first day. In one scene there were glass jars containing entrails and bits of human bodies, supposedly. Of course, they'd been to the butcher's shop for hearts, kidneys and livers. Imagine all that under the hot lights after two or three days!

Were the 50s a good time to get a career going in British films?
It was good for me when I started doing 'A' pictures like *A Town Like Alice*. An actor is never secure, though. The only time I felt secure was when I had the ATV contract. I left RADA in 1951 and you could say I've been semi-retired ever since! But, in the 50s everybody was making films. Elstree, Shepperton, Pinewood were doing the big 'A' features and all the small studios like Wimbledon and Merton Park were making second features, so there was a lot of work around. If you'd done a stint in rep and had a decent agent, you could get a job.

Did you come to play in the two Jack Lee films because you were an Australian?
After *A Town Like Alice* Joe Janni told me that I'd got the job because, after RADA, I'd understudied Michael Denison and Ronnie Lewis in a play called *The Bad*

Samaritan, by Willy Douglas-Home. Virginia McKenna, with whom I'd been very friendly was in that play. When they sent the script of *A Town Like Alice* to Ginny (whom I used to call 'my English rose', she's a lovely lady and a wonderful actress), she agreed to do it and suggested I would be ideal for the part of Ben. I was doing a children's film in Norfolk when I got a call from my agent to go to see Jack Lee and Joe Janni at Heathrow Airport. They were on their way to Australia to do location shots for *A Town Like Alice*, and Joe offered me the part of Ben.

A Town Like Alice was all done with back projection against the 'jungles' of Pinewood. It was drizzling with rain and so cold, we used to have to sip brandy to keep ourselves warm. While I was at Pinewood I changed uniforms and nipped across to another studio to do one scene for *Reach for the Sky*, playing Muriel Pavlow's brother or cousin.

After that I think Peter Finch gave Jack Lee the book *Robbery Under Arms*, suggesting that he and I could play the Marsden boys. When Jack decided to make the film, John Davis, Rank's Managing Director, insisted that contract artistes be used for the leads. I was offered the much smaller part of the brother of one of the girls and said I'd do it if we were going to film in Australia. Joe

Vincent Ball (centre) in *A Town Like Alice*, 1956

Janni said we wouldn't be going to Australia and, when I said I didn't want to do it in that case, I didn't hear from him for a couple of weeks. Then he asked me to lunch at Pinewood with himself, Jack Lee and Finch, and Joe asked me to be in the film for old times' sake and I agreed.

After they had been in Adelaide for a couple of weeks I got a call to come out there. I flew to Adelaide (after two weeks in Sydney) and was given a hotel room and a big car for another two weeks, then told to join the unit at Wulpina Farm. Ultimately, I was filmed saying one line. I had been in Australia ten or eleven weeks, being paid all the time, and when I returned I shot my scenes at Pinewood!

It was great working with Peter Finch and, after the filming, we knocked around together for about four or five years. He was very generous – never had any cigarettes or any money, but he would take twenty people to 'Casa Pepe' in the Fulham Road for dinner and just sign for it.

How did you get involved in making *Summer of the 17th Doll*?
John Mills asked if I would coach his daughter Juliet in an Aussie accent, because she was going to test for the part of Bubba. I also offered to do the test with her, playing Johnny Dowd opposite her, believing the part of Johnny had been cast. As it happened, I was working on the day of Juliet's test and couldn't do it with her. Then John asked if I would give him a hand with his script. So we worked all morning, had lunch, and that night I got a message from my agent. He'd received a telegram from Hollywood which said, 'Availability Vincent Ball, Johnny Dowd, January, Australia'. He explained that it meant they wanted me for the part. They asked for a clip of film of me and I suggested they get a copy of *A Town Like Alice*. They got a copy in New York and the next day I was offered the part of Johnny Dowd. When Burt Lancaster dropped out of the film the budget went right down. We shot it all around Sydney, didn't go to Queensland at all. They changed the ending, of course, and made it into a nice Hollywood-type ending.

Come on George (1939), *Dancing with Crime* (1947), *Esther Waters*, *Quartet* ('The Alien Corn'), *Once a Jolly Swagman* (1948), *Dear Mr. Prohack*, *Boys in Brown* (1940), *The Blue Lamp*, *So Long at the Fair*, *The Woman in Question* (1950), *Blackmailed* (1951), *Penny Princess*, *Hunted*, *The Gentle Gunman* (1952), *Appointment in London*, *Desperate Moment* (1953), *They Who Dare*, *Doctor in the House*, *The Sleeping Tiger*, *For Better, For Worse* (1954), *The Sea Shall Not Have Them*, *Simba*, *Doctor at Sea*, *Cast a Dark Shadow* (1955), *The Spanish Gardener* (1956), *Ill Met By Moonlight*, *Doctor at Large*, *Campbell's Kingdom* (1957), *A Tale of Two Cities*, *The Wind Cannot Read* (1958), *The Doctor's Dilemma*, *Libel* (1959), *Song Without End*, *The Angel Wore Red*, *The Singer not the Song* (1960), *Victim* (1961), *HMS Defiant*, *The Password is Courage*, *We Joined the Navy* (guest) (1962), *The Mind Benders*, *I Could Go on Singing* (1963), *Doctor in Distress*, *Hot Enough for June*, *The Servant* (1963), *King and Country*, *The High Bright Sun* (1964), *Darling* (1965), *Modesty Blaise*, *The Epic that Never Was** (1966), *Accident*, *Our Mother's House* (1967), *Sebastian*, *The Fixer* (1968), *The Damned*, *Justine*, *Oh! What a Lovely War* (1969), *Death in Venice* (1970), *The Serpent* (1972), *The Night Porter* (1973), *Permission to Kill* (1975), *A Bridge Too Far*, *Providence* (1977), *Despair* (1978), *The Patricia Neal Story** (1981), *Daddy Nostalgie* (1990).
* Made for television, some cinema release.

Though he would not care for the description, Dirk Bogarde was almost certainly the most popular British film star of the 1950s. During the 1960s and after, he devoted himself increasingly to more obviously taxing roles, especially in the films of Joseph Losey and Luchino Visconti, and won a new reputation as one of the world's most authoritative film actors, but this should not cloud his achievement in the 50s. True, there are no doubt more complex demands made by roles such as Barrett in *The Servant* or Aschenbach in *Death in Venice*, but the days at Gainsborough and Pinewood have their rewards as well. Apart from two bit-parts, he began as a star and has stayed one for forty years. In the early films, he shows a striking intensity as the sensitive pianist in 'The Alien Corn'

sequence of *Quartet*, offers a vivid contrast to the homely Ealing virtues as the vicious thug in *The Blue Lamp*, is a convincingly romantic hero in *So Long at the Fair* and a sympathetic fugitive in *Hunted*. Among the many felicities of *Doctor in the House*, his likeable Simon Sparrow provides a crucial credible centre, and it is this film which began his long and successful association with the team of Ralph Thomas and Betty Box over the next decade. His playing of the homosexual barrister in *Victim* in 1961 seems, with hindsight, to have been a decisive step away from the 'idol of the Odeon' roles and towards the mature triumphs of the ensuing decades.

Interview date: July 1990.

How did you get into *Dancing with Crime* in 1947?
By the grace of God, after the war I got into an actors' reunion thing when you had the chance to be in a half-hour play once a month, to which agents and managements would come. I played Jesus Christ in my demob suit, and from there got an 'overnight-star' job in the theatre, in *Power Without Glory*. But £5 a week really wasn't enough to live on, so a friend told me to see someone else who was sympathetic to actors who had been in the war. I was given a job in *Dancing with Crime*, in which I had to be a policeman. My uniform

didn't fit so they pinned it up in the front and you only ever saw the back of my head. I came back on the bus that afternoon with £20, whereas my take-home pay from the theatre (which was much harder work to do) was only £5.

You then starred in *Esther Waters* and have remained a star ever since. How do you feel about being a 'star'?
I dislike it now. It's a word that belonged to another period. I had been a serious actor in the theatre, and there was a terrible snobbery about film actors, film

stars. It didn't require anything except that the girls had to be pretty and have good tits; and if a guy was OK-looking they could get him to do anything. But there *is* something called 'star quality'; you have to have 'watchability'.

What sorts of contracts were you under up until the end of the 50s?

I signed my contract with Rank in February 1947 – it's burned into my head. It was for £3,000 a year, with a modest annual increase, for a minimum of three films a year and they had the contractual right to dump me every July. I said I would agree to those terms if I could go back to the theatre at least once every two years if I got something I wanted to do. They agreed, but I didn't realise I had to add the time off to the end of the contract. In the end I was seventeen, not seven, years with Rank, and had to buy myself out for £10,000. My only choice was that, out of every four films submitted, I had to do three.

Esther Waters and Once a Jolly Swagman were both made for Ian Dalrymple's Wessex Films. What do you remember of this unit?

I liked Ian. He was an erudite and intelligent man and a man I could talk to. I would never have signed a contract unless it had been for him. Then I found out he was under the umbrella of Rank, and Rank in those days were what they are now: businessmen who didn't know anything about making movies, so they employed people who did and gave them the chance to do it. The whole system broke up in the early 50s and it failed because Wessex didn't know how to handle it.

Esther Waters must have cost a fortune; I mean, my costumes were made by a Savile Row tailor and I was an unknown creature! Since then I've been working in films for peanuts so I can see the difference. *Esther Waters* was a gloomy movie but then I was a gloomy subject and wasn't capable of carrying it. At the end of the film, my co-star, Kathleen Ryan, gave me a silver brandy flask which I still have, saying 'To hell with Esther Waters!'

You had a range of roles in Esther Waters, Once a Jolly Swagman, Quartet, and Boys in Brown. What did you learn from these?

Nothing, except never to do it again – that is, not do what the directors told me to do. I think *Quartet* was my second film and I remember being so disheartened by the fact that I had done *Esther Waters* and ahead of me were two terrible roles with which I wasn't going to be

able to do anything. One was the motorcycle rider in *Swagman* and the other was in an Arnold Bennett story called *Dear Mr Prohack*. So I went to Sydney Box, then head of Gainsborough studios, and pleaded to be allowed to be in *Quartet* before the other movies came out, because if I hadn't done that I would have been sacked. Sydney Box was kind enough to let me be in it; I think he was rather overcome by this crawling amateur pleading with him! But I knew I could work in the part of a sensitive pianist, whereas I was totally wrong for the rest of the stuff.

Was it The Blue Lamp that established you as a major British film star?

Yes, no question of that. I'd worked with the director Basil Dearden before – on the stage. When he got *The Blue Lamp* he wasn't sure I could do it, but it worked. It was the first of what we would call today *cinéma vérité*: the first true, on-location, movie we had ever made. I think they built the policeman's flat, but everything else was done in Paddington Green Police Station and the White City dog-racing track. I had never before had to act outdoors, but then I realised this was how to do it. Some of it was done in the sleazier parts at the back of Regent's Canal, which has mostly been pulled down now as it was nearly all bombed stuff.

The whole of the chase at the end of the film was shot during a greyhound derby at White City and nobody was told that we were shooting a movie. It was a crowd of 30,000 and I had to run through it; some people were taking a razor at me! My clothes were torn to shreds. When Jimmy [Hanley] and I had to run across an electric railway track at one point, all we were told was that we hadn't been given permission because it was too dangerous. We had to cross the live tracks and I can remember the faces of the train drivers coming out of the tunnel and seeing a man and a policeman in uniform, standing between the tracks. We never got any danger money in those days! There was a very good actor in it called Pat Doonan, who eventually killed himself. He would have been one of the great British character actors.

What are your recollections of working with Anthony Asquith, first in The Woman in Question?

He didn't want me at all in *The Woman in Question*, I think he wanted William Holden, but he was forced by Rank to use a contract artiste. I was one and Susan Shaw and Jean Kent were also. I don't think he really enjoyed working with me then, but we went on to work together later and became very close. We tried to do one film together which was aborted, a film about Lawrence of Arabia. Asquith and Terence Rattigan were working on the story of Lawrence from his youth at Cambridge right through until his death. I wasn't anything like Lawrence, but they had detected in me the kind of sensitivity they needed for this part; a blond wig was made and we were going out to do this wonderful script. I had tremendous help from Geoffrey Woolley, whose father was *The Times* correspondent during Lawrence's First World War campaigns. Geoffrey gave me all his father's personal correspondence between himself and Lawrence, which has never been published.

For some reason, we were never told why, ten days before we were due to shoot on a huge BP petrol compound in the desert (which King Feisal had given permission for us to use), Rank pulled the plug. It destroyed Asquith and it practically destroyed me. Rattigan then turned what remained of his work into a play called *Ross*.

So there we all were, the whole team, and Asquith felt we couldn't just lose everything, so he said we must find an alternative within the next ten days. The only thing we could find ready to go was a script, adapted from Shaw's *The Doctor's Dilemma*, and a lot of the people who were to have been in 'Lawrence' were employed in that, and Leslie Caron joined us. It was a very good film; one of the most definitive Shaw productions I have seen. But nobody went to see it. They all thought it was a *Doctor in the House* sequel, sat through the first ten minutes with all that discussion going on and then walked out. It *is* all argument and people have a very short attention span as audiences.

I liked *Libel* very much. What do you think of it.
I haven't seen it, but I think it was a load of shit. *The Doctor's Dilemma* was a success for Metro in America and they asked us to do something else straight away, because we still had the studio space, the whole crew, Bob Krasker lighting, everyone who had been employed for 'Lawrence'. The only thing they could come up with was *Libel*, for which they were in the process of working on the script. We got Olivia de Havilland, Robert Morley came back, and we just went tramping on. It was certainly melodrama; we knew it was and we hammered it up to the elbows. We had to do something because of the failure of *The Doctor's Dilemma*, and *Libel* was quite a success.

Speaking of full-blooded melodrama, can we go back to *So Long at the Fair*?
I didn't like that film but I had to do it, and, at that point, I was very much in love with Jean [Simmons]. Rank thought it was a great idea to encourage their two juvenile stars and we were given this film which was supposed to launch our engagement. Unfortunately, by the time the film was finished Jean had fallen in love with Stewart Granger, thereby ruining the publicity effort. The story of *So Long at the Fair* is perfectly true; it was all right and the kids went to see it because Jean and I were pretty; and it was the first time I had the chance to use my own voice rather than an Irish or a Cockney one. It was also my first association with Betty Box as a producer.

What were the special strengths of the Betty Box-Ralph Thomas team?
They knew just what the public wanted. We were just coming out of the doldrums of post-war austerity and audiences wanted to laugh, to be 'taken out of themselves', to see things that were glamorous. I did four or five of those 'Doctor' films and Betty, in particular, fought for me to be in them, although the studio didn't want me. I had been noted by critics, but I hadn't become the major star that Rank had hoped I'd be. Betty and Ralph had seen me in a couple of plays and realised that I could play comedy. The studio believed I could only play spivs and Cockneys, but Betty and Ralph put me in tweeds and let me speak in my own voice and the rest was history.

Doctor in the House was such a runaway success, I think, basically because it was a ragbag of all the old doctor jokes which everyone in hospitals knows, real student jokes, cleverly strung together by Richard Gordon [author]. Betty and Ralph had the script rewritten by Nicholas Phipps; I changed my character's name to Simon Sparrow because I thought it was funnier, and so it stayed. The one stipulation I made was that I had to be a *real* doctor; I would do things that were funny, but would never instigate anything funny. We had two doctors always on the set; if any of us had to perform an operation or some medical procedure, there was always someone there to explain exactly how to do it. I wouldn't put a stethoscope to a body until I knew exactly how it was done and what I would have said. It was very strictly controlled. It was an enormously happy film to make. There wasn't a bad-tempered face on the set.

You were in a couple of the more serious Box-

Jean Simmons and Dirk Bogarde in Terence Fisher and Antony Darnborough's *So Long at the Fair*, 1950

Thomas films, including *A Tale of Two Cities*. Did you feel Sidney Carton was a very good part?
Yes, we all thought we were doing something unusual. We saw the Ronald Colman version and knew that we had to lick it. I don't know why, but ours didn't work. It was the best I could do at the time; I chose Dorothy Tutin for Lucy Manette and we had very good stage actors – Cecil Parker and Christopher Lee before he became a monster. But then Betty and Ralph made one capital error, which was not to make it in colour. If it had been in colour, people would still watch it today.

Did you steep yourself in Dickens for the film?
No, I knew about Sidney Carton from school; I didn't sit there sweating my arse off reading it. Tibby Clarke's scenario was excellent, in that it typified the essence of

the book so I didn't have to read the book itself. I have involuntarily read books of which I have then made movies; I read *The Singer not the Song* long before the movie, which was a travesty of what it should have been. So was *The Spanish Gardener*, which was a perfectly straightforward novel by A.J. Cronin, which was also ruined as a movie. Some of it's quite good, I suppose, but I saw it and was heartbroken because it just wasn't true.

How did you find working in *The Spanish Gardener* with the boy Jon Whitely, with whom you'd worked in *Hunted*?
He was five-and-a-half when I first worked with him and we were together for three months. He and I were almost the only two in the film and I was with him all the time; I

actually tried to adopt him because we became so devoted. All that we did together was extemporary, we just invented it.

We didn't have much rehearsal; I hate rehearsals unless it's something technically complicated, such as in *The Servant* where I had about forty-one camera changes to make while laying and unlaying a dinner table. Then I do want to know exactly where my props are so that it all happens on cue. I always insist on a technical rehearsal, when no emotion is happening, just saying the lines. The crew has to know what you are doing and sound has to know that you may turn your head as you say a line, but you don't put the guns in until the red light is on.

Did you find Michael Powell a good director of actors when you made *Ill Met by Moonlight*?
That's a very difficult question. He was wonderful, but he was a real bastard! I have discovered that the great directors do not direct; or you don't think they're directing. They leave it to you to get on with it and, if you're wrong, they will have a few words with you, saying something like, 'Do you have a reason for doing that?' And if you have a reason, they will very often agree to try it your way. Visconti never told me anything on *Death in Venice* – he took it on board that I had known what I was asked to do. It is only fussy directors, and not very good ones, who give you all those instructions.

I very much liked *Cast a Dark Shadow* in which you played an unusually unwholesome hero.
The unwholesomeness of the hero was what was fun about it. The film was a failure though. It was the first time I had come under another star's name – Margaret Lockwood's – and it just died, which was a pity because it was a very good movie and I had persuaded Maggie to do it. I remember being on tour in Cardiff with a play and seeing a poster for *Cast a Dark Shadow* and it had 'Dirk Bogarde in *Cast a Dark Shadow*' and, at the very bottom, 'with Margaret Lockwood'. They had altered the billing order because they saw it was dying and that astoundingly her name had killed it, though it was probably her best performance ever.

I have never seen *The Singer not the Song*, but it has acquired a cult reputation.
Yes, especially in Europe, in France and Germany. It is about a young Mexican bandit who, with his gang, holds a small Mexican town to ransom. Then a young Canadian priest, on his first mission, comes in to try and

disarm the situation; the bandit falls in love with him and that is basically the story. It was a terrible script and they put John Mills in as the priest when it should have been someone like Paul Newman as he was in those days. I should have been in blue jeans and beat-up old jacket, driving an old Chevy, and there I was in black leather and riding a white horse – I did the whole thing for camp and nobody had any idea what was happening! Mylène Demongeot played the girl who was in love with the priest and who then kind of falls for me – you know, a berserk three-hander.

Victim was really the first commercial film to deal openly with homosexuality. What do you recall now of how you all approached it?
It was the first time a man had said he was in love with another man on the screen. It was not in the script, I wrote that bit. The script was intended for another actor, but he turned it down because he said, if he played this part, it would prejudice his chances of a knighthood. Basil Dearden called me on Christmas Eve and told me he was in a jam. Now, [Michael] Relph and Dearden had already made some controversial films including *Sapphire* and *A Life for Ruth*; and this was the one they were going to do about homosexuality.

I said to my father that I thought I would do this movie because I had always wanted to create a fuss in the movies, and this one was about homosexuality. My father's response was 'Dear boy, don't do it. It's so boring because we get it on television all the time in documentaries. Do something interesting like *The Mayor of Casterbridge*!' Then he said, 'Remember that your mother lives in a very small village and it is rather difficult with the neighbours'.

So I went back to Basil and agreed to do the film on condition that we put in a scene at the end in which the man says to his wife that, yes, he did love a boy. We then couldn't find anyone to play the wife; until Sylvia Syms, bless her dear little heart, finally said, 'No problem. It's a wonderful part and I'd love to play it', which she did.

Janet Green had written the script and very kindly agreed to allow me to write that one little scene. Originally it was to have ended with us all going off to the Old Bailey, with nobody having said a word. All that happened was that a photograph was shown of me in a car with some young man. It was total rubbish, so we put in the extra scene and it went off like a humdinger. It was a commercial success because, in a way that we hadn't anticipated, it touched upon something that affected a lot of people. Women wrote in their hundreds – tragic letters saying '*That*'s what was wrong with my husband/ brother/father' and they hadn't known. I was applauded in England for my 'great courage'.

In 1954, after Joseph Losey was accused of 'un-American activities', you made a film for him called *Sleeping Tiger*. How difficult was it for Losey in England, working under a pseudonym?
It was totally impossible for him. He got out of America just in time, otherwise he would have been shopped and put in prison. He worked for a while in Italy, then came over here with Carl Foreman. He and Carl got together and got hold of a crummy script written by another McCarthy throw-out whose name I can't remember, and they tried to get it made. Joe's only chance was if he could get a star name to play the boy in the film. I had already made three films that year and was knackered; there was no money available, and so I didn't want to do it. However, the woman in charge of contract actors at Rank, Olive Dodds, felt it might lead to something very important for me. So I agreed to meet Mr Losey and he ran *The Prowler* for me. I saw about twenty-four minutes of it and told him I'd do the film.

So, I joined forces with Joe; Alexis Smith came over from America. She was shattered when she arrived at my house to see Joe sitting there; she had thought the director's name was Vic Hanbury, which was Joe's pseudonym. She was very concerned at making the film with him, given the charges of 'un-American activities' against him, but she stayed – and remained my friend ever since, a wonderful woman. So we made the film, it was a success and Joe made a lot of money. After that, we didn't work together for about ten years, although I got him a contract at Rank which he just about forgave me for, finally!

Do you think that, as far as British cinema is concerned, the 40s and 50s were a boom period?
Certainly the early 40s were of vast importance for Britain. That's when Powell, Pressburger, Dearden and a number of others began to surface and Ealing came out with modest-budget films. I think it began to crack apart as soon as I came in! The moment the war was over, we lost our way a little. It went on for a couple of years I suppose, but, by the early 50s, we were smug and complacent and we had lost the track. I am glad that I was fortunate enough to be in before the gate closed; at least I was able to work with some of the best doing their best.

Roy Boulting

As director:

The Landlady*, *Ripe Earth**, *Seeing Stars** (1938), *Trunk Crime*, *Inquest* (1939), *Pastor Hall* (1940), *Dawn Guard**, *Thunder Rock* (1942), *Desert Victory** (1943), *Tunisian Victory** (co dir) (1944), *Burma Victory** (1945), *Fame is the Spur* (1947), *The Guinea Pig* (1948), *Singlehanded*, *High Treason* (1951), *Seagulls over Sorrento* (1954), *Josephine and Men* (1955), *Run for the Sun* (1956), *Brothers-in-Law* (1957), *Happy is the Bride* (1958), *Carlton Brown of the F.O.* (1959), *Suspect* (1960), *A French Mistress* (1960), *The Family Way* (1966), *Twisted Nerve* (1968), *There's a Girl in My Soup* (1970), *Soft Beds, Hard Battles* (1973), *The Last Word* (1979).
* Documentaries or shorts.

Roy Boulting and his twin brother, John, formed one of those director-producer teams which thrived in British cinema during the 1940s and 50s. Like their friends, Sidney Gilliat and Frank Launder, they regularly interchanged roles, so that it is possible to think of 'the Boulting brothers' as a unit for a good deal of the period. In fact, Roy's directorial career is the longer and more varied of the two. He began with short films before the war and made two distinguished feature films, *Pastor Hall* and *Thunder Rock* in the early years of the war, before his involvement with three major wartime documentaries. In the post-war years, there were socially committed dramas (*Fame is the Spur*, *The Guinea Pig*), several films for American companies, and then, in the latter half of the 50s, a string of very popular satirical comedies which took swipes at the army, the law, the unions, the church and the civil service. These films made excellent use of what came to seem like a Boulting repertory company, including Ian Carmichael, Richard Attenborough, Terry-Thomas and others. Whether in comedy or drama, the Boulting films typically exhibit a vein of social commitment which gives coherence and weight to their output.

Interview date: October 1989.

How did you and your brother go about setting up Charter Films?

When John came back from the war in Spain, I proposed that he join me in setting up a film company of our own. War would be coming to England soon enough, so I thought let's get started before that happens. In six years he'd lifted himself from office boy in Wardour Street to one of Ace Films' principal salesmen: he knew his way around Wardour Street. In the office, he'd be boss: on the floor, the last word would be mine. And that was the start of Charter Film Productions.

How do you account for its extraordinarily long life as a production company?

I'd say that it was probably due to the speed with which we learned to avoid repeating the mistakes of the beginner. Our first film – of hideous memory – was titled *The Landlady*, and we learnt several lessons from it. Lesson

One: read and assess any script you are offered, alone, apart and without assistance. Never allow an author to act it out for you: he may be a better actor than he is a writer! Lesson Two: never permit a technician to alter your judgment of how a scene should be played unless he can provide a good and convincing reason. Lesson Three: never allow the prospect of profit to determine a creative decision.

As we absorbed into our film-making philosophy these and other lessons learned in the tough school of experience, so we earned a reputation for being a couple of 'toffee-nosed' bastards, arrogant, opinionated, inflexible and difficult. The fact that the films we chose to make proved successful, despite opposing advice, only served to baffle and exacerbate. The longevity of Charter Films, then, may be attributed to lessons learned and acted on; a readiness to stand or fall by our own judgment; a measure of talent; and a hell of a lot of good luck!

After the disaster of our first film and the sale of two one-reel documentaries, we made a film called *Consider Your Verdict*, based on a BBC playlet by Laurence Housman. In contrast to the frustrations of filming *The Landlady*, all moved forward as if on oiled wheels. The film opened at London's first art house, the Academy, in support of a sombre but magnificent French film, *Quai des Brumes*. It ran there for over six months before playing across the country on the Odeon Circuit. The critics lauded the film with a generosity that even we felt was excessive. Although only a supporting feature, it earned more than ten times its cost. And that is how the Boulting Brothers and Charter Films started fifty years of film-making.

You sometimes made films for other companies. Were these one-off deals?
In 1945 when we emerged from the Services, there was little in Charter's financial kitty. Largely due to their cinemas, Rank and ABPC had enjoyed five prosperous war years, and both were now into production. Two Cities was just one of the production companies taken over by Rank. The Headman was a volatile, extravagant but engaging Italian, Filippo Del Giudice. He invited us to make *Fame is the Spur* for him. Despite a splendid cast – Michael Redgrave, Rosamund John, Bernard Miles, etcetera – a sixteen-week schedule, and an exorbitant cost (over which, unhappily, we had little control), the film proved to be a disappointment. It received a mixed press – and died at the box-office. That was in 1946.

At the end of the 40s, I directed *High Treason* for Paul Soskin's Conqueror Films, also a Rank-controlled company. Soskin's first approach came with a 'thriller' titled *First Spy, Second Front*. I pointed out that the war was over, that a more topical 'thriller' could be taken from the headlines of any newspaper any day of the week. He solemnly picked up a morning daily. I, with equal solemnity, seized on a headline. He agreed. And, together with Frank Harvey, I went away and wrote the screenplay of *High Treason* – not, by the way, our title. Cast with then largely unknowns, it was of its genre a pretty good example.

John and I had learned that freedom from interference in choosing and making a film only comes when you have a financial stake in it. For this reason alone, from time to time, I would stagger off to Hollywood with John's agreement, to make a film. Whatever I earned went into Charter Films. It bought us time, independence and sufficient finance to invest in the films we

wanted to make. They were brought to me – *Single-handed* by 20th Century-Fox, *Seagulls over Sorrento* by MGM, *Run for the Sun*, by RKO – in the early 50s. If not subjects I would have chosen myself, I do not regard the results as, in any way, dishonourable; and the experience was both illuminating and valuable.

Happy is the Bride came towards the end of the 50s. We were already tied to British Lion. It was brought by my old associate, Paul Soskin and the NFFC [National Film Finance Corporation], who had an investment in the project. Lion wanted me to do it, and it was a great success.

What attracted you to filming Robert Ardrey's play *Thunder Rock*?
It seemed then that it justified everything that was being fought for in the war. There we were; France had collapsed; all our allies were powerless. Today, I think it's very hard to convey to people just how perilous the time and the scene was then. Ardrey had written this play which was put on in 1938 in New York. It had failed lamentably, and was then put on in this country. John and I saw it and felt that this play could explain – to America in particular – what time and history required of them. The British Ministry of Information felt as we did, that it should be made, and, in 1941, Sam Eckman who was the head of MGM in this country, said he wanted to finance the film. I was in the Army and John was in the RAF, and we were taken out of the services for six months to make *Thunder Rock*.

It's full of fascinating, fluid movement between present and past, between reality and fantasy ...
Yes, it is. I remember talking with Mutz Greenbaum [a.k.a. Max Greene], the most brilliant and versatile lighting cameraman I have ever worked with, and saying, 'This is a film about the past that has to be related to the present – that's its purpose. But when dealing with characters from the past, I don't want them to be 'film ghosts', double exposure figures. I want the past to be as present and as solid as the figures of today. But, in some way, odd – strange, unnatural'. And we sat throughout the day discussing this.

Suddenly, I heard a voice say: 'Roy! I am thinking, I am thinking now of many years ago in Germany. We are lighting a film with the same problem: the characters are ghosts but must look real. So I tell the producers, then you must build the set at an angle, tilt it, the camera, too, so that on the screen all will be normal, the set appear level. But it is the characters who will seem

Michael Redgrave and Lilli Palmer in *Thunder Rock*, 1942

strange. As they move, they are the ones who are tilted in response to gravity, their bodies real, their movements strange, ghostlike'. What a bloody marvellous idea, I thought – and how simple! Good, I told him, we'll have a go. The towering lighthouse interior was built at an angle of 120. Literally and metaphorically it worked like a dream – testimony to Mutz Greenbaum's brilliance as a lighting cameraman. That was the visual secret of *Thunder Rock*.

How influential were your wartime documentaries in opening up post-war opportunities to you?

I doubt that many people thought about 'post-war opportunities' in those days. About coming through with one's skin intact, perhaps. But I did get a kick out of the making of *Desert Victory*. It happened quite by chance. Just returned to the Army from 'civvy street' on the completion of *Thunder Rock*, I was up in the War Office one day, seeking information on something or other, when I encountered a Major Woolley, who couldn't help me with the information I sought, but revealed that *his* job was to keep a day-by-day diary on the course of the war in the Middle East.

What I didn't know at the time was that Major Sir Leonard Woolley happened to be the most distinguished British archaeologist of the age, and knew that area like the back of his hand. The British Eighth Army had recently been driven back over the Egyptian border by Rommel, and was now dug in at El Alamein, awaiting a

further onslaught. Quietly and graphically, he outlined what the implications would be if Rommel, once again, smashed through our defences: Egypt would be lost; all the oil riches of the area, on which our industries at home depended, would fall to his hand; and, with virtually nothing there to impede them, the Germans would be in a position to drive up into the Crimea and join with Van Paulus's army about to drive down from the north. As he told it, the battle, when it came – whether resulting in victory or defeat – would determine the whole course of the war.

I returned to AFU [Army Film Unit] headquarters at Pinewood Studios, knowing what I had to do. And there *was* a battle. It commenced on the night of 25 October 1942 and ended ten days later on the morning of 5 November with Rommel's Afrika Corps in full retreat, their Italian allies gladly surrendering in their thousands. During those ten days, Major [David] Macdonald's front-line cameramen had been sending back nearly a million feet of film recording the first victory of British arms on land since the start of the war. At Pinewood, the AFU was in a state of frenetic activity. Three reels outlining the background and prelude to the Battle had already been cut. I had written and shot a reconstruction of the night of 25 October to intercut with actual scenes of the thousand-gun barrage with which it opened.

A short time later, after a rapturous response from the Secretary of State and others at the War Office, *Desert*

Victory opened at the Odeon, Leicester Square to a cheering audience, and a glowing press on the following morning. My old friend, David Macdonald, sent back from the desert by General Montgomery to see that justice was done to the feats of the Eighth Army – and, perhaps, himself was promoted Lt Colonel overnight, and flew off to the States the next day to promote its future there. In America, the film triumphed again. *Desert Victory* was awarded an 'Oscar' as the documentary film of the year. And I looked like being pegged down at Pinewood for the duration.

After the war, what sort of impulses led you to *Fame is the Spur* and *The Guinea Pig*?
As peace broke out, I think we held, with many others, a belief that, after all people had endured, it must result in a more just and equitable society. That this sentiment was felt by the overwhelming majority had already been reflected in the landslide Labour vote at the first postwar elections.

Fame is the Spur was a cautionary tale, however, that warned of the dangers to which the political idealist is vulnerable on achieving power; the difficulty facing every politician elevated to government when trying to reconcile the original 'dream', with the harsher imperatives involved in 'trying to get things done' and the subtle seductions offered by society to someone who has become a public figure.

Howard Spring's central character, Hamer Radshaw, who rises from poverty to Prime Minister, was clearly inspired by the fate of the late Ramsay MacDonald. Played immaculately, I think, by Michael Redgrave, he emerges as a sad, rather than unsympathetic character, reluctant to face his gradual abandonment of early principles, but doing so briefly, when his dying wife, played by Rosamund John, gently reminds him of his early ideals. However, after five years of death, destruction and austerity, *Fame is the Spur* was far too grim for an audience now seeking escapism and peace. It flopped.

The Guinea Pig, on the other hand, though with strong political overtones and serious purpose, was a huge success. It was adapted from an entertaining, if untidy, play written by Warren Chetham-Strode. It also gave Richard Attenborough, who had just played the young boy gangster, Pinkie, in Graham Greene's *Brighton Rock*, an opportunity to demonstrate his versatility in the role of a working-class boy of fourteen, sent to a posh English public school. Just twenty-four years old when the film started shooting, he brought it off triumphantly, although many were deeply sceptical at the outset.

Chetham-Strode's play was sparked by educational recommendations to the Government in the Fleming Report. This urged that bright scholars, no matter what their background or financial circumstances, should be admitted to the advantages of a public school education. John and I found the play's basic situation intriguing, contemporary, exciting.

We bought the play and invited the author to work on the adaptation to film. I felt that a weakness in the play was the dialogue and characterisation of those – particularly the boy's parents – who were 'working-class'. The words they spoke, their response to the situation, didn't ring absolutely true. Without knowing it, Chetham as author, had patronised his characters, the boy's father – an ex-Sergeant Major – and mother, in a paternalistic fashion that neither would have accepted or allowed.

So, I turned to my ex-neighbour and friend, Bernard Miles, and asked him to come and work on the screenplay with the author. It was hardly a meeting of minds. Nor was it a marriage of convenience, with each recognising the other's strengths. The solution came when I took over three offices in a row with inter-connecting doors. I placed Warren on one flank, Bernard on the other. Working independently, as each completed the draft of a scene it would be brought in and placed on my desk. I took what I thought was good from both – and much was – although the merging of two such opposing talents proved far from easy, and, for the first time in my career, I took a writer's credit on the screen! Strangely enough, no seams showed in the finished work, which says much for the basic worth of the original play.

What do you recall of another unlikely-sounding screenplay collaboration – Graham Greene and Terence Rattigan on *Brighton Rock*?
Greene and Rattigan! Chalk and cheese, would you say? But the joint screen credit was determined, not so much by a collaboration, as by a prior contract. *Brighton Rock* had been purchased jointly by Anatole De Grunwald (who would produce), Anthony Asquith (direct) and Terence Rattigan (to adapt and write a screenplay). It was hardly their cup of tea: the undertones of Graham's highly idiosyncratic Catholicism eluded Terry, while the gentle, cultivated 'Puffin' Asquith found the brutal milieu, the savage action, extremely uncongenial. Finally, defeated, they gave up on the subject. Those hardier roughnecks, the brothers Boulting, arrived on the scene and acquired the film rights from them. A condition of the sale was screen recognition of Rattigan's aborted script.

Having read it, we wrote it off and decided to turn to the author himself. Graham was somewhat unsure but, pressed, agreed to have a go. What he eventually came up with may have been a trifle 'rough' as a final screenplay, but it was all that we had hoped for, containing as it did, the distilled essence of a story that was pure 'film' from beginning to end.

John, whose second feature film this would be as director, was delighted. In Brighton, in search of location backgrounds, I traipsed up and down the Palace Pier and across the pebble beaches; discovered the dramatic web of narrow lanes between clock-tower and sea front; scoured the sleazy area around Brighton's Kemp Town; found those pubs the race gangs had haunted on the eve of a meeting; and trudged up on to the Downs to take pictures of the race track and the sites where, with razors and knives at the ready, the 'Nottingham Lads', battling with the 'Brighton Boys', brought notoriety and shame to Brighton.

At the end of a month, I sat down to incorporate all this detailed research into Graham's screenplay. Two weeks later, the final work had been broken down loosely into shots, I returned to London and handed over the blueprint – the shooting script – to brother John. With casting complete, he took the film to the floor – and handled a quite sensitive subject in a quite masterly fashion. Generously, no objection was raised to Terry's name appearing up on the screen credits; but adaptation and writing glory were, in truth, entirely Graham Greene's.

These films of yours seem unusually realistic in the context of British cinema of the time.

I think that from the very beginning of our film-making, John and I sought to convey, in subject, or technique, or both, a feeling for the truth. We shied away from the trite escapism to which pre-war British films had been wedded. War itself had brought liberation and a national identity to the British film for the first time in its history. We didn't want to lose that. Even when, in the middle 50s, we turned a satirical and jaundiced eye on the pillar institutions of the Establishment – the Army, Law, Foreign Office, City of London and Trades Unions and, finally, the Church – we were not abandoning our role as critical commentators on Society, we were merely demonstrating that it is possible to be extremely serious without being solemn.

How successful do you believe the British industry has been in establishing (a) a studio system and (b) a star system?

There has never been a studio system here since after the war when Rank and ABPC sought to establish that kind of Hollywood image. I don't think either a studio system or a star system is important to developing a sturdy film industry. I think the idea of an actor or actress grabbing attention *is* important and we should seek to hold this, but that is what film is all about – to understand that somebody has star qualities. If we can keep them within this country, that is worth doing.

Were you ever aware of difficulties with theatre-trained actors adjusting to film?

From time to time, less so today. Our most vivid encounter on this subject was when John and I, aged twenty-three, decided to cast Sir Seymour Hicks, aged seventy-one, as a German general of World War I vintage, in *Pastor Hall*. Now Seymour belonged to the old school of theatre, was by repute 'difficult', and was used to having his own way. So, you can imagine, I approached him with suggestions very gingerly indeed.

I thought things were going pretty well until the very last scene of the day, when perhaps age and fatigue combined to produce an explosion. He wanted to know why I employed him since I wouldn't allow him to act! A moment's thought and then I suggested that he play the scene exactly as he wished. He brightened up at that but I went on to ask if he would indulge me, and film it again, playing it this time in the way I thought more effective. His doubts returned. 'Look, Sir Seymour', I said, 'we'll see both takes in tomorrow morning's "rushes". Whichever one you judge to be the best, I promise to use in the finished film'.

At 8.30 the next morning, Seymour came and sat himself down in a theatre packed with the film crew. We ran the 'rushes'. Eventually, the disputed scene came on. As Seymour, looking magnificent, hammed it up, first there came titters and then outright laughter. The *second* take restored the situation. Seymour – doing nothing, as he thought – held the unit in pin-drop silence, so moving did they find his performance, and they gave him a round of applause.

Later, Bernard Miles had a scene with Seymour, and I said certain things with which Bernard didn't agree at all. At the end of the day Bernard came to me and told me Seymour had said to him, 'Bernard, don't argue with the boy – he *knows*! Mind you, it isn't acting, of course'.

As producer:

The Upturned Glass (co-prod), *Dear Murderer, When the Bough Breaks* (1947), *Miranda, The Blind Goddess, Here Come the Huggetts* (1948), *Vote for Huggett, Marry Me, It's Not Cricket, The Huggetts Abroad* (1949), *So Long at the Fair, The Clouded Yellow* (1950), *Appointment with Venus* (1951), *The Venetian Bird* (1952), *A Day to Remember* (1953), *Doctor in the House, Mad About Men* (1954), *Doctor at Sea* (1955), *Checkpoint, The Iron Petticoat* (1956), *Doctor at Large, Campbell's Kingdom* (1957), *A Tale of Two Cities, The Wind Cannot Read* (1958), *The 39 Steps, Upstairs and Downstairs* (1959), *Conspiracy of Hearts, Doctor in Love* (1960), *No Love for Johnnie, No, My Darling Daughter* (1961), *A Pair of Briefs, The Wild and the Willing* (1962), *Hot Enough for June, Doctor in Distress* (1963), *The High Bright Sun* (1964), *Deadlier than the Male, Doctor in Clover* (1966), *Nobody Runs Forever* (1968), *Some Girls Do* (1969), *Doctor in Trouble* (1970), *Percy* (1971), *It's a 2'6" World Above the Ground/The Love Ban* (1972), *Percy's Progress* (1974).

In *Odd Man Out: James Mason*, Sheridan Morley quotes Mason as saying of Betty Box: '. . . she sailed with her tide and became the most sensible and hardworking producer in the British industry, where she remained one of its few survivors'. She is modest about her own 'creative' capacities and prefers to stress the producer's housekeeping role. Her films came in on schedule and budget. Furthermore, she knew what the public wanted and, in over thirty films made in collaboration with director Ralph Thomas, the public generally speaking proved her right. After cutting her teeth on over 200 training and propaganda films during World War II, as assistant to her brother Sydney Box, she then moved with him to Gainsborough. Here she made a string of popular films, including the Huggett family series, and, still in her twenties, she was in charge of production at Gainsborough's Islington studios. It was she who saw the potential of *Doctor in the House* and, once settled on a secure run of box-office successes, held out to make more problematic enterprises such as *No Love for Johnnie*. It may be that what the British cinema today really needs is a producer with her shrewd, no-nonsense approach to the task.

Interview date: September 1989.

Was your first film work as assistant to your brother [Sydney Box] during the war?

Yes. I came into the business in early 1942 when my brother was making a lot of documentary and propaganda films for the War Office and the Ministry of Information, training films for the Army, and films for the British Council which went all over the world. He had about ten film units covering all these various subjects. I was the dogsbody who made the tea and fetched the rushes from the station, went to the laboratories, and eventually learned how to do the budgets, and I suppose, in three years from 1942-5, I did about ten years' hard work.

I was very lucky indeed to be given that chance to learn. I would never be able to do that now, because of the trade unions! Then towards the end of the war the only entertainment films made were supposed to be films that aided the war effort. And Sydney, who always wanted to make feature films, seized the opportunity to make things like *The Flemish Farm* which were of help to the war effort.

When the war ended, he said to me, 'I'm going into feature films now and I'd like you to come with me'. I was very anxious to learn and very quickly did, because of the background he'd already given me on documentaries. After his enormous success with *The Seventh Veil*, he was making two follow-ups when J. Arthur Rank asked him to take over Gainsborough. Partly because of British quota and partly because there were people coming back from the war wanting their jobs back, he went on to make about twenty films a year, for two years at Shepherd's Bush, and I took over Islington, both of which belonged at that time to Gainsborough Pictures. I made a dozen or so films at these studios, before Gainsborough closed down and we all joined Rank's major operation at Pinewood studios.

How did you view the producer's function?

As a producer I had to find the subjects, the director, and someone to write the script; to cast it and to see it right through to delivery into the cinemas. I watched all the costs and made sure the money I'd been allocated was sufficient. I didn't overstep the budget and I was a very good housekeeper in that way.

Had I had, perhaps, more faith in my creative ability, I might have decided occasionally to risk spending a little more. But I just felt that I had to present, to the people who trusted me, a good product for the money they gave me. I think a producer has to tie together the best creative ability, produce the best artistic effort he can, for the money at his disposal. Maybe it was an unfair advantage I took, but I always found it a bonus rather than a disability being a woman film producer!

Is *Dear Murderer* the first film on which you are credited as a producer?

Just before that I finished off the last picture that Sydney had financed and organised at Riverside Studios, where we made *Seventh Veil*. It was a film called *The Upturned Glass*, and he said to me, 'I have promised Arthur Rank that I'll take over Gainsborough and make all those films. Therefore you've got to do *Upturned Glass* for me'. And I said, 'I can't produce it'. He insisted I could and, if I remember rightly, I was given an Associate-Producer credit with James Mason on that. Then I went on to Islington and did *Dear Murderer*, a run-of-the-mill detective story. I remember that my present husband, Peter Rogers, worked on the script and that it was not an easy one to do.

Eric Portman and Jack Warner were both very special in their own way – Eric Portman was one of the best actors I ever worked with – but he and Jack Warner didn't get on very well together. They were always fluffing and we would get to Take 20. I'd say to Arthur Crabtree, 'Oh, for goodness' sake, break the scene up'. There were great pages of dialogue in those days and Arthur, as a cameraman, hadn't quite got the director's finesse. I had to more or less force him to break the scene up into smaller pieces.

How did you find working at Gainsborough? It seems absolutely central to 40s British cinema.

Yes it was, but I worked at the poor man's studio at Islington. Shepherd's Bush, which is now the BBC, had

five stages and every facility you could want, because it was built as a film studio. But Islington had only two stages, one on top of the other, both very small. On the top stage where we obviously had to do half the work, everything had to be taken up in a very antiquated lift. You couldn't get a bus up there, or a car beyond a certain size, and it was a very difficult studio to work in. But we managed; we made our films on time.

It was my job to ensure that the studio was always working, that the technicians and the craftsmen got paid every week, and that I had a film ready to go the day I finished the previous one, which, I think very few producers have to do nowadays. But it was great fun to do it; I was young, and most of the technicians were relatively young, so we got through it.

The worst time of all was the winter of 1947, when we not only had the coldest winter I think we've ever had, but power cuts the whole time. I had to hire a generator from a fairground to provide electricity to go on shooting else we would have had to stop. We all froze, but we carried on. I remember we were working with Patricia Roc and Rosamund John and Bill Owen on *When the Bough Breaks*, and they were wearing summer clothes – poor Pat Roc in little cotton dresses. But nobody grumbled and we finished the film.

Gainsborough closed down when Rank finally took over the whole set-up; and I moved to Pinewood Studio when Sydney moved over from Shepherd's Bush. It was at Pinewood that I made my last film under the Rank contract deal that I had at Gainsborough. It was *So Long at the Fair*, and that was when I first met Dirk Bogarde. I loved working with him and Jean Simmons. The film was made partly in France on location and here at Pinewood.

Did you spend the rest of your career here at Pinewood?

I worked from Pinewood from 1949-79, but a lot of that time I was on location. I remember being in France in 1948 and going to a restaurant in a little village up above Cannes where there was a French film unit making a film on location. I watched them and, as I had my lunch, I listened to them talking and thought, this is what I've missed in shooting film. I've always been stuck in a studio. From then on my aim was to shoot as much film as I could outside, because I reckoned you got so much more screen value for the same amount of money. So from then I made between thirty and forty films at Pinewood studios and more than half of most of them were made abroad. I think I got much bigger-looking films by

Dirk Bogarde, Maureen Pryor and Amy Veness in *Doctor in the House*, 1954

shooting them outside on location.

Did you find your range of opportunities at Pinewood satisfying?

I never had an enormously inflated idea of my own importance and ability. I always thought I was very lucky to be able to say to Rank, 'I like this idea for a story, can I buy it? Can I make it with this or that star?' and they nearly always said yes. Very often they would say the most successful film you've made for us so far is *Doctor in the House*. You can make that one which we're not 100 per cent sure about if you will also make another 'Doctor'. So I had to make a 'Doctor' every year or two. Well, there are only so many jokes about doctors and so many situations you can put them into and I felt, although the public didn't seem to show it, that they were getting repetitive.

When I made *Conspiracy of Hearts*, which I rather like, they didn't want me to make it and said, 'It's religion, it's nuns, it's wartime, who wants to know? Tell you what, make us another 'Doctor' and you can do it!' And the interesting thing was that that the three top box-office films in the UK that year were the 'Doctor' film, *Conspiracy of Hearts* and a 'Carry on'.

You had an enduring association at Pinewood with director, Ralph Thomas. How did it begin?

It started at Islington when I did *Miranda*, one of my happiest films. Rank said to me, 'We've got a new man just out of the army and he's going to do all the trailers.

His name is Ralph Thomas'. I said, 'Right, I can show him the film Thursday'. So Ralph came down; I'd never met him before, but he was obviously very knowledgable about film, and I discovered that, as a very young man, he had worked in films as a clapper-boy and then an assistant cameraman and an editor. He was very wise about the way the story worked and he was very helpful. I didn't see him again until I did my next film, which I think was *So Long at the Fair*. He came to do the trailer for that, and again I found him artistically very helpful.

When I came to make my first independent film, which was *The Clouded Yellow*, I teamed up with Ralph to direct it. By that time he had directed a couple of films for my brother. We were both fairly new to the game but were keen and knew what we were doing. He was a very hard worker, very clever artistically, and my sort of technician. Eventually we formed our own little company together and that's why it says 'A Betty Box-Ralph Thomas Production' on our films.

Within the Rank organisation and made at Pinewood?

That's right, Rank fully financed us. I bought the book *Doctor in the House* from a bookstall and read it on the train coming back from a film-showing in Cardiff. I thought it would make a good film. I rang the publishers from Victoria Station and was told who the agent was. The agent said, 'Oh, I sold it six months ago, to ABC'. The agent also told me that ABC's option expired in a couple of weeks. So I said, 'Don't say a word when it expires and I'll buy it'. And of course they didn't make it and I bought it. When I bought the option, ABC said to me, 'You'll never be able to make a film, it's just a string of anecdotes'. And even Sydney agreed with them. But I said, 'I think I know how to do it. I'll take four students through the three of four years of their training as medical students and make that the story'. I was very lucky because I got a wonderful man called Nicholas Phipps who wrote the script. There wasn't a great deal of the book in it, except for the characters. The main idea really wasn't in the book.

When we showed it to the press, Leonard Moseley who was the *Express* critic said to me, 'You know you've got a winner here'; and, of course, in six weeks in the Odeon Leicester Square, it more or less paid for itself. I think it was the youthful gaiety of it that made it so popular, and it was something everybody knows about – doctors, hospitals, illness. We had people write from hospitals all over England saying, thank God you've shown hospitals as places with some humour.

You had a marvellous cast . . .
I wanted Robert Morley to play the surgeon. I rang up his agent and she said, 'I'm afraid he's £15,000 pounds'. Well, I couldn't pay that; then I remembered dear old Jimmy Justice and I thought, he can do it! He doesn't have to do very much except be himself, so we got him for £1500. The day I started shooting, I was running the first day's rushes, when I got a call from Earl St John to say, 'Betty, I've just come back from the board meeting, they're very worried about *Doctor in the House*. They don't at all like doing hospital films. Your budget's £100,000 – can you cut it down?' I said, 'I don't know how, I'm paying Dirk what you pay him under his Rank contract, which is too much for my budget. And I've got Kay Kendall on her Rank deal, but I'll do my best'. I made it, I think, for £97,000. I never told Ralph that they were moaning about the £100,000. And, of course they took much more than that in six weeks.

We had a very good quartet in Dirk, Donald Sinden, Donald Houston and Kenneth More. I did the 'Guinness is good for you, as good as a *Doctor in the House*' poster, with all four of them at the bar drinking their Guinness. Guinness put the poster up all over the UK, and that was worth a fortune in free publicity – just good luck.

Among your more serious films was *No Love for Johnnie*, which seems to me a courageous and cynical film.
I'm not a political animal, although I am more so now than I was then. Then I wasn't in the least interested. I'm still very surprised that Rank let me do it, that they didn't tell us, 'We don't want to be involved with that sort of thing', because, as an organisation, they were very politically conservative. Perhaps they liked the Peter Finch character being so corrupt because, after all, he *was* left-wing! I must say I liked the story very much. I was very sad that Wilfred Fienburgh, who wrote the book, was dead before we made the film. He crashed his car when he was driving home from the House of Commons one night.

The film wasn't as financially successful as a lot of films I've made, but I enjoyed making it very much. I loved working with Peter Finch. He was drunk some of the time, and not always very easy, but I was very fond of him. Ralph and I both knew how to work with him.

You made a lot of films with Dirk Bogarde. What was your experience of working with him?
I found him very . . . what's the word? He *gave* a lot, almost too much. But he had great integrity artistically. He decided what he should give in a part and did his best to give that, though he really wasn't suited to some of the films I did with him. Ralph had a clear idea of what he wanted and Dirk didn't always agree, but they respected each other's opinions.

I've recently seen him again in your version of *A Tale of Two Cities*. Why did you do it in black-and-white?
That was Ralph's and my fault. We saw one or two French films around that time like *Gervaise* and I remember thinking they were wonderful films and they were in black-and-white. And I thought, I can't see *Tale of Two Cities* in colour. Looking back I realise what an idiot I was. At that time Rank would have said OK, if I'd told them I wanted to make it in purple. What we didn't realise was, that very soon, we were going to depend quite a lot on television sales. And they paid nothing for black-and-white. So we dropped £100,000 straight away, which, in those days, was a lot of money.

We shot in Bourges in central France for four or five weeks, and it poured with rain the whole bloody time. It was fated from beginning to end. It was unbearably hot until the day we started shooting, and then the heavens opened. All the costumes were wet, and everything was muddy and sets fell down in the street. But of course Dirk was very good indeed, and he was certainly handsome!

As co-screenwriter (with Sydney Box):
Alibi Inn (1935), *29 Acacia Avenue*, *The Seventh Veil* (1945), *The Years Between*, *Daybreak*, *A Girl in a Million* (1946), *The Man Within*, *The Brothers*, *When the Bough Breaks*, *Dear Murderer*, *Holiday Camp* (1947), *Easy Money*, *Good-Time Girl*, *The Blind Goddess*, *Here Come the Huggetts*, *Portrait from Life* (1948), *Christopher Columbus* (1949).

As director:
*The Happy Family (1952), **Street Corner* (1953), *To Dorothy a Son*, *The Beachcomber*, *Simon and Laura* (1955), *Eyewitness* (1956), **The Passionate Stranger* (1957), **The Truth About Women*, *Subway in the Sky*, *This Other Eden* (1959), **Too Young to Love* (1960), *The Piper's Tune* (1962), *Rattle of a Simple Man* (1964).
* Co-screenwriter with Sydney Box.

It was not easy for a woman to be a director in British films in the 1950s and Muriel Box was virtually the only regular, mainstream practitioner. She had had a long experience in film-making – as continuity girl, screenwriter and co-producer with her husband Sydney – before directing her first film, *The Happy Family*. Thereafter, she worked steadily throughout the decade, often using the formulas of popular genres to foreground her interest in women's lives. *Street Corner*, for instance, was conceived as a female reply to *The Blue Lamp*.

Her best film is probably *Simon and Laura*, adapted from Alan Melville's successful West End play, satirising various aspects of television which was becoming a major threat to cinema by the mid-50s. *The Passionate Stranger* is a well-cast romantic comedy; *To Dorothy a Son* and *Rattle of a Simple Man* were broader comedies adapted from stage successes; *The Beachcomber* is derived from a Maugham short story; and *Eyewitness* is a neat thriller largely set in a hospital. They are business-like films from a woman who knew the business better than most.

Interview date: October 1989.

Before starting to direct you had a very busy career as screenwriter and producer. Did you always want to direct?
Yes, I actually started to direct in 1950, as a freelance. I never dreamed I would be allowed to direct; the position of women in films was very precarious at the time. Hardly any woman had achieved the position of director on a film – it was unheard of – and I felt I was very lucky to be offered the chance. I had been a continuity girl for a long time, and this, of course, involves assisting the director to cut his film. I knew the business backwards from about 1925, ages before I was the script director at Gainsborough.

When Sydney Box founded his motion picture company in 1939, I believe it produced propaganda and training films . . .
Yes, Sydney started the company and it flourished. He was very much in touch with the Government and they knew that he was a very efficient producer. The films were all paid for by the Government, although you never got the money until months after the films had been made. I remember one film was called *Road Safety for Children* and my husband said I should write and direct it. All the scripts had to be passed in embryo form. Sydney took my script up to Elton, the Minister for Information, who said it was very good, but he couldn't accept the idea of a woman director, so we had to find another director in a hurry. Ken Annakin was chosen to do it; he was young and fresh, although he only knew a tenth of what I did about films then. But women had to take second place.

According to my count, you and Sydney Box co-authored twenty-two screenplays, including *The Seventh Veil* in 1945.

Yes, we got an Oscar for that. I used to do the over-all plot, then Sydney would start work on it and 'diddy it up' wherever he could. Then I'd have another go at the script, then he'd do a further one; it would usually go through five or six stages. We were starting to produce then, the first one we did was *29 Acacia Avenue*.

You had an enormous success with *The Seventh Veil*.

It was that film which propelled us into Gainsborough Studios. The idea for it came simply enough. Sydney was doing one of the propaganda films for the Army or the RAF, and he was at lunch with people connected with it. One of them was a doctor who tended the shell-shocked prisoners and very badly injured men, and he mentioned that he used narcosis; the patients were put under a drug and were then questioned and examined while they were unconscious; in this way the doctors could find out things the patient himself didn't know, and they could gradually form an opinion about his case. The doctor said they had achieved some wonderful cures with men who had been badly shell-shocked.

I said later that it would be a wonderful idea for a film, if you had an artist who had some terrible accident and was crippled with a psychosis like that. Sydney told me to write it and we would start work on it! The first draft was very rough, just a few pages, and we gradually developed it. We got hold of a psychiatrist who knew about the technique to come to the studio to demonstrate it to everyone there. I am still stunned by the film's success! It opened at the Leicester Square Cinema and we were astounded to see queues all around the cinema. It was the first film about psychiatry, so perhaps it was the originality which attracted people. It was a good story, too.

Perhaps there was something comforting about the notion of a film which suggests solutions to problems.

Yes, whenever a woman tries to commit suicide as she did, you know there is something terribly wrong with her, and the Herbert Lom character was able to go back over her childhood and find out how it all built up from that.

Was it an easy film to cast and make?

We got nice people, the ones we wanted. The terrible constriction was the war being on, bombs falling while we were shooting and water dripping through the roof where it had been damaged by bombs. The rationing of clothes was another problem – I hadn't enough coupons to dress Ann Todd well enough to suit the part. I went around the secondhand shops to find what I needed. Up until the last minute I had no frock for the scene where she wears a debutante gown in Venice. She was very particular about her clothes and was right to be, because she had good taste. I finally found a dress and sent it to the costume designer to get her approval. I shut myself in the lavatory rather than face Ann in case she rejected the dress! I was so astonished – and relieved – when she was delighted with it and wore it in the film! Ann was only difficult because she wanted the right thing for the part.

This was followed by two further collaborations with director Compton Bennett, *Daybreak* and *The Years Between*. What sort of director was he?

He never sought publicity. If he had any publicity it was what accrued to him from directing other films. Sydney got more credit for directing *The Seventh Veil* than Compton did.

Compton went to America and directed *The Forsyte Saga*, but, after that, he had a bad deal over there, and eventually his contract was cancelled.

You were associated with several other directors in the 40s including David Macdonald (*Good Time Girl*, *Christopher Columbus* and others). What do you recall of him?

Christopher Columbus was a calamity, but we couldn't avoid it happening. We didn't want to do it at all, but were pressed into making it. The script had been paid for by Gainsborough Pictures, and when we got there in 1945 they asked us to make it. I got in one or two other authors to help us work on it, but it was doomed from the start. The whole unit went out to the Caribbean with the *Santa Maria*. They were sailing the ship around, and lost it! Later it caught fire! You wouldn't believe the things that happened on that film. There was trouble with the artistes, everything. The first rehearsal we called was for a preliminary run-through of the script, to give the artistes an idea of the film as a whole. We called the whole cast to the Dorchester but Fredric March, who was Columbus, didn't turn up nor did Mrs March [Florence Eldridge] who was playing Isabella! We waited an hour or more, then I sent off the first assistant to find them. Freddie was very apologetic, but said he couldn't possibly come until their contract was signed. People in England knew that if Arthur [Rank] was financing a film, he would never break his word, and his word was enough. But it wasn't enough for Freddie; he had too much experience of broken words in Hollywood.

Arthur was very generous, and also very frank about things which he disagreed with. For instance, *Acacia Avenue* was tried out and was a great success, with laughs all the way through. But Arthur didn't like it because he didn't approve of the Dinah Sheridan/Jimmy Hanley couple trying to sleep together. He thought it would be a bad example for young people, and said he would prefer to shelve it; he would pay us for our work anyway. Sydney and I argued that the cast and the director would be very upset at being shelved, but Arthur was adamant. The film was eventually released two years later, but not by Arthur. Fortunately it did very well because we had all our money in it.

Arthur was an extraordinarily nice man, very honest. His high moral stance was very rare! He had a good grasp of the importance of stars, but was really a stranger in a strange land as far as films were concerned.

None of the big epic films made in Britain at that time was really popular. Why not?

It was probably a combination of dud scripts and the fact that they didn't ring a bell. The film that cost us most money was *Bad Lord Byron*. It was meticulously researched and several authors worked on it; Dennis [Price] was very good as Byron, but people didn't go for it. I could understand the academics wanting something more literary, but we couldn't have that if we wanted mass audiences. I thought it was a reasonable saga of his life, and was very disappointed because we worked like stink on it.

How do you feel about *Good-Time Girl*? Were you forced to have that moral frame to the story?

We felt we had to justify the story in some way because, at that time, the girls were really going haywire over the Americans. I worked very hard on the script, and went to homes for delinquent girls to make it realistic. After it was filmed, the censor got his hands on it and he was an absolute bastard! He objected to certain scenes, including the one where the girls in the home – Jean Kent and Jill Balcon – have a fight. It was dreadful to have cut it. I was pleased with Jean Kent's performance, and it was a very good cast all round. Again, the director was David Macdonald. I liked him – he was a good, sympathetic director.

You directed your first film, *The Happy Family*, for London Independent.

That was just a cover name for our independent producing company. When we left Rank at Pinewood, Sydney wanted to start up on his own and wanted me to direct. We operated out of any studio where we could get space. *The Happy Family* was from a West End play. It got very good reviews in America, much better than here. George Cole was in it, as a very young man. We were always terribly insistent on getting the cast right.

Was your next film, *Street Corner*, meant as a kind of female answer to *The Blue Lamp*?

Yes, I thought *The Blue Lamp* had had too long a run for its money because it never mentioned women and how they co-operated in doing police work. It was about time women had a chance to show what they did, and the film was specifically designed to show their work. It was a mixture of a documentary and a crime story.

How difficult was it for a woman to operate as a director in the 50s?

Terribly difficult. They were prejudiced against you from the very start. I went to my agent, Christopher Mann, and told him I had made several films and got good notices. I had always wanted to make a film in Hollywood and asked Chris to put me up as director to any of the Hollywood producers who came over here – as they often did at that time. He sighed deeply and said, 'Muriel, I wish I could tell you different but, if I mention the name of a woman as a director, they just turn away and look out of the window'. That was absolutely true. There were only two in Hollywood – Dorothy Arzner and Ida Lupino. They elbowed you out.

Even with my last film (*Rattle of a Simple Man*) for which Sydney had got me the contract, they were still worried about the woman director aspect. This was three weeks after we had booked the studio space. One of the officials at ABC said they hadn't used a woman director before and were chary of it. They would have preferred not to go ahead with the film if Sydney insisted on my directing.

The stage-screen relationship is closer in Britain than in America. Has the British stage tradition worked against the cinema's interests?

They more or less worked hand-in-glove. For instance, with *Simon and Laura* I had seen Ian Carmichael do the part on stage and thought he would be wonderful in the film, so I insisted on having him even though Rank wanted a more established 'star' name. I knew the cast I wanted – Kay Kendall, Peter Finch and Thora Hird.

Ian Carmichael, Peter Finch and Kay Kendall in *Simon and Laura*, 1955

Normally the casting is left to the director but Rank had no hesitation in saying if they disagreed with you. But, with Ian Carmichael, I really dug in my heels because I knew he would be excellent in the part.

You directed some very diverse stars in your next few films. What do you recall about working with Ralph Richardson and Margaret Leighton in *The Passionate Stranger*; Laurence Harvey in *The Truth About Women*; and Van Johnson and Hildegarde Neff in *Subway in the Sky*?

I could tell you heaps of stories! We got Ralph Richardson by the skin of our teeth. Sydney took him the script and he read it and liked it, except for the ending. He typed out some ideas for a different ending, but I didn't like them. I had worked on the script for months and didn't think Ralph's ending was as good as our own. Now Ralph was easy about whether or not he did the film, and we only had a few days left before filming was due to start. He was still very keen on his idea, so I said to Sydney that the only way out was to shoot alternative scenes for the two endings and somehow cut them together. We set out doing the film, knowing that I had to do the alternative scenes on different days. Ralph was unaware that we were shooting alternative endings. We didn't dare tell him! Margaret Leighton was in on the secret. She was splendid, she knew Ralph!

The Truth About Women was the most difficult film I ever made, and Laurence Harvey was the most difficult artiste. I don't know whether his stardom had gone to his head, or whether he was just like that. It was a lovely cast, too, considering the money we spent. The film was reasonably successful, but the Rank group wasn't behind us as it should have been. The publicity people knew that I was doing a comedy and they expected belly laughs, but it wasn't like that; it was ironical, pure satire really. It was mainly to show up the situation of women that I agreed to make the film at all.

Van Johnson was a very charming man, but Hildegarde Neff was a pain in the neck. She was the first artiste who ever refused to take a direction I gave on the floor. I asked her to do another take because she hadn't done the first one correctly, a reaction shot to Van Johnson. I had to cajole her to do the shot the way I wanted, and as we shot it I could see she was determined to do the complete opposite. Eventually I had to cut around her, which was very hard.

What has interested you most in your career as a director? Is it the directing of the actors?

That is by far the most important thing, I believe – and the honest and right interpretation of the story. The director's job is to ensure that the best artistes interpret the script as best they can; you have to be clear about what your team are giving you. They come to the director and say 'This is how I see it . . .', and if you don't see it the same way you have to tell them. As a woman, I never had any trouble with the units at all. With artistes sometimes, yes, and certainly with the distributors, although not always.

Dora Bryan

Odd Man Out (1947), *The Fallen Idol, No Room at the Inn* (1948), *Once Upon a Dream, Now Barabbas, Adam and Evelyne, The Interrupted Journey* (1949), *The Blue Lamp, The Cure for Love, No Trace, Something in the City* (1950), *Files from Scotland Yard, The Quiet Woman, Circle of Danger, Scarlet Thread, High Treason, No Highway, Lady Godiva Rides Again* (1951), *Whispering Smith Hits London, 13 East Street, The Gift Horse, Time Gentlemen Please!, Mother Riley Meets the Vampire, Made in Heaven, The Ringer, Women of Twilight, Miss Robin Hood* (1952), *Street Corner, The Fake, The Intruder* (1953), *You Know What Sailors Are, Fast and Loose, The Crowded Day, Mad About Men, Harmony Lane* (1954), *As Long As They're Happy, See How They Run, You Lucky People, Cockleshell Heroes* (1955), *The Green Man, Child in the House* (1956), *The Man Who Wouldn't Talk, Carry on Sergeant, Hello London* (1958), *Operation Bullshine, Desert Mice* (1959), *Follow That Horse!, The Night We Got the Bird* (1960), *A Taste of Honey* (1961), *The Great St Trinian's Train Robbery, The Sandwich Man* (1966), *Two a Penny* (1967), *Hands of the Ripper* (1971), *Up the Front* (1972), *Apartment Zero* (1989).

Although Dora Bryan engagingly claims not to remember half of the fifty-five films she has made, it is safe to say that no filmgoer of the 1950s has ever forgotten her face or voice. Perhaps it is not surprising that the titles of the films often elude her: by her own account, she was rarely sent a script before turning up to do her day's shooting and she would learn her part in the make-up room. She played tarts with hearts of gold, conniving hussies, 'refeened' receptionists, vicious trollops, and a range of characters called Mavis, or Maisie, or Winnie, or Glad, or Pearl. In a few minutes' screen time, she could transmute dross into pure gold. Her approach to her career was

to take what came along: she was – and still is – always busy on the stage, and film was really the icing on the cake. Nevertheless, apart from many two-minute delights, she did have more substantial roles in *The Fallen Idol, The Cure for Love* (in which she is irresistibly spiteful), as Glad, the warm-hearted barmaid in the dull war film, *The Gift Horse*, as Gladys (again!) the Sultan's knitting wife in *You Know What Sailors Are*, and above all as the aging tartish Helen in *A Taste of Honey* ('Every wrinkle tells a dirty story'), for which she won the BAFTA Award.

Interview date: July 1990.

You seem to have mastered a great range of regional accents. Did you make a specialty of this?

No, but when I was making all those films in the 40s and 50s the parts were always written for little Cockney girls. I was living in London and I can pick up accents, so, although I was born in Lancashire, I found that a Cockney accent came more naturally to me than my own. In fact, when I came to do *Cure for Love* with Robert Donat and had to use a Lancashire accent, I felt a bit phoney; I never had that broad an accent, so I felt as if I were making fun of my upbringing. I was more comfortable doing a Cockney accent. I did do a 'refeened' accent in some films, but people knew it was a pseudo-lady talking like that; for instance, in *The Great St Trinian's Train Robbery*, the refined lady I played sounded so

'fraffly genteel' I felt she would lapse into broad Cockney at any moment.

You made your screen debut with a small part in *Odd Man Out* . . .

Yes, Carol Reed saw me in *Peace in Our Time*, in which Noel Coward had written a part for me, and he gave me a nice little bit in *Odd Man Out*. It wasn't a speaking part but it was a telling little part of a young blonde girl in a telephone box. My next film was *Fallen Idol*, again for Carol – and a much better part.

The Fallen Idol really fixed you in the minds of people. How did you come by the part of the warm-hearted tart Rose?

I'd already done the small part in *Odd Man Out*, but this was the first real filming I did. I have very strong recollections of it. I know I had to get up terribly early to get to the studio by 7 o'clock for make-up. I lived in Piccadilly in those days and, having done a show at night, I was always terrified I wouldn't wake up. I used to have two alarm clocks set for 5 o'clock. There were no hired cars or anything, I went to Denham by public transport. On my first day I had on high-heeled shoes, a little red suit and a plastic mac. At that hour of the morning there was no one about to ask where the studios were, so there I was walking through fields of snow in the depths of winter. I got there late. Nobody cared, but I was so keen to be good on my first day.

I had no script, and had no idea what sort of part I was playing until Carol Reed met me on the set and explained the story to me. He told me the sort of feeling he wanted, said there were a few lines of dialogue, but added that if I didn't like them I could say whatever I wanted. I asked him what I should wear and he said, 'Oh, what you've got on'. I was horrified to think I was playing a prostitute in my own clothes!

Carol was a very gentle director, lovely. I don't recall much about the little boy in the film, except they had a bit of trouble with him. Over the weekend his mother had his hair cut! Imagine what effect that had on continuity! I did my bit of filming all on one half-day. It was very quick, concentrated filming.

Bobby Henrey and Dora Bryan in *The Fallen Idol*, 1948

Did you ever reach a stage where you could pick and choose your parts?

No, I just took whatever came along. That's always been my motto – do everything you can, don't get choosy! It's amazing with some of the things you are offered, you think there isn't much to it and it turns out to be the best thing you've done. That's happened to me a few times, such as doing Mistress Quickly in *The Merry Wives of Windsor* [Open Air Theatre, Regent's Park, 1984]; I thought I'd have a crack at Shakespeare and I was so happy when I pulled it off.

You seem to have been a female version of Raymond Huntley in that you were instantly recognisable when you came on . . .

Oddly enough, the lady who used to clean for me also cleaned for Raymond Huntley; she used to say to me, 'Oo, you've not done any filming this week Miss Bryan – Mr Huntley has. He's had two days down at Pinewood and got £100 a day!'. She used to go through his papers!

Did it worry you that you were often confined to small cameo roles?

Oh, no. To me my job was in the theatre anyway, so filming was extra, a bit of fun, a day's work for £100 which was a lot of money then. Nobody asked me to do more major roles; if they had I would have done so, because if they wanted you enough they would allow for the fact that you had to be at the theatre in the evenings.

You had a much bigger part in Robert Donat's *The Cure for Love*.

Yes, that was a long part and was a lot of work, because Robert was often ill. Sometimes we would hang around all day because he couldn't work. So that took us six months. I was in *Traveller's Joy* in the theatre at the time and Yvonne Arnaud got very cross about it because I was filming every day, and had to get to the studio by 7 o'clock every day in case Robert was all right. He chose me for the part; I wasn't tested, although Diana Dors was. I think they were a bit wary of me because I was working in the theatre as well – they didn't allow for my stamina!

What was your view of Robert Donat as either a director or an actor?

As a director I don't know. Apart from Carol Reed telling me to 'think a part' I really haven't had the experience of a director helping me with a role. I liked Robert as a man, and Gladys Henson, who played my mother, was wonderful; we got on so well and shared the same sense of humour.

Did it matter much to you who was directing?
No, not at all. I didn't even care what the script was. It was just a matter of getting down to the studio and meeting fresh faces. Half the time I would get to the studio without even having seen the script. In my case, the parts were never long enough to worry about. I could learn them while I was being made up! It was always a big surprise when I went to see the film because usually I would have no idea what the film was all about.

You have what amounts to a starring role as Gladys, the Sultan's wife, in *You Know What Sailors Are*. Was this fun to do?
That was a good part and I looked nice. There were other films going on at the same time and the people working on them couldn't wait to get on to our set because it was all glamorous girls around a swimming pool! Akim Tamiroff, lovely man, was in it and dear Shirley Eaton, too. I enjoyed that film; there was a very nice atmosphere. All I had to do was sit there, knitting or something, surrounded by my husband's concubines. But I didn't seek the part out, it came through my agent.

What do you remember of playing a mermaid in *Mad About Men*?
I remember nearly drowning in that film, because of the tail. It was made at Shepperton and I can remember being wheeled down a corridor in a bath chair with the tail on. They had an enormous tank which was supposed to be the sea, with all these fish swimming around in it. By the end of the day, all of the fish were dead because Glynis [Johns] insisted on the tank water being so hot! When they put me in the water, the tail shot up because it was buoyant, and I went down. It was a very nasty experience, splashing around in the bottom of the tank. They eventually fished me out, by which time Glynis had gone back to her dressing-room (in her bath chair) very fast. So they sent for Dunlop, who had made the tails, and I was sent home 'suffering from shock'. After that they put weights in the tails and we got used to them.

In 1958, you sang 'That Deadly Species the Male'

in one of the most peculiar British films I know, *Hello London*, directed by Sidney Smith and starring Sonja Henie. Whose idea was this oddity?
I don't remember. What I do remember is going to the studio and seeing the ice on one of the stages, and the ice was black. I met Sonja Henie and I recall she had a tiny body, rather a big face, and wore a navy-blue dress with white Peter Pan collar and cuffs, like a little girl. Other than that I don't remember a thing about it. Oh, yes, Sonja had oxygen tanks in her dressing-room!

After a few more service comedies, such as *Desert Mice*, you had what is, perhaps, the best role of your film career *A Taste of Honey*. How did you come by this?
Basil Dearden directed the service comedy, *Desert Mice* (and *The Blue Lamp*). I think he felt actors got in the way of his films! He was nice to me because I didn't give him any trouble, but generally I don't think he liked actors very much.

A Taste of Honey was certainly my best film role – and I even had a script! I've no idea how I came by the role but, thank goodness, Tony Richardson chose me. Perhaps I shouldn't say 'thank goodness' because I didn't do many films after that. I enjoyed doing that part very much, but I didn't realise the film would be such a success. It was filmed at Salford in Manchester and also in a big attic over two garages in London. The seafront stuff was all shot at Salford Docks.

I saw the film again last year and loved it. It's interesting to see a film in black-and white now, after everything being in colour for so long; it adds something, gives it a documentary look. I remember Tony Richardson giving a lot of direction to Rita [Tushingham], but it was her first film. With me, I think he cast me to be me as he sees me. It's odd that, having won a BAFTA award for the film, no one asked me to do another film for such a long time.

You did a couple of thrillers – *Hands of the Ripper*, for Hammer, was one.
Yes, that was a nice part. I played a medium and ended up being stabbed through the stomach, and hung on a door for a little while.

The Young Mr Pitt (1941), The Silver Fleet (1943), A Matter of Life and Death (1946), Black Narcissus (1947), The Small Back Room (1948), Madness of the Heart (1949), The Reluctant Widow, Prelude to Fame (1950), Tom Brown's Schooldays, Scarlet Thread, Life in Her Hands, Hell is Sold Out, Four Days, The House in the Square (1951), My Death is a Mockery, The Gambler and the Lady (1952), Young Bess, Star of My Night (1953), The Night of the Full Moon, Profile, Secret Venture (1954), Handcuffs, London (1955), Hand in Hand (1960), Night of the Eagle (1962), Hammerhead (1968), Wolfshead: The Legend of Robin Hood (1969), Private Road, Twins of Evil (1971), Nothing But the Night (1972), Craze (1973), The Abdication (1974), One of Our Dinosaurs is Missing (1975), The Elephant Man (1980).

Representation of the erotic was never the strong point of British cinema, but there is a moment in *Black Narcissus* which, forty-odd years later, still seems remarkable in that respect. Kathleen Byron as Sister Ruth, in a Himalayan convent, mad with lust for the District Commissioner, suddenly appears out of her nun's habit, in a low-cut dress, applying lipstick to her mysteriously beautiful face. It remains a brilliant study in suppressed sexuality suddenly asserting itself and it is to the undying discredit of British cinema that it never gave her another comparably exciting role. With half a chance, she might have been a great melodramatic heroine: she had wit, intelligence, sensuality and a flamboyant streak that she often used to salvage inferior roles. However, to be grateful for what we got, there is a clutch of films for Michael Powell which she rightly sees as the high point of her film career; and *Prelude to Fame* gave her some scope as a selfish obsessive manipulating a small boy's life. Though wickedness or madness possibly brought out the best in her, she was also a more interesting than usual straight lead in *The Small Back Room* and *Life in Her Hands*, both of which she imbues with individuality and appealing sympathy. The screen has wasted her appallingly in the last two decades.

Interview date: June 1990.

How did you come to make your film debut in Carol Reed's *The Young Mr Pitt*?

While I was still at the Old Vic Drama School I came up to London to try to find an agent; I met John Gliddon, who was Deborah Kerr's agent, and he sent me to see the people who were doing *The Young Mr Pitt*. They gave me a part and, after that, I used to go around saying 'I had two lines opposite Robert Donat!' I did very little after that because of the war and I was working for Censorship.

Your next four films were all made by Michael Powell. Would you agree that these gave you your most exciting opportunities?

Oh yes, one wasn't aware of it at the time but I remember, when I was offered *Black Narcissus*, Michael Powell sent me a telegram saying 'We're offering you the part of Sister Ruth; the trouble is, you'll never get such a good part again'! He had a very caustic way of talking. He was more or less right though – it's still my favourite role.

Though *The Silver Fleet* was technically directed by Vernon Sewell, how involved was Michael Powell as producer?

I suppose Michael watched everything that went on, but Vernon directed us. He was very kind and helpful. I was terrified, up to a point, and he was very encouraging. This was good because when I came to work with Michael I really had to be able to hold my own. I didn't think Micky was a great director of actors; I thought he used to put people down and upset them. It was only later, looking back at the way he directed, that I realised he was determined to get something from you and didn't mind how he did it. All he wanted was the best for that particular scene. At the time, I always used to fight with him. He wanted me to overstate the madness in *Black Narcissus* and I used to argue with him that the character didn't *know* she was mad. For one scene I argued with him about what I wanted to do and he walked off the set, saying to Jack Cardiff that I would tell him what I wanted; so I did. Jack set it all up and called Michael back to the set and he just said, 'Shoot it'. Afterwards he said, 'It wasn't what I wanted, but it was very good'. I was lucky starting with Vernon Sewell; I think if I'd started off with Michael I would have come unstuck.

Did you feel *A Matter of Life and Death* was angled towards cementing Anglo-American relations?

I thought we were trying to be friends with all nations – particularly in that big courtroom scene with the jury lining up. I think Micky was trying to do a United Nations thing in it, seeking friendship between other nations besides the Americans and the British. The sets were fantastic; poor Kim Hunter had to run up that

staircase, which was the most horrifying thing. There seemed to be miles of it. Michael was very good in his direction of those huge crowds and he was lovely to his technical crew.

I think your performance as the neurotic Sister Ruth in *Black Narcissus* is one of the most remarkable in British films. How do you feel about it now?

I saw it quite recently and was quite convinced, even by myself, but a hell of a lot of it was the photography, and the music was fantastic, almost like a ballet. I didn't realise when I was stalking Deborah that there would be all that music. Although I had read the part, I didn't realise until I started doing it that it had such strength and power. To prepare for the part, I wanted to go into a convent, but Michael said, 'Oh no, we haven't got time for all that nonsense!' I thought she was quite sane really, just doing a lot of inward thinking. I think she *is* a bit touched by the time she takes off the habit and gets into the red dress to visit Mr Dean [David Farrar] in the

Kathleen Byron and Deborah Kerr in *Black Narcissus*, 1947

bungalow. She's planning her escape. I think that's the beginning of the real switch to madness, which could have been avoided if he had been at all sympathetic, but he just sent her back.

What do you recall of working with Deborah Kerr and David Farrar?
Deborah, who was a very big star, was absolutely charming throughout, and as helpful as possible. It was only my third film and the previous ones had been tiny parts. She used to whisper to me, 'Don't argue with him, just say "Oh, what a marvellous idea!" and then do exactly what you want to'. She was very shrewd! Later on I met other leading ladies who were not so sweet!

David Farrar lives near Durban now. About ten years ago, when I was out there in *Separate Tables*, he told me he simply gave up his career once they started offering him parts as uncles or fathers of the leading ladies. It's a shame. He was a very strong actor and had a very rugged approach. Again, I wasn't impressed at the time by what he was doing; it's only now that I can watch him and think what a marvellous performance he gave.

How much latitude did Michael Powell give you in creating your own performance?
He expected you to have a feeling about it all and he wasn't going to tamper with that very much; but visually, it had to be the way he wanted it. I remember a shot in *Black Narcissus* where I say about Mr Dean [to Deborah Kerr], 'All the same, I notice you're very fond of seeing him' or something like that; it could have been said several ways, but Michael wanted me to say it right across the table, in a quite grotesque position, almost as if suddenly the devil had popped out. I didn't think it was necessary, but that was how he wanted it done. I must say that after him I could cope with *any* director!

It must have been a shock to have an almost conventional leading lady role in your next film, *The Small Back Room*.
Yes. I nearly lost that part because of the censorship – you couldn't have people living together and that was the whole thrust of the story, that he wouldn't marry her because he was not happy with himself. They had offered me the part and sent me the script; then I discovered the couple were to be engaged. I argued against it and sent Micky a letter saying I thought he had buggered up the whole story! Then I thought, "What have I done?!' But they thought about it and agreed I was right.

I also remember on *The Small Back Room* that Micky

said I was to wear those Dior 'New Look' clothes, with yards and yards of material in the skirts. I argued with Micky saying that the film was set in wartime and we just couldn't get the material then; but Micky wanted me to look glamorous so he said, 'If they remember that you wore the "New Look" during the film, then you've failed as an actress'! I enjoyed playing that un-neurotic character because I thought she had a nice lot of strength and quality. That and the *Black Narcissus* part were two wonderful roles and such a contrast.

You were 'wicked' again with Margaret Lockwood in *Madness of the Heart* . . .
I got a bit fed up with those 'mad, bad and dangerous-to-know' parts. I was a very nasty and dangerous character in *Madness of the Heart*. I did enjoy it, although the film was hard work because we did a lot of swimming around in a tank in the studio at Denham. I got jaundice from it. I didn't actually do the riding sequences in the South of France; they had a young boy with a wig on doing those. Margaret Lockwood wasn't very easy to work with. I know from other people that she can be very charming and sweet, but I'm afraid our relationship was never very easy or cordial. Desmond Dickinson was the cameraman on *Madness of the Heart* and he said to me one day, 'You're only allowed close-ups in profile or if your face is distorted in anger – but we're getting round it!' Margaret had a great deal of power then and she certainly influenced which takes or prints could be used.

Did you ever feel anyone was looking after your career in films?
Not really. I owed a great deal to John Gliddon at the start of my career; he used to push for me but, later, of course, by the time I was in my thirties, when nothing much was happening, I had children anyway.

I was asked to do a film for MGM; my agent sent me a script which was for *Young Bess* and I called him back saying it looked all right. He said it should be quite fun for me, going over to Hollywood, whereas I had thought it was to be made in the MGM studios in England. I was pregnant at the time but I went to Hollywood anyway, not telling anyone that I *was* pregnant. MGM were pleased with the way the film was going and wanted to write scenes in for me with Charles Laughton; they thought I was very odd when I said that wasn't a good idea and that I wanted to get home! I might not have liked working there forever because I found it very unreal, but the time I spent there was very pleasant.

Do you remember the director Fergus McDonell, for whom you made *Prelude to Fame*?
I did like him, although he was very subdued. He was quite correct in everything he wanted done, never gave you a false move. We were doing it all on the Independent Frame technique, in which you had to make everything coincide with scenes of the Opera House in Rome behind you, or going along in the car – terribly technical, and it didn't last. It was quite a difficult film to do. McDonell spent a lot of time with the little boy and with the musical side of it; he was quite musically knowledgable, I think. He was very careful, and never very inspiring. My part was very unsympathetic. The film was based on an Aldous Huxley story ['Young Archimedes'] and my character was a bit cobbled; she was a rich selfish woman and had to have some motivation because she wanted success – for herself, not for the boy.

You made a lot of films at this time, including six in 1951. What sort of choice did you have over your parts then?
I tended to take what was offered. Some of them were quite good parts. Lewis Gilbert directed *Scarlet Thread* with Laurence Harvey, who was impossible even then. If he hadn't got the camera on him he wouldn't bother to act. I do remember Philip Leacock who directed *Life in Her Hands* – he was very charming. The film was made on a shoestring; it was more or less a documentary made by the Crown Film Unit to recruit nurses. I actually got Paul Dupuis to come in and sing on it, as we were quite friendly at that time. Oh, and I had to learn to drive for that film – just so that I could crash into an ambulance!

Discord, Anne One Hundred (1933), *Two Days to Live* (1939), *They Came by Night, Let George Do It, Charley's Big-Hearted Aunt, Neutral Port* (1940), *Inspector Hornleigh Goes To It, Kipps* (1941), *The Young Mr Pitt, Uncensored* (1942), *The Man in Grey* (1943), *Fanny by Gaslight, 2000 Women, Madonna of the Seven Moons* (1944), *They Were Sisters* (1945), *Men of Two Worlds, The Magic Bow* (1946), *The Root of All Evil, Time Out of Mind* (1947), *My Own True Love, Broken Journey* (1948), *The Golden Madonna, Appointment with Danger* (1949), *The Woman with No Name* (1950), *Mr. Denning Drives North* (1951), *Mandy* (1952), *The Net* (1953), *It's Never Too Late, Child in the House* (1956), *Indiscreet, A Lady Mislaid, The Young and the Guilty* (1958), *Oscar Wilde* (1960), *Battle of the Villa Fiorita* (1965), *Twisted Nerve* (1968), *Oh! What a Lovely War* (1969), *The Walking Stick* (1970).

Phyllis Calvert had already made ten films before she became a household name in the 1943 period romance *The Man in Grey*. Along with her co-stars, Margaret Lockwood, James Mason and Stewart Granger, she became identified with the Gainsborough melodramas that enjoyed so remarkable a success in the mid-40s. She was usually cast in the good-girl, English-rose mould, and it says much for the intelligence of her playing that she held her own in these roles and made them interesting. She made the most of the showy role of the schizophrenic heroine of *Madonna of the Seven Moons*, was sympathetic and believable as *Fanny by Gaslight* for

Asquith, and made good use of Launder and Gilliat's dialogue in *2000 Women*. All three of these were released in 1944, the peak of her Gainsborough period.

She had, perhaps, her best role in Alexander Mackendrick's *Mandy* in which she showed a tough-minded understanding as the mother of the deaf-and-dumb child. In 1958, in *Indiscreet*, she played the first of a series of incisive character roles – on screen, stage and television.

Interview date: October 1989.

Your career seems to divide into pre-Gainsborough, high Gainsborough and post-Gainsborough, with a side-track to Hollywood ...
I think that's a marvellous idea but I always think that my Gainsborough days were war days and, of course, the war did break up one's life. Oh, Gainsborough was wonderful – I don't say all their films were wonderful, but they made *Kipps*, *The Young Mr Pitt*, and all the Launder and Gilliat pictures. The ones that made money were the ones we were in – *The Man In Grey*, *The Wicked Lady* ...

In the early stages of your career you worked with a number of notable comics including George Formby, in *Let George Do It*. What do you recall of this?
Well I was learning my craft. The parts weren't all that terrific, but I loved doing comedy and I made friends of

Richard Murdoch and Arthur Askey. George Formby was protected by Beryl, so I didn't really get to know him. He was a strange creature. He seemed to be quite brainless, but he was a brilliant technician. In one number he was singing and undressing at the same time, getting into pyjamas, cleaning his teeth, getting into bed and putting the light out on the last bar of the song. He never deviated; he was absolute perfection. It's hard to believe now, but he was the highest paid entertainer in his day.

In 1941 you co-starred with Michael Redgrave and Diana Wynyard in *Kipps* for Carol Reed. Did this feel suddenly like the big-time?
I have never felt like that in my whole life. I did my job and that's it. Originally for *Kipps* I was cast for the Diana Wynyard part [Helen] and Margaret Lockwood was going to play the maid. I went to have my clothes fitted, all

these beautiful clothes that Cecil Beaton had designed for Helen Walsingham, when they told me Margaret didn't want to play the maid's part and they'd got Diana as Helen and I was to play the maid. I burst into tears. Everybody in that film was playing a character who was acting a part – they were trying to get on in society, or trying to be a different person – the only 'real' person in it was Anne, the maid, and that is how I got such good notices!

As for Carol, he didn't give a lot of advice, but he encouraged one to be courageous. If it didn't work he would say 'No, try . . .' but half the time your courage was your creativity.

You worked for him again in 1942 in _The Young Mr Pitt_.
Yes, he was under contract to the same company. They cut a lot of me out of the film eventually. They put me in as a love interest, but there wasn't really any of that. I had played the Cockney maid in _Kipps_, so they wanted me to use me again, though Robert Donat, who had seen the clippings from _Kipps_, said I was completely the wrong person to play a duchess. One day I was standing outside the studios waiting for my car and he walked out. I had never met him. He looked me up and down and went back into the studio. He went straight to Maurice Ostrer and said 'I've just seen the girl I want to play the part!' The film was propaganda really. It was during the war and they made it to keep the spirits up.

Your period of intense Gainsborough activity began with _The Man in Grey_ in 1943. Did it make household names of you, Stewart Granger, Margaret Lockwood and James Mason?
Margaret was already a household name, but it certainly did that for the rest of us. _The Man in Grey_ was also the first Gainsborough film to make a great deal of money. Don't forget it was wartime and people wanted films to make them forget the war. I suppose it happened at just the right moment. It is the only film that has had two West End premières. It had one première, got terrible notices, went through the provinces and made so much money that it had to come back to London and be premièred again.

How far were Leslie Arliss as director and Ted Black as producer responsible for its success?
Arliss, not at all. We all said we would never work with Leslie again and I never did, although the other three did. He was a lazy director; he had got a wonderful job

there and he just sat back . . . Ted Black was the one who would watch it, cut it, and know exactly what the audience would take. I don't say he wanted to do really good films, but he knew where the money was and he made all those escapist films during the war.

Was there a lot of care devoted to costumes, settings, historical period?
Tremendous, yes. Elizabeth Haffenden was the main costumier and she was very clever. She did a great deal of historical research on the costumes all the time, and of course we had Cecil Beaton – you couldn't get higher than that! He did _Kipps_ and _The Young Mr Pitt_; Elizabeth did _The Man in Grey_. Don't forget, I was an antiquarian bookseller and I had a tremendous collection of costume books, which we made use of when we did _Fanny by Gaslight_.

Was the modern 'frame' story at the auction to permit a happy ending?
It was in the original book; I suppose they wanted the family to go on, to feel that all wasn't lost. We can put up with sad things when there isn't a war on, but it is difficult to be entertained by something sad during a war. You needed something that had a beginning, a middle and a happy ending and that's what they did. They weren't great films, but they filled a gap at that time.

This was the first of a number of 'good girl' roles for you. Did you yearn for wickedness, or were you just as happy making a career out of goodness?
I was _not_! I was under contract for seven years and at the end of those seven years, it took me _ten_ years in the London theatre to prove that I wasn't just the girl that all the troops wanted to marry, that I could act. I played all sorts of rather vicious parts after that, but it took me ten years to get rid of that image, which had stuck to me like Araldite. I do think it is much more difficult to establish a really charming, nice person than a wicked one – and make it real.

Do you feel films like _Fanny by Gaslight_ and _Madonna of the Seven Moons_ showed goodness as finally triumphant, but also allowed audiences to experience the thrill of wickedness along the way?
Oh, yes, indeed, although of course there wasn't the sort of sexual permissiveness there is today. At that time you

Mandy Miller, Phyllis Calvert and Jack Hawkins in Alexander Mackendrick's *Mandy*, 1952

couldn't have two people on a bed together unless their feet were on the ground! But in *Madonna of the Seven Moons* we got away with it by having a very dark room, with the two heads on the pillow – there was just a light on our faces made by the cigarettes we were smoking. You couldn't see the foot of the bed, it was too dark. Sex wasn't talked about in those days; it was there, implied, we all knew it happened.

Whose idea was the final image of you with the cross and the rose?

I think that was our director, Arthur Crabtree. If that film had been made today, you would have seen the rape, the passion on the bed, but *then* it had to be imagined. Arthur was a very good cinematographer, but there weren't enough directors, and so people who were scriptwriters or were behind camera were suddenly made directors, and they had no idea about actors at all. It wasn't that Crabtree was an unsatisfactory director, just that we found ourselves *very* satisfactory – we did it ourselves. But the fact that he had been a lighting cameraman was wonderful for us, because he knew exactly how to photograph us.

With *Fanny by Gaslight*, *2000 Women* and *Madonna*, 1944 was a big Gainsborough year for you. I admire *Fanny* most of these films . . .

Yes, I do too. I'm not very good at watching my old films, but I did watch that. It was a little slow but it holds together even nowadays I think, and it was a fascinating story. I adored 'Puffin' [Anthony] Asquith, but I think he reached his peak some years before *Fanny*. Remember *Pygmalion*? But then, maybe he was like me and had to earn a living, so he did the films he was asked to do. Of course, the director OKs everything, decor and so on. It was a marvellous cast, and Wilfred Lawson was my favourite actor, I loved working with him. It's lovely to work with someone you have admired. In my young days I had great heroes, but when you work with them they are just ordinary people. But Wilfred Lawson never lost his magic.

They Were Sisters would, I suppose, have been rather insultingly called 'a women's film' at the time, but it had a powerful performance from James Mason. Very dangerous and destructive.

Oh yes, and this subject has come out so much into the open lately. Then, such things were suppressed, now you never stop reading about people being bashed about. Yes, it was a very good performance. Dulcie Gray was very good too – a very under-rated actress, I always thought.

After making several films with Launder and Gilliat as screenwriters, you were directed by Launder in *2000 Women*. How did you find him as a director?

I loved Frank and Sidney; we were tremendous buddies *before* I did *2000 Women*. They asked me to play the nun who falls in love with the airman, and I said I just couldn't do that. That broke up our friendship. Pat Roc played the part I was originally cast for. From then on I didn't see much of them – they didn't like me turning down a part they had written for me, which I can understand. I enjoyed playing Freda Thompson though. It was a great film to work on, except that Renee Houston and Flora Robson didn't get on at all. And Thora Hird – and her little girl, Janette Scott – was in it too. Thora told me she didn't know how to keep Janette off the stage and I told her not to try, it was a talent that ought to be encouraged. And there was Betty Jardine who died in childbirth. She was a great young character actress in those days, very clever indeed.

Men of Two Worlds must have seemed a change of

**pace to you. Was Thorold Dickinson notably
different from the other directors you had
worked for?**

I loved him. I enjoyed being in the film enormously. One
thing that worried me was that all my clothes were so
beautifully pressed and that didn't seem right if I was
supposed to be in the jungle. They told me I would have
had all sorts of people doing those things for me. It was
all rather tricky because we had American negroes and
African negroes who used to have great fights on the set.
They spent a year in Africa doing the exteriors, although
I didn't go, then a year in the studios after that. It was
the most expensive film ever made in England at the
time, £2m or something.

It was a Government-sponsored film and it was to
show what we were trying to do in Africa, trying to get
people out of the villages and into the big towns so they
would have education and health. And, of course, we
were fighting the witch-doctors. It was done with very
high-minded notions. I didn't know Thorold very well,
but he coped with the situation marvellously. Thorold
was very good with the coloured actors. He left the rest
of us to our own devices pretty much.

**Someone has summarised the Paganini life story,
The Magic Bow, as 'Violinist's childhood
sweetheart lets him wed French aristocrat'. What
do you think of it?**

I tried to get out of it. It was the *last* thing I wanted to do.
I rang Granger up and asked him if he thought we should
do it. I didn't want to do it. It was absurd – I made more
laughs out of that film than any other, and the way
Granger played the violin! He had the leader of the
London Philharmonic bowing and someone else doing
the fingering, and he had a little man standing underneath . . . Maggie was cast in it, too, and we both went
along to see Rank himself on Park Lane. There was a
long onyx table in the room and he was sitting at the end
of it, a very big man. We came in through the door and
Margaret went around one side of the table, and I went to
the other. Then he stood up and said, 'I hear you've

coom ter talk about more brass'. Mostly, he was absolutely charming. He was very nice, until I signed a contract with America and he turned my photograph to the
wall. He admitted that in *Time* magazine.

**You made a film for Independent Film
Producers, directed by Ladislas Vajda, called
Woman with No Name, with the young Richard
Burton . . .**

At the time he couldn't act for nuts! I had just seen him
do *The Lady's Not For Burning* and thought he would do
for this part so I cast him (I was co-producer). He told
me he had saved some money and had just taken out a
mortgage on a house. It had three floors; he had the
middle flat and he intended to let the upper and lower
flats. He said, 'I will never have to work again!' That's
sweet, isn't it?

**How did you find working at Ealing again (in
Mandy) for the first time since 1940?**

(Sandy) Alexander Mackendrick was a perfect director
of actors. He was the first person who let me cry naturally. In the early days if you were to cry, you had to
have tears streaming down your face but no frowning or
looking ugly. Sandy was a wonderful director. Then he
went to America. I think *Mandy* was a very moving film.
Sandy really was sensitive to actors. He was the first
man who had directed me since Carol Reed. There was a
long time in between!

**When you worked with Ingrid Bergman and Cary
Grant in Stanley Donen's *Indiscreet*, had you
made a conscious decision to play character
parts?**

I was very lucky as far as character parts go: *Mandy* was
my first break; my second was theatrical, when Wendy
Hiller came out of *Crown Matrimonial* and I went in to
play Queen Mary. Those two gave me the entrée into
character parts, which is difficult, because they always
expect you to go on being glamorous. But I liked the part
in *Indiscreet* very much.

Ian Carmichael

Bond Street (1948), *Trottie True, Dear Mr Prohack* (1949), *Ghost Ship, Time Gentlemen Please* (1952), *Meet Mr Lucifer* (1953), *Betrayed* (1954), *The Colditz Story, Storm Over the Nile, Simon and Laura* (1955), *Private's Progress, The Big Money* (1956), *Brothers-in-Law, Lucky Jim* (1957), *Happy is the Bride* (1958), *Left, Right and Centre, I'm All Right Jack* (1959), *School for Scoundrels, Light Up the Sky* (1960), *Double Bunk* (1961), *The Amorous Prawn* (1962), *Heavens Above!, Hide and Seek* (1963), *The Case of the '44s* (1964), *Smashing Time* (1967), *The Magnificent Seven Deadly Sins* (1971), *From Beyond the Grave* (1973), *The Lady Vanishes* (1979), *Diamond Skulls* (1989).

For about five years, Ian Carmichael was one of the 'hottest' stars in British films. He came in towards the end of the British cinema's most prolific period, but between 1955-60 he established himself securely in the popular imagination. His image was essentially that of slightly bumbling innocent abroad in a corrupt world, but he combined this with a capacity to play the romantic element convincingly. As a result, he was indisputably a leading man rather than a character comedian. It was Muriel Box's persistence in casting him in *Simon and Laura* that initiated the series of slightly frazzled young men on whom he worked skilful variations over the next few years. However, it is with the Boulting Brothers that his name is inextricably linked – as the more or less sane centre of their satires on various British institutions. Stanley Windrush, the character introduced in *Private's Progress* ('Feeling a little fragile, sir', he confided to his sergeant), made him a major British star, and he repeated the role three years later in *I'm All Right Jack*. The 'silly ass' strain is less apparent in *Lucky Jim*, and *Happy is the Bride* gives him a more or less straight romantic lead; he adapts well to their different demands.

Interview date: September 1989.

At the start of your film career, you had unbilled roles in three late 40s films. Do you remember these parts and how you got them?
Through my agent. They were bit-parts, one-day parts, and I felt a little lost. I remember being on location in Camden Town for *Trottie True*. The director was Brian Desmond Hurst and, at one point, the cameraman asked me 'What are you doing here?' and I said, 'Well, the director's just told me I've got to do so-and-so, but in this bit of script they sent me I do something else'. Hurst heard this, turned round, and absolutely snapped my head off with, 'Will you bloody well learn to do as you're told?' I never looked favourably on Brian Desmond Hurst from that day onwards.

You were in *Meet Mr Lucifer* (1953) and *Simon and Laura* (1955) which satirise television. Did

50s British cinema respond well to the threat of television?
I think they were terribly frightened of it for a long while. Front office was very reluctant to let contract players appear on television, fearing it would do them infinite harm. It took a long time for them to realise they could sell their old movies to television. As for *Simon and Laura*, I've done that in three different media – stage, cinema and television. When Muriel Box directed the film for Rank, she had a hell of a battle with them, because she wanted me to play my original part in the movie. They, however, said, 'We must have a name that means something in the cinema'. On the stage the stars were Roland Culver and Coral Browne whose names would have meant nothing at provincial cinema box-offices. So, in the film, there were Kay Kendall and Peter Finch and myself and Muriel Pavlow. Muriel Box

fought for me and I was the only one from the theatre production who went into the movie. Then, a few years later, when I repeated it on television I moved up one, and played Simon.

I did some television direction for the BBC in the early days, and had enough experience to know that, in many ways, the technical aspects of *Simon and Laura* were incorrect. It has hardly ever been shown again, and I wondered if it was, in regard to television, technically all old-hat.

In 1954 you made your only American film, *Betrayed* with Clark Gable and Lana Turner. Did you find notable differences between American and British film production methods and attitudes?
Again, it was the star system. I had a very good part in *Betrayed*, a tip-top light comedy juvenile role written by Ronnie [now Sir Ronald] Millar. But it was an American company (MGM), it had an American director, with very big American stars, and I never got a look in. They never did the reverse shots, I had no close-up, and they gradually whittled my part down. I vividly remember my only scene with Lana Turner. She was ill in bed in hospital, and I went in to take her some flowers. I was standing at the end of the bed talking to her and the camera was either over my shoulder or close on Lana Turner. This was my experience with a Hollywood company.

You made several films in rapid succession. Were you being carefully groomed?
No I wasn't. I got parts purely as a result of my name coming to the fore a bit in the theatre, as with *Simon and Laura*. Then came the Boulting Brothers, and that was an entirely different matter. They'd got two subjects: *Private's Progress* and *Brothers-in-Law*, and they wanted a man to play both parts. I'd just done *Simon and Laura* on the stage. I thought that, once I'd got out of revue and into a play (it was my first for a long while), there might be a chance for me to get into the cinema, because casting directors in those days didn't look upon revue performers as actors. Then suddenly I got these two parts from the Boultings and told them what I just told you. They said, 'You're quite wrong, dear boy, we gave you the part because we saw you do that undressing-on-the-beach-sketch in a revue. We knew then we wanted you, but we couldn't remember your bloody name'.

Did you find noticeable difference between the methods of the two Boulting Brothers?

Yes, but they were both splendid directors. I found that many actors who worked for the Boultings usually *preferred* the one they worked for first, but they were *liked* by everybody. It was John who first directed me in *Private's Progress*, and when you're inexperienced in the cinema you really want all the help you can get from the director and John gave me that. I found him very sympathetic and tactful. He could bring out a performance without ever raising his voice. But this is not to say that Roy isn't very good, too. In those days they used to take turns to direct and produce, because they both enjoyed being on the floor. You always talk of the Boultings as a team, as 'the Boulting Brothers'. There was never any kind of conflict between them.

How influential was the Stanley Windrush character in your career?
Enormously. It was the big break for me, into national as distinct from West End theatre recognition. As soon as I read *Private's Progress*, I thought, 'God, this is a funny part', and I fancied myself playing comedy. It was a bit overshadowed five years later when I did *I'm All Right Jack* because I was repeating a performance. We all were, with the exception of Peter Sellers who was brought in new and fresh. He was given a tremendous part and did it brilliantly.

***I'm All Right Jack* is, perhaps, one of the most cynical British films. What, if any thing, is it in favour of?**
I think the Boultings would like to feel they were exposing the frailties of both sides in industry, but I don't think there's any doubt that the unions were a bigger target than management. They provided such material with their pomposity and follies. It was about time somebody took them down a peg and the Boultings did it. But they didn't neglect having a go at management, too. The film still works because it is so topical.

You also made *Lucky Jim* for the Boultings.
There was trouble with *Lucky Jim*. I don't think I named names in my book, and I would hate to do so now, but a triumvirate got hold of the rights to *Lucky Jim* – the late Patrick Campbell, who was a journalist, his then-lady friend, who eventually married him, and the director I prefer not to name. They'd got this script and they asked me to play Jim. The first fortnight we were in one set – the big quadrangle in the University – and it was on the large stage at MGM. I was finding the director intimidating, because, whereas the Boultings whispered in my

ear, he was apt to stand behind the camera and shout, which I didn't like very much. The production company worked through British Lion, who were distributors, and by now the Boultings were on the Board of British Lion, and were not happy with the daily rushes.

After two weeks British Lion sacked the three of them, including the director, and on the following Monday morning John Boulting took over. It was a ten-week schedule, of which two weeks had gone. Now John was hamstrung inasmuch as we were already in production on the floor and he had to largely accept the existing script. The Boultings always believed you should start with a script and work to it. So John was stuck with that script. Then there was terrible trouble with an actor called Hugh Griffiths. He hadn't liked the changeover and was a pal of the original director. Generally speaking, it was a bloody mess. At the end of it all, not a bad movie came out, which was lucky, but it was a bit of a

hybrid. For my part, I'd done two greenhorns, two innocents abroad, and was most anxious not to do a third. I did want to try and give the character a bit of backbone and John helped me. If the overall product still looked as if it was in the same mould, as I suspect it did a bit, that is because there *was* a similarity in the script and he was another man against authority.

What do you recall about working with the great Robert Hamer in *School for Scoundrels*?
He was very, very unhappy because he had just been taken off the bottle. One was aware all the way through the film that he was being nursed along by the producer, an American called Hal Chester, who used to pick him up every morning, bring him to the studio, and take him home every night to make sure he *went* straight home. He managed to last for about eight weeks. Then, when I came down for a night shoot in London, he was absol-

Ian Carmichael and Maureen Connell in John Boulting's *Lucky Jim*, 1957

utely sloshed. The producer sent him home and directed that night's work himself. He then brought in a new director to finish the film, a man called Cyril Frankel, who never actually got a credit. In the weeks I did with Hamer, I felt that the *effect* of his alcoholism was on him – he was beyond his best powers.

In your last film for the Boultings, *Heavens Above*, yours is a guest appearance. Did you do it as a favour to them?

Entirely. They rang up my agent and Roy said – they were excellent salesmen, the Boultings – 'You know this is John's major opus, he has spent ages on it. It is so sad that we can't find a big part for Ian in it, but there's one small part he *could* play. I wonder if he would like to', and told me what it was [the new vicar who replaces Sellers at the end]. They were very fair, and paid me very well for doing it. I did it as a favour because I owed them so much *and* wanted to be in the movie.

Were satisfying film roles hard to come by in the 60s?

Very much so. I was very 'hot' in the 50s and the early 60s, and seemed to be first choice for anything that was funny, but, as a result of the Boulting pictures, I had a high standard and didn't want to make inferior movies. Like so many actors, I kept saying, 'Will somebody please find me a nice Cary Grant-type part. Can I please have a *North by Northwest*? But they never came, and, by the mid 60s with the new wave that came, that sort of part rather dropped off. When a film called *Hide and Seek* came along, I was sure this was going to be it. It was produced by Hal Chester who'd done *School for Scoundrels*, and had a superb script. However, it turned into a chaotic mess, with Chester breathing down the neck of the director, Cy Endfield, and ran weeks over schedules. It was an enormous disappointment for me – I don't think my one chance for a gear-change even got a London showing or press show.

Were the later 50s the key part of your career?

Oh, yes. They included the happiest five or six years of my career. There *was* a studio system, there *were* contract artistes. I was in on the tail-end of that, and as an actor I was terribly happy, working the hours I liked and doing something I loved.

George Cole

Cottage to Let (1941), *Those Kids from Town* (1942), *The Demi-Paradise, Fiddling Fuel** (1943), *Henry V, Journey Together* (1945), *My Brother's Keeper, Quartet* (1948), *The Spider and the Fly* (1949), *Morning Departure, The Happiest Days of Your Life**, Gone to Earth* (1950), *Flesh and Blood, Laughter in Paradise, Scrooge, Lady Godiva Rides Again* (1951), *The Happy Family, Who Goes There?, Top Secret* (1952), *Will Any Gentleman?, The Intruder, Our Girl Friday, The Clue of the Missing Ape* (1953), *An Inspector Calls**, The Belles of St Trinian's, Happy Ever After* (1954), *A Prize of Gold, Where There's a Will, The Constant Husband, The Adventures of Quentin Durward* (1955), *It's a Wonderful World, The Green Man, The Weapon* (1956), *Blue Murder at St Trinian's* (1957), *Too Many Crooks* (1958), *Don't Panic Chaps, The Bridal Path* (1959), *The Pure Hell of St Trinian's* (1960), *Dr Syn Alias the Scarecrow, Cleopatra* (1963), *One Way Pendulum* (1964), *The Legend of Young Dick Turpin* (1965), *The Great St Trinian's Train Robbery* (1966), *The Green Shoes* (1968), *The Vampire Lovers* (1970), *Fright* (1971), *Take Me High* (1973), *The Blue Bird* (1976).
* Short film. ** Unbilled.

From cheeky resourceful Cockney kid to awkward or inhibited young man to St Trinian's 'Flash Harry' to TV's sensationally successful Arthur Daley, George Cole has hurdled the decades with effortless ease. He was immediately noticed as the Cockney evacuee in Asquith's *Cottage to Let*, repeating his stage role in his first film and holding his own with some distinguished talents, including Alastair Sim who was to be a continuing influence in his career. Briefly moving as the boy in Olivier's *Henry V*, he played a string of sharply differentiated young misfits throughout the late 40s and early 50s. In doing so, he showed himself equally adept in comedy (as the timid bank clerk in *Laughter in Paradise*) or drama (as the obsessive kite flyer in an episode of *Quartet*). In fact the St Trinian's role, starting in 1954, really obscures by its popularity the range of his film work during these busy decades just as the cult success of Arthur Daley in the 80s, a marvellously detailed study in incorrigible deviousness, has probably obscured for many people the fact that it was preceded by nearly forty years of the most solid kind of film success.

Interview date: June 1990.

You are one of the few child actors who went on to a successful adult career. How did you come in to acting?
It's a terrible story really, one which I would be careful not to tell my children if any of them were planning to go on the stage. I left school at the age of fourteen, on a Friday; during the evenings I used to sell newspapers around the streets, and, on that particular Friday night, I looked through the London evening newspapers I had been selling and in one of them there was an advertisement for a boy, wanted for a big musical in London. I went up to the West End the next morning and, although I didn't get the part, I got the understudy's job, and I never went home again. People say what wonderful parents I must have had, to let me do it. I sometimes think they must have been bloody awful parents, not to have come after me!

Did Anthony Asquith choose you to play the Cockney boy in *Cottage to Let* as a result of seeing you play the part on the stage?
Yes, I think so. It was my first play as well as my first film; and I was a Cockney so there wasn't a problem there. The idea of going on the stage, being a rude little boy, being paid for it, and having people clap you for it — I don't think I took in what it was all about.

What do you recall of working with Laurence Olivier in *The Demi-Paradise* and in *Henry V*?
I don't recall very much of *The Demi-Paradise* except being terribly in awe of Olivier; but *Henry V* was a wonderful experience. Olivier's direction was extremely detailed; I wasn't aware of what being directed was all about when I did *Cottage to Let*. Olivier would play everybody's part, showing you what he wanted done with

a scene, but he never played it anything like you were going to play it. I did tell one journalist that I was rather hurt Kenneth Branagh hadn't called me back for my original part [that is, the Boy!]. I had one line that was cut by the censor (which shows what censorship was like in those days); one character had a Frenchman down on his knees and he called me in as his interpreter. He said 'Tell him I'll ferret him, I'll fur him, I'll ferk him' and then I had to say 'I dunno the French for 'ferk'!

Did you ever have coaching from Alastair Sim, as one source suggests?
Not really. I did *Cottage to Let* with him as a play and while we were playing at Wyndham's Theatre the London Blitz started, which closed all the theatres. Alastair thought that my mother and I should get out of town to avoid the bombing and he found a place for us,

very near to where he and his wife lived. Well, my mother couldn't stand the country so she came back to London, and we (that is, Alastair and all the cast) took *Cottage to Let* around all the Army camps.

I then did about six plays and three or four films with him and, although I can't say he actually coached me, you can't work with someone like that without learning something. He was a most wonderful comedy actor, with incredible timing. He was also extremely generous with other actors, provided they were pulling their weight. He once said to me during a scene from *The Green Man*, 'If that's all you're going to do, then I'll just have to take over the scene'. I realised then I hadn't really looked at the scene and wasn't doing nearly as much as I could with it.

Your post-war films seem to present you as a shy, awkward young man, as in 'The Kite' episode in

George Cole and Alastair Sim in Frank Launder's *The Belles of St Trinian's*, 1954

Quartet and in *My Brother's Keeper*. Was it helpful to have an image established in that way?

I think I did develop that image, but I doubt if you can think like that until you *are* established and can afford to turn things down. I just took what came along. I think the young man in *Quartet* wasn't so much shy as a bit nervy and introverted. Sadly, they couldn't use Maugham's ending, again because of the censor. In the original story he went to gaol – and kept going back – for refusing to pay his wife maintenance. It didn't have a happy ending.

What do you recall of some very distinctive directors you worked with at the end of the 1940s – Robert Hamer, Roy Baker and Michael Powell?

I recall little of Robert Hamer other than that he was very nice. The film was *The Spider and the Fly* in which I really consider I played Eric Portman's walking stick; it was a dreadful part. I think the drink was beginning to undermine Hamer by that time.

Roy Baker is astonishing: in 1948 we made *Morning Departure* and the year before last he did the *Minder* special! For *Morning Departure* I had a very good part in the original script. The important aspect of my character was that he was a Jew; the money for the film, however, finally came from Jewish businessmen who didn't like the way the others behaved towards this character. Originally, Dickie Attenborough's hatred of me was supposed to be because I was Jewish, but in the film you're left wondering why he hates me. It was a pity to alter the script in that way because it would have set up a very interesting situation. There was no anti-Semitic feeling while the submarine was all right; it was only when it was in trouble that the conflict arose – either he goes or the Jew goes. It was an interesting film, though, in showing the breaking down of class barriers towards the end. Now, of course, there *has* been a considerable breaking down of those barriers, as in the introduction of regional and working-class accents on television.

As for working with Michael Powell, I didn't like him at all. He was fine to me but he would reduce actresses to tears; he even tried with Jennifer Jones. He tortured one particular actress, kept making her do re-takes which were totally unnecessary. He was more interested in the visual aspects of a film than in the actors and he was often horrid to them. I am a great admirer of his work but I didn't like that side of him.

You worked often with the team of Launder and

Gilliat. What were the special pleasures of working with them?

They always had a good script, although terrible money. If Alastair was in the film, it was even worse money because he got most of it! They were wonderful people to work with; Sidney Gilliat was very much the intellectual director and Frank was the down-to-earth one. Sidney always produced Frank's films and vice versa. When you were doing a film with Frank, Sidney would go mad because, at the end of every take, Frank would say, 'That was lovely, just do another one'. Sidney would say, 'Well, if it was so lovely, why are we doing another one?' It was just a habit Frank couldn't get out of.

Between the films each directed I think there was probably a difference in subject matter; I don't say that Frank couldn't direct one of Sidney's scripts or vice versa; either of them could have directed the *St Trinian's* films but it was always Frank. *Green for Danger* was another Alastair film and that was a Sidney Gilliat film. What I'm saying is that I don't think Sidney would have directed a *St Trinian's* film; I think I'm right in saying Frank directed all of them. Frank directed a film called *Lady Godiva Rides Again* – that could have been Sidney but it was more suited to Frank. *Green For Danger* couldn't have been Frank, it had to be Sidney, and *Gilbert and Sullivan* was another which had to be Sidney's. I think Frank enjoyed the broader comedy.

What do you think was the key to the success of the *St Trinian's* films?

Basically I think the first one, *The Belles of St Trinian's*, was the best, with Alastair as the headmistress and as the brother. They did have wonderful casts and were great fun to make. The scripts were not as good by about the third or fourth film; they did another one about five years ago which I couldn't do it because I was in *Minder*. It was awful – X-rated, topless girls – they had ruined the whole idea. The early ones had a real understanding of farce and I would say the script was the most important thing about them. But it was all there, in Ronald Searle's cartoons. That character of Flash Harry was in the cartoons. Ronald Searle has him coming around the wall at an angle that is physically impossible to do – worse than 45 degrees.

You made several films for Mario Zampi. Would you agree that for an Italian he had a remarkable grasp of British comedy?

Oh yes, wonderful, but I think he had the knack of finding the right scriptwriter. Jack Davies and Michael

Pertwee wrote those scripts for *Laughter in Paradise*, *Top Secret*, *Happy Ever After* and *Too Many Crooks*. Pertwee was first-rate; he wrote practically all of Mario's films. Those were very good comedies and Zampi was very nice to work with. In those days of course, most films were 'family' films, and they had a good audience.

I recently saw *Will Any Gentleman?* again and found it very fresh and funny. How do you rate it among your films?
I enjoyed doing it; it was a contract film for ABC. I had certain disagreements with them because they wanted me to play it rather like the man who had created the part, Robertson Hare, and I wouldn't do that. I think I was fairly arrogant as a youthful actor, digging my heels in and very blinkered about my attitude. I can remember some terrible rows about them wanting me to copy someone else's performance.

How did you feel about the steady stream of Hollywood actors pouring into Britain all through the 50s?
I think we had feelings about it, but we can't have had very *much* feeling because the only way the film was going to get distribution was if it had American stars. We were grateful that these films were being made. One American who became a close friend was Dick Widmark – I did *Prize of Gold* with him. Admittedly some of the people who came over here to make films weren't huge stars but, in the case of someone like Tom Conway,

these were people who made 'B' pictures and the picture would only get distribution if it had an American name in it. The whole thing would be sold as a package – you would have an Yvonne De Carlo film and with it a Tom Conway film, as a package. I don't think Yvonne was a particularly good actress, but she was fun. She got good direction here and got better parts than in America.

I am struck by the way you keep adapting to each period. How much of it was chance and how much clever calculation?
People think you plan things and you like to think you do, which is absolute rubbish because you don't. I do feel I have become aware, about three times in my career, that it is time to change direction. There was the *Life of Bliss* character, a young bachelor; then there was *St Trinian's*, which couldn't be more different.

One change I made very consciously was when I was offered the television series, *A Man of our Times* in 1966; I had been playing a man of twenty-five for forty-two years and suddenly here was my first opportunity to play a middle-aged man, which I did. Of course, as soon as I made a success of playing a forty-year-old, every part I was offered from then on was a forty or forty-five-year-old. That went on for quite a while and then came *Minder*, and I suddenly went from forty to whatever Arthur's age is (he says he's the same age as Paul Newman) and suddenly I am into my fifties, which is very nice.

Sidney Cole

As Editor, unless otherwise noted:
Freedom of the Seas, Mr Cinders (1934), *Royal Cavalcade* (co-ed), *Dance Band, Midshipman Easy* (1935), *Lonely Road* (1936), *High Command* (1937), *Spanish ABC** (co-dir, co-ed), *Behind the Spanish Lines** (co-dir, co-ed) (1938), *Roads Across Britain** (dir), *Gaslight* (1940), *Pimpernel Smith* (sup ed) (1941), *Nine Men* (sup ed), *The Bells Go Down* (sup ed), *Undercover* (sup ed), *Went the Day Well?, San Demetrio London* (sup ed) (1943), *Halfway House* (sup ed), *For Those in Peril* (sup ed), *They Came to a City* (assoc prod, co-scr) (1944), *Dead of Night* (assoc prod) (1947), *Against the Wind* (assoc prod), *Scott of the Antarctic* (assoc prod) (1948), *Train of Events* (co-dir) (1949), *The Magnet* (assoc prod) (1950), *The Man in the White Suit* (assoc prod) (1951), *Secret People* (prod) (1952), *The Angel Who Pawned Her Harp* (prod, co-scr), *North Sea Bus* (scr) (1954), *Escapade* (assoc prod) (1955), *Sword of Sherwood Forest* (co-prod) (1960) *The Kitchen* (prod, scr) (1961).
* Documentaries.

Sidney Cole was a key member of the Ealing family during its most productive years (1942-52). He had been an editor at several studios during the 1930s, and in 1938 he went to Spain with Thorold Dickinson and others to make documentaries. His Leftist sympathies, which he traces back to his time at the London School of Economics, made this work important to him, and no doubt helped him to find Ealing a sympathetic home when he returned there in 1942, after editing Dickinson's *Gaslight* and Leslie Howard's *Pimpernel Smith*. His most frequent Ealing collaborators were the Basil Dearden-Michael Relph team, Charles Frend and Charles Crichton, and his role varied. He was sometimes supervising editor, often associate or co-associate producer; he was also co-author of at least one screenplay (*They Came to a City*) and directed the most characteristically Ealing episode of the portmanteau film, *Train of Events*. From 1935 onwards he was active in the Association of Cinema and Television Technicians.

Interview date: June 1990.

Did the documentary work you did in Spain during the Civil War have any connection with the Grierson-dominated documentary movement in Britain in the 30s?
Not really. I had worked with Grierson in the early days and I knew him, not only in the context of the documentary film movement but also on the Council of the Film Society. But, except in the most general terms, those Spanish films didn't have any connection with Grierson.

What do you recall of two films you edited in 1940 – Thorold Dickinson's *Gaslight* and Leslie Howard's *Pimpernel Smith*?
They are very, very different. Of course, I knew Thorold very well from Spain and *Gaslight* was a great pleasure to work on. I was very nervous when I started to edit it. I showed Thorold the first sequence I'd cut, which was the prologue of the film; Thorold looked at it and said, 'Well, that wasn't quite what I had intended', so I apologised. He ran it again and then said, 'Oh, I see what you've done'. He had had a chronological sequence in mind and I had cut it purely on a visual basis of increasing and accelerating action, so that it had a mounting rhythm in terms of what was happening and was not related to chronology or the topography of the house. Thorold made a few small suggestions and that totally restored my confidence. What happens with directors who are also editors is that they like to have a good editor with them because they shoot material that can *be* edited.

Pimpernel Smith was the first film Leslie Howard had directed and he had great style as an actor which came over in the way he directed; but he safeguarded himself by asking me (as Supervising Editor) to be on the studio floor all the time during shooting so that he could ask me questions or I could tell him if I thought I needed another shot. I found when I was editing it that Leslie's style – as an actor and as a director – more or less dictated the way I edited it.

What do you regard as the editor's essential contribution?

An editor can help to make a good film even better; he can make a mediocre film look reasonably good, but there is very little he can do about a film which is absolutely terrible anyhow! I think the editor is very important, either in carrying out to its maximum possibility the director's intention, or in rescuing things that, for various reasons, haven't quite come off. In my youth as an editor, there was a surprising number of directors who desperately needed a good editor to try and do something with the material they had shot.

On what basis did you rejoin Ealing in 1942?

I went in as a supervising editor, when there were a number of young editors who needed guidance. At Ealing we always had several films going at the one time and it was the fashion to have a supervising editor then. Film terminology is always difficult but, for instance on *Pimpernel Smith*, it could be said that I was the editor and the so-called editor was an assembly cutter or assembly editor. It's a little unfair to him, but what happened on that film was that, as supervising editor, I spent a lot of time actually on the studio floor with Leslie; the editor would make the first assembly of a sequence and then I would look at it and make suggestions, then he would make any changes I had suggested. At a later stage I would take a reel myself and alternate, then we would look at it together; we would then switch things around as necessary. In short, I made sure that I worked physically on every reel, although the editor had done the preliminary putting-together, in most cases, of that particular sequence.

Michael Balcon wanted a supervising editor and I was known in the industry so he asked me in. Leslie was starting *The First of the Few* about the Spitfires when he discovered I had gone to Ealing; he told Balcon he wanted me on his film, so that in my first year at Ealing I was working both on *The First of the Few* and at Ealing.

During your time at Ealing you are variously described as editor, producer, director, and co-author. Do you have any preference among these roles?

Not really. On the whole we were very co-operative at Ealing, which was part of the pleasure of working there. I worked on one very well known film called *Dead of Night* which started with Charles Frend and myself

deciding we would like to make an anthology film on the works of writer M.R. James, ghost stories which were very chilling and frightening. Then we decided that the stories weren't as visual as we had thought when viewed in film terms. Everybody got interested in the idea and we had very interesting script discussions; it finally evolved into what it is and involved practically the entire studio – except, oddly enough, Charles Frend, who was by then making another subject. We shot it with two units and shot in parallel; there was a kind of friendly rivalry between the two units. When the film was put together I wasn't specifically the supervising editor; I was one of the associate producers who had a lot to do with the editing. That's why it is difficult to answer your question because, as associate producer or producer, I feel one of the most important things is to be there all through the editing process including the dubbing stage, to the final print. So I suppose I would have to say I like being a producer, because then I am involved in the scripting and in the editing as well, even if I am not billed as script-writer or editor.

A lot of Ealing films have your name or that of Michael Relph as associate producer. Did that mean that technically Michael Balcon was producer?

Yes, that's correct. Michael never wanted to take the title of executive producer; I think that was partly because in the early days he didn't get credited and when he was totally in charge he wanted the credit as producer. In many cases films were made because a producer and a director went to him and told him what they would like to do; if it was a novel or a play he would buy it. He would then want to approve or himself suggest the top casting and he would see the rushes every day. Beyond that he didn't interfere – not at all in the editing. He backed his judgment of us by letting us get on with the job.

Another name which crops up in your earlier years is that of Sergei Nolbandov, director of *Undercover*, now perhaps the least remembered name in the Ealing canon. Was he out of touch with the wartime spirit of Ealing?

Yes, he was a bit. I don't know much about Sergei, but he was a nice chap. One of the early films I did there was *Undercover*, an extraordinary film about Yugoslavia. The main character was someone called Mikhailovich who, at that time, was supposedly heading the Yugoslav Resistance to the Germans; when the film was nearly

John Clements and Googie Withers (foreground) in *They Came to a City*, 1944

finished the previous British ambassador to Yugoslavia came down to see it and said it would never do because our aid was then going to Tito. The aid which had been going to Mikhailovich had in fact been used to fight Tito. It was a rather old-fashioned film and didn't fit in with the way the younger directors were working.

Of course, the big influence at Ealing in those days was Cavalcanti. He had not only a feature background which he had before he went into documentary, but he also gave documentary a great sense of style. One of the first things I did at Ealing was to edit his *Went the Day Well?*, which has stood up remarkably over the years and was regarded enormously highly in the United States. He knew how to shoot to be edited, therefore we were very much in tune as to how the film should be put together.

You were associate producer on *They Came to a*

City **which seems a most daringly uncommercial venture. How did it come about?**
This was in the immediate post-war period and there was a great deal of feeling around that, now the war had ended, there was going to be a new world opening up. Priestley always had his ear to the ground and he wrote the play which was quite successful. It used the same cast as that which ultimately appeared in the film. I saw the play and, being a socialist, I thought it was extremely interesting and captured the mood of the moment. I went to Balcon and suggested making a film of the play. Priestley was very well known as a screenwriter as well as a playwright, and several of his books and plays had been turned into films by the studio, so Balcon agreed and we made it, very cheaply. I've no idea how it fared commercially.

You worked on four films for Charles Frend, *San*

Demetrio London, Joanna Godden, Scott of the Antarctic and The Magnet. Did you have a particularly sympathetic working relationship with him?

Yes. Somehow we gravitated together. We found we agreed on a great number of things and that's how we came to work together quite often.

Scott of the Antarctic took us about two years altogether; both Charles and I had boyhood memories of the Antarctic expedition and we both felt it had epic quality, so we went to Balcon and told him we wanted to make the film. It was one of the biggest productions Ealing had tackled at the time. We got a great deal of co-operation from the Polar Research Institute at Cambridge, from Professor Debenham who had actually been on the expedition. We did a great deal of research as to where we needed to shoot and we found that for some purposes we needed to shoot at the Aletsch Glacier in Switzerland, running down from the Jungfrau; and for other things we went just north-west of Bergen in Norway, to the place where Scott himself actually went to try out his motor-sledges before he decided not to take them. So we really had a tough time with the picture because it was very cold on location and occasionally the cameras would stop turning.

Joanna Godden was also made almost entirely on location, which really became something of an Ealing tradition. That's where Cavalcanti and Harry Watt, myself to some extent, and Charles Crichton had a considerable influence.

You worked with Crichton twice — For Those in Peril as supervising editor and Against the Wind as associate producer.

For *Against the Wind* we needed a French girl to play one of the parts. We went to Paris and saw a film with Simone Signoret, after which we met her in the bar of the Hotel Georges Cinq. She was the only leading actress whom Michael Balcon agreed to cast without having seen or met her, because we phoned him with such enthusiasm from Paris. A very debated piece of casting was that we persuaded Jack Warner to be in it; there is a very good scene in which Simone Signoret as the radio operator with a group of Resistance fighters is listening to London and gets the news that there is a traitor in the group, who is Jack Warner. She turns to Jack, who is sitting there quite calmly, and shoots him. It was a tremendous shock to audiences, Jack Warner being so much loved by them.

Your one directorial assignment was the Engine-Driver sequence in Train of Events; it seems to me the most characteristically 'Ealing' sequence of the four stories.

It probably is because of its being down to earth, about working-class people and shot on location. We thought we'd try to do a 'portmanteau' type of film; the stories aren't connected, of course, as they were in *Dead of Night*, where it all gels together and becomes quite frightening.

How did you find working with Alexander Mackendrick at the end of your time there?

The film was *The Man in the White Suit*. Unlike most other directors I worked with, I had some clashes with Sandy; however, they were fruitful clashes. *The Man in the White Suit* was so full of meaning that all sorts of small things became debatable in it. We had long discussions about the attitude of union representatives for instance. I remember Sandy saying it was probably one of the most important films he had been connected with. Some of my friends criticised the film for the way it portrayed union attitudes but I thought Mackendrick was right in the way he approached it, because the Alec Guinness character is an innocent, a naive person and an idealist who doesn't realise any of the social implications of what he is doing.

Ealing was like a repertory company of actors, wasn't it?

Yes it was, and it was successful in creating stars with whom audiences fell in love. I always remember travelling on a train and two young girls were reading *The Evening Standard*. One of them scanned the cinema listings and said to her friend, 'Oh, a Googie Withers film! I must go and see it!'. And I thought, 'Well, Ealing did that'. Googie was remarkable, very strong.

If you were asked what you saw as the highlight of your career, do you have something which stands out for you?

I like to think back on certain films such as *Dead of Night*, *The Man in the White Suit* and *Scott of the Antarctic*, but I think looking back can become rather self-indulgent. Most of my films I like to remember but, most of all, I like to remember that I have been very fortunate in having spent my working life in a sphere which I enjoyed and always wanted to work in.

Passport to Pimlico (extra) (1948), *Malta Story* (1953), *The Love Lottery, Svengali, The Embezzler, Forbidden Cargo* (1954), *Passage Home, Handcuffs, London* (1955), *The Black Tent, Eyewitness, Yield to the Night, House of Secrets* (1956), *High Tide at Noon, Campbell's Kingdom* (1957), *The Silent Enemy, Nor the Moon by Night, Sea of Sand* (1958), *Life in Emergency Ward 10, Sapphire, Upstairs and Downstairs* (1959), *The Angry Silence, Cone of Silence, Doctor in Love* (1960), *Payroll, No, My Darling Daughter* (1961), *A Pair of Briefs, The Mysterious Island, Life for Ruth, The Iron Maiden* (1962), *The Captive City, The Stolen Hours* (1963), *Life at the Top, Sandra* (1965), *Modesty Blaise* (1966), *Star!* (1968), *Twinky, The Royal Hunt of the Sun, Country Dance* (1969), *A Town Called Bastard* (1971), *Vault of Horror* (1973), *Inn of the Damned, Ride a Wild Pony* (1975), *The Irishman* (1978), *Turkey Shoot* (1982), *Stanley* (1983), *Appointment with Death* (1988).

Considering that Michael Craig's screen career began to gather momentum just as British films were beginning to lose theirs (that is, in the mid-1950s), he managed to run up an impressive number of credits in the decade that followed. The last of the Rank contract artistes, he made about twenty films from 1956-66. Though he grew tired of the handsome young professional men he was always being called on to play, he brought to these often bland leading roles an easy charm and authority. Along with his brother Richard Gregson, Richard Attenborough, Bryan Forbes and Guy Green, he was one of the driving forces behind *The Angry Silence*, a film he saw as offering him a distinct break from the lightly likeable roles in which he had become a star. Unfortunately for him, as he points out, he had acquired the wrong sort of image to be acceptable to the new wave of realist directors who came along at the end of the 50s. Despite his modest and articulate disclaimers about his career, he was never less than a convincing screen presence, and in the 1978 Australian film, *The Irishman*, he gave a fine character performance in the title role.

Interview date: October 1988.

You became a film star after several years on stage. How did you get your first break in films?

During the 50s the Rank Organisation and indeed ABPC [Associated British Picture Corporation] ran these studio programmes that they hoped were a carbon copy of the American system, whereby they had a stable of young people under contract. The Rank Organisation scouts came to see a play I was in at the Oxford Playhouse and I was offered a seven-year contract, in the summer of 1954. That sounds OK, but there was an option at the end of every year, which was on their side. They could drop you if they wished. That's how I got started at Rank: I signed in August or September and, about a week later, I found myself playing a part in a picture they were doing with Finch and Diane Cilento, *Passage Home*, about a ship and its crew. Then I got my first lead in *House of Secrets*, a sort of James Bond thing. It was a huge part, with various leading ladies, love scenes and fights, and all that idiot stuff. Some of it was filmed in Paris I remember.

Did the 50s seem a good time for a budding film star in Britain? Did you have a sense of a sturdy industry?

It depended on how naive you were. Television was just coming into real significance as a competitor to the film business, and Rank believed that competition could be beaten by making good family entertainment. However you define that, the end product was bland and dated and hadn't very much to say. I did five films at Pinewood which are exactly the same: the same writers, same directors, producers, camera team, actors. In one I'd be a doctor, in another I'd be an architect, whatever. Same jokes. Same character people. Well, there's a limited life for that kind of product. Anyway, after a series of rows over one thing or other, the lively talent went off and did independent production. The same sort of thing was happening at ABPC and the studio idea was breaking down.

When I first was under contract in 1954, there were forty-odd people under contract to Rank; when I finished in 1961 there was me and Dirk [Bogarde], who I think had a different kind of deal.

Was anyone looking after your career in the 50s?
No. For example, when I did *The Angry Silence* which I'd also written, so I had a big stake and interest in the whole project, they first of all refused to let me play my character, because they said it wasn't the kind of character they had been grooming me to play, which was the up-market, upper-class juvenile lead. This chap was a bit of a wide boy, a layabout with Cockney accent and so on. And weak. I had the most terrible bloody row about that. Finally I did it because I said, 'I'll go to the

press, you know', and it would have looked a bit daft if they'd stopped me.

How did you get the roles you had then?
Through the studio. If a picture came into Pinewood the pressure would be on – a lot of them were Rank pictures anyway – and the producers and directors would be persuaded, if possible, to use Rank contract people. The reason I lasted all that time, and was quite well-known (though I don't think my being in a picture ever specifically sold a ticket, even in England), was that they would loan you out, under the terms of contract, and I did several pictures for other people, Romulus, ABPC, Fox, whatever. And their loan-out price on you would be your year's salary, so, in my third year, when I did a picture for Romulus, I was getting £4000 a year, and the cost to Romulus was £4,000 for me. Rank was then clear. They'd got their money back on me and I went on

Michael Craig, Sidney James and Madge Ryan in Ralph Thomas's *Upstairs and Downstairs*, 1959

to do another three pictures for them that year, so they had me in three pictures for nothing. If I was loaned out again as I was in another couple of years, we would split the overage.

Yours looks like a typical 50s career in the kinds of films you were in. War stories, colonial adventures, frivolous romantic comedies, and so on. How did you feel about this at the time?
It was very difficult. Take the reason *The Angry Silence* got made. I was doing a war picture in 1958 or 1959 called *Sea of Sand*, with Dickie Attenborough. The director was Guy Green whom I'd worked with on *House of Secrets*. We were having lunch just before we went off to Libya to make the film, and I said, 'Honestly Guy, I think it's pathetic. Here we are more than ten years after the war has finished, and we're still making pictures about it. Why aren't we making pictures about what's happening now?' 'Such as?', he asked. I said, 'Well when I was in Rep in York, a chap there had refused to join a strike, because it wasn't a union-called strike, it was a wildcat strike, and he'd been sent to Coventry, not just him, but his family, too, and it'd gone on for a year or more and he finally gassed himself. He couldn't take it any more'. 'That's the sort of thing we should be making movies about'. He said, 'Why don't you? Have you written any of that?'.

Then, by coincidence, Dickie had just formed a company with Bryan Forbes called 'Beaver' and they were looking for a subject. I spoke to Dickie about it when we were on location out in the desert, and he said, 'Get me your script'. So when I got back, I bashed it out with my brother [Richard Gregson]. First draft, story outline and first script. And Dickie, by this time, with Guy Green again, coincidentally, had gone off to make a picture called *SOS Pacific*, in which they met Pier Angeli. She was so engaged by the script of *The Angry Silence* that she asked Dickie if she could be in it, playing his wife. Now it hadn't been written for an Italian obviously, and we couldn't have afforded to pay Pier Angeli her sort of money, but she really wanted to do it. Then Bryan did the shooting script and that's how it got made. We all did it for nothing – £1000 each, against a percentage, which still owes me a few pounds.

You then did *Doctor in Love*. Did you simply have to do this?
Well, Dirk had decided he didn't want to do any more 'Doctors', though he later went back to them. *Doctor in Love* was really nothing to do with me, but it was the top

money-making film in England that year. It was quite fun you know, and, anyway, I didn't have any choice about it.

To an outsider, what looked like your more serious roles were in films like *Sapphire*, *The Angry Silence*, and *Life for Ruth* in the early 60s. What do you recall about these?
I made *Angry Silence* because I knew what I wanted to do. I certainly wasn't going on playing those architects or doctors. But it wasn't very easy. In actual fact, most actors don't have much option, we do what we get offered. There's never been bundles of scripts coming through my letter boxes. I've never been out of work much, but that's partly because I've done what came along.

In the 60s, I worked for Visconti, Joe Losey, and Bob Wise, three of the most successful directors ever, but the pictures I did with them were probably their least successful films. Now that's the luck of the draw. But, I liked *Sapphire*. That was Basil Dearden and Michael Relph, at Pinewood, where they had a sort of independent status because of their track record from Ealing, and they had a certain amount of autonomy. And *Life for Ruth* was made by them as well. There was the same writer, too, Janet Green.

I *did* choose to do *Life for Ruth* because my contract with Rank was finished then. It was, I think, in 1961 and I was under contract to Columbia for two years. Basil knew what kind of picture he wanted to make, and Michael was a very good producer. I remember Basil talking to me once on *Life for Ruth*, which was quite a hard picture to do. I said, 'I'm a bit worried about this', and he said, 'Michael old chap, you are the actor, we pay you to know how to do these things. I would no more expect to tell you how to play this scene, than I would expect you to tell me how to direct'.

What do you recall of the other directors you worked for?
Guy Green was a friend of mine; he taught me a lot about lighting as he began as a cinematographer, and won an Oscar as David Lean's cameraman on *Great Expectations*. As for Joe Losey, I thought he was a pretentious, very over-rated director. I did a picture for him called *Modesty Blaise* and I found him no help. Ralph Thomas was enormously supported by Betty Box, who was a very good producer. I think most of Ralph's pictures were done with Betty. They were a team for years, that whole Box-Rogers-Thomas clan, and Muriel Box, who was

Betty's sister-in-law, directed me in *Eyewitness*.

What do you remember of Philip Leacock's *High Tide at Noon*?

Phil was in favour, then, because he'd made a very successful and charming picture called *The Kidnappers*, which, like *High Tide*, was set in Nova Scotia. It had the same writer, Neil Paterson. There were a lot of problems with it, because we didn't go to Canada, we shot it in the west country. Also, Betta St John, an American dancer in *South Pacific* at Drury Lane, was cast as the girl, and she hadn't told them that she was four months pregnant. By the time we finished shooting the picture she couldn't be shot below the shoulders! Flora Robson and Pat McGoohan were also in it, but I don't remember much about the film except that it was about lobster fishermen, and the last line was, 'The bugs [vernacular for lobsters] are crawling'. There must be a happier line than this to bring down a curtain!

What about *The Silent Enemy*, directed by William Fairchild?

Yes, he wrote the script, too. It was nearly all shot in Gibraltar and Malta – all the water stuff was. It was about a real person, 'Buster' Crabb who foiled the Italians who had this flotilla of midget submarines that were banging off all these ships in the harbour just across the bay from Gibraltar. I loved working with Larry Harvey in it; he was a wonderful bloke. He always got a bad press because he baited them, he used to send them up, and they couldn't stand it. He was one of the wittiest and most relaxed people I ever met, but as soon as he got in front a camera he became all stiff and started to 'act'. I never admired him as an actor. He was OK as Joe Lampton, but the part carried him rather. He was his own man, Larry. The crew always loved him, you can always tell from that. He lived this wonderful sort of elegant life-style, even on location, which used to annoy people, but I thought it was very funny.

From the mid 60s you appeared in a number of films that seemed to be much more consciously aimed at international markets. Was this a conscious decision on your part?

No, it's just the way it happened. There were fewer pictures around and I found that I couldn't get cast by the new directors. They'd seen enough of me. I'd had seven years of Rank pictures and I consciously tried to break that image by going back into acting at Stratford and doing plays and so on. I never worked for any of those directors, Schlesinger or Jack Clayton or Lindsay Anderson either in a movie or on stage, which I regret. They didn't want me, so I did what there was to do. They wanted Albert Finney or Tom Courtenay. They wanted a different type, a different look.

One of the names most closely associated with the Rank Organisation during the 1940s and, particularly, the 50s was that of John Davis. He had early turned to accountancy 'because it taught general management', and he became involved with Oscar Deutsch, having responsibility for keeping the records and management accounting in good order. Eventually he became Managing Director for Deutsch's Odeon Cinemas chain, which was bought by Rank after Deutsch's death. In the late 40s, Davis worked closely with Rank in devising strategies to remedy financial difficulties. These made him a sometimes unpopular figure in the eyes of creative personnel who queried his policies. However, Davis insists that he never interfered with creative decisions, and makes clear that his first loyalty was always to Rank, whom he greatly admired. His knowledge of the British film industry, from a managerial point of view, is unique and would repay further documentation.

Interview date: July 1990.

Your name is always associated with the Rank Organisation. When did you and Mr Rank, as he was then, meet and in what circumstances?
The Dorchester Hotel in London has a big reception area and I was told to go there to meet Arthur Rank. I was standing on one side of the vestibule and he was standing on the other side; I was wondering to myself who that was and thinking I wouldn't like to cross swords with him because he looked a very austere person. It turned out to be Mr Rank and that was in March 1938. I found out in later years that he wasn't austere at all.

I had worked as accountant to Oscar Deutsch in the 1930s and later became Managing Director of his Odeon Cinemas chain. Arthur Rank became associated with Oscar Deutsch only twelve or eighteen months before Deutsch's death and it was agreed in principle that when Oscar died his estate would sell his interest to Arthur Rank. When Arthur realised how important film was in the life of a nation, and that the American film industry largely had a stranglehold throughout the world, he decided to take them on to show the British way of life as compared with the American. He wasn't anti-American at all, though.

What would you say to an account I've read somewhere that yours and Mr Rank's qualities were complementary — that is, his unbridled optimism was complemented by your more cautious approach?
Our relationship was complementary for a much deeper reason: he believed in the things I could do and I believed in him. I have never known such a fine man

whose attitude towards life applied to everything he did. He was undoubtedly a happy man himself. He was a man of great vision as far as the film industry was concerned. One of the problems was that many of the people whom he trusted completely to make films didn't share this vision. On the one hand you had those who thought the only things you could make were so-called 'English films' — small comedies and the like; and on the other hand, there were people wanting to make international pictures, neither of which was the answer to the question. When he got to grips with the film industry, he realised the importance of supplying his people with the latest equipment; he relied on them to produce the actual film. He was not a picture-maker and never tried to be, although he enjoyed films. That was my situation, too.

In box-office — and artistic — terms, British cinema reached a peak in the mid-40s. How difficult was it to arrange overseas distribution, especially in the US, even for the best of such films?
It was my responsibility at that time to go out and acquire cinemas all around the world or make distribution arrangements, so that these films could be shown. It was particularly difficult in America, but that's another subject, it's very complicated. You must have international markets. Because of the strength of the American industry, if one is to compete with them one must have a strong foreign market as well as a domestic one, if the producing country has only a limited population. You couldn't include the Commonwealth coun-

tries in that context. I had to go to Canada where the circuit was dominated by an American corporation (the name of which doesn't matter), and they were trying to block any foreign film of any sort from coming in.

With hindsight, it seems to me the 40s and 50s were a sort of boom period in British cinema. Is that how it seemed to you in your managerial position?

The question you raise is difficult to answer briefly. At the end of the Second World War, this country was, for all practical purposes, bankrupt, and certainly insofar as the US dollar was concerned. The Government was looking for ways to save dollar payments to the American companies. At that time Arthur Rank and I were in America and were told by the American industry that the British Government intended to bring in legislation which would restrict the flow of dollars to America.

At that time the Americans thought incorrectly that Arthur Rank was sponsored by the British Government. We were trying to negotiate with the Americans to arrange for British films to be shown in the United States with the support of their industry. They told us that they would support any scheme which conserved dollars, *provided it was voluntary* and not by legislation. They were afraid that, if it was by legislation, other countries, also short of dollars, would follow the same road. Arthur agreed to send me back with a message to the Chancellor of the Exchequer. I spent a whole day sitting outside the Cabinet Office and was not seen by anyone until the end of the day, when I was told that the problem was settled. Consequently, I could not convey to the Government that they would get voluntary support from America if they produced a scheme which would control sending dollars to America.

In a nutshell, the Government intended to impose legally an *ad valorem* duty on all foreign films imported, basically American. The *ad valorem* duty was to be calculated by estimating what a film would earn, and this had to be deposited with the British authorities before the film could be released to the public. This, of course, would involve large sums of money which the Americans either didn't have or were not prepared to put up.

Sir Stafford Cripps and Mr [Harold] Wilson came to see Arthur, at which meeting I was present, saying that the country desperately needed his help to provide British films to replace the American films whose import would be restricted. Needless to say, Arthur agreed to support them. We were told we 'would be taken care of'

when the *ad valorem* arrangement came to an end.

We stepped up film production (in retrospect, beyond the capacity of the creative people), and ultimately incurred a loss of some £20m. The problem was further complicated by international politics. The Americans at the end of the Second World War were very generous in providing Marshall Aid to help restore Europe's economies and industries. Many Americans thought that we, the British, should only receive Marshall Aid if we were allowing films into this country, with the Americans having the right to remit dollars to pay for them. The outcome was that the Americans sent over one of their top people to negotiate a deal with the British Government, which cancelled the *ad valorem* duty, without, as far as I know, consulting any members of the British industry as to the effects of doing so.

The fact was that a large backlog of American films, many of them great box-office attractions, flooded into the British market without any restriction, which explains the disaster with which we at Rank were faced. We had to work our way out of the problem without any help from the Government, but fortunately the National Provisional [now National Westminster] Bank gave us a lot of help which enabled Rank over a period of time to pay off the bank with slow recovery.

Do you think the whole concept foundered because the British public always wanted to see American films anyway and because it was impossible to fill the gap with British-made films?

It really goes deeper than that. The real question was that the British Government could not afford the dollars that the importation of American films incurred. They produced a lot of money and we (that is, the British film industry) could not afford to pay the dollars back to America, because we were desperately short of hard currency, particularly dollars, at the end of the war. As to whether we could fill the gap with British-made films, Arthur Rank was pressed very hard to do his best, which he did. Some films were good, some were not, and that created the problem.

When you were appointed managing director of the Rank Organisation, it had just suffered a loss of about £8m. How did you go about reversing this trend?

The effect of the *ad valorem* duty and the promises which were made to slowly bring back American films meant, in round figures, we lost £20m towards the end of the 40s. The broad issue was either to reverse that trend or go bust. In order to reverse the trend I had to make myself very unpopular to start with, by cutting every penny of expenditure that could be saved and selling everything that wasn't directly needed by the organisation for it to continue.

What was your attitude to those independent production companies that operated under the Rank umbrella (for example Cineguild, The Archers and so on)?

They were independent units which approached Rank for the projects they wanted to make. They were ideal film-making conditions and this was the great thing about Arthur Rank: he was convinced this was the way films ought to be made and I think it was right. But the producers didn't play their cards very well and some took Arthur's approach as a sign of weakness, whereas it was giving them adequate facilities and opportunities to be creative. By the early 50s that set-up had essentially dwindled away. Much of the film production was at Pinewood, which had by then become the best-equipped studio in Europe. Arthur Rank's approach was always 'I will give you the tools; you make the product'. It was very attractive to film-makers – or should have been.

I gather budgets were meant to be kept modest. If producers wanted to do something more

extravagant, how would they persuade you?

They would use the subject matter and whether or not we could get a partner to come in – say, an American or European distributor. There was never a general limit on budgets, though. We tried to work with budgets which were realistic and then expected producers to keep to them. We would consider each project and the marketing people would express their views as to its potential. They would look back at another film of a similar type to see what it had done and then attempt to measure the potential of a new film against its performance – whether a particular director had a good track-record, things like that. If the budget of a film was higher than we thought would enable it to recover its cost, we would suggest to the producer that he should get an American distributor, or maybe a European, to participate in the cost of the film.

How much time did you spend in the actual studios?

When you're running a large organisation you can't divide your time that way; it's all intermixed. I spent a lot of time at Pinewood, of course. I didn't want to exercise any influence over the kinds of films we made. Arthur Rank and I had one intention only and that was to make what today we would call 'clean' films which would be successful at the box-office.

MICHAEL DENISON:
Tilly of Bloomsbury (1940), *Hungry Hill* (1947), *My Brother Jonathan, The Blind Goddess* (1948), *The Glass Mountain, Landfall* (1949), *The Franchise Affair, The Magic Box* (1951), *The Tall Headlines, Angels One Five, The Importance of Being Earnest* (1952), *There Was a Young Lady* (1953), *Contraband Spain* (1955), *The Truth About Women* (1958), *Faces in the Dark* (1960).

DULCIE GRAY:
Banana Ridge (1941), *2000 Women, Victory Wedding*, Madonna of the Seven Moons* (1944), *A Place of One's Own, They Were Sisters* (1945), *Wanted for Murder, The Years Between* (1946), *A Man About the House, Mine Own Executioner* (1947), *My Brother Jonathan* (1948), *The Glass Mountain* (1949), *The Franchise Affair* (1951), *Angels One Five* (1952), *There Was a Young Lady* (1953), *A Man Could Get Killed* (1965).

* Short film.

Dulcie Gray had already given several fine screen performances before Michael Denison returned to Britain after war service and, by lucky chance, found himself starring in Harold French's *My Brother Jonathan*, in which his wife had already been cast. Denison became an overnight film star in what proved to be the year's most popular film, and this initiated a series of co-starring films for him and Dulcie Gray, including two for Lawrence Huntington (*The Franchise Affair* and *There Was a Young Lady*).

Dulcie Gray emerges very well from her time with Gainsborough: her servant role in Bernard Knowles's charming 'ghost' film, *A Place of One's Own*, is refreshingly free from stereotype, and she makes a genuinely moving figure of Charlotte, the gentle wife driven to alcohol and suicide by her brutal husband (James Mason) in *They were Sisters*.

Michael Denison was delighted to be in Anthony Asquith's elegant film version of *The Importance of Being Earnest*, in which he had exactly the right touch as the dandy Algernon, making the most of some of Wilde's best epigrams.

Together the Denisons scored popular successes in the romantic melodrama, *The Glass Mountain*, and the war drama, *Angels One Five*. Whether on film, stage, radio or television, they have had two of the busiest careers of any British actors.

Interview date: October 1989.

Are you pleased with the balance you've achieved among stage, screen and television?
DG: Yes, I think so. I would rather have done more classical stuff, but it didn't come my way for various reasons. I enjoy all the media, so I think I've been extraordinarily lucky to have been a part of all of them. I think Michael loves straight theatre even more than I do; I certainly think it is the cradle of all acting, but of course some things are the same in all media. You are working on the truth of the character that you're portraying, and it is really the kind of projection that is the basic difference. In the theatre you have to *think* towards the dress circle, whereas in television and even more so in films, you have to think as though the camera is very close to you, so of course you don't project so broadly.

I remember James Mason telling me I must never forget that, in close-up on film, my face would probably be eight feet high, so that was already enlarging my performance; I didn't have to go any further than that. I believe it is easier to make the transition from stage to film than the other way about, unless one is obstinately going to say, 'This is trash – the *theatah* is the great thing and I can't possibly . . .' and all that stuff.

A lot of notable British films have been written by playwrights and novelists. Do you think the British cinema of the 40s and 50s is really a very literary cinema in some ways.

Yes, I think so, especially the Ealing comedies. Gainsborough, which was my kind of stuff, was rather low-brow, but it was very 'film-y', full of story. The best of the Gainsborough films, even if they were called 'weepies' or 'women's films, had stories to tell – and the public loved them!

MD: It's interesting what you say about a literary cinema. In my comparatively brief cinema experience, I think every film I did except perhaps one was based on novels. *The Importance of Being Earnest* was based on a play, of course. *The Glass Mountain* was somebody's brainchild and was purely cinematic from that point of view. But *My Brother Jonathan*, *The Franchise Affair*, *Hungry Hill*, *Landfall*, were all based on novels. I think that meant there was a good narrative skeleton to those films.

What sort of association did you have with the Rank Organisation?
Very little. But I admired the way Rank tried to establish a deal for British films to be properly distributed in America. His talks were very successful and he was on his way home when the Government – Stafford Cripps was the Minister involved – put an embargo on American films coming into Britain. The Americans thought Rank had taken them for a ride when it was really the Government's doing. Dulcie was with Gainsborough before it became associated with Rank, then she went to Korda and I was with Associated British.

Korda seems to have been the one great entrepreneur.
DG: He was a one-off. He was a quite extraordinary man. I had decided not to sign with him for various reasons, and I went to see him to tell him so – and signed within ten minutes! He had enormous charm and a very kind, piercing logic, and I was very happy with him. The thing about our contracts was that they were one-sided. We couldn't opt out once we had signed, but they could sack us at any time, or at least on a yearly basis. A seven-year contract was actually one year guaranteed and six options on their side!

MD: This didn't worry me because I had emerged from the Army – to be signed for a seven-year contract which the press people described as a £55,000 contract! That was the aggregate which I would be paid if I lasted the full seven years. In fact I was being paid £25 a week in the first year but, in comparison with Army pay, I went from penury to what I thought was pretty well off!

DG: In my first year at Gainsborough, I earned £600 for several little pictures. My contract was with Gainsborough Studios, but they were thrilled if they could loan you and make money out of you. That is how they lost Audrey Hepburn years later: Michael and I had seen Audrey at Ciro's, dancing with six other girls, and she was outstanding. We took Robert Lennard, the Casting Director of Associated British, to see her. They were about to do a remake of *The Good Companions* with Michael and myself and couldn't find a girl to play the Jessie Matthews' part. We urged them to use Audrey, whom they had put under contract. But the film was made without her (and us) and, within six months, Audrey was making *Roman Holiday*. She was loaned out, and was lost to British films.

Mr Denison, apart from *Tilly of Bloomsbury* **in 1940, you played one supporting role in** *Hungry Hill* **before being given the title role in** *My Brother Jonathan*. **Did this seem like an awesome responsibility at the time?**
It seemed very exciting, after six years in the Army. About half-way through my Army career, I was coming back from Northern Ireland on forty-eight hours' leave. I rang Dulcie to tell her and she said, 'Oh well, I'll cancel the film test then'. I told her not to and went along with her instead. They hadn't provided a man to play the scene with the girls being tested so, rather than have someone stand there reading from a script, it was an advantage to have me as an actor do it. It was a love scene, a typically British love scene! So I did the scene, albeit with my back to the camera, with Dulcie and the other girls.

Three years then elapsed while I was in the Army, and Dulcie was approached to do *My Brother Jonathan*. It was hanging fire rather and Dulcie enquired of the casting director, Robert Lennard, what was going on. He said they were trying to find an unknown to play the long leading part. He asked her if she recalled the young man who had played opposite her in the film test she had done three years earlier. She replied, of course, that he was her husband and was at home, just back from the Middle East. As a result of that I was tested, got the part and a long-term contract with ABPC. I was loaned for *Hungry Hill*, because they took quite a long time to decide whether to take the risk of giving me Jonathan.

What do you think of the notion that *My Brother Jonathan* **is really an allegory of the rise of the National Health system in post-war Britain?**
I think all I felt was that it was a bloody good part to

play! It was, of course, written well before the war; whether the makers thought they were catching a mood or not I honestly wouldn't know.

DG: But Francis Brett Young was definitely on that side – that's what he would have wanted.

MD: Yes, it was strongly autobiographical; he had been a GP fighting abuses in medical care in the West Midlands as a young man, but that was pre-First World War period. Of course, considerable works in the literary field will have messages for all time, even though they are rooted in their period.

My Brother Jonathan was the first film you made together. Were you promoted after that as a team, or did you seek work together?

We have always enjoyed working together, but Dulcie's already strong film reputation meant that I was riding in on that, which was very good for me after having been away for so long. They cashed in on the team idea with *The Glass Mountain* and then, for various reasons, it didn't last. I think I contributed to that because, having been away from the theatre for a long time, I was very grateful to films for persuading *theatre* managers to employ me. I think the studios looked for opportunities to co-star us, and publicity sold us as the cosiest couple unhung, all that his-and-hers stuff with the thatched cottage in Essex. I did one film on my own, a terrible thing called *The Tall Headlines*, in which I played twin brothers one of whom was a maniac!

Of your films together, which one do you think gave you the best opportunities?

DG: We became rather fond of *The Franchise Affair*, which was not as good as the novel, but then the novel was particularly good. It had a marvellous cast, including Kenneth More giving an early appearance on celluloid as a garage mechanic.

The director was Lawrence Huntington, with whom you both did several films. What is your recollection of him?

MD: I think of him with great affection. He was a very funny man and splendid with actors.

DG: We were very fond of him. He knew what he wanted from you, but seemed relaxed, friendly and easy-going. He was very much underrated, as I think a lot of directors were.

Do you remember *Faces in the Dark* which has this plot synopsis in 'The British Film Catalogue':

'Man helps mistress drive her blind husband mad by moving his house from Cornwall to France'? It's based on a story by the authors of *Vertigo*.

MD: Best forgotten! I remember nearly meeting my end because I very properly drove my car off the road into a lake, where I was to drown. It was actually a gravel pit, and the arrangements for the car to sink were rather too effective! I just managed to get out of it and they put in a dummy instead. I did three pictures with Mai Zetterling – that one, *The Tall Headlines*, and *The Truth About Women*. I admired Mai a great deal. It's a pity that at least my first two films with her were rather claptrappy.

You starred in Anthony Asquith's film of *The Importance of Being Earnest*. What was his aim in making the film as he did?

Michael Denison with Dorothy Tutin in Anthony Asquith's *The Importance of Being Earnest*, 1952

I think he felt that it was essentially a theatrical piece, and that is why he 'topped-and-tailed' it, with the curtain going up on a glamorous first-night audience and all that. Virtually the only changes he made – apart from some cuts, I suppose – were putting in the railway journeys, Algy going Bunburying, and Lady Bracknell coming on the train, too. They were going to have me ride down Piccadilly in the morning – I come on first in riding breeches, you remember – but they called that off when they realised the confusion it would have caused.

I loved Asquith as a director. He was an interpreter and that is how I like my directors to be. I like them to know the script and the subject. He obviously loved the play, loved the wit and the shape of it, and loved the characters. He was completely in tune with the subject and, indeed, with the players. He didn't guide us much, in my recollection. I remember the first day's shooting – that long bit with the cigarette case – and we filmed it in quite large chunks, which was different from the normal method of filming. There are lots of quite long takes in it, not a lot of elaborate cutting.

The play is a masterpiece of artificiality which, on screen, must have posed real problems.
I think it goes back to what I said. It is a masterpiece and, provided it is faithfully done, it will continue to speak.
DG: I think it was because of its artificiality that Puffin left it as a theatrical piece.
MD: I think my only hope of screen immortality is due to the fact of Edith's (Evans) presence in the film. We once did a television version of it with Martita Hunt, who was a wonderful actress, but she was so determined not to do the handbag bit as Edith had done it that she whispered it, which was legitimate but wrong. It was like playing a major chord pianissimo.

Was it an harmonious film to make?
It was very happy. I think one of the important tasks of a director is a public relations exercise, and Puffin was admirable at that. I don't think any of that company was awkward. Darling old Margaret Rutherford was an eccentric, but she was a most lovable person. The cameraman was an absolute ace [Desmond Dickinson].

One of your last films was *The Truth About Women*, directed by Muriel Box, produced by Sydney Box and, I think co-written by both. What was your experience of working with them?
That was the only time I worked with them; they were

very nice to me and I thought the film was directed very efficiently. I enjoyed it very much. I had not been a fan of Laurence Harvey in his early days – largely on the disgraceful grounds of the way he dressed and wore his hair. This was when he had just arrived as a contract artiste at ABPC. So when I was asked to do this film with him I initially didn't want to, but I made myself do it and told myself to enjoy it. He welcomed me on a location shot in the early morning by saying, 'How lovely to see you. We are going to have a marvellous lunch so we can really get to know each other'. He charmed the birds off the trees, and we became enormous friends. That is my principal recollection of the film – the joy of working with Larry Harvey.

Miss Gray, did you feel those 40s Gainsborough films gave you a good start?
They didn't quite know what to do with me. I was taken on at Gainsborough on the strength of my stage performance in *Brighton Rock*. I think they had decided I was 'a stage actress' and they had made up their minds about me. I was sacked after *They Were Sisters*. It was the most extraordinary day. I woke up to find that James Agate, the top *theatre* critic, had done a notice of the film and said what a tremendous performance I had given. Then I was rung up to be told the Ostrer brothers wanted to see me. I went by bus, but on wings as well – and they sacked me on the grounds that they didn't want that sort of reality in films! The notion of Charlotte taking to drink, yes, but they didn't want me to look so plain; they wanted her to look pretty in her agony, which I thought was absurd. She was, after all, taking drugs and alcohol and was suicidal. It didn't seem to me she would have had her hair done just before she committed suicide! I was stunned, particularly in view of the superb notice which I had just received. I went home and burst into tears. Then the phone rang and it was Eric Portman. He asked me to be his leading lady in *Wanted for Murder*, so, in next to no time, I was working with him, for the first time with co-star status. He was a darling to work with – a fine actor and very funny.

What do you recall of working with James Mason?
There is a very strange strain among critics in England: they don't like success. I remember James saying that one of the reasons he went to Hollywood was because he knew he'd be rubbished every time he did anything here. Once he went to America he was accepted as the marvellous film actor he was. I don't mean to be unkind but, while being immensely lovable and endearing,

Dulcie Gray with Derek Farr in Lawrence Huntington's *Wanted for Murder*, 1946

James wasn't very funny – unlike practically every other actor. James was, in a way, dull; he was kind of 'sturdy'. But put him into a film and he was inventive and amusing. There was a marvellous moment in *They Were Sisters* when he was talking to me and decided to look at his teeth in a mirror. It was a bit of business he put in himself, and it was so wonderfully cruel, when my character was in agony and pain and needing his help, and that was his reaction to it. It had nothing to do with the script. The moment James was in a play or a film he had this amazing invention, often a cruelly comic invention, that welled up inside him. He was immensely helpful, easy-going, just what one dreams of in a co-actor.

Another person for whom I had a huge affection was Margaret Lockwood, who sadly became a total recluse in later years.

You made *A Place of One's Own* with her and for former cameraman Bernard Knowles.
I enjoyed doing it very much. I think the powers-that-be may have been a little shocked at my playing the 'below-stairs' character without turning it into a caricature.

Did you enjoy working with Arthur Crabtree, another former cameraman?

Yes, very much. You see, they did know about their cameras, which was great for actors. There was a revolution going on at Gainsborough all the time – every cameraman wanted to be a director, and quite often was.

I loved working at Gainsborough, being so fond of Maggie and James and I was having a quite glamorous start. But it never felt terribly secure and, of course, I was there in its last days. The Boxes came to Gainsborough after I had left. I did do a film for them, however, with Valerie Hobson, called *The Years Between*. That was directed by Compton Bennett; he was very good, too. Those directors weren't greatly inspired, except perhaps Lawrence Huntington, but they were marvellously efficient – they knew it all.

When I was doing *They Were Sisters* I had to come down the stairs crying; I had to do several takes for various reasons, and I finally did one when I wasn't actually crying, and they said, 'That's it!' I said to Arthur Crabtree how sorry I was, that it was the only time I hadn't actually been crying, and why was he going to use that particular take? He showed me eleven rushes and in some of them I hadn't actually hit my light, so all my crying went for nothing; the one they chose had me perfectly lit.

You made two starring films in 1947 before *My Brother Jonathan*. What do you remember about working with Leslie Arliss in the first of these — *A Man About the House*?

He was under-estimated, I think, because he did *The Man in Grey* and that was his style, and he was being rubbished by critics all the time. He helped very much indeed on the characterisations. He was shrewd, very kind and absolutely on one's side, and he had a very firm, clear vision of Maggie [Johnston] and me.

It is my great regret that that film wasn't in colour, it was so beautifully photographed. It was all shot on location in Amalfi and Positano. It was decided to hold the opening at Eastbourne, I think, and there was a huge motorcade with a star in every limousine. The film was an absolute flop and Leslie saw at once why it had failed with the audience. He decided which scenes were failing and he was absolutely right; he cut those scenes and the film was then a great success.

It was also Dame Lillian Braithwaite's last film, wasn't it?

Yes. She was doing *Arsenic and Old Lace* at the time, with Mary Jerrold at the 'Duchess', and she came down to do a few days with Felix Aylmer. I was deeply shocked because she was an old woman and a great star, yet they didn't have a chair for her. I tried to arrange one for her; they said they hadn't got any more, so I said she must have mine. After the film was over I received the most enormous basket of flowers, with a note saying, 'I noticed, dear. From an autumn actress to a spring one, with love'. I realise now that this is part of the difficulty of growing old: that the parts are fewer and you are very lucky to be able to keep going at all.

Did you see the second of those starring films, *Mine Own Executioner*, as a serious film about psychiatry or as a romantic thriller?

I didn't really see it as either. I played an awful lot of put-upon wives in those days! I really don't see things from the outside when I get a part; my main concern is to try and be that woman. I found her rather upsetting to play; she needn't have been so awfully inadequate. She was so in awe of her husband that I had to invent a background for her to be able to play her. Why does she put up with his having all these affairs? I think she knew she was inadequate but it wasn't ever explained,

because he was rather cruel to her even though he was going through trouble himself. In that film poor Kieron [Moore] was totally miscast. He was a splendid actor in *Man About the House*.

How did you feel about having an American star such as Burgess Meredith, because there was no special reason for his character to be American?

The special reason was that Paulette [Goddard] had come across to do *An Ideal Husband*! That's why he came over; their marriage was on the rocks and finished immediately afterwards. I don't think British actors resented him doing that major part, though. Korda had a very special standing with us all; he was the greatest entrepreneur of that time, so in our eyes he could do no wrong.

I liked Anthony Kimmins as a director; he was a very positive man. He loved the script and seemed to like us, too. I was lucky in that I got on very well with all my directors. It's easier that way! I knew I wasn't Arthur Crabtree's type, but then I knew I was a misfit in Gainsborough.

People such as Kieron Moore, Margaret Johnston, Christine Norden, Barbara White looked as if they were being groomed for big things, but never really reached the top of British screen stardom — why do you think that was?

Kieron was miscast twice in *Mine Own Executioner* and as Vronsky opposite Vivien [Leigh] in *Anna Karenina*, and that killed him. He could have done splendidly had he been cast right; he was a complicated man. Margaret? I think I will pass. Barbara? Wildly pretty, very clever and rather self-effacing. Perhaps she just retired into marriage with Kieron. I can't understand why she wasn't promoted. I don't know how good Christine was, how much range she had; I didn't get to know her well, simply because they were either using her or me and we hardly ever met.

Did you simply find fewer congenial opportunities in films by the mid-50s?

Oh, the British film industry more or less packed up. I think the heart went out of British pictures, and it wasn't a dream factory any more. I am immensely grateful for the opportunities I had and I enjoyed myself very much indeed.

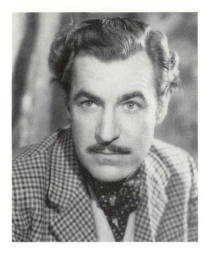

Return of a Stranger, Head Over Heels, Silver Top (1937), *Sexton Blake and the Hooded Terror, A Royal Divorce* (1938), *Danny Boy, Penn of Pennsylvania, Sheepdog of the Hills* (1941), *Suspected Person, Went the Day Well?* (1942), *The Dark Tower, The Night Invader, They Met in the Dark, Headline, The Hundred Pound Window* (1943), *For Those in Peril, Meet Sexton Blake* (1944), *The World Owes Me a Living, The Echo Murders* (1945), *The Trojan Brothers, Lisbon Story* (1946), *Black Narcissus, Frieda* (1947), *The Small Back Room, Mr Perrin and Mr Traill* (1948), *Diamond City* (1949), *Gone to Earth, Cage of Gold* (1950), *The Late Edwina Black, Night Without Stars, The Golden Horde* (1951), *Duel in the Jungle, Lilacs in the Spring, The Black Shield of Falworth* (1954), *The Sea Chase, Pearl of the South Pacific, Escape to Burma* (1955), *Lost* (1956), *Woman and the Hunter* (1957), *I Accuse!, Son of Robin Hood* (1958), *John Paul Jones, Watusi, Solomon and Sheba* (1959), *Middle of Nowhere, Beat Girl, The Webster Boy, The 300 Spartans* (1960).

Like Kathleen Byron with whom he twice – memorably – co-starred, David Farrar's finest hours in British cinema were in the films he made for Michael Powell, and *Black Narcissus* provided him with a major turning point in his career. As the caustic, insolent Mr Dean, the British agent deputed to keep an eye on the Himalayan convent, his scenes with Byron and Deborah Kerr carried a sensual charge rare in British cinema at the time. This was followed by two further striking roles for Powell: as the lame bomb-disposal expert in *The Small Back Room*, and as the swaggering squire in *Gone to Earth*. These opportunities came after a decade of – mostly – second features, in which

he established himself as a strongly masculine presence of a kind British cinema needed. The vein of sensitivity that was sometimes allowed to surface in these films worked well with the easy strength that was his hallmark, and resulted in fine performances in Basil Dearden's *Frieda* and Lawrence Huntington's gripping version of *Mr Perrin and Mr Traill*, as well as in the Powell films. It was a pity he elected to retire in 1960, when he might so well have found a niche in the new social realist films of the early 60s.

Interview date: December 1990.

Were you already established on the stage before you entered films?

I don't know about 'established', but my wife and I did a repertoire of mainly costume plays, with some success, before films tempted me somewhere about the middle 1930s. A chap called Victor Hanbury, then head of RKO Radio Pictures in Britain, came to my dressing-room and offered me a small part in a film they were making at Shepperton Studios. Then followed a long apprenticeship of small parts in big films and big parts in small films until the outbreak of war put a stop to all this.

When I saw myself on the screen for the first time, I realised I had no idea at all of film-acting technique, which really wants naturalness or 'underplaying'. And, of course, on the screen, they can shoot a scene a dozen times and it is a miracle if your best performance coincides with everything else being right – camera,

lighting, sound and so on.

What sort of film roles were you offered at this time, when war broke out?

There were some I prefer to forget, but I was certainly pleased when I got an offer to play the lead in *Sheepdog of the Hills*, even if my co-star *was* a sheepdog and he had the title role. It was a lovely acting part with everything in it – lots of pathetic blind stuff (I played a vicar who'd lost his sight) and noble self-sacrifice at the end. I also enjoyed the two months' location in Devonshire. Then, in 1942, I got my army call-up papers and was about to be sent to a camp in Paignton, when Warner's were just starting a film called *Night Invader* in which I'd already been signed to play the lead. Perhaps it was felt I was more useful providing entertainment than in soldiering, because the producers got the War Office to request me to return my call-up papers.

Went the Day Well? still seems a very interesting film. What do you remember about it and the director Cavalcanti?

I thought it was a bad title because I doubted if many people knew where the quotation came from. But it was a good film and Cavalcanti was a charming person who spoke English with a strong Brazilian accent. It was an Ealing film, with a lot of location work, including some at Henley where we worked with a regular army company. I played a Nazi posing as a British officer. My fan-mail suggested that, although they were impressed with what they described as a fine 'acting' performance, they disliked my playing a brutalised part.

After several films for Warner's, you were back at Ealing for *Headline*.

I enjoyed that. It was a thriller with a good script and was set in the newspaper world I knew from my own days in journalism. Before *Headline* was finished I was already contracted to make *For Those in Peril* for Ealing. Ealing had distributed *Headline*, but the film was made at Hammersmith Studios. *For Those in Peril* was an Ealing production, and it turned out to be a great film which got marvellous notices from all the critics. It was about the Air Sea Rescue service which did wonderful work during the war. I had a fine part as the tough skipper of the launch and we shot it in the Channel under actual combat conditions. Charlie Crichton, who directed the film, and who was something of a sailor, used to like watching us turn green in a rough sea.

Unhappily, the film was not booked to go into any West End cinema. Perhaps it was because of its awkward length (it was only sixty-seven minutes long), too short for a West End first feature, though it was booked throughout the provinces. I felt I'd given my best film performance to date, but there were no cables from Hollywood! Perhaps if it had been padded by a further thirty minutes and if we had introduced a feminine interest, it might have been a success at the box office as well as with the critics.

What do you recall of the three films you made for British National at this time — *The World Owes Me a Living*, *The Trojan Brothers*, **and** *The Lisbon Story*?

I made *The World Owes Me a Living* at Elstree where I was very happy working. It was from a novel by John Llewellyn Rhys, a young author who was killed during the war, and it was about the growth of aviation between the two world wars. We spent weeks on location doing the flying sequences and I very much liked playing opposite Judy Campbell who was a grand actress and a lovable person. The director was an unusually inventive man, Vernon Sewell, the first that I had known to lay tracks for continual shooting of up to several minutes.

The other two films you mentioned had to wait till I got back to London after a tour with ENSA of camps and gun-sites in a play called *Jeannie*.

The Trojan Brothers was taken from a novel by Pamela Hansford Johnson. It had a powerful subject – the fatal attraction of a Cockney called Sid for a worthless woman. In the end he's driven mad by her heartlessness and finally strangles her. I was all for playing the film 'as per book' but the producers wouldn't let me strangle my leading lady and, despite my protests, changed it to a happy ending. However, I treasure a letter from Miss Johnson which finished by saying, 'I liked your Sid better than mine'.

The ABC circuit snapped it up and the film was very popular and financially successful. But, as it didn't get a West End showing, it didn't add an inch to my stature. However, I had the great pleasure of working with Bobby Howes in it: we played a horse act, with me as the fore-legs and Bobby as the hind-legs, which led him to say, 'I feel such an arse!'

Patricia Burke was my leading lady in both *The Trojan Brothers* and *The Lisbon Story*. It took hours to get her hairdo right, leading to jokes about Burke and Hare. *The Lisbon Story* had a long run on the London stage, but the actual film had a new story about my escapades as an intelligence officer. Pat and Richard Tauber and others added some charming and attractive songs and the film filled two West End cinemas.

Would you agree that your career entered a new phase with *Black Narcissus*?

Yes. The producer and director was, of course, Michael Powell. I was about to sign a Hollywood contract, with Universal-International to play Grieg in *The Song of Norway*, when the phone rang and I was asked if I would like to read the script of Mr Powell's next picture. It was *Black Narcissus*, and, when I read it, it seemed too good an opportunity to be true. I had a meeting with Powell and Emeric Pressburger, his scripting partner; there was a period of anxious waiting, then I was asked if I would test for the part of Mr Dean. It seemed a long time before Micky told me, 'The part is yours', and I never even signed a contract till long after the film was finished.

I can honestly say that every day of shooting that film was an exciting adventure, mainly due to Micky's creative ideas. It was an outstanding, fully satisfying artistic creation. People could scarcely believe that the whole film was shot in the studio, with profiles and smoke-screens against the skyline to give the effect of the dizzy height of the Himalayas. In some of the 'snow scenes', Sabu and I were wearing bear-skin coats in the middle of a heat wave!

You made two further films for Powell and Pressburger — *The Small Back Room* (1948) and *Gone to Earth* (1950). Do you regard these three films as the highlight of your career?
Artistically yes, though I would also include my Ealing films, *Frieda*, with Mai Zetterling and *Cage of Gold* with Jean Simmons. My journeys to Hollywood also constituted another sort of highlight — money and glamour, and the star treatment as only Hollywood can do it.

I was still working on *Mr Perrin and Mr Traill* when Micky was ready to start *The Small Back Room* early in 1948. We shot the location scenes first in Dorset. We did the bomb-defusing sequence there which many critics thought one of the most thrilling things ever seen on the screen. It was a long and difficult sequence, most of it shot at about 5 a.m., in early March, as I remember, with a biting east wind coming in off the sea. And the artificial foot I wore to play the part of Sammy Rice was so uncomfortable that I couldn't help limping anyway. But it was a great part and worth all the discomfort in the end. Once again, we had excellent notices.

What about the two films you finished before *The Small Back Room* — *Frieda* and *Mr Perrin and Mr Traill*?
Frieda was made for Ealing studios, with some location work in Oxford. It actually opened to great success in New York when I was there to publicise *Black Narcissus* for the Rank Organisation. The premières of the two films were on two consecutive nights. *Frieda* was a good film that had wonderful notices in both Britain and the States. I attended its premières in London, New York and Stockholm.

Before I did *Mr Perrin and Mr Traill*, I was unemployed for eight months. This was because one deal for me to star in a film version of *Precious Bane* fell through and also because the Archers and I did not see eye to eye about the character they wanted me to play in *The Red Shoes*. Because, under my contract, I had to be paid for a film anyway, I agreed to do *Mr Perrin and Mr Traill*. This didn't turn out too badly, and was very popular, but I was never mad about it.

Did you like playing the raffish, 'glamorous' cad as opposed to James Donald's sterling 'Ealing' virtues in *Cage of Gold*?
Funny you should ask that. Michael Balcon wanted me to play the 'good guy' but it stood out a mile that the 'baddie' was much more exciting, and I had quite a job to talk him into it.

After a busy time in Hollywood and several more British films in the 50s, you had three films released in 1960 — *Beat Girl*, *The Webster Boy* and *The 300 Spartans* — and then retired. Why did you stop when you were just over fifty years old?
People find that a mystery. But I'd played leading roles in about fifty films and might have been getting a bit blasé with all the artificiality — I'd just finished a flamboyant role as Xerxes for 20th Century-Fox in *300 Spartans*, which played for seven months in London's West End. I always felt the ideal was to get to the top, stay at the top, and get out at the top. This time also coincided with some problems, not least the death of my agent, Haddon Mason of Filmrights, who had been my manager for twenty-five years. This left me feeling a bit lost. I was tired of the hassles and battles, and conceit might have come into it, too — I'd always been the upstanding young leading man and I was afraid of the parts that were being hinted at for uncles, or for the girl's father instead of the lover! I just felt, 'the Hell with it all', and walked out into the sunset.

Ralph Michael and David Farrar in Charles Crichton's *For Those in Peril*, 1944

As actor:

The Tired Men (1943)*, *The Small Back Room, All Over the Town, Dear Mr Prohack* (1949), *The Wooden Horse* (1950), *Green Grow the Rushes* (1951), *The World in His Arms* (1952), *Appointment in London, Sea Devils, Wheel of Fate* (1953), *The Million Pound Note, An Inspector Calls, Up to His Neck* (1954), *The Colditz Story, Passage Home* (1955), *The Last Man to Hang* (1955), *Quatermass Experiment* (1955), *Now and Forever, The Extra Day, It's Great to be Young, The Baby and the Battleship, Satellite in the Sky* (1956), *Quatermass II* (1957), *The Key, I Was Monty's Double* (1958), *Yesterday's Enemy* (1959), *The League of Gentlemen* (1960), *The Guns of Navarone* (1961), *A Shot in the Dark* (1964).
* Documentary

As writer/producer/director:

The Black Knight (co-w), *Cockleshell Heroes* (co-w) (1955), *The Baby and the Battleship* (co-w), *The Black Tent* (co-w), *House of Secrets* (co-w) (1956), *I Was Monty's Double* (w) (1958), *The Captain's Table* (1959), *Man in the Moon* (w), *The Angry Silence* (w), *The League of Gentlemen* (w) (1960), *Whistle Down the Wind* (d) (1961), *Only Two Can Play* (w), *Station Six Sahara* (w), *The L-Shaped Room* (d, w) (1962), *Of Human Bondage* (w), *The High Bright Sun* (w), *Seance on a Wet Afternoon* (d, w, co-p) (1964), *King Rat* (d, w) (1965), *The Wrong Box* (d, p), *The Whisperers* (d, w) (1966), *Deadfall* (d, w) (1967), *The Madwoman of Chaillot* (d) (1974), *The Slipper and the Rose* (d, w) (1976), *International Velvet* (d, p, w), *Sunday Lovers* (d) (1980), *Better Late than Never* (d) (1982), *The Naked Face* (d, w) (1984), *The Endless Game* (d, w) (1988).

Bryan Forbes, as actor, director, producer and screenwriter, has maintained one of the busiest careers in the British film industry, and in the last two decades he has emerged as an author of distinction. He began in the late 1940s when there was plenty of work for a versatile character actor, taking whatever was offered and giving individuality to roles large and small. He was especially memorable as the unhappy girl's seducer in *An Inspector Calls*, and he worked with some of the most prolific directors of the period, from Michael Powell in 1949 (*The Small Back Room*) to Basil Dearden in 1960 (*The League of Gentlemen*, for which he also wrote the sharply ironic screenplay). Since 1960, he has been influentially involved as director of a number of distinctive realist films (for example, *Whistle Down the Wind* and *The Whisperers*) and, with Richard Attenborough, as co-founder of Beaver Films, initially set up to produce *The Angry Silence*. From 1969, he spent three frustrating years as Head of Production and Managing Director of Elstree Studios for EMI. He has shown himself persistently willing to try his arm in demanding ventures.

Interview date: October 1989.

Were the late 40s and 50s a good time to get an acting career going in British cinema?

Yes, it was very easy really. I literally went from film to film, because the film industry was booming. The Rank Organisation particularly had made a concerted effort. Old Lord Rank, who was much abused, I think wrongly, poured millions in to try to make a British film industry and to break into the American market. Rank and ABPC, to a lesser extent, and other periphery studios, were pouring films out. There must have been well over a hundred films a year made, because we still had 'B' films, of which I made some.

Rank had a lot of people under contract, myself included. The first big role I ever had was in *All Over the Town*, which was made for Wessex Films, an off-shoot of Rank under Ian Dalrymple, who was a very gentle man, probably to his own disadvantage.

I was never a star, I was a feature player. I got work through being *in* work, because I was also working in the theatre at the same time. They had to shoot around me on matinée days. If they were on location, of course, and the film was being shot down at Lyme Regis, like *All Over the Town*, obviously I wouldn't have got the job if I'd have been in a play. But if I was in a play and they were filming at Pinewood or Elstree they would let me off in time to get back to the theatre. This kind of arrangement provided the British film industry with an enormous reservoir of talent which they could tap. People, especially Americans, often asked, 'How did you manage to get Ralph Richardson to play such a small role?' But British actors tend, even enormously exalted actors, if they aren't doing anything else and they like the part, not to count the words, whereas American stars tend to feel a bit too proud to accept anything other than a major role.

Did any of your early films give you special satisfaction?

I suppose my best role was in Guy Hamilton's film of the Priestley play, *An Inspector Calls*. Though I was never a star, I had some interesting roles, in *The Wooden Horse* for instance. For this film, I originally had an eight-week contract and we arrived out in Luneberg Heath, shortly after the war. It was 1948. Although there must have been five-hundred disused prisoner-of-war camps of one description or another, this being the film industry, they decided to clear fifty acres of Luneberg Heath and build a totally new one! So, we hung about for six weeks with nothing happening and the script being re-written, then we shot for about two weeks.

Because the negative came back to England to be developed, we didn't see the rushes very early. When we did see them, there were all these shots of Leo Genn, David Tomlinson, Tony Steel and me, but the rest of the high-ranking RAF officers were cast with displaced persons. So you panned past Leo Genn and me, for example, and suddenly there were Mongolian Wing Commanders with flat noses and fake moustaches, which looked totally ludicrous. The producers saw this, junked the whole lot, and ordered a re-shoot. So, if you can believe it, my eight-week contract became fourteen months.

What are your recollections of working with directors such as Philip Leacock, Guy Hamilton, Ronald Neame, Roy Baker, Carol Reed?

Carol is the one who stands out for me. I liked the others and got on with them all, but I can't remember getting a lot of direction. When they cast you, they assumed that you knew your job. They certainly knew theirs; they were all marvellous technicians. But Carol, for whom I did *The Key*, was my mentor, somebody I admired extravagantly and I'm sure he influenced my own work when I became a director.

Once an actor himself, Carol understood actors very well. He wasn't a showy director. When I got the chance to direct I went to him and said, 'Is there a secret? Can you give my any tips?' He said, 'Yes, never humiliate an actor and never cut until he's exited frame'.

Those are two very good rules. Film isn't a theatrical medium. I think what you need is a visual eye and a great deal of sympathy with actors. It's very lonely for actors out there in front of the camera; the actor has nobody he can feel any response from except the director. Really, I think the director has to have the feeling, the *taste*, and set the style of the movie.

How did you find the American stars who were always being brought over to Britian in the 50s?

I suppose the one I worked with most was Alan Ladd, a monosyllabic and very withdrawn character. He wasn't rude, just very withdrawn and, I think, very unhappy. I worked on three of his films: *The Black Knight*, *The Red Beret*, *Hell Below Zero*. That's how my screenwriting career started, with Irving Allen and Cubby Broccoli. The first credit of any note I had was *Cockleshell Heroes*, for [Jose] Ferrer, whom I didn't get on with terribly well.

What did you feel about the preponderance of war films still being made throughout the 50s?

I think it was inevitable. The war was so long and so hard — we suffered four years of nothing but reverses — that I think it was only natural afterwards to use that material to say, as it were, 'Listen we've won, you know'. And a lot of the prison-of-war stories were quite extraordinary – *Colditz*, and *The Captive Heart*, and the conception of *The Wooden Horse* and the way they executed it, were good stories in anybody's book. It's not unnatural for people to want to pat themselves on the back when they've come through a long war which, in this country, don't forget, involved all the civilians. People just wanted to say, 'Jesus, we came through it'.

What did you think of the 'new wave' of British cinema in the late 50s?

The revolution started with John Osborne. I think I was never a star because I was born in to the wrong class, as it were, and, in my day, people like Tom Courtenay wouldn't have carried a spear, because you had to have a rather plummy accent. I was once turned down for a part in *The Cruel Sea* – nice letter saying 'Can't cast you because we've decided you're not officer material'! Then, suddenly, after Osborne had written *Look Back in Anger*, a few others were writing not for the old-school-

Bryan Forbes in Guy Hamilton's *An Inspector Calls*, 1954

ties sort of accent, but for the provincial accents, for Albert Finney in *Saturday Night and Sunday Morning*, and Rachel Roberts. Suddenly you didn't have to have a BBC announcer's voice; and you could write about a hero who wasn't six-feet tall, and get him cast. You could do films which showed a much more realistic picture. I think it came out of a 'new wave' of younger directors, younger writers.

I turned the class thing around in *The League of Gentlemen*. I took the epitome of British stiff-upper-lip acting, and I do not mean this in a derogatory sense because I think Jack Hawkins was a considerable actor, and turned it on its head. I made Jack a cashiered officer who was a crook, and every word he spoke in my screen-play was the reverse of what you'd expect him to say. I'll give you an example. There was a scene between him and 'Paddy' [Nigel] Patrick when Paddy asks, 'Is that your wife?' Jack says, 'Yes', and Patrick, because Jack appears to be living alone, asks, 'Is she dead?' 'No,' Jack replies. 'I'm sorry to say the bitch is still going strong'!

Do you think the middle-classness of 40s and 50s British cinema helps to account for its not acquiring the mass audience of the average American film?

Yes, but in addition to that we didn't really make use of the country. I mean we still built Bond Street on Stage 4. It wasn't until about the time of *The Angry Silence* that, instead of building a bit of a factory at Pinewood, we went to Ipswich and went into a factory. We shot actual sound. When I made *Whistle Down the Wind*, we went up to Manchester and shot in a real farm in a real barn. That was my first film as a director. Having said that, I think there are some films which *have* to be made in studios and it's a great shame that studios are closing because we'll always need them.

What is your attitude to the ways in which the Government or its instruments have intervened in British cinema?

Well, I think in direct ways they could help us but don't. You get very little co-operation when shooting in London, for example; in fact, you're actively discouraged. When I was shooting *Seance on a Wet Afternoon* I was arrested. Some ridiculous by-law says you can't put a tripod on a pavement. However, the Eady Plan undoubtedly helped us and I was sorry to see that go.

The Americans helped to wreck the Eady Plan. What happened was, the moment the Eady Plan was introduced, there were back-door routes through which Americans could come here and finance films through

British companies, because they weren't allowed by law to be American companies. These companies would then get Eady money which would then go back to the American financiers, instead of flowing back into the industry. Most people took the Eady money and ran, but Allied Film Makers and Beaver Films used the money to go back into business.

Nowadays, to make a British film industry you want a minimum of £100m injected into it. No Governments are really interested in cinema. Wilson pretended to be, and took credit for it when he was Minister of Trade, but I think it was a political gesture rather than a gesture in favour of the British film industry. Nobody since has been interested at all.

The Angry Silence still seems to me to be a very important British film. What attracted you to it and what was the nature of your involvement?
Well, Dickie Attenborough, Pier Angeli and Guy Green had come together on another film and, while they were out in the desert somewhere, they were all fairly fed up with the way their careers were going, saying 'We're going down a cul-de-sac. OK we're getting work but where's it going?' Just at that time my wife Nanette [Newman] said to me, 'Look, there's a marvellous story here that you should write about a railwayman who'd been sent to Coventry, and eventually, after three years of nobody talking to him, he committed suicide'. I was dickering with that idea when they all returned from location, and Michael Craig and Richard Gregson had come up with a famous story of a man who was sent to Coventry, a different story from mine. So we said, 'Let's not fight. Let's not make two films. Let's join forces'.

I was attracted to the story and wanted to make it very tough – not the usual thing of treating the British workman as if he were the salt of the earth. I felt there were two sides to the thing. Afterwards, Dickie and I were much attacked by the unions. The film was black-listed by the miners' union, and we had threatening letters sent to us. To this day, some people have never forgiven us, but I felt the film was just as hard on management as unions. I made management seem absolutely crass, because it didn't see what was coming. The whole philosophy of the film is that if you can't be different, you are nothing. It's a plea for the individual. The character supports the strike in the first instance, then thinks it's gone stupid, which so many of the strikes in those days did. I mean, the film industry was in anarchy as a result. The Angry Silence was the beginning of a partnership between Dickie and myself, which resulted ultimately in Allied Film Makers.

That was a second company you formed?
Yes. I thought that was a very innovative idea which came with the blessing of John Davis. We went to him and said, 'Listen, we're not really getting a fair share because the distributor takes the cream. We'll make films and we want to form a distribution company as well. We're the people who supply the product, it's wrong to be excluded'. And he said, 'Well put your money where your mouth is, and whatever you can raise I'll multiply it by five and we'll give you a differential on the distribution of 2 per cent off the top, which is the important piece of money. And so we all put in £20,000 each, I think, and raised £100,000 and he made it up to £500,000. We made *The League of Gentleman* and *Whistle Down the Wind*, both of which were enormously successful in their own time.

Did The Angry Silence actually make any money?
It still makes money. It cost £98,000 and, I think, to the last accounting period, it had made about £200,000 profit. Now that's not a vast profit, it's not Indiana Jones! *The League of Gentlemen* cost about £172,000 and made probably £300,000 to £400,000 profit. However, if you more than double your initial cost, it's not bad in business terms.

The idea of having Pier Angeli as Tony's Italian wife is interesting in that working-class setting.
Again this was a move away from having some little mousy English housewife which would have been the norm. I think it was the first time that working-class dialogue was actually colloquial as opposed to a sort of pastiche written by somebody who wasn't, like me, working-class, but was trying to emulate working-class dialogue.

Do you think the 40s and 50s constitute a sort of boom in the British film industry?
Yes, I mean cinema-going was a habit, and the habit grew substantially during the war when it was basically the only form of entertainment. Also, in those days, a British film could get its money back within this country, and that's another reason why the British film industry boomed. Today, if you don't make it in America, you can never, in most cases, hope to get your money back.

Harry Fowler

Those Kids from Town, Salute John Citizen, Went the Day Well? (1942), *Get Cracking, The Demi-Paradise* (1943), *Give Us the Moon, Don't Take It to Heart, Champagne Charlie* (1944), *Painted Boats* (1945), *Hue and Cry* (1947), *Trouble in the Air, A Piece of Cake* (1948), *For Them That Trespass, Now Barabbas Was a Robber . . .* (1949), *Once a Sinner, She Shall Have Murder, Trio, Dance Hall* (1950), *Scarlet Thread, There is Another Sun, The Dark Man, Madame Louise, Introducing the New Worker*, High Treason* (1951), *Angels One Five, At Home with the Hardwickes* (Six short films in the British Movietone News Series), *I Believe in You, The Pickwick Papers, The Last Page* (1952), *Top of the Form, A Day to Remember* (1953), *Don't Blame the Stork!, Conflict of Wings, Up to His Neck* (1954), *Stock Car, The Blue Peter* (1955), *Fire Maidens from Outer Space, Behind the Headlines, Home and Away* (1956), *Town on Trial, Lucky Jim, Booby Trap, The Birthday Present, West of Suez* (1957), *Soapbox Derby, The Supreme Secret, I Was Monty's Double, The Diplomatic Corpse* (1958), *Idol on Parade, The Heart of a Man, The Dawn Killer, Don't Panic Chaps!* (1959), *Tomorrow at Ten, The Golliwog, The Longest Day, Lawrence of Arabia, Flight from Singapore, Crooks Anonymous* (1962), *Clash by Night, Just for Fun, Ladies Who Do* (1963), *70 Deadly Pills* (1964), *Life at the Top, Joey Boy, The Nanny, Doctor in Clover* (1965), *Secrets of a Windmill Girl* (1966), *Two by Two* (1968), *Start the Revolution Without Me* (1970), *The Prince and the Pauper* (1977), *High Rise Donkey* (1979), *Sir Henry at Rawlinson End* (1980), *The Little World of Don Camillo* (1981), *Fanny Hill* (1983), *Big Deal* (1986), *Chicago Joe* (1990).
* Documentary.

Harry Fowler's extraordinarily prolific career is a testimony to one who believed in taking every opportunity that was offered, even though he was aware of the limitations imposed on a Cockney actor in British cinema. Since most British films, certainly in the 40s and 50s, were largely middle-class affairs, he often found himself relegated to stereotyped cameo roles. However, he always managed to imbue these with a lively individuality and, when given the chance of something more substantial, he showed himself more than equal to the occasion. Ealing gave him his best roles in films such as *Champagne Charlie, I Believe in You*, and, above all, as the leader of a bunch of Cockney schoolboys which routs a gang of crooks in *Hue and Cry*. He was also a notable Sam Weller in *The Pickwick Papers*. In addition to the the many supporting films he made was a steady trickle of 'A' films such as *High Treason, Lucky Jim*, and *Lawrence of Arabia*.

Interview date: June 1991.

You are described as having been a newsboy and as having worked in radio before coming into films . . .

Yes, I began my working life in 1941 selling newspapers in London's West End and I used to sell them in clubs which were frequented by actors and BBC producers. One of these was the producer of 'In Town Tonight', a very popular interview programme. He asked me if I'd be prepared to relate my vicissitudes (his exact words to a near-illiterate newspaper boy!). So I asked how much I'd get for it and he said two guineas. Considering I was earning eight shillings a week, I agreed!

I was interviewed on a Saturday night by a man called Roy Rich, and, at that time, somebody was casting a picture about British evacuees. They had already cast a boy called George Cole and were looking for another one. They heard this broadcast, contacted the BBC immediately, and within two days I was doing a film test on the set at Elstree. Again, my first question was 'How much do you get for this?' and they said '£5 a day'. There was no way I was going to fail that film test and that's how it all began. The film was *Those Kids from Town*, starring Jeanne de Cassalis, who was very helpful to me. Bernard Miles' wife, Josephine Wilson, played the kind lady who took in the evacuees.

Do you recall anything of the director, Lance Comfort?

Yes, Lance was the epitome of what I, as a thirteen-year-old Cockney, saw as 'a posh gent'. A nice man, but my memories of him aren't all that bright, since I knew nothing about film directing then. Years later, at the end of his career, I made *Tomorrow at Ten* for him, with John Gregson and Robert Shaw – a cops-and-robbers thing.

You played twice with George Cole. What do you recall of working with him?

George had a professional approach to acting, whereas I was as raw as could be. I didn't meet him on *The Demi-Paradise*, which had Laurence Olivier playing a Russian. His leading lady was Penelope Dudley Ward, a lovely woman, and, again, everyone struck me as being very 'posh'. I was told I should take elocution lessons but that would have defeated the purpose – I was cast by these men because they heard a genuine Cockney voice.

Certain directors would say to me, 'Don't pronounce it like that – say "aren't", not "ain't"'. Otherwise, they said, they wouldn't get the American market because Americans wouldn't understand broad Cockney. Firstly, they weren't getting the American market anyway, and, secondly, I was brought up on a series of films about the East Side kids where I couldn't understand a word they said. That didn't stop me going to see the films though!

I think it was a legacy of the theatre; it was undoubtedly middle-class and most of my roles throughout my working life, certainly up until the 60s, had me as the obligatory Cockney, just as you had the obligatory negro in American films. Cockneys and working-class characters were never allowed any intellectual horizons, whereas America and France were making pictures with working-class people as heroes. My idol was Jimmy Cagney, but there were no Jimmy Cagney pictures made here, so I had no aspirations regarding roles.

As soon as I finished my ten days on the first film I went straight into another picture called *Salute John Citizen* for Maurice Elvey, simply because I happened to be on the next set at British National studios. The more I appeared, the more obvious it was that I was the 'real McCoy', and there were enough people about who wanted the genuine article to keep me busy. I had an agent, but I don't think he had to *look* for parts. Sometimes I might only have a few lines but, once you build up a good track record, that's the way it is.

How did you find working for Ealing, starting with Cavalcanti's *Went the Day Well?*

Ealing was like a university for me. Cavalcanti was an enigma: as a South American he could not have been expected to have a great knowledge of English life, yet he was chosen to direct *Went the Day Well?*. But they couldn't have chosen anybody better, because often outsiders will see more, because they are inquisitive. *Champagne Charlie* was a perfect example of what I mean: it was about British music halls in the last century, strictly an English subject, but I don't think anybody could have made it as well as Cavalcanti. Tommy Trinder was one of the stars (Stanley Holloway was the other) and he was a very down-to-earth Cockney from the music halls. Betty Warren was in it too, a lovely lady and very helpful to me.

You are well remembered for Charles Crichton's *Hue And Cry*. How did you come to do this?

By the end of 1944 I was nearly eighteen and, the war still being on, I was called up. I went into the Air Force and, at that time, Tibby Clarke was writing a script about a gang of kids with me in mind. The film industry had a very good liaison with the Board of Trade, so I was temporarily released from the Air Force to make *Hue And Cry*. Part of its classic status is that it has actual film of London as it was in the immediate post-war years, when the bomb sites were still evident. The climax takes place on a bomb site adjacent to Cannon Street Station, which today is a massive skyscraper. Charles Crichton was a great technician as far as film directing was concerned but, equally important, was the producer Henry Cornelius, who was outstanding with the kids, taking their inhibitions out of them so that they gave great performances. And Alastair Sim must be one of the great film actors of all time. He had that underlying sinister quality, but, at the same time, he was a kind, lovely man. I think that was the first time Jack Warner played the villain and he loved it. I remember Jack telling me: 'Never turn down anything, because every time you appear on that screen it's an advert; to be a character actor at eighteen is worth being; stars come and go, but as a character actor you'll work until you're ninety'.

What do you recall about Crichton's semi-documentary *Painted Boats*?

We made it in a very picturesque part of Northamptonshire, a place called Stoke Bruerne, a major junction on the Grand Union Canal. I think the Board of Trade wanted to show the kind of work the canal boats were doing, lugging steel, coal and wood up and down the canals as part of the war effort. It's worth seeing again now because, outside of myself and an actor called Bill Blewitt (who, in fact, wasn't an actor but a Cornish postmaster) the rest of the cast were talking in plum in-the-mouth English, which doesn't really fit for a bargee.

You were back at Ealing in 1952 for *I Believe in You*, Basil Dearden's film about probation officers. What did you feel about the film's approach to its subject?
Sewell Stokes wrote the book and I met him. As part of preparing for the role I actually stayed in a Borstal at Rochester for two nights; that was an experience to say the least – people were in there for all kinds of things, including capital crimes. It would have been a very dour sort of film but for Cecil Parker, who was a marvellous man. It was all shot on bomb sites, rain-laden cobble-stone streets at night and in the depressing atmosphere of the court.

Ursula Howells gave a great performance as the inebriate society girl, and I think it was good to put that into the film. It showed that probation officers did not only deal with lower-class delinquents. As for Celia Johnson, a marvellous lady! If you met her in a super-market, you'd think 'She's probably a vicar's wife'. It was great to watch her working, to see the transition from this ordinary lady to this great actress. She had a wonderful face and eyes yet she used them modestly, you never saw her over-act. She was a theatre actress who took the screen by the horns.

Throughout the 50s you did a mixture of 'A' films and supporting films; what were some of the obvious differences between the two?
There was much more time taken over an 'A' film. To light a shot for an 'A' film could take two hours, whereas to light a 'B' film they'd give you the script and a candle!

Jack Lambert, Harry Fowler and Jack Warner in Charles Crichton's *Hue and Cry*, 1946

I know I sometimes gave better performances in 'B' pictures, often because the parts were bigger and meatier, but the pay was 50 per cent less than for a smaller part in an 'A' picture. You were pampered on 'A' pictures; sometimes you even got a canvas chair with your name on it! The 'B' picture lark was a marvellous game; the sheer speed of making them before the money ran out in some cases made for very good work.

You made three 'B' films for Lewis Gilbert, *Once a Sinner*, *Scarlet Thread* and *There Is Another Sun*.
Yes, Lewis undoubtedly learned his trade on those, all three of them are good films. He was a working-class boy himself, and another of those gentle, kindly directors. *Scarlet Thread* was a good film and Kathleen Byron was marvellous in it; Lewis adored her and he was right to, she was a wonderful actress whose potential was never fully realised. Lewis could see it, but he didn't have the power then that he achieved later.

What recollections have you of several directors who are not much heard of today — John Paddy Carstairs, Wolf Rilla, and Vernon Sewell.
Paddy Carstairs was a frustrated actor if ever I saw one. The one thing you never did when you were working for him was look at him, because he was doing your role behind the camera – very disconcerting! If you were to draw a caricature of the 'film director' for *Punch*, it would be him. He was the right man for the job, doing those cheerful comedies.

I always thought Wolf Rilla was kidding! He was always very self-conscious in the part. *Stock Car* didn't need directing, it was more a montage of library footage about these battered old cars smashing into each other. Wolf interspersed it with shots of unrecognisable actors in goggles and helmets, sitting in the cabins of these cars and saying trite dialogue.

I did *Home and Away*, with Jack Warner and Kathleen Harrison for Vernon who went from film to film but didn't make a great impact on the industry.

Montgomery Tully was another director, but he was getting on and in failing health by the time I worked for him in *Clash by Night*. I spent the first two weeks of that picture handcuffed to Terry Longden, which was agonizing for both of us. It wasn't a bad little picture at all; Tully did a good job on it.

To return to 'A' territory, you played Sam Weller in Noel Langley's *Pickwick Papers*. Was this a role you really enjoyed?
Yes, very much. I'd like to do it again because I think I could give a better performance than that. However, it was a great prestige picture which got a Golden Bear Award in Moscow. The part of Sam Weller, like the gravedigger in *Hamlet*, is one of those great philosophical comedy roles. One of the joys of the film was that you were working with the *crème de la crème*. Every part was played by somebody who was talented to their fingertips, like Hermione Gingold and Hermione Baddeley, and I was actually going to work with George Robey, whom I only knew from cigarette cards.

Noel Langley wasn't a film director really, although he wrote some great things. It would have been a different film if directed by David Lean who had done those early Dickens films. I later worked for David Lean on *Lawrence of Arabia*; the entire cast and crew respected and admired him as the maestro.

As actor:

Hypocrites (1923), *East Lynne on the Western Front*, *The Officers' Mess*, *Jealousy* (1931), *The Callbox Mystery*, *A Safe Proposition*, *When London Sleeps*, *Tight Corner* (1932), *Yes, Madam*, *Night of the Garter*, *The Umbrella*, *I Adore You*, *Mannequin* (1933), *Faces*, *Murder at the Inn*, *How's Chances* (1934), *Radio Pirates*, *The Girl in the Crowd*, *A Fire Has Been Arranged* (1935), *Two on a Doorstep* (1937).

As director:

Dead Men Are Dangerous, *Cavalier of the Streets* (1939), *House of the Arrow* (1940), *Jeannie*, *Major Barbara* (co-dir, uncredited) (1941), *Secret Mission*, *Unpublished Story*, *The Day Will Dawn* (1942), *Our Film* (short), *Dear Octopus* (1943), *English Without Tears*, *Mr Emmanuel* (1944), *Quiet Weekend* (1946), *White Cradle Inn* (+ co-sc) (1947), *The Blind Goddess*, *Quartet* ('The Alien Corn'), *My Brother Jonathan* (1948), *Adam and Evelyne* (+ prod) (1949), *The Dancing Years*, *Trio* ('Sanatorium') (1950), *Encore* ('Gigolo and Gigolette') (1951), *The Man Who Watched Trains Go By* (+ sc) (1952), *Isn't Life Wonderful?*, *The Hour of 13*, *Rob Roy, the Highland Rogue* (1953), *Forbidden Cargo* (1954), *The Man Who Loved Redheads* (1955).

Harold French's films are above all 'actor's films' and in his modest account of his career he would claim to have been essentially an actors' director. When one considers the quality of the performances he elicited, this claim is amply borne out: Barbara Mullen in *Jeannie*, Wendy Hiller in *Major Barbara*, Felix Aylmer in *Mr Emmanuel*, Dirk Bogarde in *Quartet*, Michael Denison in *My Brother Jonathan*, and Claude Rains in *The Man Who Watched Trains Go By*. If there is no obviously great film among his credits, there is, equally, no film that is less than entertaining and a number of them have real charm and sharp compassionate observation. Surviving the hazards (along with David Lean) of putting *Major Barbara* together under Gabriel Pascal's ostensible direction, French then made a trio of lively war films before hitting his stride with *Dear Octopus*. All French's work in the Somerset Maugham films is distinguished, especially perhaps in the Raymond Huntley-Betty Ann Davies vignette in *Trio*. He doesn't care for his last film, *The Man Who Loved Redheads*, but he and Gladys Cooper ensure that its last few minutes provide a fitting swansong.

Interview date: July 1990.

After acting in a lot of films, were you really wanting to direct by the late 30s?

Yes, I was. I directed a lot of plays, too, including *French Without Tears*, which was Rex Harrison's first big success; then I was doing *Major Barbara* and the chap we had in it wasn't very good, so I persuaded Gabby [Gabriel] Pascal to play Rex. I co-directed quite a lot of that with David Lean.

Pascal knew nothing at all about directing and in the end he paid me quite a lot of money *not* to have my name mentioned as a director of it. Gabby hadn't the slightest idea – I mean, sometimes he would look through a viewfinder the wrong way around! But he had the money and he had the ear of George Bernard Shaw, which he got for £1! I think Shaw was amused – and bemused – by

Pascal. I only met Shaw the once when he came to the set at Denham. I asked him about the character of Undershaft – whether he was honest, merely a money man, or whether he had any integrity at all, and Shaw replied, 'I haven't the slightest idea, but he is amusing'.

I ended up shooting the first quarter of the film, then Gabby wanted to be producer, director, the whole caboodle. So I told him I was fed up and David Lean shot the rest of it himself, about three-quarters of it I suppose. Gabby took a lot of credit but it was David mostly.

Was *Jeannie* the film that established you as a director?

Yes, that was after *Major Barbara*. The producer, Marcel

Hellman, was very generous and forced me through into a major picture. I don't think the distributors wanted me, they wanted someone well-known. It made a star of Barbara Mullen, who was terribly good, though we thought she would have become a bigger star. Bernard Knowles was the cameraman; I valued his co-operation. If I got in a muddle in a crowd scene, he always knew how to move the camera. We also had Anatole de Grunwald and Roland Pertwee as the writers, so we had a very well-credentialed film.

You made three war films in 1942 with Bernard Knowles as cameraman — *Secret Mission*, *Unpublished Story* and *The Day Will Dawn*. Did you value that sort of continuity?

Yes, because I believed in teamwork. It was very difficult to make pictures at that time, because we had so little equipment. We didn't have zoom lenses or anything like they have nowadays. I made a picture called *Dear Octopus* with a lot of people sitting around a table; we didn't have a crane, so the carpenters built a structure in the middle with the camera stuck up on top of it, and we turned the camera around.

***Dear Octopus* is a charming film. Were you pleased with it?**

Yes, I'd liked the play and thought I could make a picture of it. I think I did some of it well. When you think about it, *Jeannie* was a success because Jeannie was Cinderella. There is also a touch of that about the

Harold French (r) directs Stewart Granger and Jean Simmons in a scene from *Adam and Evelyne*, 1949

Maggie Lockwood character in *Dear Octopus* – the secretary who marries the son of the house.

I remember Celia Johnson in *Dear Octopus*, of course. She could read the dictionary to me and I'd blub if she wanted me to. She played one very moving scene with the children around her; it was quite a long scene and I decided to do it in one shot because of the children. We rehearsed it, then I shot it in one take and printed it. By this time Celia's tears were rolling down her face. I told her she had been marvellous to get into the mood so quickly. She said, 'I'll tell you honestly, I do want to catch the 3.45 bus and I knew damn well if I'd dried you'd do it again, so I put the lot into it!' It was quite true, she wanted to get back to Henley before the rain started!

It was a lovely film to make, a very harmonious cast and I loved working with Mike Wilding – and Roly Culver, too, who was in many of my pictures. I was delighted to get away from making war films, to make something light and frothy. It was just what the public wanted. Of course, Margaret Lockwood was the big star at that time and she was charming to work with.

You went on to make *English Without Tears* which reunited you with Terence Rattigan. Did you find him especially congenial to work with?
Oh, yes, we were enormous friends until his death. But as for *English Without Tears*, that was a bit of wickedness on Tolly de Grunwald's part because it wasn't good and made no real sense. Tolly, who was a lovely old villain, had found a backer and he persuaded Terry to lend his name to it and, of course, Terry, who was then in the Air Force, needed the money. By the time we were shooting I knew it wasn't Terry's dialogue. Penelope Dudley Ward was in it and she had a lovely comedy sense with a very light touch.

In 1944 you made *Mr Emmanuel* which seemed an unusual film for you. Was it a personal choice?
Yes, it was, I thought it was a very good story. Louis Golding was quite a big name as a novelist then, and a very nice man. It was a rare starring role for Felix Aylmer. He came to audition for it and, while I admired him as an actor, I told him I felt the part needed a Jewish actor. He said 'But I *am* a Jew!', and I had no idea, nor I think did many other people. He did it very well, I thought. It made a lot of money on the art-house circuit in America; the Americans were very sympathetic towards the exiled Jew at that time.

After a two-year gap you directed *Quiet Weekend*. Were you sought out by the producer?
By Warwick Ward, yes. I did two or three pictures with him. I don't know why I did it – the money, I should think. I must confess I wasn't ever really dedicated: I got by and I worked hard while I was doing it, but I think I might have been a better director had I been more choosy. *Quiet Weekend* is pleasant enough in its silly way. We had some good actors – Marjorie Fielding and Frank Cellier and so on – who'd been in the play. Glynis Johns was in the play, too, but her part was played in the film by a charming young actress called Barbara White, who just disappeared shortly after.

You then made two films with very British actresses, Madeleine Carroll at the end of her career in *White Cradle Inn* and Claire Bloom in her first film, *The Blind Goddess*.
White Cradle Inn was my original story and I also co-authored the screenplay and directed it. We made it at Hounslow Studios and on location in Switzerland, where filming had to stop because the money had run out. I didn't mind as long as they paid the actors, which they did; I didn't get all my money from that one. I got on well with Madeleine Carroll, but I didn't think she was a very good actress, frankly. I don't think Ian Hunter was terribly good either – a bit stolid. It would have been a better picture with a stronger man. But Michael Rennie was marvellous in it. I liked that film because I thought it had a lot of atmosphere, because I used Swiss actors quite a lot. Having been an actor myself, I could encourage actors and help them; I think I was 'an actors' director' more than anything else.

I'd forgotten *The Blind Goddess*. Claire Bloom's role was a secondary one, but she stood out in it; I thought she was going to be a star. I chose her personally when she auditioned for the part. I don't think the film was successful, but it got Claire noticed.

The next film you made was a very big box-office success – *My Brother Jonathan*. What do you recall of that?
It made more money than any other picture in England that year. It was a great success and it made Michael Denison a star. I didn't actually choose him, although I approved of him. It had a good story once again. I had read the novel, and I believe in staying as close as I can to a novel when I adapt it for the screen.

One film I liked, which you haven't mentioned, was *Adam and Evelyne*, which I produced and directed for

Two Cities. At that stage I could pick and choose and I really liked that one. I became producer because Paul Soskin, who was to have produced it, didn't like the fact that I had employed an actor called Edwin Styles for the part of the valet; I thought he was quite good and he got on well with Jimmy [Stewart] Granger in his first comedy role. Paul said he wanted to go back to America and would I take over as producer. I didn't mind but I told him I knew nothing about money. So I used to get a list each day of expenses which I would put in a desk and lose. But I did enjoy that film and I adored working with Jean Simmons, a lovely actress.

Did you enjoy doing segments of the Somerset Maugham films *Quartet*, *Trio* and *Encore*?

Oh, very much indeed. I particularly liked doing 'Sanatorium' in *Trio* although, again, I don't think I did it as well as I should have done. I should have been more honest about the disease than I was; I was concentrating on the romance too much. I should have made them more ill. When I saw it again some time afterwards it didn't suggest to me a nursing home. I should have done it as a background thing, them looking at their handkerchiefs to see if there was blood on them – that's the sort of thing Lean would have done. The part with Raymond Huntley and Betty Ann Davies as husband and wife together was marvellous though. So was Michael Rennie – Guy Rolfe was originally cast for the part, but he was dropped when, sadly, he actually came down with con-sumption like the character in the film.

I did 'Gigolo and Gigolette' for the *Encore* film. A stunt man dressed up as a girl did the dangerous dive sequence and I did it as a very long shot from the top of a ladder. We shot it all at Pinewood and I went to France just for a few wild shots. There's a good little scene with a couple of old troupers backstage – Mary Merrall and a lovely European actor, I forget his name [Charles Goldner].

Your last film is one of my favourites of the 50s – *The Man Who Loved Redheads* – and then you suddenly stopped making films.

Oh, I didn't like that film – I didn't enjoy making it or seeing it. I got on all right with Moira [Shearer] but I didn't think she was quite strong enough. I felt we were under-cast. You couldn't meet a nicer man than the leading man, John Justin, but I really wanted Kenneth More. But it wasn't a very good play [Terence Rattigan's *Who is Sylvia?*], and Terry did the screenplay as well. Of course, Gladys Cooper steals the whole thing in the last ten minutes. She wasn't a film actress very often, in this country at least, so she just said 'I'm in your hands, tell me what to do'.

I quarrelled with Korda about that film. I had a clause in my contract with him that he wasn't to come on the set, but he did come a few times and suggested very old-fashioned ideas. His days as a great producer were pretty much over by then and he was tired.

As director:

Sailors Do Care* (1944), *The Ten-Year Plan** (1945), *Arctic Harvest**, *Under One Roof** (1946), *Fishing Grounds of the World**, *The Little Ballerina* (1947), *Marry Me* (co-sc only) (1949), *Once a Sinner* (1950), *There is Another Sun*, *It's a Small World*, *Scarlet Thread*, (1951), *Emergency Call* (+ co-sc), *Cosh Boy* (+ co-sc), *Time Gentlemen Please* (1952), *Johnny on the Run* (+ pr), *Albert RN* (1953), *The Good Die Young* (+ co-sc), *The Sea Shall Not Have Them* (+ co-sc) (1954), *Cast a Dark Shadow* (1955), *Reach for the Sky* (+ co-sc), *The Admirable Crichton* (1956), *A Cry from the Streets*, *Carve Her Name with Pride* (+ co-sc) (1958), *Ferry to Hong Kong* (+ co-sc) (1959), *Sink the Bismarck!*, *Light Up the Sky!* (+ co-sc) (1960), *The Greengage Summer* (1961), *HMS Defiant* (1962), *The Seventh Dawn* (1964), *Alfie* (+ pr) (1966), *You Only Live Twice* (1967), *The Adventurers* (+ pr, co-sc) (1970), *Friends* (+ pr) (1971), *Paul and Michelle* (+ pr, story) (1972), *Operation Daybreak* (1975), *Seven Nights in Japan* (+ pr) (1976), *The Spy Who Loved Me* (1977), *Moonraker* (1979), *Educating Rita* (+ pr) (1983), *Not Quite Jerusalem* (+ pr) 1984), *Shirley Valentine* (+ pr) (1989), *Stepping Out* (+ pr) (1991), *Annie II* (1993).

* Documentary.

Lewis Gilbert is a survivor, a fact he attributes to his never having been under contract and therefore free – and, as it has turned out, able – to do what he wants. After experience as a child actor in the 1930s, he cut his teeth as a director on documentaries and ten second features before his first 'A' film, *Albert RN*, in 1953. Since then he has worked successfully in a number of genres, with an emphasis on war subjects in the 50s. With *Reach for the Sky* and *Carve Her Name with Pride*, two celebrations of wartime courage, he scored popular success. Gilbert seems less a director who imposes a strong personal stamp on every project he undertakes than one who makes a shrewd assessment of the material at hand and approaches it with a craftsman's eye to making it viable entertainment. Two of his early films, the village comedy, *Time Gentlemen Please*, and the thriller, *Cast a Dark Shadow*, hold up remarkably well for just such reasons.

Interview date: July 1990.

Your first feature film, after wartime and post-war documentary experience, was the children's film, *The Little Ballerina* in 1947. Did you enjoy working with children?

Yes. They had just started to make films for children and wanted feature films. I had a background of feature films as well as documentary experience, so that's how I came to do one of the earliest children's films, under the aegis of Mary Field with whom I'd worked at Gaumont-British. The film had a very good cast – people like Martita Hunt and George Carney – and because of my feature film background I knew these people and was able to ask them to be in it. The budget was almost nothing so they did it as a favour, really.

I suppose your real directorial career began in 1950 with *Once a Sinner*.

Yes, with Pat Kirkwood – it's sad that her career foundered because she was very good. In those days, in order to get established you had to start at what I call 'Poverty Row' film-making; I mean, we were making films in those days for about £15,000. It was all good experience, even though the films were pretty trite stuff, which hopefully someone would spot and give you something better to do. I never had an agent in my life – I think I got *Once A Sinner* because the producer, John Argyle, had seen *The Little Ballerina*; he approached me and asked if I would like to do his film. It's very difficult today for someone to break in because there isn't that kind of cheap film to cut your teeth on; you're not allowed to fail now, it's all or nothing.

I recently saw *Time Gentlemen Please* again ...

That was made for the company, run by Grierson and

John Baxter, called Group Three, with Michael Balcon in the background. They raised money so that new directors, new cameramen and writers could get a chance at making films, a very laudable idea. It had a very strong cast – people like Hermione Baddeley and Raymond Lovell, whom I'd worked with before. We would only have paid them something like £25 a day but that was pretty good money when you think that the average working man's wage was about £6-7 a week. A lot of them would have been working in the theatre at the same time. Hermione Gingold was playing a prostitute in *Cosh Boy*; she was middle-aged by then and was wearing a dreadful wig for the part. I was doing night shooting with her the night my son was born; we left the studio at about five o'clock in the morning and I gave her a lift because her car hadn't arrived. I suddenly thought to myself, here I am on the night my son is born, driving along with someone who looks like a dreadful old prostitute – if anyone sees me I'll be shot to ribbons!

With *Albert RN* you clearly entered the 'A' film category. Where did you come across that story?
It was a play, but it was clearly a much better film subject than a theatre piece. We built the camp out on Headingly Heath, a whole POW camp with barbed wire and so on. I think it gives you some insight into the economics of film, because that film which had Jack Warner, Anthony Steel and a lot of other stars, cost £80,000 at a time when something like 20,000,000 people a week went to the cinema. Now it would take £4m or £5m to make a film like that and there are only about 2,000,000 people going to the cinema each week. You couldn't get your money back in England on a film like *Albert RN* today, although we did when it was made.

By this point, you'd established two important working relationships – with producer Daniel Angel and screenwriter Vernon Harris.
That's right, yes. Vernon Harris, who died only a couple of months ago, worked with me on almost every film I did over nearly forty years. In those early days we very often did the complete screenplay together. Vernon's real strength was as a script editor. We would lay out the scenario together and we would then usually depend upon a dialogue writer to supply the dialogue. Daniel Angel was more on the financial side, raising the money and so on. Usually, with the bigger films like *Reach for the Sky* and *Albert RN*, he bought them himself. I bought *Carve Her Name with Pride* myself, but I brought Daniel in because he always called on me. It was a good part-

nership but after six films, which were all successful, you want to go your own way.

Then I did a couple of films with Ian Dalrymple, whom I liked very much, as producer. But they were always *my* films. By the time I left Angel I had learned a hell of a lot about film finance, so I went my own way after that. Sometimes, as with *A Cry from the Streets*, which was a very successful film, Ian owned the book and I went to him and said I would like to do it; but I raised the finance for it. So I am very much involved in the business side of making films and I think that's why I've survived, because I'm not dependent on anyone in that sense.

Did you make *Cast a Dark Shadow* because you were attracted by Janet Green's play, *Murder Mistaken*?
Yes, I had seen it in the theatre. At the time, I was doing *The Sea Shall Not Have Them* and I mentioned it to Dirk Bogarde, who knew the play. I think Janet Green had, in fact, asked him to do the play but he wasn't doing plays at that time; Derek Farr did it. It was a very interesting plot, very claustrophobic. I think it was the best thing Margaret Lockwood did – she was great in the film. The film was reasonably successful but, by then, Margaret had been in several really bad films and her name on a picture was rather counter-productive. It was a great shame because, after *Cast a Dark Shadow*, she could have started a whole new career as a character actress. Dirk is still one of my absolutely favourite actors. He is a lovely man to work with, a marvellous actor – and now a marvellous writer as well.

War films tended to dominate 50s British cinema. Why, do you think?
After the war Britain was a very tired nation, worn out by five or six years of war. The war films were a kind of ego boost, a nostalgia for a time when Britain was great, because it was rapidly overtaken economically by other countries, particularly by Japan and West Germany whom it had just defeated. I chose my war films because they were great stories – *Reach for the Sky* in particular. This was extremely successful in the English-speaking countries but, oddly enough, the Rank Organisation was unable to get anywhere with it in the US. They had thought to use its success as a vehicle for setting up their own distribution network in the US, but it didn't work. Yet, when I did *Sink the Bismarck!* a few years later it was very successful in America; it's very difficult to ascertain why one film succeeds and another doesn't.

We had a very interesting experience recently: it was the fiftieth anniversary of the Battle of Britain and they chose *Reach for the Sky* to show at a one-night première in aid of the war charity of the RAF; and it was a sell-out night. They ran the film, which was thirty-five years old, and it was like a time warp. I sat there, not having seen the film myself for about thirty years, and it was a really strange experience. All the young faces coming up on the screen are now old men. Muriel Pavlow was at the anniversary and I saw her again for the first time since making the film. Beverly Brooks [who played Bader's early girl-friend] was also there, married now to Viscount Rothermere.

Did you have a lot to do with Douglas Bader when you were making *Reach for the Sky*?
Oh, yes, and was he difficult! He was difficult in the sense of wanting himself to be depicted in a certain way.

He knew I was in the RAF and, when we couldn't get anyone to adapt the book, he said I should do it. So I did and then, when he read the script, he said I had made a terrible hash of it because I'd cut out a lot of his friends. I pointed out that the book contained hundreds of names and I had to cut it down or else the film would run for three days. He said, 'That's your problem. If you don't get my friends in, I won't double for the film', because he was going to double for Kenneth More in long shots. I explained to him that wouldn't stop the film being made; I said that we could undoubtedly find someone with a disability similar to his – which we did. In fact, a number of his friends had helped me with the script, although we didn't tell Douglas that. Douglas wasn't in the film at all.

He was an incredible man for all that. He was the only man with that sort of disability who had ever walked without sticks. The film was really as much about the

Bill Owen and Virginia McKenna in Lewis Gilbert's *Carve Her Name with Pride*, 1958

triumph over adversity as it was a war film. Kenneth More wasn't my first choice for the part. The first choice was Richard Burton, who wanted to do it until he was offered *Alexander the Great* at three or four times the salary, and chose that. Laurence Olivier actually told Kenneth More that the only person who could play it was Bader himself, but Kenny was adamant he could do it.

Carve Her Name with Pride is a very grim story. How much license did you and Vernon Harris feel you could take with the story?
We didn't take much license with it. One night we invited to dinner R.J. Minney who had written *Time Gentlemen Please*. He told us the story of Violet Szabo and we thought it would make a wonderful film, so he sent me his proof copy of the book and I bought it. Virginia McKenna really wasn't the right type for it, but she was under contract to Rank and they wanted to use her. Ideally, it should have been someone like Diana Dors, who was much rougher, because Violet was a Cockney who had lived in Brixton, a very poor area of London. In fact, Virginia was wonderful in the film and got several awards for it. She had Odette as an adviser on *Carve Her Name with Pride* which was very useful, especially as Odette, having already had a film made about her life, understood a bit about film-making. Some of the dialogue we fictionalised, of course, but most of the film story is true, including the fact that Violet spoke perfect French because she used to spend every summer in France with her French grandmother. A lot of the film was set in France, but we shot it all in England around the Pinewood area.

When you adapted The Admirable Crichton did you study the original closely?
No, we made it as a vehicle for Kenny More who was a very big star. I would say it was freely adapted from the Barrie play to suit Kenny, and it was a very successful film. I don't think you owe total allegiance to original text because you are, in a sense, making something that is very different.

I was very fond of Kenny as an actor, although he wasn't particularly versatile. What he could do, he did very well. His strength was his ability to portray charm; basically he was the officer returning from the war and was superb in that role. The minute that kind of role went out of existence, his popularity as a box-office star began to go down. In something like *The Greengage Summer*, he was somehow too normal – it didn't quite work; that's a role Dirk should have played because you could well imagine a girl of fifteen or sixteen falling in love with Dirk.

Speaking of The Admirable Crichton, I think, until the late 50s, British cinema often seemed uncritically middle-class and snobbish.
I think that's true and I think it changed for two reasons: first, the censorship changed, and second *Look Back in Anger* showed that working people could have lives of their own, and not just come in to say, 'Dinner is served'. I suppose the cinema reflects its own time and, prior to then, working-class people just didn't 'exist' in the West End or the cinema.

Marius Goring

Rembrandt, The Amateur Gentleman (1936), Dead Men Tell No Tales, Consider Your Verdict (1938), The Spy in Black, Flying Fifty-Five (1939), Pastor Hall, The Case of the Frightened Lady (1940), The Big Blockade (1941), The Night Invader (1943), The Story of Lilli Marlene (1944), Night Boat to Dublin, A Matter of Life and Death (1946), Take My Life (1947), The Red Shoes, Mr Perrin and Mr Traill (1948), Odette, Highly Dangerous (1950), Circle of Danger, Pandora and the Flying Dutchman, The Magic Box (1951), So Little Time, Nachts auf den Strassen, The Man Who Watched Trains Go By, Rough Shoot (1952), The Mirror and Markheim (voice only) (1953), Break in the Circle, The Adventures of Quentin Durwood, The Barefoot Contessa (1955), Ill Met By Moonlight (1957), The Truth About Women, The Moonraker, Family Doctor, Son of Robin Hood, I Was Monty's Double (1958), Whirlpool, The Angry Hills, The Treasure of San Teresa, Desert Mice (1959), Beyond the Curtain, The Unstoppable Man, Exodus (1960), The Inspector, The Devil's Daffodil, The Devil's Agent (1962), The Crooked Road (1964), Up from the Beach (1965), The 25th Hour (1967), Girl on a Motorcycle, Subterfuge (1968), First Love (1970), Zeppelin (1971), The Girl in the Yellow Dress (1978).

Marius Goring so often played sinister foreigners that it comes as a surprise to find that he is wholly English. In a very long career in films, dating back to the 1930s, when he was not playing Nazi officers he was often seen as neurotic or ambiguously decadent characters. On the rare occasions when he played 'leading man' roles, he still invested them with a memorable suggestion of strangeness. Goring rightly regards the films that he made for Michael Powell – especially *A Matter of Life and Death* and *The Red Shoes* – as the highlight of his screen career, but he was also memorable in Lawrence Huntington's *Mr Perrin and Mr Traill*: only in his mid-thirties at the time, he suggested a lifetime of disappointment and frustration. He was extremely busy throughout the 50s, while maintaining an almost unbroken commitment to the stage.

Interview date: June 1990.

As well as doing broadcasts for the BBC's European and World Service during the War, did you also make a number of films, including Roy Boulting's *Pastor Hall*?
No, that was made before the war broke out although it wasn't released until about 1940. The Chamberlain Government wouldn't allow it to be released. It was about German concentration camps and, although it was completely true, it wasn't considered a good idea to insult the Germans! If Churchill had been in power he would have said 'Nonsense! Show it everywhere!'.

You have made about sixty films for the cinema. Do you have any personal favourites?
Oh, yes. I made a film in 1939 with Michael Powell, *The Spy in Black*, but I was unable to make many films during the war because of my broadcasting and other commitments. After the European war came to an end, Powell and Pressburger came up with *A Matter of Life and Death* and offered me a marvellous part. I made four pictures in all for them; I think those films were in a totally different category from any others I've done. Powell and Pressburger were such a delight to work with, so inventive, and they gave actors great scope.

But back to *The Spy in Black* – there was a book that came out before the 1914-18 war, *The Riddle of the Sands* by Erskine Childers. This presented an imaginary invasion of Britain which could happen should there be a war with Germany. Powell took the proposition and decided to make a film about a submarine coming into Northern Scottish waters and blowing up British warships. The amazing thing was that, although the film was pure fiction, the war had only been on for about three weeks when a German submarine did come in and blow up one of our ships.

Did Powell give his actors a lot of guidance?
No, he really left things to the appropriate people. At

least, he always gave the impression that they were doing it all and he was just checking up on what was going on. With me, as an actor, Powell would simply let me get on with it. I wrote an obituary for him when he died, because a lot of people wrote that he was horrible to actors whereas I thought he was marvellous.

There was a scene in *The Red Shoes* where I, as the composer, halt the orchestra, without permission from the conductor, because I think they aren't playing my music properly. Michael told me about this scene one morning and said we would shoot it that afternoon. I asked him what was going to happen during the scene and he said, 'Oh, I thought you'd tell me that'! Then he looked at his watch and said, 'You've got half an hour; fix it up yourself with the orchestra. You'd better hurry up'! I remembered that Sir Thomas Beecham was rehearsing in the building that day, so I went in to listen. Beecham was very witty and his musicians loved him. At one point he stopped the orchestra and asked the first cello if he had a 'b' or a 'b-flat' in a particular bar; the cellist replied that he had a 'b-flat' and Beecham said, 'Yes, it does make quite a difference, doesn't it?'. The orchestra laughed, and I wrote all that down and showed it to Powell. He thought it was fine, so that's what we shot.

How much in evidence was Pressburger around the studio at this time?

He was certainly in evidence; he did all the scripting, although sometimes Powell would make a contribution as well. Pressburger also did quite a lot on the business side of things. What he never did was direct. As time went on though, he felt he would like to direct a film on his own and it was this which really broke the partnership up. They never worked together again and it didn't do Pressburger any good, because he couldn't direct – and *Peeping Tom*, of course, finished Powell. It's a great movie, but we were all so shocked by it then.

Perhaps no British director has quite had Powell's extraordinary visual sense. How much was this the work of Jack Cardiff?

Powell always said that Cardiff was the greatest cameraman in the world and he did such things with colour – I wouldn't say people *can't* do it today, but it never seems as good as what Cardiff did. The whole technique – such as in *A Matter of Life and Death*, with the idea of having a mixture of black and white and colour – was so good. In fact, I had a line in that film which was originally, 'One is so starved for colour up there' and, during a run-through, I said, 'One is so starved for Technicolour up there', and Powell said, 'That's good, leave it in'. So that was my contribution.

I understand *The Red Shoes* was a big

Mary Jerrold and Marius Goring in Lawrence Huntington's *Mr Perrin and Mr Traill*, 1948

breakthrough for British films in the USA, although Rank thought it wouldn't succeed there.

Yes, it was very successful, but Rank thought the picture was awful. He said, 'Nobody is going to go and see this nonsense', which shows you he really didn't know anything about films. He even decided he wasn't going to finish the picture, so Powell asked Alexander Korda to bail him out, and he finished the picture financially and arranged the distribution. It still had Rank's name on it but, as he was still convinced nobody would go to see it, Rank didn't even give it a première showing in England. Then a filmhouse in New York picked it up and it played there for a year. After two or three years, the money came pouring in.

What do you recall of the other Powell-Pressburger film you made, *Ill Met By Moonlight*?

It's not in quite the same class as the others. We were going to make the whole thing in Crete, so we went out there, but it was a very bad time because the good wartime relationship between the British and Greek governments had passed away completely. All the cameras and the materials that we had taken out to Crete were stolen, so Micky Powell said it was useless trying to film there. We shot it in the South of France instead. Micky had lived there as a boy and knew it well, so he was able to choose locations which no one could tell weren't Greece.

I greatly admire your performance as the increasingly deranged schoolmaster in *Mr Perrin and Mr Traill*. What did you think of Lawrence Huntington as a director?

I got on very well with him, but he just seemed to disappear. I don't know what happened to him. He understood actors very well and, above all, he had a great sense of humour. I don't remember much about the film other than that Lawrence and I had a very enjoyable time together making it. The man who produced it was a German refugee, Alexander Galperson. He knew my work from the theatre and it was his idea that I should play the part – as a change, because most of the time when I wasn't working for Powell I was playing Nazi officers. When I was asked to do the film I read Hugh Walpole's novel first, then agreed to do the part.

In 1951 you made two films with American directors and stars: Jacques Tourneur's *Circle of Danger* with Ray Milland and Albert Lewin's

***Pandora and the Flying Dutchman* with Ava Gardner. Did you find their way of working different from what you'd been used to?**

No, basically it was just the same. I loved working with Jacques Tourneur, but *Circle of Danger* was one of those odd pictures that I haven't seen since it was first made.

Pandora and the Flying Dutchman was made at Pinewood. Lewin was a very remarkable man: he had been a professor of English and somehow got a job as a sort of permanent producer with MGM. He had a deal whereby he was allowed to direct one picture every two or three years and, apart from that, he was just supposed to give advice.

James Mason, who I had known since I started at the Old Vic, was in *Pandora*. His one ambition had always been to get into films in America – an ambition I didn't share. I wanted to stay in England. Also I had never envisaged myself as a film actor, I preferred the theatre. As for Ava, she was totally delightful – we had great fun together. There was none of the 'great star' about her, she was absolutely natural. She was very good in the next movie we did together, *The Barefoot Contessa*, which we made in Italy. Joe Manckiewicz the director was an inspiring man to work with, a very good actor's director, and some of the dialogue he gave us was extraordinary. He seemed to fade out just like Powell and Pressburger.

You had almost a conventional romantic lead role in a film called *So Little Time*, directed by Compton Bennett.

It was a touching little film, yes, my favourite apart from the Powell films. The story originally happened in Poland, but it was changed to Belgium for the film. I played a Nazi officer who falls in love with Maria Schell, who was beautiful and extremely good. It was soon after the war and people still thought that every German was a horror. It was probably the first picture that dared to suggest that all Germans weren't 'Nazi swine', but its timing was wrong. I think if it had been a year later, it would have been all right.

Were the 40s and 50s a good time to pursue a film career in Britain?

Oh, yes, from the late 40s. It was a period of immense vitality, invention and drive. I had a contract with Rank during that time, until he decided to throw the business up. I can't say I think much of my later films. I have done some television work I've enjoyed much more than most of my films – for example, *The Old Men at the Zoo*.

Stewart Granger

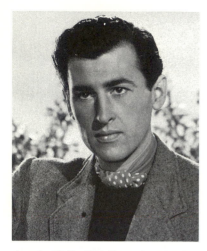

A Southern Maid (1933) Over the Garden Wall, Give Her a Ring (1934), Mademoiselle Docteur, So this is London (1937), Convoy (1940), Secret Mission (1942), Thursday's Child, The Lamp Still Burns, The Man in Grey (1943), Fanny by Gaslight, Love Story, Madonna of the Seven Moons (1944), Waterloo Road (1945), Caravan, Caesar and Cleopatra, The Magic Bow (1946), Captain Boycott (1947), Blanche Fury, Saraband for Dead Lovers, Woman Hater, Adam and Evelyne (1948), King Solomon's Mines (1950), The Light Touch, Soldiers Three (1951), The Wild North, Scaramouche, The Prisoner of Zenda (1952), Young Bess, Salome (1953), All the Brothers Were Valiant, Beau Brummell (1954), Green Fire, Moonfleet, Footsteps in the Fog (1955), Bhowani Junction, The Last Hunt (1956), Gun Glory, The Little Hut (1957), The Whole Truth, Harry Black (1958), North to Alaska (1960), The Secret Partner, The Swordsman of Siena (1961), Commando, La Congiura dei Dieci, Sodom and Gomorrah (1962), The Shortest Day, The Legion's Lost Patrol (1963), The Crooked Road, Frontier Hellcat/Among Vultures, The Secret Invasion (1964), Rampage at Apache Wells, Old Shatterhand (1965), Red Dragon, Target for Killing, Requiem for a Secret Agent (1966), The Trygon Factor, The Last Safari (1967), The Wild Geese (1978), The Adventures of Baron Munchausen (1987).

Stewart Granger became a household name in British films after co-starring with Phyllis Calvert, Margaret Lockwood, and James Mason in *The Man in Grey*. He was a dashing hero in a string of subsequent melodramas made for Gainsborough Studios, though he would have preferred to have had the meatier, more villainous roles that often fell to Mason's lot. Although he does not value these films, he was a very important ingredient in their success. Nevertheless, his best performances in British films, in roles that gave him more scope, were either in different vein (for example, as the spiv-like Ted Purvis in Sidney Gilliat's *Waterloo Road*), or at other studios (for example, *Saraband for Dead Lovers* at Ealing, *Blanche Fury* for Cineguild, and the attractive comedy, *Adam and Evelyne* for Two Cities). Hollywood capitalised on his flair for costume drama and action adventure and he was solidly successful in these genres throughout the 1950s.

Interview date: June 1991.

As far as I can tell, your fifty-year career in films began with work as an extra in 1933. How did this come about?

I started training to be a doctor, but since the training was long and I was not a dedicated fellow, I gave that up and went to work for a firm that made tickets and ticket-punches for the buses. After a quarrel with them, I left. A friend asked me whether I had a car and a decent wardrobe – and, on that basis, I became a film extra at a guinea a day. Then I had go to the doctor with a cut finger and I met his wife, Susan Richmond, who taught at the Webber-Douglas School of Dramatic Art. My grandfather had been an actor and she asked, why didn't I apply for a scholarship?

How valuable did you find such training when you came to films?

Twelve to eighteen months at acting school is valuable, but not to learn how to act. They teach you techniques such as how to walk through a door, pick up the telephone and drink a cup of tea; technical things like the use of make-up and how to learn dialogue. But to act, you have to *do* it. I learnt acting in the reps. The audience teaches you – particularly timing. You have to have an innate sense to act.

Your screen career really got started when you were invalided out of the war . . .

Yes. In fact, I did films like *Convoy* and *Secret Mission* while I was still 'Grade E' – that is, in the process of being invalided out, but not quite out. John Clements told me there was a part going in *Convoy* and that's how I came to be in that with him and Clive Brook. But the cinema world is not easy. It is full of envy from little people – heads of studios, for example, who hate people for their attractiveness. I don't regret my film career, but medicine would have had more dignity. Actors are shackled to others. I was always fighting with people. I was resented because I was liked by the press. And it was boring being an actor who was confined to swash-buckling hero roles, as I was for most of the time, and playing characters, like Beau Brummell or Scara-mouche, that weren't based in history but were tailored to fit my image. My career in the USA was better for me than my English one – for example my role in *King Solomon's Mines*. After that I was offered *Quo Vadis*, but I refused to sign the contract so it was offered to Robert Taylor instead. My divorce ruined me and sent me out of the USA. I went to Europe where I paid no tax, but I ruined my career in lousy films. My last real film was *The Last Safari*, which was the worst film ever made in Africa.

I was not a dedicated actor. After a forrty years absence, I have recently gone back to the theatre to play in *The Circle* with Rex Harrison and Glynis Johns on Broadway. It got good notices, ran for six months – and then had two months on the road.

What do you remember about *The Man in Grey*?
I got a call from Gainsborough Studios while I was doing a play [*Rebecca*], and they sent me a script. Robert Donat had suggested that they should try me. I knew if I got the part in *The Man in Grey* it would make me a star. I tested, and was given the part straight away, before the tests were ready to view. I went on doing the play at the same time. I was just out of the army, where I had learned to speak my mind. My battalion had been wiped out – I felt guilty for surviving and for making films during the bombing.

How happy were you with those Gainsborough melodramas – *Fanny by Gaslight*, *Madonna of the Seven Moons*, and so on?
I didn't like *Fanny* and *Madonna* – they both had drippy characters. At least *Fanny* was directed by Anthony Asquith who was a sweet man. I would have liked to play the villains in these films – someone with character, with balls. James Mason was luckier than me – he played the villains and later got into character parts. In *All the Brothers Were Valiant* in America, I had an OK villain's part in a bad film, but I was generally cast as the hero because I had good looks and a good voice, and I could wear costumes. But so can most English actors because they come out of a theatrical tradition, the greater part of which calls for this ability to wear period costume. And at Gainsborough we were lucky to have Liz Haffenden,

who was a wonderful designer, to do our costumes. I was also lucky in this respect at MGM in Hollywood.

Certainly Asquith was much the best of the directors I worked with at Gainsborough. I mean [Arthur] Crabtree and [Bernard] Knowles, both sweet men, were really cameramen, and Leslie Arliss was a writer. Apart from Asquith I really had a bunch of bloody awful directors at Gainsborough. And, you know, they were terrible films – *Caravan*, *Madonna of the Seven Moons*, and so on. My alibi for doing them was that it was wartime and they provided the escapism that people needed.

Were you pleased with the change offered by Sidney Gilliat's *Waterloo Road*?
Waterloo Road was made in ten days, while I was also making *Love Story*. Well, we had the set, the clothes, the dialogue, so we just got in and did it. It was hard work. Gainsborough was bombed while we were making *Love Story*, which, as I say in my book, was a load of crap – and a smash hit! *Waterloo Road* was better than that and the famous fight was well done. It was difficult,

Phyllis Calvert and Stewart Granger in Leslie Arliss's *The Man in Grey*, 1943

though, because I was a heavyweight boxer and Johnny Mills was a good bit lighter than I was. Anyway, we had a pro to help us with telegraphing the punches, and so forth, and it ended up looking realistic.

What do you recall of filming two lavish costume melodramas in Britain – *Blanche Fury* **and** *Saraband for Dead Lovers***?**
Blanche Fury was a silly story, too grim and melodramatic, but it's a wonderful-looking film. It was photographed by Guy Green [and Geoffrey Unsworth] who did David Lean's Dickens films. I enjoyed working with Valerie Hobson, a lovely woman, but the film didn't work.

Saraband was a sweet film, though, and it's one I'm quite proud of. But, whereas Gainsborough loved stars, Ealing didn't like them – there, the production was the star. *Saraband* was their first big colour film. I said I would do it, but I wanted Marlene Dietrich, whom I loved, for Clara. I felt I couldn't be brutal to Flora Robson. Flora was a great actress, but she'd never been beautiful and it was hard to be cruel to a woman who was never beautiful! That's why I wanted Dietrich for the part. The opening sequence was planned in great detail. Françoise Rosay wanted to rehearse . . . but in the end this wasn't used. You see Koenigsmark, whom I played, was introduced as penniless, and this was cut out because it involved Jewish moneylenders.

Director Harold French was pleased with *Adam and Evelyne***? How do you feel about it?**
The story-line of *Adam and Evelyne* was mine – I worked on an idea based on the old silent film, *Daddy Longlegs*, and when I had the outline completed, I contacted the writer Noel Langley to collaborate with me. I wrote it for Jean Simmons, and it was a very good vehicle for her. It was a sweet film, a charming light comedy.

How did you come to go to Hollywood for *King Solomon's Mines***?**
I was bitter because I was making no money in the movie industry in Britain and was highly taxed there. So I went to America where the tax was a bit better. But acting was hard work for little reward. I did all my own stunts in *Scaramouche*, some of them quite dangerous and got dysentery when filming in Africa.

Were you pleased with the way MGM went about building you up as an international star?
MGM certainly did not build me up. After *King Solo-

mon's Mines* I made *Soldiers Three*, a cheap film. They ruined my career. I made them do *Scaramouche*. *Solomon* was a cheap film to make. They didn't realise what they had. It only cost a million dollars. They had nature, animals, mountains, Africa . . . and they suddenly realised they had a smash hit. My best film, for them, was *Young Bess* – for the costumes, the cast, the story.

Was it very different from working in England?
Hollywood was more professional than British studios. The studio staff loved stars, the English resented stars. It was the technicians who counted in England; English crews were bolshie. The plug was pulled on the dot of 6 p.m. They killed the British film industry – the electricians, the carpenters and so on. In the USA and in Europe the crew were on your side. They loved stars because stars provided them with work. I liked those crews as fellows. In England left-wing shop stewards dominated. They hindered not helped. In USA the crews were efficient, well trained . . . they wanted the film to be a success. I was too forthright in England and ruined my career there. James Mason, too.

What do you recall of *Beau Brummell***, the film you returned to England for in 1954?**
Prince Philip told me that the joke about the royals – George III, to be exact – was the Queen's favourite. But everyone said it was a tasteless choice for the Royal Command Performance!

How did you find working with Fritz Lang on *Moonfleet***?**
I hated working with Fritz Lang – he was a Kraut and it was a bloody awful film. I wanted to produce and act it in Cornwall, and I made them buy the book. MGM turned it into a big colour film. *Moonfleet* was not Lang's type of film – it is a romantic child's film. It wasn't a bad part though.

How do feel now about the British cinema of your period?
Early British films are embarrassing. The war brought out the best of British cinema: Powell, Lean, Carol Reed. But the Labour Government didn't take the tax off after the war and the industry was stifled.

I am not proud of my British films. I had no choice of films, I was always under contract. I was a good costume actor, but I shortened my career because I made the wrong choices. I missed *Quo Vadis* and *Ben Hur* and I had the physique for them.

As screenwriter (or co-screenwriter) only:
The Maid of the Mountains, Innocents of Chicago (1932), *No Monkey Business* (1935), *Good Morning Boys, Public Nuisance No. 1, All In* (1936), *Okay for Sound* (1937), *Oh Mr Porter, Alf's Button Afloat, Convict 99, Hey, Hey, USA!* (1938), *The Frozen Limits, Old Bones of the River* (1939), *Band Waggon, Ask a Policeman, Charley's (Bighearted) Aunt, Gasbags* (1940), *Inspector Hornleigh Goes To It, Hi Gang!, I Thank You* (1941), *Back Room Boy* (1942), *London Town* (1946), *Paper Orchid* (1949), *Happy-Go-Lovely* (1951).

As director (other functions noted in brackets):
The Nose Has It* (1942), *Miss London Ltd* (+ co-sc) (1943), *Give Us the Moon* (+ sc), *Bees in Paradise* (+ co-sc) (1944), *I'll be Your Sweetheart* (+ co-sc) (1945), *Just William's Luck* (+ co-sc) (1947), *William Comes to Town* (+ co-sc) (1948), *Murder at the Windmill* (+ sc) (1949), *Miss Pilgrim's Progress* (+ sc), *The Body Said No* (+ sc) (1950), *Mr Drake's Duck* (+ sc) (1951), *Penny Princess* (+ pr, sc) (1952), *Life with the Lyons* (+ sc), *The Runaway Bus* (+ pr, sc), *Men of Sherwood Forest, Dance Little Lady* (+ sc) (1954), *They Can't Hang Me* (+ sc), *Break in the Circle* (co-sc, uncredited), *The Lyons in Paris* (+ sc), *The Quatermass Experiment* (+ co-sc) (1955), *The Weapon, It's a Wonderful World* (+ sc) (1956), *Carry on Admiral* (+ co-sc), *Quatermass II* (+ co-sc), *The Abominable Snowman* (1957), *Camp on Blood Island* (+ co-sc), *Up the Creek* (+ co-sc, uncredited), *Further Up the Creek* (co-sc) (1958), *Life is a Circus* (+ sc), *Yesterday's Enemy, Expresso Bongo* (+ pr) (1959), *Hell is a City* (+ sc) (1960), *The Full Treatment* (+ pr, co-sc), *The Day the Earth Caught Fire* (+ pr, co-sc) (1961), *Jigsaw,* (+ pr, sc) (1962), *80,000 Suspects* (+ pr, sc) (1963), *The Beauty Jungle* (+ pr, co-sc) (1964), *Where the Spies Are* (+ pr, co sc) (1965), *Casino Royale* (co-dir), *Assignment K* (+ co-sc) (1967), *When Dinosaurs Ruled the Earth* (+ sc), *Tomorrow* (+ sc) (1970), *Au Pair Girls* (+ co-sc) (1972), *Confessions of a Window Cleaner* (1974), *The Diamond Mercenaries* (1975), *The Shillingbury Blowers* (1980), *The Boys in Blue* (+ sc) (1983).

* Short film.

In terms of sheer output and range, it seems unlikely that there will ever again be directors like Val Guest. After writing numerous screenplays throughout the 1930s for most of the popular comedians of the day, he then began a forty-year career as director in 1942. He has worked in virtually every popular genre – comedies, musicals, war films, thrillers, science fiction, costume adventures and so on – and in this respect he resembled, perhaps more than anyone else in British films, the craftsman-like energy of the Hollywood directors of the studio years. At their best,

Guest's genre films, such as the urban thriller, *Hell is a City*, exhibit a fine, unpretentious realism and there is vigour and inventiveness in his science fiction works. There are also several engaging comedies starring his wife Yolande Donlan, and a whole string of other lively entertainments. 'Lively entertainment' is what, one feels, Val Guest was always aiming at – and very often provided.

Interview date: July 1990.

When you became a director, you were also more often than not the author or co-author of the screenplay. Was this the arrangement you favoured?

Yes, in fact, of all the films I have made as a director, there are only two I haven't written as well. I started as a writer/director at Gainsborough and always felt I would

rather do the writing myself so that, if it went wrong, there was only me to blame. And of course I'd had a wonderful chaotic time in the 30s writing for all those great comics like Will Hay and the Crazy Gang. I had also produced quite a few of my films. Yolande [Donlan – Guest's wife] and I started our own company and every now and then I had a specific subject which I liked, so I would do it for our company. It gave you control and made you think a little harder; you learned to wear different hats for different departments. It wasn't that difficult, because, as writer, I knew exactly what I wanted to see on that screen.

How did you come to start your directing career at Gainsborough?
The start of my career as a director is a little strange. Although I had done some second unit stuff for Marcel Varnel, from whom I learnt a great deal, I hadn't really been a director as such. I then received a request through the studio that the Ministry of Information would like me to write a short picture about sneezing – 'sneezes spread diseases and so stops the ammunition'. I found out that they had sent the job to six other writers first, but all their stuff had been turned down and finally they sent it to me. I put on an Academy Award performance, saying 'How dare they send it to me seventh?!' and I refused to do it unless, if what I wrote was accepted, they allowed me to direct it. So they agreed to this and that was my first job as a director.

It was put on at the Odeon cinema in Leicester Square with a Rita Hayworth/Victor Mature musical, *My Gal Sal*. That was lucky for me because the musical got terrible notices and two critics said that the best thing on the bill was the MOI short about sneezing [*The Nose Has It*]. I had done this with Askey, having written it for him. That's really how I got my Gainsborough contract to write and direct.

Was Gainsborough a good studio to work at/for in the 30s and 40s?
Gainsborough was a great studio to work for. There was a lot of work and we went from one picture to another, from one type to another, and it had a happy family atmosphere. I would think Gainsborough was as near as dammit to a solidly based studio system, because there was real continuity. In a different style, Ealing also had a continuity and a studio-based system. I think it helps a film industry enormously to have two or three units that are continually turning out products.

Between 1949 and 1952 you made four more sophisticated comedies with Yolande Donlan, the American stage star you married. Did you enjoy this change of pace?
Yolande was a sophisticated player and I wrote the films – *Miss Pilgrim's Progress*, and so on – for her. I must say that once you get into a line of pictures that are success-

ful, nobody wants you to leave that particular genre. On a number of occasions I wanted to get away from broad comedy to do a thriller or something, but nobody wanted to know about that. So, being able to do pictures of more sophistication, with something of a story to them, helped me to break through and I did enjoy the change of pace.

Mr Drake's Duck is something of a perennial favourite in England; they bring it out every Christmas. The idea of the duck laying the uranium egg came from a very short BBC playlet by a man called Ian Massiter. It had nothing whatever to do with the story of the film. It was just the *idea* which I bought from him.

Did you have control over casting? Players like Reginald Beckwith, Anthony Oliver, and Wilfred Hyde-White crop up again and again in your films.
I had, I would say, 80 per cent control but the final control came from the American distribution company which insisted on a star name and put forward its preferences as to stars. The players you mention were part of my film rep company; I used to write parts for them in every film I made. I kept a whole lot of them going for quite a long time – Sid James was one of my 'rep' people, as were Leo McKern, A.E. Matthews and certainly Wilfred Hyde-White. Tony Beckwith was actually a partner in Yolande's and my film company and also one of our closest friends.

Someone recently remarked that you are, of all British directors, the one who made genre films with as much flair and energy as Hollywood did. What do you feel about such an assessment?
I'm thrilled that somebody said that of me. I always tried, once I got away from that comedy kick, to make every film I did which had any sort of thrill content or serious content, as much *cinéma vérité* as I could. I tried very hard in all the pictures that I made to give a certain reality. I did make a lot of different genres. We had a wonderful success with *The Day the Earth Caught Fire*. After that, what do you do! Incidentally, I am just about to remake it. So, for my next film I did *Jigsaw*, a police thriller which I still think is one of my better films. I can't say I have a preference for one particular genre. I like doing comedy, but I would rather do something more serious, particularly a thriller of some kind if it was a good one.

You were immensely busy throughout the 40s and

Richard Wordsworth in *The Quatermass Experiment*, 1955

50s. Was it a good time to be a director in Britain?

Yes, I was busy and it was a good time to be directing. I was lucky to be around then because I met up with Jimmy and Michael Carreras and they asked me to join the Hammer fold. I joined up with Bebe and Ben Lyon to make *The Lyons in Paris*, which started me off and I did about thirteen or fourteen pictures with Hammer, one of which was *The Quatermass Experiment*. I had done about three pictures for Hammer and was going to Tangier on holidays when Anthony Hinds (the producer of *Quatermass*) asked me to read some scripts based on the television series. I took the scripts with me and more or less forgot about them. I wasn't too interested in science fiction. Once I'd read them I couldn't wait to do a film of them.

What do you recall of your work with other famous comics in the 50s — Ben Lyon and Bebe Daniels, Peter Sellers, Frankie Howerd and others?

Ben and Bebe were very close friends of ours and we spent a lot of time with them. Bebe was the brains of the family and she used to write all their television and radio scripts. They were lovely people to work with.

As for Sellers, I had decided he should be put into a starring role in *Up the Creek*, but I had a terrible job selling him to the people at Wardour Street because no one had heard much of him except as a radio comic. I finally had to go to my old friend Jimmy Carreras who pointed out that Hammer didn't do comedies but that, if I really wanted to do this one, they would back me as long as I had someone well-known alongside Sellers. I suggested David Tomlinson and Jimmy OK'd that. It was a big hit; it made Hammer a lot of money and Sellers went on to do great things. He was also a great chum of ours, but he made his life a hell.

I saw Frankie Howerd in a revue at the Palladium; afterwards I told him I'd love to put him into a film. He said he would only do a film if it was a mystery/thriller, so that if the comedy was no good, at least the thriller would be! I talked to Margaret Rutherford, a great fan of Frankie's, and asked if she would co-star with him which she was happy to do. So I wrote the story, *The Runaway Bus* for him and her. Frankie would only sign his contract on condition he didn't get top billing, because he didn't want to be blamed for anything, so Maggie had top billing. After the first day's rushes Maggie came to me and said she refused to take top billing over Frankie, so that was that!

What seem to me to be two of your finest films

come right at the end of the decade – *Expresso Bongo* and *Hell is a City*. Do you rate these highly?

Yes, both are very much favourites of mine. If I had to pick favourites of all my films I would say *Yesterday's Enemy*, *Hell is a City*, *The Day the Earth Caught Fire*, *Jigsaw* and *Expresso Bongo*. With *Expresso Bongo* we had a terrible job getting people to agree to do it; I had seen it on the stage and it was Yolande who said we should film it. Paul Scofield was very good, but he wasn't enough of a *film* name. Originally someone had thought of Peter Sellers to play that part on screen, but nobody really wanted to know about that either. Finally they accepted Larry Harvey, so that's how it happened. I thought he did an extremely good job in that. Again, most of the cast were part of my repertory company – Eric Pohlman, Barry Lowe and so on. And, of course, Yolande.

Expresso Bongo was your first collaboration with Wolf Mankowitz. Did the fact that he wrote the book make writing the screenplay easier?

We worked very well together. I admired enormously his turn of phrase, wit and his bite. So we joined up and, at various times in my film career, subjects came up about which I thought, 'Wolf would be great to work with on this', and I pulled him in and we did them together. His having written the book for the play didn't make writing the screenplay easier, because there were a lot of things in the play that we couldn't use on the screen or decided not to. For instance, the second half of the play took place in the South of France and I thought that was all very musical comedy. So we brought that to London and made it take place at the Dorchester, in the Oliver Messel Suite, the balcony and the terrace. Wolf understood that we had to undo various things from the stage version and strengthen various other things for the film,

but it didn't make it any easier to write the screenplay.

Hell is a City carries a caption thanking the Manchester Police Force. Did you have any problems filming in Manchester? Were you aiming at something like a thriller with documentary touches?

Manchester Police were wonderful; they gave us everything we wanted, all the help in the world – after they had checked me out! They checked out that I had made a picture in Brighton with the police, who said I was all right. We didn't really have any problems filming in Manchester; the police roped off streets, even loaned us a lot of their men. It was a tough film to make in that it was all on location, but we didn't have any trouble. I wanted to give it a newsreel quality. I tried desperately to get the quality of realism about the streets, houses and crowds. I was aiming for documentary touches. I thought the strident music was wonderful; it was written by Stanley Black, who had written a lot of music for me and who is brilliant on film scores.

Would you agree that the 40s and 50s were a 'boom' time in British cinema? What do you think were its great strengths and weaknesses in this period?

Yes, it was a boom period. Its great strengths were that Britain was beginning to find its feet, knowing that it could get a world market if it tried hard enough, so everyone tried that little bit harder. It's a terrible thing to say, but I think the unions were the weakness. They put up so many barriers, one way and another, that eventually they drove all the American companies out of Britain. They also made life very difficult when there was only a shoestring budget with which to make a movie.

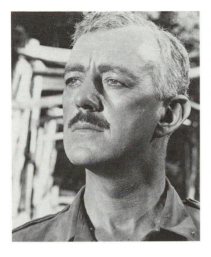

Evensong (1936) *Great Expectations* (1946) *Oliver Twist* (1948) *Kind Hearts and Coronets, A Run for Your Money* (1949) *Last Holiday, The Mudlark* (1950), *The Lavender Hill Mob, The Man in the White Suit* (1951), *The Card* (1952), *The Captain's Paradise, Malta Story* (1953), *Father Brown, To Paris with Love* (1954), *The Prisoner, The Ladykillers* (1955), *The Swan* (1956), *Barnacle Bill, The Bridge on the River Kwai* (1957), *The Scapegoat, The Horse's Mouth* (1958), *Our Man in Havana* (1959), *Tunes of Glory* (1960), *A Majority of One* (1961), *HMS Defiant, Lawrence of Arabia* (1962), *The Fall of the Roman Empire, Situation Hopeless but not Serious* (1964), *Doctor Zhivago, Hotel Paradiso, The Quiller Memorandum* (1966), *The Comedians* (1967), *Cromwell, Scrooge* (1970) *Brother Sun, Sister Moon* (1972), *Hitler: The Last Ten Days* (1973), *Murder by Death* (1976), *Star Wars* (1977), *The Empire Strikes Back, Raise the Titanic, Little Lord Fauntleroy* (1980), *Lovesick* (1983), *A Passage to India* (1984), *Little Dorrit* (1987), *A Handful of Dust* (1988).

Alec Guinness claims that he has never felt happy playing parts too like himself, and perhaps this accounts for his having been, since his early thirties, one of the screen's great character stars. One thinks of his Fagin in *Oliver Twist*, the larcenous bank clerk in *The Lavender Hill Mob*, the unctuous and incompetent criminal in *The Ladykillers*, the obsessed Colonel Nicholson in *The Bridge on the River Kwai*, and the boisterous and boorish Jock in *Tunes of Glory*, to choose but five variously memorable roles from the 40s and 50s alone. In this period, he is perhaps most closely associated with that remarkable run of Ealing comedies, beginning with his virtuoso appearances in *Kind Hearts and Coronets,* and he makes some interesting discriminations among the Ealing directors. As well as nearly fifty films, he has also done a great deal of remarkable work on stage and television.

Interview date: October 1989.

After appearing as an extra in Victor Saville's *Evensong* in 1936, you made no further film until 1946. Did you feel it important to establish yourself on the stage first?

The stage was my prime interest then. I had no ambition to be a film actor and a screen career seemed unlikely to come my way. I'd done an adaptation of *Great Expectations* before the war and this had been seen by David Lean and Ronald Neame. I went into the Navy during the war, and when I came out they were preparing their film of *Great Expectations*. They remembered my performance on the stage and asked me if I'd go into their film as Herbert Pocket. I thought of film as a much greater mystery than the theatre and I felt a need to begin in films with a character I knew something about.

You came into British cinema at its absolute peak. Did your involvement with Cineguild and David Lean and Ronald Neame seem exciting at the time?

Cineguild [semi-independent production company under the Rank umbrella] certainly seemed to make very stylish and entertaining films. David Lean and Ronald Neame's films seemed a breath of fresh air in the British film scene. In the films of *Great Expectations* and *Oliver Twist*, they surmounted the difficulties of telling those long complex stories in about two hours each. I think they achieved a great success in telling them so swiftly and stylishly.

To jump forty years, what differences did you feel in filming *Little Dorrit* for Christine Edzard?

One of the main changes is that people have got used to very long entertainments. They feel they're serving the cause of culture if they're sitting on their arses for hours at a stretch. However, with *Little Dorrit*, you knew you were in for some sort of marathon. There was real interest in feeling the difference between a film where you could luxuriate in the leisureliness of the atmosphere, as compared with the tightness of David Lean's story-telling.

Great Expectations was perhaps the first of the great post-war international successes for British films. How would you account for these?

Well, British films at that time *were* a bit classy, not just the Dickens' films, but Lean's other film of that period – *Brief Encounter* – was also a great success. It was an artistic success here and in America, even if not a huge box-office success. There was a sense of a breakthrough into something new. And one mustn't forget the work of Carol Reed.

Valerie Hobson thought David Lean was not a great director of actors at this point, but that he'd been very lucky in his casting of the Dickens' films. Would you agree?

I think they simply cast the films as well as their budgets would permit. They were just concerned to get the best and most suitable people available. And, of course, with Dickens, it helps if you can get actors who do the larger-than-life stuff well, and I think Lean had a lot of people like that.

What did you make of the fact that *Oliver Twist*, in which you starred as Fagin, was initially banned in the US on grounds of 'anti-Semitism'?

I wasn't aware of *Oliver Twist* being banned in the States. But I do remember being at a large party in New York when a sort of doyen of the critics said to me, 'I'd rather give my child a dose of prussic acid than let her see this film'. In Austria, a Russian military audience walked out in bulk in protest against *Oliver Twist* as an anti-Semitic film, which is ironic when you reflect on their bad record for anti-Semitism.

Rank wanted Fagin played as a straight character; he

Alec Guinness and John Mills in *Great Expectations*, 1946

wasn't interested in the descriptions in the book or in the original illustrations. I wanted to copy the illustrations and, as far as I know, my interpretation caused no disturbance in this country. We all fell over backwards so that the film wouldn't be thought of as anti-Semitic. The word 'Jew' isn't used in the film. My chief personal recollection of playing Fagin was the business of the make-up. I had to be at the studio (Pinewood) by 6.30 a.m. every day because the make-up took three hours to apply, and filming would start between 9 a.m. and 9.30 a.m.

Apart from Cineguild, your other crucial film connection of the 40s (and 50s) was with Ealing. What was it like to work there?

I suppose you could say it had a cosy atmosphere in many ways. It was smallish, modestly and pleasantly run, and turned out good things. Balcon had a bunch of young directors who were seen as up-and-coming, and they were always consulting with each other. There were innumerable meetings when a new film was mooted. The Ealing films were tasteful, perhaps in some ways too much so. Their posters were something quite new, much more elegant than film posters usually were and some people didn't care for this. Now, of course, they're collectors' items.

Kind Hearts and Coronets **still seems the blackest and funniest of the Ealing comedies. What attracted you to it most?**

The script reached me in France where I was on holiday. I read two pages and burst out laughing. I'd been offered two parts (I mean, to play both), I read this extremely stylish script, and sent off a telegram asking if I could play all eight of these characters [the Ascoygne family] if they hadn't already been cast. Well, the director and others were intrigued by the idea and that's how it came about. I think it was a great example of *comédie noire*.

You described its director, Robert Hamer, in your autobiography as your 'very good friend' who 'spoke the same language'. What were his special qualities as a director?

Hamer was a man of great sensitivity and wit, and he had a fine sense of style, though he was not perhaps a very brilliant technical director. He disliked close-ups, he liked distancing things, and he was very good and appreciative with actors. He could see what actors were trying to do and he encouraged them in the working out of their own performances. He was a very intelligent

man and I was very fond of him.

Am I right in thinking that the 'one rather awful' and 'one quite dreadful' films you did for him were, respectively, *The Scapegoat* **and** *To Paris with Love***?**

There was a lot of script trouble on *The Scapegoat*, and they brought in Gore Vidal and Kenneth Tynan, others perhaps, to try to fix it up. Hamer was certainly drinking and a bit unreliable by this time, but in the final cutting they chopped the story around and made utter nonsense of it. It was a good story at first but it had nothing to do with Daphne Du Maurier's conception. To make sense of the plot, the Bette Davis character should have been much more austere. But she spat out her lines and she, or someone else, insisted on her being all 'flounced up' instead of the severe woman she should have been.

As for *To Paris with Love*, it was a case of a totally wrong director. The original American script for it wasn't bad and I hoped that Hamer would make it sharper, more European. However, he had a miserable drink problem by this time, and, really, the film needed someone brasher, more extrovert to deal with it.

In 1951 you made two of Ealing's flagship comedies, *The Lavender Hill Mob* **and** *The Man in the White Suit***. What was the secret of their success?**

Perhaps there was something liberating in the idea that everything is going to be all right, that there's a chance for ordinary people to break out. I suppose they're intelligent nonsense. I think *The Man in the White Suit* is an absolutely terrific film. It's very sad that Sandy [Alexander] Mackendrick gave up and went to Hollywood. He was always intelligent, always had something to say. Now *The Man in the White Suit* is a minor classic, but I remember the headline in the *Observer* (I think) at the time: 'Ignoble film'. It had been quite misinterpreted by the critic who'd expected nothing but joyful laughter. *The Lavender Hill Mob* is a very good-natured film with a well-told story. Charlie Crichton had a very good eye for cutting, and a feeling for the idea of getting away from drab reality into a world of fancy.

What distinctions do you make among the Ealing directors?

Hamer had an amused, cynical view of things; Mackendrick was an enthusiast, who took a strong political line; I never got to know Crichton well; [Charles] Frend was a chum: he was always very worried, a charming man, but not all that good a director. I did *Barnacle Bill* for Frend, out of friendship for him (not usually a good idea in film) and it was a mistake. I would have been happy to do it as a diatribe against the sloppiness of British life, not just as a jolly comedy which is how it emerged.

I wonder what you remember of *Last Holiday*, *The Card*, and *The Captain's Paradise*, three engaging, non-Ealing films of the period.
Priestley's script for *Last Holiday* was very good in a simple, straightforward way, but the film was not very well directed. It was efficient enough and the final effect was quite pleasing, but it could have had more punch. It turns up on TV quite often and I'm interested in how films like it, from this period, are often much more appreciated than they were at the time.

I never felt I was the right actor to play Dendry in *The Card*. They should have had someone more obviously tougher. I think I treated it too lightly and I have never been happy playing parts too like myself.

The Captain's Paradise had a nice script and was very enjoyable to make, especially the experience of working with Celia Johnson. I also enjoyed working with Tony Kimmins who was a very easy-going director. Rex Harrison told me that the part had originally been offered to him and I'm sure he would have been more suitable. I suppose Yvonne de Carlo was cast to boost the American sales.

Is *Bridge on the River Kwai* an early example of the internationalisation of British films?
I suppose so, considering that Sam Spiegel was its producer. The original script was ridiculous, with elephant charges and girls screaming round in the jungle. When David Lean arrived, with a new screen writer, it became a very different thing. I saw Nicholson as an effective part, without ever really believing in the character. However, the film paid off: it was a huge success and I got an Oscar for it, though I don't think it made an enormous difference to my career.

I admire your performance as Jock Sinclair in *Tunes of Glory*. How do you regard it among your work?
As it turned out, I was very pleased with it. Initially, I'd been offered the John Mills character, but I made the wild suggestion that I should play the hard-drinking, hard-swearing man. The impossible appeals to me more than the obvious. I thought it was a very good script, with excellent dialogue and character.

What are your impressions of working with Carol Reed on *Our Man in Havana*? And how involved was Graham Greene?
As I remember, Graham Greene was around for some of the time in Cuba, but I didn't enjoy doing the film very much. I didn't get on awfully well with Carol Reed. When you arrived on the set, you found everything had been worked out to the finest detail. Also I thought there was a big tactical error in the Cuban boy-and-girl romance and there was a lot of strange angling of the camera. The story wasn't told in the simple way that it should have been. I like to find something in a part that I can contribute each day and I felt Reed was inclined to over-direct. He rather threw me when he said early on, 'We don't want any of your character acting'. I felt my concept of the character – not filmed – was closer to Greene's.

I never liked playing myself. It's important for me to get some hook to hang my character on. I want to know what I should look like. If I'm frustrated in this, I worry that I won't get to know what's inside. I'm a practical man as far as my work is concerned.

How would you respond to criticisms that British cinema has been too literary, too class-bound, too tied to the theatre?
It certainly has been too literary, but I must say it is refreshing to read a script that is well-written. As for it being too tied to the theatre, there have been films of stage successes in the past which led to a great deal of staginess on film. But I do think there was a break away from this during the time of Reed and Lean who'd seek to tell a story more visually. I think the theatre connection often made British films seem very talkative. About the 'class-bound' criticism, I'd say one gets just as weary of seeing working-class types on the screen as one did of upper-class ones. In the time that you're talking about, films were about people who *did* have servants who were often comic when they weren't pathetic. In terms of changes in film, there was a whole batch of socially refreshing films at the end of the 50s.

Guy Hamilton

The Ringer, (1952), *The Intruder* (1953), *An Inspector Calls* (1954), *The Colditz Story* (1955), *Charley Moon* (1956), *Manuela* (1957), *The Devil's Disciple*, *A Touch of Larceny* (1959), *The Best of Enemies* (1961), *The Party's Over* (1963), *Man in the Middle*, *Goldfinger* (1964), *Funeral in Berlin* (1966), *The Battle of Britain* (1968), *Diamonds are Forever* (1971), *Live and Let Die* (1973), *The Man With the Golden Gun* (1974), *Force 10 from Navarone* (1978), *The Mirror Crack'd* (1980), *Evil Under the Sun* (1982), *Remo Williams: The Adventure Begins* (1985).

Unlike many British directors of the period, Guy Hamilton was never a screenwriter, or cameraman, or editor, before turning to direction. He had always wanted to direct and, along the way to achieving this goal in 1952, he became the most sought-after assistant director in the business. When he did begin to direct, he turned out a string of highly entertaining, carefully crafted films in a range of popular genres. His first, *The Ringer*, derived from Edgar Wallace, showed a great deal of unpretentiously deployed craftsmanship and makes excellent use of a strong cast. He had three varied successes with his next films: *The Intruder*, an intelligent version of Robin Maugham's novel of post-war malaise; *An Inspector Calls*, which gave new life to Priestley's morality play; and the very popular POW film, *The Colditz Story*. And *Manuela* is an erotic melodrama of a kind unusual in British cinema, with a remarkable performance from Trevor Howard as the obsessed sea captain. There is a real gift for narrative and an unobtrusive sophistication at work in the best of Guy Hamilton's films.

Interview date: July 1990.

You made some of the most entertaining British films of the 1950s. How did you arrive at that phase of your career?

When I came out of the Navy in one piece, I knew what I wanted to do. Having been lucky enough to work for Carol Reed who really was my 'father' as a director I became a third and then a second assistant director. I learned a lot from Carol Reed, working on films such as *The Fallen Idol* and *The Third Man*, and for John Huston on *The African Queen*. It was a wonderful training. I also learned a lot from *bad* directors.

The trick I discovered was not to be an assistant director, but to be the director's *assistant*. There are certain things the director is not interested in doing and you have to cover for those, while watching very carefully for the things he passionately cares about. In this way you become very valuable to him because you sense his needs. Some of the films I did as assistant director were Launder and Gilliat's *State Secret*, Tony Kimmins'

Mine Own Executioner and Jean Negulesco's *Britannia Mews* (as well she might!).

The problem, then, was how to become a director because there were plenty of directors but not many good assistants. I was under contract to Alexander Korda, a remarkable man, a combination then of British Lion and London Films, but we were taking much too long to make pictures. I said to Korda that I could make a picture in three weeks. There was a series of 'B' pictures being made and that was how I got my first break as a director. My first film, *The Ringer*, took three weeks for rehearsal and shooting.

You had a continuing association with producer Ivan Foxwell.

I got my chance as a director making 'B' pictures but I was looking to make an 'A' picture; I was lucky enough to come across Ivan who had been in the Army and had had a very similar career to my own beforehand. He didn't want to direct and I didn't want to produce, so we made an excellent combination. We took the idea for *The Intruder* to Korda and that was my start. It was a happy experience for both Ivan and myself. We decided to team up again, and I wanted to do *The Colditz Story*, having always been intrigued by POWs and their escape attempts. Ivan had a real knowledge of pictures – I like a hands-on producer – and was willing for us to work closely together.

The Ringer was your first feature film as a director, for which I believe you were contracted to London Films.
That's right. Carol Reed was very instrumental in helping me. He said 'Don't make the picture you want to make; make a comedy thriller. You'll miss some of the thrills, some of the laughs, but with a bit of luck there'll be something left'. So he suggested I make Edgar Wallace's *The Ringer*, which was all on one set and could be done in two weeks. It had been made before as *The Gaunt Stranger*. Our version was a 'B' picture so it went out as bottom of the bill on a double feature; as such it was successful.

Your next two films were also adaptations – *The Intruder* from Robin Maugham's novel *Line on Ginger*, and *An Inspector Calls* from Priestley's play. How do you approach the business of adaptation?
The Intruder was a script that was brought to me in more or less a 'go' situation, subject to Jack Hawkins agreeing to me being the director. There were a lot of pressures, such as 'My goodness, Jack, how can you work with Guy? He's just a new director and you're a big star . . .' and so on. I offered to step aside but I had lunch with Jack one day and it turned out that the actual problem was a small one, to do with the homosexual overtones in the original novel which had been removed from the script. Maugham and his partner, John Hunter, had concocted the screenplay, and structurally there wasn't much of it we had to change.

I didn't really want to do my next picture *An Inspector Calls* because I'd discovered *Dial M for Murder* and I wanted to do that. It was, however, ultimately sold to Hitchcock. And, as a contract director, I had to do the Priestley play instead. I was happy doing it; I had a nice cast and it was fun doing vintage Priestley. I was left very much alone because A.D. Peters and Norman Collins were not hands-on producers. There's something about that play that undoubtedly works. I considered

myself as the handmaiden of Priestley, for whom I had an admiration, and I tried to be honest to his play. The girl, played by Jane Wenham, doesn't actually appear in the play; she's just talked about.

From the point of view of adaptation *A Touch of Larceny* was the very opposite to *An Inspector Calls*. *A Touch of Larceny* was a thriller which was written very seriously and which I thought was utter rubbish but, turned around, was terribly funny. I asked Ivan if I could make it as a comedy; he saw the point and off we went, working with Roger MacDougall who was a lovely writer. In that case we showed little respect for the novel. I adored working with Vera Miles, a very underrated acress, on that. Again I had a very strong cast – James Mason, George Sanders, Harry Andrews and so on. Of that period, it is definitely my favourite film.

The Intruder is one of a small group of films which seemed to be reappraising post-war British life. Did you see it that way?
It came not so long after we were all demobbed and I felt very much at ease with all the characters, because I'd met them all in one form or another during the war. Lindsay Anderson came up to me not long after the film was released, and said, 'You've let the side down'. He meant that the burglar rejoined the Establishment when he really should have turned on the Colonel.

Elsa Martinelli and Trevor Howard in Guy Hamilton's Manuela, 1957

You then did _The Colditz Story_. Unlike many British directors of the period, you didn't make many war films. Was this your choice?

Yes. After _The Colditz Story_, which was my personal baby, I felt a bit too closely involved to do war films. I had too much admiration for certain things and hated a lot of war films which seemed to me too facile and not dealing in any way with the truth, so I steered well clear of them. Eric Portman and John Mills were the backbone of _The Colditz Story_, all the rest were basically new boys. It was Lionel Jeffries' first film and Ian Carmichael wasn't a well-known screen actor then.

Was the business with the geranium a sort of quotation from _La Grande Illusion_? Or the first meeting between the opposing officers?

As a small boy I had been greatly smitten with _La Grande Illusion_ and you can't avoid recalling things you've admired. But I was really more influenced by Pat Reid who was in Colditz and wrote the book the film was based on. I also enjoyed doing those scenes in Polish and French because, having already explained to the audience beforehand that a Polish soldier is to be court-martialled, then doing the scene in Polish without subtitles, it works very well as a touch of realism.

The real importance of _The Colditz Story_, apart from its being a big success, was that it was essentially a comedy about something that, up until that point, you could not make fun of – POWs. I was absolutely determined to show that Colditz was exceptional _and_ could be very funny – and it worked.

How did your collaboration on the screenplay, with William Douglas Home and Ivan Foxwell, work?

Essentially, Ivan and I supplied the structure and Willy, who was a playwright, supplied the dialogue. He had been a distinguished officer himself and had a fine dry humour; he had been in an officers' camp and was able to supply the right humour and the right dialogue.

How would you react to my idea that Trevor Howard in _Manuela_ gives the best performance in a Guy Hamilton film?

That's for other people to judge. It was a very personal film. Ivan and I were at the height of our powers, very cocky. I enjoyed working in black-and-white, enjoyed Trevor, enjoyed the whole thing. It was my first taste of real melodrama. For a British film I think the film is unusually direct about the destructive power of sexu-ality; until then, sex in British films had been mostly very well-behaved. _Manuela_'s a very French film in mood. It was probably influenced a little by all the films I'd seen in my childhood in France (and shouldn't have seen, because of my age). It rather shook the critics and the public. It was fairly strong meat and had the Censors right on edge. Otto Heller was the cameraman. I chose him because I always liked his black-and-white work. I pushed him a little bit, but then gave him a free hand and he did a lovely job.

How was your next film, _The Devil's Disciple_ set up?

Sandy Mackendrick had just made that marvellous picture, _Sweet Smell of Success_ for Hecht-Hill-Lancaster in the US, and they'd come over to make _The Devil's Disciple_ with Sandy directing. The grosses of _Sweet Smell of Success_ were very disappointing and Burt Lancaster and Kirk Douglas started to niggle, so they fired Sandy who had been shooting for about three weeks. MCA who were my agents told me they wanted me to take over. I refused to take over from Sandy and was given a stern lecture to the effect that I would never be a serious director until I had worked with some international stars . . . Someone would have to direct the picture so it might as well be me . . . So, in the event, I did it.

The terrifying thing was that I found it so easy to be a 'traffic cop' with no 'gut' in the project. I'd never done this before and won't do it again. All you can do is follow the blueprint. How did I find working with such 'heady talents? Both 'made love' to me and I could see, straight away, that whichever way I came down I was going to make an enemy for life. So I said, 'Don't ask me, fellows, because, if it was my picture, Kirk would be playing Burt's part and vice versa'. There was a stunned silence and for the rest of the day they were in corners, looking through the script at the other's part! That kept them apart and off my back for the rest of the picture.

Eva le Gallienne was in the film and she'd only made two or three pictures. She was a very distinguished lady, and I don't think she terribly approved of these two clowns who were not my favourite people at that time (and I'm sure they said the same of me). Burt I found irritating because he'd say things like, 'What did George Bern_ard_ Shaw mean in this scene? I think we're missing some of the kinetic values', and he'd go on and on. Then you'd pick him up and say, 'Burt, I think we're losing some of the kinetic values', and he'd say, 'Ah, shit, kid, it's only a _movie!_'

Sir Anthony Havelock-Allan

As producer only, except where otherwise indicated:
Badger's Green (1934), *Love at Sea, Murder by Rope, The Scarab Murder Case* (1936), *Cross My Heart, Cavalier of the Streets, Missing—Believed Married, Lancashire Luck, The Fatal Hour, Holiday's End, The Last Curtain, Mr Smith Carries On, Museum Mystery, Night Ride* (1937), *Incident in Shanghai, Lightning Conductor, A Spot of Bother, This Man is News* (1938), *The Lambeth Walk, The Silent Battle, Stolen Life* (assoc pr), *This Man in Paris* (1939), *From the Four Corners* (+ dir) (1941), *In Which We Serve* (assoc pr) (1942), *This Happy Breed* (co-pr) (1944), *Blithe Spirit* (+ co-sc), *Brief Encounter* (1945), *Great Expectations* (+ co-sc) (1946), *Take My Life* (1947), *Blanche Fury, Oliver Twist* (exec pr), *The Small Voice* (1948), *The Interrupted Journey* (1949), *Never Take No for an Answer* (1951), *Meet Me Tonight* (1952), *The Young Lovers* (1954), *Orders to Kill* (1958), *The Quare Fellow* (1962), *An Evening with the Royal Ballet* (+ co-dir), *Othello* (co-prod) (1966), *The Mikado* (co-prod), *Up The Junction* (co-prod) (1967), *Romeo and Juliet* (co-prod) (1968), *Ryan's Daughter*, 1970.

The name of Anthony Havelock-Allan is most firmly associated with the critical and commercial triumphs of the Two Cities and Cineguild production companies from 1942-8 – that is, with filming the works of Noel Coward and Charles Dickens, from *In Which We Serve* to *Oliver Twist* in the major period of prestige in British cinema. However, Havelock-Allan had already produced more than twenty films in the 1930s, chiefly for Paramount British. If most of these films were 'quota quickies', they also nurtured many talents which would find their place in the story in the ensuing decades. He entered 'A' film production with *This Man is News*, and thereafter was one of the most influential producers in British films. His recollections of the Coward and the Dickens films valuably complement those of other surviving collaborators. He should also be remembered for two films he made starring his then-wife Valerie Hobson: the sombre, sensual melodrama, *Blanche Fury*, which looks remarkably fine today, and the tense home-under-seige thriller, *The Small Voice*, which introduced Howard Keel to the screen.

Interview date: June 1990.

After a very busy producing schedule in the 30s, you began the 40s by directing and producing *From the Four Corners*, a documentary. What was it about?

It was a propaganda film, a three-reeler and it had Leslie Howard, an Australian, a Canadian and a New Zealander. Leslie met them in Trafalgar Square and began to explain what relevance various things in London had to Australia, New Zealand and Canada; he explained the historical significance of various English places and monuments. It was sponsored by the Ministry of Information.

I would like to know about your involvement with Two Cities and Cineguild, starting from *In Which We Serve*.

Del Giudice was sent off to an internment camp at the beginning of the war, but, for the good reason that he was a staunch anti-Fascist, he was later released. He found two backers, Major Arthur Sassoon and Colonel Crosfield, and said he wanted to make a big propaganda film, and that he wanted to approach Noel Coward. I had met Noel, so Del and I went to see him and asked him if he would write a story, like, perhaps, his *Cavalcade*. He said he would think about it.

Two weeks later Noel rang to say that he had an idea for a big propaganda film. He had dined with Lord Louis Mountbatten who had told him the story of HMS *Kelly*, the destroyer of which he had been captain. Del got the money for the film, I was to produce, and I suggested that David Lean was the best possible person to act as technical director; he was a great editor with a great story-telling sense on film. Noel said he wanted Ronnie Neame as cameraman, so we all met and Noel agreed to do the script.

Three months later Noel produced a script, which would have taken eight-to-ten hours on the screen. It started some time before the war, in the Caribbean, then went to the China Station before the war, then there were some scenes in the Café de Paris with some socialites – all long before anything happened to do with the war! When we explained that it was too long, Noel told us to take it away and do something with it. We decided simply to tell the story of one ship, the *Kelly*, from the laying of its keel to its 'death' off Crete. We came back to Noel with it and he approved our story line. Mountbatten was involved and got for us all the help we needed.

When we came to discuss who would play the part of the Captain, Noel said *he* would. I didn't think that was very good casting, and Del Giudice told him this; Noel, however, said 'He's perfectly right, I'm not, but I want to play it and Tony's going to produce it!'. So we went on from there and, in fact, Noel gave an excellent performance, even though he was not anyone's idea of a 'sea dog'. The commissioning speech, the speech to the survivors in Alexandria, was almost word-for-word Mountbatten's own.

We then did *This Happy Breed*, turning the play into a screenplay; when new dialogue was required Noel wrote it. By that time I had come to the conclusion that all of us ought to be getting on to the bandwagon which was just starting; Arthur Rank thought it was fair that directors and producers should have a percentage of any profits that their films made, which was a new idea. He was a splendid influence on the business; one has only to think of the films he made possible, and the opportunities he gave to independent producers – Powell and Pressburger, Launder and Gilliat and ourselves – some of whose films were for all time.

In Which We Serve offers an interesting reflection on the class situation in Britain at the time. Do you think British cinema has been too middle-class for wide acceptance?
When you think of it, the few British films that have been international successes operate on that basis. *A Matter of Life and Death* was about the officer class – nobody in Heaven talked with Cockney accents, all the angels were clearly upper-class! The divisions in the Dickens films are absolute, because Dickens wrote in the framework of a class system which was far more marked in his day than in ours.

Brief Encounter is about a couple of middle-class people and it seems to work everywhere, including America. Noel almost invariably wrote about the upper classes or, if he wrote about the lower classes, always did so from an upper-class point of view. Funnily enough, the one thing that David Lean would have changed in *Brief Encounter* if he had had the chance was the comic scenes with Joyce Carey and Stanley Holloway, the 'lower orders'. But Noel was an extremely skilful theatre writer and he knew that the story would have been intolerably sad without those scenes. They provided some relief from the central situation which was building up to be increasingly painful, both for the audience and for the two principals for whom the audience feels deep sympathy.

Your next three films were all based on Coward plays: This Happy Breed, Blithe Spirit, and Brief Encounter. How did this trio come about?
After *In Which We Serve*, there was still a desire to have some kind of propaganda edge to whatever we made. Noel had written *This Happy Breed* which had run in London and it was, in a way, a piece of propaganda for the British people, for their stoicism, the humour and so on, so we decided it would make a good film.

After *This Happy Breed* Noel gave us *Blithe Spirit*, a tremendous plum of a play that had run for two or three years in London and New York, and had toured all over America. Noel stipulated who was to play in it and because of that we were in a straitjacket on casting. The point of the play is a middle-aged man well into his second marriage, having long ago put away the follies of his youth with his sexy first wife, and suddenly being 'woken up' by her reappearance as a ghost. Rex Harrison was not middle-aged; and Kay Hammond, though a brilliant stage actress, didn't photograph well and also had a very slow delivery, which was difficult in films.

When we started shooting scenes with Kay and Rex it became obvious that Constance Cummings [the second wife] looked more attractive to the average man in the street than Kay. This upset the whole play. The other thing was that Noel didn't want us to 'open it up' too much; in fact we played forty-eight minutes in one room; all in all, the film was a failure. Better casting would have been Cecil Parker the actor who played it on stage after Noel. Margaret Rutherford, who drove Noel mad in the theatre because she never gave the same performance two nights running, was wonderful in it. I saw five other women playing the part, none of whom was in the same street when it came to getting legitimate laughs.

Celia Johnson and Trevor Howard in *Brief Encounter*, 1945

When we finished *Blithe Spirit* we didn't know what to do, because David Lean wasn't keen on directing comedy. Noel suggested there might be something in the *Tonight at 8.30* plays, so we read them all, and the only one we could see expanding into a film was 'Still Life'. We decided to have a go at it, did a rough script and Noel supplied the new dialogue we needed; the play had been a half-hour play and the film, now called *Brief Encounter*, was to be an hour-and-a-half, so we needed more visuals and more words. At one stage during *Brief Encounter*, Noel was in India with an entertainment troupe; we managed to get cables through to him saying that we needed thirty seconds of dialogue for the scene in the boat and we got a cable back giving us two lines of dialogue, saying, 'This runs forty-eight seconds; if you

want to shorten it, take out the following words . . .'!

Then David didn't want to do any more Coward films. He wanted to do *Great Expectations* because he had seen a production of it in the Rudolph Steiner Hall in which Alec Guinness had played Herbert Pocket. He had been very impressed by the book and the story and by Alec. I still think it is the finest of all the Dickens adaptations ever made.

What do you remember of the relative involvement of David Lean, Ronald Neame, Kay Walsh, Cecil McGivern and yourself in the screenplay?

David, Ronald and I wrote the screenplay and the other two provided additional dialogue; the three of us did all the first draft screenplays up to *Oliver Twist*. We would do the draft and then David would do a final shooting script from it; somehow it worked for the three of us to combine in that way. Kay was very good at dialogue, too, particularly when we hadn't written enough 'Dickens' dialogue. The same with Cecil, who worked most on a film we didn't eventually make, unfortunately – Margaret Irwin's book *The Gay Galliard* about Bothwell and Mary Queen of Scots. I think we chose well what to use and it worked.

How closely were you involved as co-producer with the art director John Bryan?

He did one lovely job for me on a film that didn't work, but looks very beautiful and stands up quite well, *Blanche Fury*. John Bryan was Art Director on that and also on *Oliver Twist* and *Great Expectations*. He worked closely with all of us – myself, David Lean and Guy Green the cameraman.

Cineguild's next venture with Dickens was *Oliver Twist* . . .

After we did the first script and preliminary casting, I didn't have much to do with *Oliver Twist*. By that time I ' wanted to make *Blanche Fury* and I thought Stewart Granger would make a very good villain rather than a romantic hero; I also wanted to do something with Valerie [Hobson].

The basis to the story of *Blanche Fury*, and its most exciting aspect, is the murder apparently committed by a gypsy woman, prefiguring *Psycho* because, in fact, it isn't a woman at all. Stewart Granger refused to play it dressed as a woman, even though we would only have seen a flash of him, so it lost that high-point scene. The director, Marc Allegret, made some splendid films before the war but did not have such success afterwards.

We took far too long over *Blanche Fury*. It cost too much money, it didn't 'work', and never attracted any great audience. David and Ronnie didn't like what I was trying to do with the film, which was along the lines of the very successful costume films from Gainsborough. I wanted to make a serious film with a better story and I thought it would make a lot of money. I found out that what I was making was a 'hard', not a 'soft' film which the others were. There was real hatred in it, as well as love, and the public didn't want it. Cineguild more or less broke up over that film.

I then formed a company called Constellation Films and made a film in Italy that was called *Shadow of the Eagle* in Britain. It looked nice, had beautiful sets, but again I wasn't pleased with it. When I came back to England we made *The Small Voice* with Howard Keel. This got very good notices, was very well received, but it didn't make much money. Our director was Fergus McDonell who was an editor for Carol Reed. Carol had suggested I give him a chance to direct. I nursed him through the film and he obviously had talent, but he was so highly strung that he could very easily have had a nervous breakdown. He went to Canada afterwards and did well in the documentary field.

Your last two films of this period were directed by Anthony [Puffin] Asquith – *The Young Lovers* and *Orders to Kill*. How would you rate him among British directors?

Puffin was never quite a great director – perhaps not ruthless enough – but he was a very very good one. I think if he'd had enough of the right material, such as several like *The Importance of Being Earnest*, it would have made a difference.

For *The Young Lovers*, I had wanted Mark Robson to direct, Jimmy Stewart to star and a very good European actress whom I intended to find. The Rank Organisation wanted me to use a young American, David Knight. Puffin was the wrong director for the film; it should have been made in that stark, realistic style that the Americans are so good at, but the Rank Organisation wanted to use Puffin. I hadn't made a film for some time and was getting lazy, so I agreed to do what Rank wanted. It was a perfectly good film, but it lacked guts; it didn't have the hard edge it needed. It was intended as a blast against McCarthyism, and was written by a noted anti-Fascist.

The next film was a story which Puffin had found, *Orders to Kill*, which again would have been better with a harder, sharper edge to it. It needed to be conceived more harshly. Both the films I did with Puffin were well-made, well-crafted, but the impact was soft and did not grip a world-wide audience. *Orders to Kill* was a very good story – how hard it is to kill an enemy when you get to know him personally – but the public simply didn't go for it. Puffin had known Lillian Gish, in Hollywood in the 20s and loved her – that's how she came to be in it.

Lancashire Luck (1937), *Pygmalion* (1938), *Major Barbara* (1941), *I Know Where I'm Going* (1945), *To Be a Woman* (voice) (1951), *An Outcast of the Islands* (1952), *Single-handed* (1953), *How to Murder a Rich Uncle* (1957), *Separate Tables* (1958), *Something of Value* (1958), *Sons and Lovers* (1960), *Toys in the Attic* (1963), *A Man for All Seasons* (1966), *David Copperfield* (1969), *Murder on the Orient Express* (1974), *Voyage of the Damned* (1976), *The Cat and the Canary*, (1977), *The Elephant Man* (1980), *Making Love* (1982), *The Lonely Passion of Judith Hearne* (1987).

Wendy Hiller has made only twenty films for the cinema in fifty years, yet few actresses have so secure a place in the history of British cinema. This is no doubt partly due to the marvellously distinctive looks and voice which have made her so instantly recognisable, and partly due to her having been seen in several films of legendary status in British cinema. No one has effaced the impression she made as Eliza Doolittle in Anthony Asquith's film version of *Pygmalion* or in the title role of *Major Barbara* three years later. The third role, which so firmly ensconced her in the affections and memories of film-goers, was that of the spoilt wilful heroine of Michael Powell's Celtic romance, *I Know Where I'm Going*, in which her materialism cracks under the claims of love. But even in less distinguished films she was always memorable: for example, as the girl seduced and abandoned in *Single-handed*, as Mrs Aylmer in Carol Reed's version of Conrad's *Outcast of the Islands* (which she dislikes), and in the Hollywood-made *Separate Tables*, for which her touchingly restrained playing as the hotel manageress won her an Oscar. Like the greatest stars, she is one of a kind; we can only wish that she had made twice as many films as she did.

Interview date: June 1991.

You have had a long and distinguished career in all the acting media: it looks like a brilliantly planned career.

Oh, no, I have to contradict you because, looking back, I can't think how I managed to be so untidy and wayward in the choice of things I did *and* the things I said no to. I suppose I started in films in a way that some people would say (and I think I now agree with them) was really rather bad luck – and that is, to have such an enormous success on your first big film, which I did with *Pygmalion*. It was wonderful in one way, but in a perfect career I would have put myself into a Drama School and acquired a formidable technical armoury, which I never had for either films or the theatre.

Even after I had made *Pygmalion*, *Major Barbara* and *I Know Where I'm Going*, I didn't think of myself as a film actress. I didn't think I ought to go to Hollywood and ought to get a long-term contract. I have been very blessed in being in three or four, perhaps five, films that have had a long life and worn well. This is usually because the director was not mannered in style, and the film is, therefore, acceptable to another generation.

You have had enormous success both in film and on stage. How do you place films in your career?

To take a purely practical attitude, I now find films easier to manage from a domestic point of view. With a play you know when a run is going to start, but you never know when it is going to finish. With a film you have a finishing date and they usually want to get rid of you on that date, because otherwise you'll cost them money. This has its satisfactory side. One thing I still can't get used to, with films and television, is what I call 'pacing' myself. As a stage actress, if you have a month's rehearsal and, perhaps, two weeks of touring, you can pace yourself. When I do a film I learn the whole of the part, of course, so that I know how I'm going to play the last scene, but it still takes me by surprise if they do the next-to-last scene first!

How did you come to make your first film, *Lancashire Luck*, in 1937?

It was a 'quota quickie', made in a fortnight. My husband [Ronald Gow] had written the script and didn't want me to be in it because he thought that would be nepotism. It was directed by Henry Cass who was a friend of ours, and it was altogether a very friendly and cosy affair. I think I played a working man's daughter who fell in love with the character played by George Galleon, a tall handsome creature and a dear boy, but I don't think he had a very successful career. George Carney played my father, as he did in *I Know Where I'm Going* – he was Lancashire as I am.

And then came *Pygmalion*?

George Bernard Shaw had seen me in my husband's play, *Love on the Dole*, at the Garrick Theatre, the first play I did in London. Then I played *St Joan* and *Pygmalion* at the Malvern Festival to celebrate Shaw's eightieth birthday, and he insisted I should play Eliza when the film was to be made by Gabby Pascal. I don't think Gabby wanted me and certainly the backers didn't, not knowing me from a bar of soap. I didn't want a long-term contract and fought against that.

I made *Pygmalion* in about eight weeks, with that very much-to-be-admired director Anthony Asquith. His straightforward classical approach to a classical piece of work is one reason, apart from the Cinderella story, for the film's success. He shared the director's credit with Leslie Howard. I don't mean to denigrate Leslie but, as one who was in practically every day's shooting, I can say with confidence that I wouldn't have known Leslie was co-directing until the day we were shooting the tea-party scene. Then, Leslie suddenly said, 'She can't play it like that. That won't work'. I didn't have the courage to say, 'Well, Mr Howard, I've played it this way with audiences and it brings the house down'. So I rushed to my dressing-room in floods of tears. That dear actor who played my father, Wilfred Lawson came in, listened to me snuffling, then just said in a very soothing voice, 'Take no bloody notice of them. Play it the way you know', and walked out! Poor Leslie must have been warned to leave me alone or they'd never get on.

I was so swollen with weeping that it would cost them

money! So we got on with it.

Why was Shaw so attracted to Gabriel Pascal?

Well, he was a beguiling creature and GBS and Mrs Shaw, being the kind of people they were, were entranced by this Hungarian. Hollywood people had been after the rights to *Pygmalion*, but, in Gabby, Shaw had someone who said he had been a distributor, and who was stagestruck and starstruck, although he came to grief when he tried to direct. Gabby had enormous charm and tried to be clever but, unlike Korda, he wasn't a bit clever. He didn't make any money for himself. He was just an old bumbler-on who had great charm, a certain appreciation of good acting, and Shaw.

We ran into problems over *Major Barbara*. We didn't have an experienced director on that – we had Harold French, a charming man who was a stage director with a great gift for directing light comedies. We spent ten months in the studio at Denham making that film. There was a small fighter squadron based there and we used to have a system of spotters. I remember spending one night there when the noise was very worrying. I wrapped my head in a towel, thinking, 'Ronnie Neame will be so cross in the morning if my face is cut!' As though if my feet were cut off it didn't matter!

Ronald Neame was a dear man and he must have been very clever. So was David Lean who edited *Major Barbara* – and directed most of it. And we had that darling actor, Robert Newton, who had trouble with his lines after lunch! He was large, and rude, and outrageous, and lovely.

There is a long gap between those two Shaw films and *I Know Where I'm Going*, some three years later.

Well, there was a war on and I had another baby; also I didn't want to go to Hollywood. If you've played in two Shaw films you're a little bit choosy and the things they asked me to do were not what I was looking for. Michael Powell asked me to be in *Colonel Blimp*, but I couldn't because my son was born. Then he offered me something very strange; then finally he came up with *I Know Where I'm Going* and that lovely actor, Roger Livesey, was dangled before my eyes; I was in love with him before I met him! The location work on Mull was heaven – well no, it wasn't really, because the war was still on and it was pretty hard going. Also Roger wasn't there. He was in a play in London. There was his stand-in and I on Mull, mucking about in boats doing the water scenes for about a month or six weeks. Having said that, a lot of the

Wendy Hiller and Robert Newton in Gabriel Pascal and Harold French's *Major Barbara*, 1941

storm scenes were actually shot in a studio tank.

Why do you think the film has worn so well?
I'm not sure. It's very unsentimental for its time and has a very modern attitude. She's a tough girl and yet is truly swept off her feet. That sort of unsentimental romance is still telling. Also the whole approach was very adult, that materialistic thing. It was also lovely to look at. I remember those beautiful colours up in the Isles.

There are conflicting attitudes towards Michael Powell. What is your feeling about him?
I didn't take to him personally. Emeric Pressburger was charming but Michael Powell was, I would say, rather a strange character. I could never warm to him. We just managed to get on without too much friction and I enjoyed playing with Roger and the rest of the lovely cast. I'm sure Michael Powell is a very good film-maker, but I have never enjoyed his films. *I Know Where I'm Going* is the warmest, most compassionate and likable of

his films and I don't say that just because I was in it. Pressburger, as a European, did very well to capture that legend. The film is very Celtic in its feel and I think Powell owed a great deal to Pressburger in that respect.

I am surprised you didn't film again for six years.
I was bringing up small children and, at that time, didn't have very good health. Then I think I went to New York. One film I never did, but would liked to have done was *The Heiress*, which I played in America with Basil Rathbone. The play was a great success and, for about a month off and on, Willy Wyler was always reported to be in the audience. However, it had been several years since *I Know Where I'm Going*, and people do come and go in films.

What do you recall of working with Carol Reed in *Outcast of the Islands*?
That was very strange. I knew Carol because he had married a very dear friend of mine, Penelope Dudley

Ward, who had played in *Major Barbara*. The film was actually a bit of a hybrid – two of Conrad's novels put together. My character was originally a full-blooded native, but they turned it into me, from Beaconsfield! My daughter in the film, Annabel Morley, should have been a half-caste, so that the story of *Outcast of the Islands* is *her* story. Carol Reed was not an intellectual. He saw life entirely visually through little squares, as did David Lean.

You made another adaptation at the end of the decade, *Sons and Lovers*. When filming a literary classic do you steep yourself in the original work?
No. I knew the Conrad books quite well, but there was no point in going back to them when I found myself cast as I was. It can be a confusion in a way, to go back to the original. I also knew *Sons and Lovers* very well. That should have been a much better film but, again, there were major concessions to Hollywood. It was Jack Cardiff's first film as a director. He was a superb cameraman, but I don't know if he was happy with it as the director. All I know is that Trevor Howard and I got on very well together, and just wanted to get our work over with and get home. Poor Dean Stockwell wanted to be analysing and talking about the inner meaning. We would say rather sceptically, 'There's no time for that. Let's get on with it'. He was a very hard-working young actor but he was out of his depth, his country and his class. It was unkind to him and unkind to the film.

Did you enjoy making the comedy thriller, *How to Murder a Rich Uncle*?
I *thought* I would because I had played with Nigel Patrick in something else and he had said that he was going to direct this film. I thought it would be rather larkish, but it turned out not to be so at all. Nigel Patrick was not as happy as a director as he was as an actor. I never wanted it to be known that I'd been in the film. Then once when I was travelling by train across America, from Hollywood to New York, we drew up at Albuquerque for a couple of hours and on the platform was a large notice saying 'Coming Next Week – *How to Murder a Rich Uncle*'. I thought, I've made Albuquerque and didn't know whether to be pleased or not!

In 1958 you filmed that very English play, *Separate Tables*, in America.
We were all English except Burt [Lancaster] and dear Rita Hayworth. She made a jolly good stab at the film, and she was a lovely creature. I have never been large, but Rita was so delicately boned she made me feel like a camel! It was, as your question suggests, a bizarre idea to transport all that was so English to Hollywood, but it was a very good film. I won an Oscar for it, but then my character was always the best part in the play.

Valerie Hobson

Eyes of Fate (1933), *Two Hearts in Waltz Time*, *The Path of Glory*, *Badger's Green*, *Strange Wives*, *Great Expectations* (US) (1934), *Oh What a Night*, *Rendezvous at Midnight*, *Werewolf of London*, *Bride of Frankenstein*, *The Mystery of Edwin Drood*, *Chinatown Squad*, *The Great Impersonation* (1935), *August Weekend*, *Tugboat Princess*, *The Secret of Stamboul*, *No Escape/No Exit* (1936), *Jump for Glory* (1937), *The Drum*, *Q Planes*, *This Man is News* (1938), *This Man in Paris*, *The Spy in Black*, *The Silent Battle* (1939), *Contraband* (1940), *Atlantic Ferry* (1941), *Unpublished Story* (1942), *The Adventures of Tartu* (1943), *The Years Between*, *Great Expectations* (1946), *Blanche Fury* (1947), *The Small Voice* (1948), *Kind Hearts and Coronets*, *Train of Events*, *The Interrupted Journey*, *The Rocking Horse Winner* (1949), *The Card* (1951), *Who Goes There?*, *Meet Me Tonight*, *The Voice of Merrill* (1952), *Background*, *Knave of Hearts* (1954).

Valerie Hobson's early retirement robbed the British cinema of one of its most stylish leading ladies. After a busy apprenticeship in Hollywood in her late 'teens, she returned to England in 1936 and made a rapid ascent to stardom in Korda's *The Drum* and three good-humoured thrillers, *Q Planes*, *This Man is News* and *This Man in Paris*.

The latter two films established what has always seemed to me her forte – sophisticated comedy for which her elegant touch so well suited her. Her finest opportunity in this vein was *Kind Hearts and Coronets*, in which her lady-like poise so brilliantly off-sets Joan Greenwood's bitchy opportunism. She was also an enterprising heroine in the adventure films she did for her favourite director Michael Powell, *The Spy in Black* and *Contraband*. She is superb as the extravagant selfish mother in *The Rocking Horse Winner*; and shows real sensuality and intensity in her performance as the eponymous heroine in that under-rated melodrama, *Blanche Fury*.

The body of her work stands up very well to the scrutiny of forty years on.

Interview date: July 1990.

I particularly admire your work in comedy. Do you recall two comedy thrillers called *This Man is News* and *This Man in Paris*, with Barry K. Barnes?

I especially remember them because while making them I met and fell in love with my first husband, Anthony Havelock-Allan. *This Man is News* had an extraordinary success. As a nation, we hadn't made a high comedy successfully until then. It was a low-priced film, shot very quickly, and made along the lines of the William Powell-Myrna Loy films. When they put it on at the Plaza, there were literally queues around the block to see it.

Yes, I liked comedy which I found more of a challenge than drama, but I played more drama, mostly costume drama. I felt happiest in high comedy, though this is harder to play on film than on stage because you don't have audience response, and it requires very careful timing.

I did two high comedies with Alec Guinness, *Kind Hearts and Coronets* and *The Card*, which were, I think, two of the most elegant British comedies made. I have always thought that the main reason for the success of *Kind Hearts and Coronets* was that it was played absolutely dead straight, very seriously. It's a matter of being aware that you are playing a funny situation, yet playing it so straight that even the tongue-in-the-cheek doesn't show. Robert Hamer, the director, a genius who died sadly young, was a very sophisticated man. To play something that requires sophisticated handling, you cannot have a naive director.

In Kind Hearts and Coronets, the whole idea of the Gascoyne family was so absurd that, if it hadn't been handled with the most delicate gloves, people would have walked out. As it is, I think it is an important film which will stand the test of time. It was very well cast and, of course, Alec Guinness was miraculous. He doesn't have the obvious greatness of an Olivier; instead he has the most subtle integrity, and is a wonderful film actor, doing the tiniest things to great effect. I think they were very clever to cast two such contrasting types as Joan Greenwood and myself as the women, and Dennis Price was marvellously 'lacy' as the murderer.

What do you remember of *The Card*, directed by Ronald Neame, and *Who Goes There?* for Anthony Kimmins?

The Countess in *The Card* was a charming but dull character, exactly as Arnold Bennett would have seen a woman of that class at that time. The female characters are very well contrasted, again, one so nice and charming, the other [Glynis Johns] so naughty and flirtatious – rather like the Joan Greenwood character in *Kind Hearts and Coronets*. The fact that they were both physically very small women seemed good casting. *Who Goes There?* was from a stage play, but I hadn't been in it. Nigel Patrick was an actor with an excellent comedy touch, perhaps slightly heavier than others but always sure. Comedy playing is very much a matter of being a couple, even more so than playing romantic leads; in a comedy you *have* to work well with your opposite number.

To backtrack, was it your two Michael Powell films, *The Spy in Black* and *Contraband*, which firmly established you as a star?

Probably yes; they were almost the first films we made at the beginning of the war and, if they were successful, then you couldn't help being successful, too. But I'm not sure if it was not the film before those two that set the seal: under Korda's umbrella, I had made *Q Planes*. This had two such rare actors in it, Olivier and Richardson, even though Olivier was nothing like the major star he was to become after *Henry V*. He didn't have a light comedy touch in those days; he was more of a straightforward romantic actor. Ralph Richardson was hardly known in films, but was magnetic.

I hear such diverse views about working with Michael Powell. What is your view of him?

Mick tried so many different things! He was a very clever man, almost a genius, and he *loved* cinematography. Emeric Pressburger and he were so closely associated they were like two bookends together. I know some people found working with Mick not such a happy experience, but he was easily my favourite director of all. He was very sharp and energetic, and his mind was like a brilliant butterfly, flitting all over the place. He was given to fits of tremendous bad temper which one knew perfectly well weren't genuine and would be immediately forgotten. He could be very sarcastic about someone's performance to try and get the best out of them; that usually has the effect of shrivelling one up, but not so with him, because it was not done from unkindness or bad temper. Alas, I only made two pictures for him, but we remained close friends until he died. Connie Veidt was in both those films and you couldn't enjoy working with an actor more. He had a riveting screen presence and yet he was not really a great actor; this is rather like some American stars who have the right physique and an amazing talent for the camera without being very interested in acting.

To move on to *Great Expectations*, what did you think of the change to a rather upbeat ending?

I didn't really have any thoughts about it. My only feeling was that anything was now possible for two young people going from the darkness into the light, away from all the nonsense and evil that had gone on over the years. I think the audience felt that way about it, too.

In 1935 I was too young to play Estella in Hollywood, but I played Estella *and* Molly in David Lean's 1946 film. In Hollywood I think I was more impressed with the sense of being in the film version of a classic; I was closer then to the reading of Dickens. The enormous attention to detail you find in the Lean version was the chief difference I found between how England approaches the classics and how it was done in America.

My only sense of relating to the original was in terms of the Victorian style, and I think this comes out in the film. In this case, at least, I think we had a perfect script – and that's all you can ask of any film whether or not it's an adaptation. You have to assume people haven't read the book. I didn't go back to the book much in 1946, but David and Tony worked very closely from it. Things were pulled out of the book and pruned, getting down to essentials.

We knew we were in a very rare film. In the immediate post-war period there was a feeling of an end and a new beginning – a tremendous feeling of a Renaissance, of a burgeoning of all the talent that had been squashed in by money restraint during the war. We had virtually *carte blanche* as far as money was concerned. I know more about this aspect than I normally would have done because I was then married to Tony Havelock-Allan who was the producer.

What do you remember about David Lean's direction?

I felt he stressed the intimacy of the story, so that it seemed enormously domestic. But I think he improved later as a director of actors. He was always a great technician - a great cutter and editor, which is how he started, but not a great director of actors – then. I didn't feel easy working with him though I was very fond of him as a friend. When he would have forty takes for a shot, it wasn't so much for perfection as for uncertainty, and, as often as not, he'd print the third or fourth take. He was one of the world's brilliant directors, but a devil on the set. Don't forget I'm speaking of over forty-five years ago! He was a charismatic person and actors were mesmerised by him; but he was lucky that the cast was filled with remarkable actors – as well as Johnnie Mills, there were Alec Guinness, Martita Hunt, Francis L. Sullivan – all carefully cast by David and Tony. Both director and producer had fallen in love with Dickens and oversaw the smallest detail.

How did you feel about playing Estella?

I think she's a very unsatisfactory character. It's easy to play someone without a heart, but harder to make people feel you're *acting* cold, instead of being just stiff and unresponsive. It's a slight, thinly written part; it's a nice idea in the book – the 'no heart' business – but it's not well developed there either. Jean Simmons's natural vivacity came out strongly and this helped the contrast with the older Estella. When you see Estella 'grown up',

Valerie Hobson and Stewart Granger in *Blanche Fury*, 1947

127(1)-66.

you feel this vivacity has been suppressed and I think this suited my particular style very well.

Whose idea was it for you also to play Molly?
It was David's idea – about a week before we started – because he said that the girl must have looked a bit like her mother, which was clever of him. I don't think I appear on the cast list as Molly, and perhaps few people realise it was me.

I very much liked _Blanche Fury_; did you?
Tony [Havelock-Allan] very much wanted it to be a success because it had cost a lot of money. It was beautiful to look at, with wonderful interiors. I had just had our son who was born mentally handicapped, and Tony meant the film as a sort of 'loving gift' that would make me back into a leading lady, which was a wonderful idea. But the film didn't work completely. We could not have done better than Guy Green and Geoffrey Unsworth as cameramen. And that, of course, is enormously important to an actress – you know, then, that you are looking the best you _can_ look. Our leading man was also particularly good – Jimmy [Stewart] Granger can do that wonderful, slightly unpleasant edge, you know, the 'attractive man with the sneer'. We also had a very good director in Marc Allegret. I don't know why it wasn't a smash hit and I was sorry for Tony's sake it wasn't.

I have seen and enjoyed all of Fergus McDonell's films including _The Small Voice_, but he seems simply to have stopped directing.
Unfortunately, I don't know where he is or what he's doing. That film is most remembered for the fact that it was the first film for Howard (or Harold, as he was then) Keel. He was over here doing _Oklahoma!_ and it was very clever of Tony [Havelock-Allan] to spot him. He was awfully good in the film as the villain with a heart. It's quite an alarming film and rather _à propos_ today.

What do you remember of _The Rocking Horse Winner_, playing perhaps your most unsympathetic role?
Yes, it was very unsympathetic but I loved doing it. It was so well-written, by both D.H. Lawrence originally and Anthony Pelissier who did the screenplay. Tony caught the fact that there are people like Hester, who love their children but who are terribly guilt-ridden because they can't manage their affairs. Both Tony Pelissier and I adored children and I remember saying to him that I found the ending intolerable – that is, the original novella's ending. I don't remember any directive from on high, any censorship that required the ending to be softened as it was. I think it finished that way because Tony and I both felt that we had to show Hester as not being made entirely of stone. It's very carefully made and very accurate about a certain class of family.

I haven't seen your last film, René Clément's _Knave of Hearts_, with famous French star Gérard Philipe. What do you remember about this?
I'm sorry you haven't seen it because it was an elegant and well-made film. Gérard Philipe was a very attractive, rather strange man who died shortly after the film was made. I played one of those endlessly accommodating wives who turn a blind eye: I actually got to keep the husband that time, although I don't think he wanted to be kept! It was a charming and very funny film.

What do you regard as the highlights of your film career?
From the point of view of success, I'd choose _Great Expectations_ or _Kind Hearts and Coronets_. But the film I enjoyed most, which was the most enormous fun and my first real little success, was _This Man is News_. I did enjoy it. Certainly the most beautiful film I was in was _Blanche Fury_, and it remains my favourite.

Sir Michael Hordern

The Girl in the News (1939), *The Years Between, A Girl in a Million, Great Expectations, School for Secrets* (1946), *Mine Own Executioner* (1947), *Night Beat, Portrait from Life, The Small Voice, Good Time Girl* (1948), *Train of Events, Passport to Pimlico* (1949), *The Astonished Heart, Trio, Highly Dangerous* (1950), *Flesh and Blood, The Magic Box, Tom Brown's Schooldays, Scrooge* (1951), *The Card, The Story of Robin Hood and his Merrie Men, The Hour of Thirteen* (1952), *Street Corner, Grand National Night, The Heart of the Matter, Personal Affair* (1953), *You Know What Sailors Are, Forbidden Cargo, The Beachcomber* (1954), *The Night My Number Came Up, The Constant Husband, The Dark Avenger, Storm Over the Nile* (1955), *Alexander the Great, The Man Who Never Was, Pacific Destiny, The Baby and the Battleship, The Spanish Gardener* (1956), *No Time for Tears, Windom's Way* (1957), *The Spaniard's Curse, I Was Monty's Double, I Accuse!, Girls at Sea* (1958), *Sink the Bismarck!, Moment of Danger, The Man in the Moon* (1960), *El Cid, Macbeth, First Left Past Aden* (narrator) (1961), *The VIPs, Cleopatra, Dr Syn — Alias the Scarecrow* (1963), *The Yellow Rolls Royce* (1964), *The Spy Who Came in from the Cold, Genghis Khan, The Taming of the Shrew, A Funny Thing Happened on the Way to the Forum, The Jokers* (1966), *How I Won the War, I'll Never Forget What's 'is Name* (1967), *Where Eagles Dare* (1968), *The Bed-Sitting Room* (1969), *Futtock's End, Anne of the Thousand Days, Some Will, Some Won't* (1970), *Up Pompeii, Girl Stroke Boy, The Pied Piper, The Possession of Joel Delaney, Demons of the Mind* (1971), *Alice's Adventures in Wonderland, England Made Me* (1972), *Theatre of Blood, The Mackintosh Man* (1973), *Juggernaut, Mister Quilp, Royal Flash, Barry Lyndon, Lucky Lady* (1975), *The Slipper and the Rose* (1976), *Joseph Andrews* (1977), *The Medusa Touch, Watership Down* (1978), *The Wildcats of St Trinian's* (1980), *Gandhi, The Missionary* (1982), *Yellowbeard* (1983), *Lady Jane* (1986), *Diamond Skulls* (1989).

One of the great exemplars of the British screen tradition of character acting, Michael Hordern has had an astonishingly prolific career on stage and on television as well. Never having been ambitious, as he says, he simply took what came along and, indeed, a great deal *did* come along. He had made over thirty films before 1956 when he, at last, had a full scale role worthy of him: that is, in Philip Leacock's *The Spanish Gardener* as the Ambassador fighting for his son's affections. His roles following this film were increasingly prominent: he was often in uniform (the Captain in *The Baby and the Battleship*, the C-in-C in *Sink the Bismarck!*), or officials of various kind (the Commissioner in *Pacific Destiny*); and there were several brushes with Shakespeare (Banquo in George Schaefer's *Macbeth*, Baptista in Zeffirelli's *The Taming of the Shrew*). Michael Hordern was one of those actors who made even bad British films worth going to.

Interview date: June 1990.

You began in films in 1939 in *The Girl in the News* directed by Carol Reed — which seems like starting at the top!

Yes, I had one line in it, during a court scene. I was the Junior Counsel and my Senior was a very famous actor, Felix Aylmer. I had to come up to him in the foyer of the Old Bailey and say 'We're on next, sir'. Not a line you could get a great deal into!

I then went into the Navy for the duration of the war. I didn't have any contact with films during that time. I came out of the Navy in 1945, having signed my own demobilisation order. I had trouble getting back into the profession. I was very frightened because I hadn't used my voice for over four years. I got terribly nervous and tightened up, so I had a course of voice-teaching over a few months, the only actor's instruction I have ever had.

I always thought of films as being in quite a different slot. In the theatre you have to project, not only voice but a whole performance. There is also the learning as you go along; you rehearse a play for perhaps four weeks, and then the curtain goes up on the first night, and all that you've learned comes out in a progression.

With films, you're as likely as not to do the last scene first, so you don't get a progression. That can be very tiresome and difficult.

What do you remember of such directors as Anthony Kimmins, Fergus McDonell and Anthony Darnborough?
On the whole I found them very helpful to me as a young actor starting out in films. There were only two famous directors with whom I did not get on and who were hopeless at any sort of tactful direction; they were John Huston and Zoltan Korda. Korda (for whom I made *Storm Over the Nile*) was absolutely hateful. He just loved having a whipping boy who was inexperienced, and I was ideal for his purpose!

With directors in the theatre or any other medium, I look for those who can use me, lead me and not direct me – someone who can say to himself, 'I see what this chap can do for me, so I'll encourage that', as opposed to Zoltan Korda who bullied one. But it was a good time then because the whole British film industry was very much alive and expanding.

You made *The Heart of the Matter* and seemed to be an ideal interpreter of Graham Greene's work. Did you admire his novels?
Yes, I have enjoyed his novels very much. That particular film was with Trevor Howard. Then I did *England Made Me* some twenty years later, which I loved. They were the only two Greene parts I did, but they were both very enjoyable to attack. Greene himself wasn't involved in the filming; I don't think I've ever met him.

You worked with many famous Hollywood names who were imported into British films in the 50s. What do you recall of them?
I remember playing Errol Flynn's father in *The Dark Avenger* and Errol played the Black Prince; Peter Finch was in it, too. Errol was a commanding presence – always drunk but pretty commanding at the same time! I don't remember any feeling of resentment among my profession towards the American imports. I think we were all too aware that they were helping to keep our industry going, by ensuring a certain amount of American distribution.

Michael Hordern and Gordon Jackson in Wolf Rilla's *Pacific Destiny*, 1956

In 1956 you had a batch of three very good and varied parts: *Pacific Destiny*, *The Baby and the Battleship* and *The Spanish Gardener*, in which you played various officials. Do you recall working on these?

I had very much enjoyed Arthur Grimble's book *A Pattern of Islands*, and what went wrong with that film was the title! *A Pattern of Islands* was such a lovely evocative title whereas, *Pacific Destiny* could have meant anything. We filmed it in Samoa. There were only four English actors in it, Denholm Elliott, Susan Stephen, Gordon Jackson and myself, and we all went to Samoa. It's a very attractive film, directed by Wolf Rilla. He's not a great director but workmanlike.

The Baby and the Battleship had some marvellous performances; and some of it was very funny. Jay Lewis produced and directed it, and he was quite a significant figure in those days.

It's an awful shame that *The Spanish Gardener* hasn't had a better showing recently. I think what really happened was that Dirk [Bogarde] was a great draw and a star, yet his part didn't really weight the film, so it was thought to be a bit of a disappointment to his fans. I found Philip Leacock a very sympathetic director, particularly with children; I knew him quite well. I was proud of that film. It was certainly my best film part to that date.

What is your approach in preparing for such a role?

I have no great theories about it; just 'learn your lines and don't bump into the furniture'. Never having been ambitious, I never felt I was working under that pressure and could take things very calmly. I have always been a quick study and that's a great advantage, particularly in films where changes are thrown at you at very short notice. I would become very familiar with a script, but wouldn't attempt to learn it until I was to use it the next day. In my experience in films I have almost never rehearsed beyond the immediate coming take; and there was almost never any business of sitting around as a whole cast, going through a screenplay.

There were a great many British war films made in the 50s and you were in *I Was Monty's Double* and *Sink the Bismarck!* to name two. Do you think nostalgia prompted them?

Yes. Nostalgia seems rather a nice word for it, but I think the war was a tremendous slice of most men's lives, men of my age, and there were many good stories to be told

and morals to be drawn. *I Was Monty's Double* was an extraordinary story; I don't think we went on any foreign locations – I was the Governor of Gibraltar, but I certainly never went there to film.

Sink the Bismarck! didn't have any location work either, as far as I was concerned. They built a big model of the ship in the huge tank at Pinewood. I have worn the uniform and insignia of every rank and rating in the British Navy except those of midshipman – some of it in anger, as it were, in the war itself – ending up as Commander-in-Chief in *Sink the Bismarck!*.

Unlike many British players, you went on working steadily throughout the 60s, almost as though you hadn't observed that the British film industry was in a decline.

So much of my work has been in the other media – theatre and/or television – that the film industry could have died altogether without my noticing. True, I did things like *El Cid*, *Cleopatra* and *Genghis Khan*. I remember *El Cid*, made in Spain with Samuel Bronston. One of the great advantages of film acting in my life has been travelling; for instance, I don't need to go on holidays to the Costa Brava because I spent two or three pleasant months there while making *The Spanish Gardener*.

I have to say that working on epics like *El Cid* with its cast of thousands, doesn't really exercise your brain very much; you simply need to be able to ride a horse!

I remember being asked by Richard Lester when we were filming *How I Won the War* whether I could ride. I said that I could, but what he hadn't told me was that he wanted me to ride a camel! I had a terrible time with that beast. I think Dick Lester thought actors were expendable! He also had me doing terrible things in a toga during *A Funny Thing Happened on the Way to the Forum*, which was filmed in Spain. I liked Dick Lester very much. We had lots of laughs during filming – and work should be fun!

Do you have a favourite film role?

No, I don't have a favourite film or any other role. I get so much pleasure from being ready to take any job and I enjoy them for entirely different reasons. I loved playing that part in *England Made Me* and enjoyed it for the fun it was, as much as I enjoyed, say, *The Spanish Gardener*. I don't do much picking and choosing of roles – that is done by the people who employ me. What they know is that I am ready to turn my hand to anything.

Raymond Huntley

Can You Hear Me Mother? (1935), *Rembrandt, Whom the Gods Love* (1936), *Knight Without Armour, Dinner at the Ritz, Night Train to Munich* (1940), *The Ghost of St Michael's, Freedom Radio, Inspector Hornleigh Goes to It, The Ghost Train, Once a Crook, Pimpernel Smith* (1941), *When We Are Married* (1943), *The Way Ahead, They Came to a City* (1944), *I See a Dark Stranger, School for Secrets* (1946), *So Evil My Love, Mr Perrin & Mr Traill, It's Hard to be Good* (1948), *Passport to Pimlico* (1949), *Trio – 'Sanatorium'* (1950), *The Long Dark Hall, The House in the Square, Mr Denning Drives North* (1951), *The Last Page* (1952), *Laxdale Hall, Glad Tidings, Meet Mr Lucifer* (1953), *Hobson's Choice, Orders are Orders, Aunt Clara, The Teckman Mystery* (1954), *The Dam Busters, The Constant Husband, Doctor at Sea, The Prisoner, Geordie* (1955), *The Last Man to Hang, The Green Man* (1956), *Town on Trial, Brothers-in-Law* (1957), *Next to No Time, Room at the Top, Carlton-Browne of the F.O., Innocent Meeting, The Mummy, I'm All Right Jack* (1959), *Our Man in Havana, Make Mine Mink, Follow That Horse, Bottoms Up!, Sands of the Desert, A French Mistress, Suspect, The Pure Hell of St Trinian's* (1960), *Only Two Can Play, Waltz of the Toreadors, On the Beat, Crooks Anonymous* (1962), *Nurse on Wheels, The Yellow Teddybears, Father Came Too* (1963), *The Black Torment* (1964), *Rotten to the Core* (1965), *The Great St Trinian's Train Robbery* (1966), *Hostile Witness* (1968), *The Adding Machine* (1969), *Young Winston, That's Your Funeral, Symptoms* (1972).

Dora Bryan recalled that, for some time in the 1950s, she and Raymond Huntley shared the same cleaning lady who used gently to chide the one for not being as busy as the other in any given week. In fact, this lady was 'doing' for two of the busiest and most instantly recognisable character actors in British films of the period. Huntley specialised in pompous civil servants, the sort of bank manager who would inevitably turn down your request for a loan, or the supercilious official who would keep his head while others all around were losing theirs ... Occasionally he was given a role that would enable him to do more than merely stamp his authority on brief cameos. When this happened he revealed himself a consummate screen actor, notably in Carol Reed's *The Way Ahead* as the prissy salesman-turned-soldier, as Geraldine Fitzgerald's chilly, mother-dominated husband in Lewis Allen's *So Evil My Love*, as the cruelly insensitive headmaster in Lawrence Huntington's *Mr Perrin and Mr Traill*; and in Harold French's 'Sanatorium' episode in *Trio*, very moving as the embittered husband, dying of TB. Huntley is a prime example of the sort of character acting that was once the glory of British cinema.

Interview date: October 1989.

What do you recall of Alexander Korda for whom you made *Rembrandt* and *Knight Without Armour* early in your film career?

I was very fond of Korda; he had such taste, which is a rare enough commodity at any time – practically extinct now! I was in a play called *Bees on the Boat Deck*, one of the five Priestley plays I did. I was very fortunate in having a small part which pretty well ran away with the play. Alex saw it and offered me a part in *Rembrandt*. It was a totally different kind of part, in fact, a pretty bad part, and the make-up and wardrobe departments turned me out looking like Bob Donat's handsome young brother! After a day or two, I went to the rushes and heard Alex say, 'No, no, I want for him to be funny, like in *The Boat Deck*!' He was so perplexed that I wasn't being funny. But he had real flair; he built the Denham Studios and they were pretty damn fine in every way. There were people whose careers Alex absolutely *made*.

You acquired a particular character image in films quite early on — rather disapproving, sometimes supercilious or downright mean ...

In the Launder and Gilliat and the Boulting days I had the image of the very pompous type, particularly in *Carlton-Browne of the F.O.* and that sort of thing. I probably have played a wider range of characters in the theatre than on film, where I sometimes felt a bit pigeon-holed.

On several occasions you worked with Carol Reed. How did you find him as a director of actors?

He was absolutely marvellous. One trusted him completely, that was the great thing. He was very quiet, had very little to say; one day, all he said was, 'Very good, just do one more. Raymond, make sure you get the laugh *with* you, not *against* you', and that was it. The part of Mr Davenport in *The Way Ahead* was very challenging, and very strenuous, one of the best parts I ever had in films. I've never forgotten that assault course! We did it all, no doubles or anything then. The film was made with the co-operation of the Ministry of Information and the War Office, because the co-writers, Eric Ambler and Peter Ustinov, were both in the Army. It was a superb film, and it stands up enormously well. Among so many others, dear old Stanley Holloway was in it. He and I later did *Passport to Pimlico* together.

You made a number of films for the Boulting brothers, and Launder and Gilliat. What differences did you feel in the films made by each pair?

I don't know that I could point to any great differences, and I could easily get mixed up as to which was which. I didn't work much with John Boulting as a director; most of the time it was with Roy.

One of the last films I made for the Boultings was *I'm All Right Jack*; I had just one small scene at the end, as the judge in the courtroom scene. It is amazing that the unions tolerated that film at the time. They might just as easily have walked out and pulled the plugs! True, it was just as critical of the bosses, but it certainly didn't pull any punches as far as the unions were concerned; and it made the Peter Sellers character look a real bloody fool. There was a studio manager at Denham at one time who I swear came off the floor the first day of production and said, 'Always be prompt, Peter [Ustinov]. A lacksadaisical director means a lacksadaisical picture which jeopardises the whole business'! When Roy Boulting was directing, he and John weren't on the floor together, but they were very sympathetically attuned to each other's thinking. The Boulting films were more politically slanted than those of Launder and Gilliat; or maybe they just took on institutions, like the unions and the clergy, and satirised them, because the subject appealed to them at the time.

Your first performance in a film directed by Launder and Gilliat was in *I See a Dark Stranger*.

I enjoyed making that, and it was such a pleasure to work with Deborah [Kerr]. She taught me a great deal. It took such a long time to set up dolly shots in those days, and Deborah would always say to the cameraman, 'Is there anything I can do to help?', which appealed to me very much. She certainly knew her business, but she was so patient and took everything in her stride, with a laugh. That film was a happy experience. It was made in 1945. We hadn't had much good food for quite a while, so when we went on location to Dublin the real meat and eggs were a treat!

Then, at Ealing, you made *They Came to a City*, which you'd done on the stage.

Yes, all the company who had played in it at the Globe Theatre had parts in the film - Googie Withers, Renee Gadd, A.E. Matthews, John Clements and so on. It was quite a popular film, although I didn't think a great deal of it myself. I think it was one of Jack Priestley's lesser plays; I think he owed a great deal to the cast for its success.

Ealing was unique, much smaller than the average studio with an intimate family atmosphere. Mick Balcon had a sort of school of directors, mostly young men gathering experience, to their great benefit, and not taking large salaries. It was very much a 'family concern' of Balcon's. I didn't like Pinewood as much as Ealing or

Geraldine Fitzgerald and Raymond Huntley in Lewis Allen's *So Evil My Love*, 1948

Denham, but I did quite a bit of work there. Denham, Alex Korda's studio, was slightly smaller. The general atmosphere and the happy times one had at Denham distinguish it in my memory from Pinewood. And Denham also had the most marvellous restaurant!

What do you remember of four other directors you worked with: David Lean, Anthony Asquith, Lance Comfort and Lawrence Huntington, on *Hobson's Choice*, *Freedom Radio*, *When We Are Married* and *Mr Perrin and Mr Traill*?
There is a shop in London which sells stills of old films and the other day someone sent me one of *Mr Perrin and Mr Traill* to sign. I hadn't seen or heard anything of this film since we made it. Lawrence Huntington was a most neglected director; I don't know what became of him, but I've never heard of or from him since. As a director I found him very good, not outstanding, but very agreeable and very competent.

When We Are Married was another Priestley play that I'd done on the stage and I don't think the film was nearly as good. It was disappointing – probably I missed some of the original cast, which was marvellous. As to Lance Comfort, I don't think he had very much individual impact.

Anthony Asquith's *Freedom Radio* was very early, at the time of the fall of France. I remember the awfulness of the occasion more than the film.

I was only just in *Hobson's Choice*, a very small part as Derek Blomfield's disapproving father. I remember David saying, 'If I had known you were available for something bigger, I should have been only too glad to offer it'. I said, 'There isn't such a thing as a small part in a David Lean production!' I admired him for his taste and style as a director, though he did later develop a terrific leisureliness about production. Personally, I would put Carol Reed ahead of David Lean, because I got more out of Carol – he was probably more of an actor's director than any of the others.

How did British actors feel about the practice of importing Hollywood players in the 50s?
I don't think we resented their presence at all. I think one simply looked for their quality. I worked with Tyrone Power in *The House on the Square* and he was a lovely actor. Ray Milland was also a very interesting case in *So Evil My Love*. He was technically superb, although as an actor I would say he was quite limited. It calls into question just what film acting is. We did a very long take, something like six minutes, which was a hell of a long take in those days. It was a very tricky thing with Ray and me together. At the end of the first take, all Ray said was, 'Joe, No.66 wants tilting'. That's Hollywood know-how. I liked Ray, got on very well with him and, as a technician, there was no beating him. He asked me to do a film a few years later, *Hostile Witness*. I'm afraid the film wasn't up to very much. But I did like *So Evil My Love*. I greatly enjoyed working with Geraldine Fitzgerald and I have very good memories of the director, Lewis Allen, who had been one of Gilbert Miller's stage managers.

I think one of the finest British films was *Room At the Top*. How do you feel about it now?
I was very dissatisfied with my performance in it – I didn't give the part nearly enough punch. The Yorkshire accent is not difficult for me; after all, I had done five plays with Priestley. But I think I was inhibited in that, and trying not to use the accent too strongly affected my whole performance. I was far too gentle. Laurence Harvey was certainly happening in a big way then! I got on perfectly well with him, but I remember that Annie Leon, a favourite actress of mine, who was playing a bit part in *Room At the Top*, once called him a 'rude bugger'!

It was a period of change and I wasn't vastly impressed on the whole. One does not always take kindly to change, and I preferred my Launder and Gilliat and Boulting Brothers times.

The Foreman Went to France (1942), *Nine Men, Millions Like Us, San Demetrio, London* (1943), *Pink String and Sealing Wax* (1945), *The Captive Heart* (1946), *Against the Wind* (1948), *Eureka Stockade, Floodtide, Stop Press Girl, Whisky Galore!* (1949), *Bitter Springs, Happy-Go-Lovely* (1950), *Lady with a Lamp* (1951), *Castle in the Air* (1952), *Death Goes to School, Meet Mr Lucifer, Malta Story* (1953), *The Love Lottery, The Delavine Affair* (1954), *Passage Home, The Quatermass Experiment, Windfall* (1955), *Pacific Destiny, Women Without Men, The Baby and the Battleship, Sailor Beware!* (1956), *Seven Waves Away, Let's Be Happy, Hell Drivers, The Black Ice, Man in the Shadow* (1957), *Blind Spot, Rockets Galore, Three Crooked Men* (1958), *Yesterday's Enemy, The Bridal Path, Blind Date, The Navy Lark, Devil's Bait* (1959), *The Price of Silence, Cone of Silence, Snowball, Tunes of Glory* (1960), *Greyfriars Bobby, Two Wives at One Wedding* (1961), *Mutiny on the Bounty* (1962), *The Great Escape* (1963), *The Long Ships, Daylight Robbery* (1964), *The Ipcress File, Those Magnificent Men in Their Flying Machines* (1965), *Cast a Giant Shadow, The Fighting Prince of Donegal, The Night of the Generals* (1966), *Danger Route* (1967), *The Prime of Miss Jean Brodie, On the Run, Run Wild, Run Free, Hamlet* (1969), *Scrooge* (1970), *Kidnapped, Madame Sin* (1971), *Russian Roulette* (1975), *The Medusa Touch* (1978), *Shooting Party* (1984), *The Whistle Blower* (1987).

In his nearly fifty-year career in British films, Gordon Jackson played in virtually every film genre, for all the major companies, and for most of the key directors of the period. He didn't regard himself as ambitious, never thought of himself as a star, assessing himself simply as a 'Scots type'. Not many would agree. He is one of those British character actors who seems never to have given a poor performance, even when he fetched up in wretched films (think of *Stop Press Girl* or *Happy-Go-Lovely*). Taken up by Ealing in 1942, he regarded his time there as the happiest experience of his career. His unaffected freshness and naturalness are very well used in such films as *San Demetrio, London* and the great *Whisky Galore!*

in which his scenes with Jean Cadell as his beady-eyed mother are among the film's funniest. The 1950s did not generally give him opportunities of the same calibre. Then, suddenly, in Ronald Neame's *Tunes of Glory* in 1960, he began a new phase of his career, appearing in international films and other major films including Neame's *The Prime of Miss Jean Brodie*. His roles in *Tunes of Glory* and as Horatio in Tony Richardson's *Hamlet* show him in two affecting studies of friendship and loyalty: perhaps for an actor so universally well-liked, by audiences and by his colleagues, such studies were as to the manner born.

Interview date: September 1989.

Before you were twenty, you were playing a leading role in *The Foreman Went to France*. How did this come about?

The first film I did was a fairly major role, but mostly I had Scots character parts. I was with Ealing Studios for about ten years on a 'peppercorn' contract. They had a little group of people – Mervyn Johns, Freddie Piper, and others – who just played little character parts and they wrote these parts in for them. They weren't stars and they weren't being built up to be stars.

Ealing was my happiest time ever, and I was very lucky to serve my apprenticeship there. It was a lovely compact little studio. There was a little group of writers, directors, all working together and wishing each other

well. People helped each other out, in fact. Sandy Mackendrick, whose first film was *Whisky Galore!*, told me that Charles Crichton had suggested that wonderful sequence of hiding bottles of whisky with singing going on. Michael Balcon had confidence in the people around him and they enjoyed working together. He was shrewd, of course; he was in the business to make money as well, but one was never conscious of that at Ealing.

Those Ealing war films, like *San Demetrio, London*, seem different from the general run — was that the documentary influence?

Oh, yes. For instance Harry Watt was there; he was straight from the Film Unit of the GPO and the John

Grierson school. Then he brought in Cavalcanti, who had a lot to do with documentary as well as doing *avant garde* films in France. The films made at Ealing before then – with George Formby, for instance – were what people wanted at the time, then suddenly the war came and there was a switch to documentary and semi-documentary. Take *Nine Men*, which was on a shoestring budget. Harry Watt was happiest when he was just given a camera and a group of actors, although he didn't even want actors, but that's another story! People used to tell him to go into a field and make a film with a bunch of farmers and see how much money he made!

What are your recollections of those Ealing directors?
Well, Harry had made some very successful documentary films without actors and he thought we were mollycoddled. Sandy Mackendrick wasn't quite sure what he was, but I'm sure when he worked with someone like Alec Guinness he was conscious of a very professional actor. Those directors weren't prone to say 'Do it this way . . . do it that way . . .'. I think a good director, once he has got the people he wants for the film, leaves them to do it themselves. But, technically, a director should know exactly what he wants from a scene from the point of view of setting up the cameras and the cutting. At Ealing, directors were technically very efficient because they had been through either script-writing departments or cutting rooms, and were not straight from the theatre.

Robert Hamer was a sad case. I don't remember *Pink String and Sealing Wax* much and I never watch me in re-runs. Of course, he really came into his own with the great classic, *Kind Hearts and Coronets*. He also shot quite a lot of *San Demetrio, London* because Charles Frend was taken ill half-way through it. But Bob was really much happier with the humorous side. He was a brilliant man and was never drunk on the set, although I think he had a big drink problem even then.

To go back to 1943 and *Millions Like Us*, you were starred above Eric Portman and Anne Crawford . . .
That was only because it was the one time in ten years that Ealing lent me out – to Gainsborough, though Launder and Gilliat were rather Ealing in their approach. It was their first film as directors and they told me they had written so many screenplays that they thought they would like to see one through. They supposedly directed together, but I think it was mainly Frank who said what was to be done.

Did you feel it was really about the classes pulling together?
I think it was rather sending up the idea of the upper class coming together with the working man. It was essentially a 'man-in-the-street' story. The Anne Crawford character was slightly jokey, the rather grand lady working in the factory, whereas Patricia Roc was just the little suburban girl. Considering I was an outsider coming in from another studio, I found Launder and Gilliat gentle and charming. They were a bit worried about my love scenes. They said I always held Patricia Roc as if she were a time bomb! Years later I made a film at Ealing called *Against the Wind* with a then-unknown Simone Signoret. Launder and Gilliat told me they were sitting in the Caprice restaurant talking about their film and how hopeless I was at holding Patricia Roc when, just at that moment, probably the sexiest girl in town – Simone – swept in with *me*!

My personal favourite of all the Ealing comedies is *Whisky Galore!*. How do you rate it?
As a Scot I thought it was great fun. Sandy Mackendrick got very depressed because it was his first film and we had pretty rotten weather. The schedule was 'If rain, indoors' and we had converted a little church hall into a studio, but the weather was so bad we eventually found ourselves sitting there with nothing else to do inside. There are some marvellous exteriors in it, though. And it had some great comic actors. If you look closely you'll see me laughing sometimes when I shouldn't be, especially in scenes with Jean Cadell, who was a marvellous woman. I find comedy terribly difficult, I can't be funny. If I come across as funny it is just because of the situation and the script.

Jean played my mother again in the sequel, *Rockets Galore*. That was a sort of Rank-Ealing film, it was just at the transition period and I was moved over to Rank from Ealing. The other film I made at Ealing with Jean was *Meet Mr Lucifer* and she played my aunt, but it wasn't up to the Ealing standard. I enjoyed working with Anthony Pelissier on that. It hadn't a very good script, and he was called in because none of the Ealing directors would touch it. But he made *The Rocking Horse Winner* and that was marvellous.

Throughout the 50s you made about thirty films – were you under a contract?
Again, it was character work. I wasn't as busy as it sounds. After my contract with Ealing ended I moved over to Rank and made one or two films at Pinewood.

Patricia Roc and Gordon Jackson in Sidney Gilliat and Frank Launder's *Millions Like Us*, 1943

But I was no use to Rank because they only wanted to build 'stars' and I wasn't the type who could be built into romantic leading man. I made a rather turgid film called *Floodtide* at Rank, then a wicked one with Sally Ann Howes called *Stop Press Girl* which, they say, is the worst film ever made. That was the end of me at Rank and I can understand why! Thereafter I was 'freelance'. I had contracts for individual films negotiated by an agent.

On *Floodtide* I met my wife, Rona [Anderson]. That film was made on the Independent Frame system, which was a good idea but was never really given a chance. They wanted to avoid the cost of building huge sets, so Independent Frame came up with the idea of going to a restaurant, filming it when it was empty, and throwing up back-projection scenes behind the actors, so that we sat on a banquette in front of this beautiful set. The idea failed because there weren't any decent scripts in *front* of it.

I made a lot of second features in the 50s, some of them terrible. In New York once, I was watching a Late Night Movie and I said to Rona, 'This is the worst film I have ever seen'. Suddenly a door opened and I walked in! I didn't even know I was in it! In those days they wouldn't send you the whole script; they only sent you your scene and you'd play it and go home. I did a second feature for the Danzigers once. I got my script two days in advance, only to find I was to play a Yorkshire boxer. I pointed out I was Scots. Danziger said, 'You can play it in anything but Jewish!'

What about Joseph Losey with whom you worked in *Blind Date*?

He was a good man, very slick and very American. I've only recently realised how tough he must have been in all that McCarthy business. On the set he seemed to be a very gentle, artistic man. I remember there was a case of temperament on *Blind Date*. I had to lead Hardy Kruger to a table, and Joe said, 'Just catch him by the arm and say, "Over this way, sir"'. Came the shot, the camera was turning and I said, 'This way, sir' and Kruger said, 'Don't touch me!'. He was a German actor over here in a leading part and perhaps he thought, 'I'll take it out on this little policeman'. But, being a practical Scot, I immediately turned to the director and said, 'You told me to do it!'

Two of your finest later performances are for Ronald Neame in *Tunes of Glory* and *The Prime of Miss Jean Brodie*. Was he a particularly good director of actors?

He *records* marvellously anything you do. He has been a stills man and cameraman. He has been through it all.

So he knows what angles he wants and all that sort of thing. Having cast the film, that's it. I remember Maggie Smith in *The Prime of Miss Jean Brodie* looking worried and saying, 'He never laughs at any of my jokes'. I told her not to worry, that he would be recording her performance beautifully – which he did, and she ended up getting an Oscar.

I did like *Tunes of Glory*. Guinness was wonderful to watch. He is a superbly technical actor. If you go for ten takes, he will be as brilliant in each one, whereas most of us wilt after three or four. At the end of *Tunes of Glory* he does a long speech when he breaks down. I was standing behind the camera, giving him an eye-line, and I couldn't help it, a tear started running down my face because he was so moving. Ronald Neame called, 'Cut, print', but Alec said no, and asked them to take a shot of my reaction. So they turned the camera around, put the lights on and Alec did his all behind the camera for me. But I couldn't do a thing as they filmed me. I stood there, as they say in Scotland, like a pound of mince! I'm an emotional actor which is very dangerous. I just couldn't turn it on for Take Two and Three.

Pat Jackson

Big Money* (co-dir), Book Bargain* (co-dir) (1936), Men in Danger* (1937), Happy in the Morning* (1938), The First Days (co-dir) (1939), Health in War* Welfare of the Workers* (co-dir) (1940), Ferry Pilot* (1941), The Builders* (1942), Western Approaches* (1944), Patent Ductus Arteriosus* (1947), The Shadow on the Wall (1948), Encore ('The Ant and the Grasshopper'), White Corridors (1951), Something Money Can't Buy (1952), The Feminine Touch (1956), The Birthday Present (1957), Virgin Island (1958), Snowball (1960), What a Carve Up! (1961), Seven Keys, Don't Talk to Strange Men (1962), Seven Deadly Pills, Dead End (1964).

One of the finest flowers of the British documentary movement is the beautiful 1944 film *Western Approaches*. It is also the finest hour of its director Pat Jackson and it influenced his feature film work in giving him a taste for using non-actors.

Nearly fifty years later, *Western Approaches* still looks remarkable: it is full of marvellous images of ships and men at sea, combining a strong sense of realism with equally strong narrative interest.

In the post-war years, Jackson fell victim to unfortunate contracts and to a studio regime he found unsympathetic, and his career lost the momentum he had established in his documentary years. Nevertheless, there are some very attractive entertainments among his later films. *White Corridors* is a rigorously observed and finely acted film of hospital life; 'The Ant and the Grasshopper', his episode in the Somerset Maugham portmanteau film *Encore*, is an elegant anecdote; and *The Birthday Present* is an unexpectedly tough-minded little drama about customs-evasion.

Interview date: October 1989.

After your 1930s documentary work with the GPO Film Unit, what sort of wartime film-making experience did you have?

When war came, the new school of documentary drama, begun with *Night Mail* in 1935, was now established, while the other – Grierson – school of documentary stayed rooted in its exposition, never liberated from the 'illustrated commentary' style. But Harry Watt was writing a history of England by the careful use of the non-actor. Not that the choice of a non-actor can be taken easily: sometimes Harry would test thirty or forty people – just like testing a professional actor – until he found the real thing.

Then the war came and *London Can Take It* was of enormous help to the GPO Film Unit because it had such a great impact. Its originators, Harry and Cavalcanti, said to us, go out and shoot any little vignettes you can. Then these were all put into some sort of shape by Stewart McAllister, a brilliant editor who cut so many of Humphrey Jennings' films. But the thing that really made it tick was the voice of the American correspondent, Quentin Reynolds. Harry got talking to him in a London pub and asked him to do a commentary for the film. Reynolds' voice added an enormous dimension to the film. McAllister edited it over three days and nights and it was out in a week. Reynolds took the film back to Washington in his diplomatic pouch. He went straight to the White House and showed it to Roosevelt, who was very moved, and influenced by it. It made Roosevelt even more impassioned to pass the Lend-Lease legislation.

We went on after that, getting bits and pieces from the Ministry of Information which was still feeling its way in how to use the medium to advance the war effort. Then, slowly, the service films came through. Watt got *Target for Tonight* to make, which had a huge impact because it was the first film of Britain striking back at the enemy. Parallel with that I was doing *Ferry Pilot*.

When Harry finished *Target for Tonight*, he left the Crown Film Unit, joined Ealing and did *Nine Men*. I was then given *The Builders*, and was very lucky in that I walked on to a building site and heard the wonderful Cockney voice of a bricklayer, Charlie Fielding. I tested him on the spot and next day started to film him. He never stopped talking, and kept on laying his bricks without even watching what he was doing. No actor could have done that!

The GPO Film Unit was formed in 1933 and, in 1940, it became the Crown Film Unit under the auspices of the Ministry of Information. Our producer, Ian Dalrymple, was a great administrator who knew how to deal with the Civil Service. He fought for us to be able to get on with the job he knew we could do. We were given more freedom than we ever had before or since.

How did you come to do *Western Approaches*?

Dal called me into his office one day and asked me if I would like to make *Western Approaches*, about the Battle of the Atlantic. The Navy had seen the RAF getting enormous publicity and éclat for *Target for Tonight* and suddenly realised they should be sharing in this. The Commander-in-Chief, Admiral Sir Percy Noble, called his great friend, the naval historian Owen Rutter, and suggested the making of a film on the Navy. Rutter wrote a twelve-page sketch of an idea, and went to see the Crown Film Unit. I agreed to do the film and then had to go to see the Admiral who took me down to the Control Room. As we went in, a WREN ran up a metal ladder that was placed against an enormous map. She went right into the middle of the Atlantic, and stuck a little red cross there. This signified a ship which had been hit, and the Navy could not divert anything to go to its rescue. The Admiral turned to me and said, 'That is going on constantly; it is a battle of attrition'.

That scene became the opening scene of the film. I had great trouble finding the key ingredient for a story of a navy at war. Then, suddenly, I had the thought: what would happen if a U-boat picked up an SOS message from a lifeboat? Then the answer came: it would use the lifeboat as a decoy. Within ten days I had the story

Megs Jenkins, Brand Inglis and Googie Withers in *White Corridors*, 1951

treatment and we had our approval. We only needed three ingredients – the lifeboat, the reaction from the U-boat and, sooner or later, a merchant ship which would pick up the signal from the lifeboat. The naval facilities would be kept to a minimum, yet these were the basic forces in the Battle of the Atlantic, interacting one against the other and creating an ever-increasing situation of suspense.

We were to use a three-strip technicolour camera which, in those days, was the size of a household refrigerator. Try to put that in a ship's lifeboat with sound, two two arc lamps, a microphone and a cast of unknown but carefully tested seamen and see how far you get! We were five months doing the lifeboat sequences and poor Jack Cardiff was violently ill most of the time! He was a hero on that film and I think he photographed it brilliantly throughout. I was very lucky to have a wonderful bunch of people from so many walks of life, united in the pursuit of a common goal. British Lion distributed the film and made a lot of money from it. Then the Ministry of Information, to their eternal shame, sold it to America for £7000 or so – peanuts. It did very well over there, too.

How did you come to do the US film _Shadow on the Wall_ after the war?
When I had finished _Western Approaches_, the Ministry of Information didn't know whether it was any good, so their Honorary Adviser, who was at that time Alexander Korda, was called in to look at it. We screened it for him and he offered me a contract. By the time I took the contract up, he had been sacked by Metro, but they wouldn't release me. I finally went to Hollywood but wanted to resign within three weeks, because it was quite clear they were never going to use me. Dore Schary, who had been brought in to 'save the studio', asked me why I thought I could come over to America and make films. I suggested they should have thought of that three years earlier! However I made _Shadow on the Wall_, which Dore didn't like and which, incidentally, was Nancy Davis [Reagan]'s first film. The great thing about working in an American studio was that the back-up was so good; if you made a sensible request, it was immediately granted.

Did you feel the 40s and 50s were a good time to be a film director in Britain?
I'm sure it was a boom period. I came back to do _White Corridors_, which we made in five weeks at Pinewood. John Davis then wanted to put me under contract but,

after my experiences with MGM, I did not want to lose my freedom by being under contract and losing the right to refuse an unacceptable assignment. It is not easy to refuse an assignment when in receipt of a fat weekly wage. I liked the story very much, and saw how I could make it more dramatic. I rewrote it with Jan Reid and built up the boy's story and character. However, when Arthur Rank saw the film he said to me, 'It's a very nice little film indeed, but I don't think the boy ought to die; I think we've got to retake all that'. I couldn't believe this and said, 'If the boy doesn't die, you haven't got a story'. He said, 'I don't know about that, Mr Jackson, but I don't think the boy should die'. Rank was a charming man, but, like so many of these people who control the industry, he had no idea!

Were you trying to get a documentary flow to it?
Oh, yes. I was lucky because I had a wonderful cast, with the melding of the amateur actor with the professional cast. You may have recognised the hospital porter as the gunner from _Western Approaches_. He was a non-actor who had been magnificent in _Western Approaches_. The matron who read the prayers in the ward and played that wonderful scene with Petula Clark was an amateur whom I'd met in the Hind's Head, Bray. The boy, Brand Inglis, had never acted before, but gave a wonderful performance!

You made another hospital-set film in 1956 – _The Feminine Touch_. Was this pure coincidence?
I went to Ealing and brought them the 'Tirpitz' story, which Mick [Balcon] loved. We went into further researches on it, but Mick felt it was a bit too expensive for him so we abandoned it. I hunted around for another subject, and felt that _The Feminine Touch_ could be made into something, so that's how it happened. I didn't really have a choice. But I loved working at Ealing. The film could have been marvellous had I been able to carry out what I wanted to do. It had some good people and one or two nice little scenes, but it wasn't a good film.

Which of your later films are you most pleased with?
The Birthday Present was an honest piece of film-making, with a lovely performance from Sylvia Syms. It was a very interesting story and a well-written script by Jack Whittingham. _White Corridors_ pleased me most because it most happily melded the documentary method with Big Box-Office and made no compromises to _become_ 'Big Box-Office'.

Rosamund John

Secret of the Loch (1934), *The First of the Few* (1942), *The Gentle Sex*, *The Lamp Still Burns* (1943), *Tawny Pipit*, *Soldier, Sailor* (1944), *The Way to the Stars* (1945), *Green for Danger* (1946), *The Upturned Glass*, *Fame is the Spur*, *When the Bough Breaks* (1947), *No Place for Jennifer*, *She Shall Have Murder* (1950), *Never Look Back* (1952), *Street Corner* (1953), *Operation Murder* (1957).

Rosamund John is always described in reference books as 'gentle-mannered' and 'pleasant' which seem wan epithets to describe her best screen work. They do less than justice to the crispness and compassion which characterise her most sympathetic roles – for example, as the firm-minded pub-keeping Toddy in *The Way to the Stars* – or to the potential for dangerous repression she suggests in *Green for Danger*. In the latter film, her surface gentleness is very cunningly used by actress and director to provide a surprising solution to a murder. As the suffragette wife of the politician who has compromised his ideals, in Roy Boulting's *Fame is the Spur*, she presents a very persuasive study in strength and dedication, and the scenes in the Swiss chalet when she is ill and dying are very moving; so, too, are her scenes of friendship with Douglass Montgomery in the *Way to the Stars*. Rosamund John made only sixteen films and was lucky that half-a-dozen of them gave her such excellent opportunities. She was also much interested in the politics of the British film industry and remains forthright in her views on it.

Interview date: September 1989.

After your 1934 debut, you returned to the screen in 1942 and made three films in a row, all for Leslie Howard. How influential a figure was he in your career?

Oh, he taught me everything I knew about film-making. I got on very well with him and luckily he didn't want to get into bed with me, as he did with quite a few people he worked with. I was playing Mrs Mitchell in *First of the Few*. Leslie made me realise that the only thing that matters when you are filming is what you are thinking and feeling, because it will all show in your eyes.

Leslie was an actor before he became a director and he saw things from an actor's point of view, but a lot of directors merely looked upon actors as being inconvenient bits of furniture. The beginning of the *First of the Few*, where he was watching the gulls, was really difficult to film because, at that time, practically the whole British coastline was covered in barbed wire. We had to go to Polperro in Cornwall to find a place where there were rocks and gulls, and we had a lorry-load of fish to attract the gulls. We tossed the fish around on the rocks and the gulls said, 'So what?' As soon as we packed up to leave for the day, they descended in clouds!

I had done a play with Robert Donat, who had wanted to make the film but was under contract to MGM. I was up a tree picking cherries at Robert's house one day when a girl I knew in an agency phoned to say Leslie Howard was looking for someone for this film. She had suggested me and I had to go straight away. Leslie said I didn't look like an actress and decided to test me for the part of the wife. I knew nothing about the film but I did the test anyway, and got the part. I've never forgotten my first appearance on the set. There was this massive crowd for the presenting of the Scheider Trophy, which was won by planes that Mitchell had designed before the war. They had this set with the winning plane – God knows how they got it in the studio – and, when I walked on to the set, I could feel a wave of people looking at me and wondering, 'What the hell has she got?' And I realised there was a lot of antagonism towards a complete newcomer.

The Gentle Sex is officially co-directed by Leslie Howard and Maurice Elvey. What did that mean in practice?

It was directed by Leslie. He was an extraordinary character; I suppose one would call him amoral. He just did what he enjoyed doing. I remember one day his daughter came on the set and took out a very nice cigarette case. Leslie said, 'Where'd you get that?' 'Don't you recognise it?', she said. 'It's one Merle Oberon gave you. Mummy had the inscription removed and gave it to me'. Leslie just roared with laughter!

Leslie's mistress, Violette, died while we were making *The Gentle Sex* and he was devastated. He asked Maurice Elvey to finish the film. I had never heard of Elvey, but everyone in the studio said, 'Oh, no, that terrible man'! He was a very pompous little man who had made a lot of indifferent films before the war.

Leslie went off to Lisbon while we were making *The Lamp Still Burns*, and his plane was shot down on the way back. He was travelling with a man the Germans thought to be Churchill and that is supposedly why they shot the plane down. Leslie had been flying around making speeches in neutral countries like Sweden, and, of course, Portugal was also neutral.

Was The Gentle Sex made as propaganda for the women's forces?

Partly; they wanted to recruit women for the ATS, and it was originally to have been made by Derrick de Marney, who played a small part in *The First of the Few*. It was about six girls who join the army. I wanted to play the Cockney girl, but Derrick said, 'No, you can't, you look all wrong for that', though I grew up in Cockney London. However, she was played by a girl called Joan Gates who married a GI and went to live in America. Jean Gillie was the good-time girl, and I was the Scots one. I used to rush off to John Laurie on another set at Denham for help with the dialogue. I think the film *did* work as propaganda, especially in America. Until that film, many people didn't realise that women were working on gunsites and driving lorries. The Ministry of Information wanted Leslie to do it, which is why he took over from Derrick.

How did you find Maurice Elvey, as the director of The Lamp Still Burns?

I was appalled. He had no idea of what to do or how to do it. The electricians would shout, 'Print Number Three, Maurice!' He was unbelievable. Stewart Granger had been given a contract and was on the rise, although no one had heard of him at that stage. He discovered he was supposed to have a head injury, which would have meant shaving off his hair and putting on a bandage like a turban. He flatly refused, so they had to change the injury to a broken rib!

Did you feel securely established as a British film star by the time of The Lamp Still Burns?

I don't think so. All I wanted to do was to work. The next film I did was *Tawny Pipit* which Bernard Miles made. It was lovely because we went up to the Cotswolds, and it was a charming film about birds, which only the British would care about – making sure the birds could hatch undisturbed in the middle of a war! Rank didn't think they would be able to sell the film to America, so it was stashed away for a while. When it *was* shown, it was wildly popular, because it was everything that the Americans thought of as English.

My personal favourite of your films is The Way to the Stars. Did you like your role of Toddy?

I loved it. It was written by [Terence] Rattigan, and had a lovely script. The war ended before the film was finished, so they scrapped a lot of the wartime stuff we'd done at the beginning and substituted the brilliant idea of the people going back to the aerodrome and seeing all the graffiti on the walls, which linked it all up. They were afraid no one would want to see a film about a war which had just ended. Originally, the script was called *Halfpenny Field* because that was the name of a place where they had an airstrip, but they decided nobody in America would be able to pronounce 'Ha'penny' so it had to go.

I can't think of another film in which there is so moving a friendship between a man and a woman, as the one between you and Douglass Montgomery . . .

This was a fascinating idea, but they had hell's own job casting it, because every American on this side of the Atlantic was involved in the American armed forces. I was very worried because it was a tricky part to play. Then someone found Douglass who was actually Canadian. We had made quite a bit of the film by that time. As soon as we started to work, he said he thought it ought to be a love story between our two characters,

Michael Redgrave and Rosamund John in Roy Boulting's *Fame is the Spur*, 1947

when the whole point of the thing was that there *wasn't* a love story! Puffin [Anthony] Asquith – my favourite director – told Douglass we would shoot it at the end, and, of course, we never did. The relationship, however, got a lot more emphasis when some of the war scenes were cut out.

Reference books describe you as a 'gentle-mannered' English actress, which I think undervalues much of your work ...

I think it's the parts I played. In those days we were much more ladylike than we are now. We used to admire French films because actresses in them were allowed to be real. English films made us unreal because the audience liked to be taken out of the reality of the war. I think they cast me as the murderess in *Green for Danger* because no one would ever suspect me! Alastair Sim was wonderful in that film, which was quite a success – surprising given the frightful novel from which it came!

Did you think of *Fame is the Spur* as a film of the

post-war Labour Government England?

No. I never thought about that. I adored it because it was 'costume' film, and, that for an actress, is much more satisfying than modern clothes. I was very impressed with Mrs Pethwick-Lawrence, the famous suffragette, who told me about her time in prison. I also met Christobel Pankhurst – God, what a bitch she was! The Boultings couldn't wait to get her off the set.

I enjoyed *Fame is the Spur* more than any other. You know how it's said to be based on Ramsay MacDonald; well, the author, Howard Spring, came on the set one day and said it was based on *any* chap who had feet of clay, and he'd taken bits from various people. I think Roy enjoyed putting over the idea that all these Labour chaps who were supposed to be holier-than-thou had, in fact, feet of clay.

What do you recall of your work as Actors Equity representative on the Working Party on Film Production Costs in 1949?

Equity fought to have a representative. Our secretary, a marvellous man called Gordon Sanderson, said it was terribly important for actors to be represented. There was a dreadful man on the Working Party, then secretary of NATKE [National Association of Theatrical and Kinematograph Employees], who always said he spoke for everyone ... well, he didn't speak for *any*body, certainly not actors.

So, Gordon fought for an Equity representative along with distributors and producers. Harold Wilson was President of the Board of Trade and agreed to appoint two extra people. He asked for a list of names from Equity, and I was amazed to get a letter saying that I had been appointed. I met Harold long after that and asked him why he had chosen me. Larry [Olivier] was one of the names on the list, but Wilson said he thought that if he had chosen Larry, people would say, 'Oh, you're just having another director, he isn't really there as an actor'. So Harold Wilson said he had appointed me because he had enjoyed my films. He also said, 'Either you weren't a Communist or you had succeeded in hiding it very well!' It was the time of McCarthyism in America and if you weren't a staunch Tory you were a goner as a rule!

It was fascinating to be a part of all that, and it was a great advantage to be a woman on that Council. All the men around the table were going on about cutting production costs, cutting wardrobe budgets, and so on. I pointed out that one of the reasons people go to the cinema is to see beautifully dressed women, that the money was not being wasted.

The Thief of Baghdad (1940), *The Gentle Sex* (1943), *Journey Together* (1945), *Call of the Blood* (1948), *The Angel with the Trumpet* (1950), *The Sound Barrier*, *Hot Ice* (1952), *Melba*, *King of the Khyber Rifles* (1953), *The Village*, *Seagulls Over Sorrento*, *The Teckman Mystery*, *The Man Who Loved Redheads*, (1954), *Untamed*, *Guilty?* (1955), *Safari*, *Crime Passionelle* (1956), *Island in the Sun* (1957), *Spider's Web* (1960) *Le Crime de M Chardin*, *Les hommes voulent vivre* (1961), *Candidate for Murder* (1962), *Men in Silence** (voice only) (1964), *Savage Messiah* (1972), *Barcelona Kill/Razzia* (1973), *Lisztomania* (1975), *Valentino* (1977), *The Big Sleep* (1978), *Trenchcoat* (1982).
* Documentary.

John Justin began his film career at the top – as the dashing Prince in Alexander Korda's *The Thief of Baghdad*, in which he was required to be handsome, athletic and romantic. He was placed under contract to Korda, but 1940 was the wrong time to be twenty-three and on the verge of a film career. He was in the RAF during the war and was released briefly to make two propaganda films – *The Gentle Sex* and *Journey Together*. It was his role in David Lean's *The Sound Barrier* that really launched his screen career and his scenes with Dinah Sheridan brought a needed warmth to the film. Hollywood (Fox) grabbed him in the mid-50s for several CinemaScope epics, but his British films were persistently more attractive, especially Harold French's *The Man Who Loved Redheads*. In the 70s he made three films for Ken Russell: having begun with Korda, and allowing for changes in taste, this must have seemed like watching the flamboyant wheel come full circle.

Interview date: July 1990.

How did you come to start in a plum part in *The Thief of Baghdad* in 1940?
I got the part because I had a very good agent at MCA who had come from Hollywood. His name was Harry Ham. One day he told me to go to Denham for a test. I was sick of auditions and was about to give the whole thing up; so I went out to Denham quite relaxed for a change. I went on to a huge stage which had a boat in the middle of it, in which there was a little Indian boy. I put on some kind of costume and got into the boat with this little boy, Sabu. He was very funny and clever and utterly unafraid of all the film people, and this helped me. The two of us sent the whole test up. Normally I would have worked much harder at it but I did it quite casually, and left assuming I had missed out.

Two days later, the front page of a newspaper had a photograph of me on it, with headlines! The publicity campaign had started and I had been cast without even knowing about it! Korda had made some very good pictures by then and this film was a particularly import-ant one because it was to be in Technicolour, which was rare then, and a lot of the special effects were very difficult to do in colour.

How did it come to have three directors' names on the credits — Michael Powell, Tim Whelan and Ludwig Berger?
It was really a Korda film. If it had been the mess it looked like being, then Korda would have been finished, so he might as well get the credit. Korda was technically the producer but he controlled the film totally and, effec-tively, directed it. Michael was the exterior director, he wasn't on the set. I can't remember Tim Whelan at all. Ludwig Berger was a very successful European director who had just won a prize for his last film, so of course Korda wanted him for *The Thief of Baghdad*.

The day we started shooting, Alex left for Hollywood. We worked for three months and then Alex came back from America, looked at the rushes, and said they were no good. Four days later we started again with a new

Moira Shearer, Joan Benham, Roland Culver, John Justin and Gladys Cooper in *The Man Who Loved Redheads*, 1954

script. He wanted Berger out but couldn't sack him, so that first day Sabu and I found them both behind the camera. Sabu had a hard enough time with his dialogue but with two directors giving contrary instructions he nearly gave up. To give just one example of the two styles of directing – a scene under Berger's direction involved June [Duprez], Sabu and me, a donkey, a bale of straw, and a short flight of wet steps. When Alex redid this scene, it filled the whole of the biggest stage at Denham and included a dozen camels, mules, horses, three elephants, 400 extras, tons of fruit and vegetables, and Sabu and me!

Georges Périnal was lighting it. He was a wonderfully talented man, but also absolutely infuriating. He was the one person to whom Alex didn't dare say anything. He would spend hours on a face and would refuse to hurry. Actresses had a bad time with him. He would approach them slowly, eyes narrowed, peering within inches of their faces, then move slowly round them. He would then step back and, throwing his hands in the air, would say in despair, 'Aah! Mon Dieu!' and walk away. When he turned, he'd find the girl in tears. I don't think he saw people as *people* really, only as objects to be lit perfectly, against great odds, but then again he did make us look good.

What was your experience of working with Leslie Howard on *The Gentle Sex*?
He was a lovely man, deeply admired by us as a theatre actor, but I didn't know him at all. He was brilliant, but nervous. I was only very briefly in *The Gentle Sex* to provide someone's love interest. They borrowed me to do it for the Army, on my Air Force pay, fourteen quid a week!

You made a curious-sounding enterprise called *Call of the Blood* in 1948. Was John Clements particularly keen to do this film? He both stars in it and co-directs it?
And wrecked it, too! It was a silly idea. It starred his wife, Kay Hammond, who was a dear lady. We did the whole film in Sicily, which was the only interesting thing about it. It was very rare in those times to do an entire picture on location. All the interiors were actually shot in houses in Sicily, with very low ceilings, and it was quite a trick to get any lighting from the top without damaging the houses. It was a terrible Victorian story about a woman doctor. Alex Korda took one look at it and, from then on, referred to it as *Call of the Bloody*!

Were you working on the stage until you came

back to the screen in *The Angel With the Trumpet*?

Yes. I was doing a play with Eileen Herlie called *Thracian Horses*, a mock Greek comedy. It went very well, so Alex came round one night, handed Eileen a blank piece of paper and told her to write her own contract, including salary. Of course, she had no idea of money – not on the scale he dealt with. What appeared to be a great gamble, Alex knew was no gamble at all. No agent would have let him get away with it, but he'd by passed the agents. Her first picture under that contract was *Angel with the Trumpet*. Eileen was a fine actress but she wasn't right for the part, and the picture failed. It was the first time I played a role which aged from twenty-two to seventy-five – but not the last.

You did that again in *The Man Who Loved Redheads*, from a Rattigan play in 1955.

Yes, that was Alex Korda again, as a result of my having played in *The Angel*. Poor Harold French, the director, had a bad time with Alex who had been starting stories about his direction because the company was too happy! Alex felt that only unhappy productions make good pictures. Nonetheless it *was* a very harmonious experience, and I loved working with Roly Culver; we both knew our stuff well enough to get the sparks flying a bit. I remember having to embrace Gladys Cooper, who played my wife, and saying to her, 'What a terrific moment in my life, to hold you in my arms!'; she was enchanting. The film didn't go down well, though. I suppose if Moira Shearer and I had been huge stars world-wide, people would have come to see it just for that but neither of us was of that calibre. I liked it, though; there were some wonderful comic actors in it and some very nice moments.

Would you agree that your film career really took off with *The Sound Barrier* in 1952?

Yes, I suppose that made me a real star. David Lean was an extraordinary man who I think hated actors, but he was a *brilliant* editor. The thing about good actors is that they don't act *with* each other but *against* each other, each one working for the best he can get out of himself, and the director is there to see 'fair play' as it were.

I remember rehearsing a crucial scene in *The Sound Barrier* with Nigel Patrick; Nigel was very fast and I kept looking across at David Lean to defend me, but he just sat there looking very blank. Finally we paused a moment and David simply said, 'Let me know when you're ready', and he walked off the set, leaving us to it.

We had no direction at all from him: we had the set, the script and we knew the story – that was it. Eventually we sent a message to him that we were ready and he simply said, 'Shoot it'. I loved him though; I don't like too much direction. I prefer to be told it's good or it's no good, particularly if I'm going over the top. With that I'm happy, I trust the director absolutely then.

Maybe you remember that sequence of the dive to break the sound barrier. David was at his wit's end to make that dive as long and as dramatic as he wanted it to be. On a grey cloudy day, with the camera tilted, he shot thousands of feet and created one of the most exciting moments in any film. Of course, it's very difficult to explain the idea of breaking the sound barrier. It had only just been done and it was brand new stuff. Someone said could the pilot push the stick forward, giving the idea that it reversed the controls, so that's what we did. I said the words, 'I'm now going to push the stick forward', and that was the great moment. It was either right or wrong, his life was at stake.

The relationship between your character and Dinah Sheridan's is important as a foil to the tensions of the other relationships.

Yes, that's the author [Terence Rattigan]. I put a bit in there too and, here again, it shows David Lean as not being a good director of actors. I suddenly knew that, because I had just broken the sound barrier, the laugh about my wife worrying about the children's clothes would really turn into a cry, so I asked David if I could do that. He agreed, but was worried in case repeating it might distress me too much! I explained that this was what I did for a living, that I was not really distressed.

Did you feel you were treated differently as a star in your American films from the way you'd been treated in Britain?

You were judged strictly on your salary level, on your billing, whether or not you had a caravan on location, all those things. At first I didn't have a caravan to myself and I mentioned this, not understanding the system. The next morning there was a caravan for me and everyone apologising. I was working on a quarterly contract, but they had thought it was a year's contract in which case my salary wouldn't have warranted a caravan! In fact, I was getting a star's salary although I was a junior star – nothing like Ty Power, who was a very big star. Korda knew how to pick stars all right, but he didn't know how to groom them. There was nothing like that in England.

Jean Kent

The Rocks of Valpre, How's Your Father (1935) Hello Fame (1940), It's That Man Again, Miss London Ltd, Warn That Man (1943), Bees in Paradise, Fanny by Gaslight, 2000 Women, Champagne Charlie, Madonna of the Seven Moons, Soldier, Sailor (1944), Waterloo Road, The Rake's Progress, The Wicked Lady (1945), Caravan, Carnival, The Magic Bow (1946), The Man Within, The Loves of Joanna Godden (1947), Good-Time Girl, Bond Street, Sleeping Car to Trieste (1948), Trottie True (1949), The Reluctant Widow, The Woman in Question, Her Favourite Husband (1950), The Browning Version (1951), The Lost Hours (1952), Before I Wake (1955), The Prince and the Showgirl (1957), Bonjour Tristesse, Grip of the Strangler (1958), Beyond This Place, Please Turn Over (1959), Bluebeard's Ten Honeymoons (1960), Shout at the Devil (1976).

When I asked Jean Kent whom she had most admired in American films, she said without hesitating 'Claire Trevor'. It seemed a very revealing answer about the kind of parts British films rarely offered women in the 1940s and 50s, or perhaps ever: gutsy, worldly-wise, generous, like the role she'd love to have played and for which Simone Signoret won an Oscar in *Room at the Top*. However, it must be said that she made the most of what came her way. She made her mark as the flashy, determined Lucy in Asquith's *Fanny by Gaslight* and had her best role ever, again for Asquith, as the vicious wife in *The Browning Version*, mining

veins of real frustration in Millie Crocker-Harris. After *Fanny*, she became established as Gainsborough's sexy bad girl who usually lost the heroine to more virtuous types, then came into her own with a series of strong starring roles in 1948. As a change of pace, in *Trottie True* she was stylish and charming as the Gaiety Girl who married a Duke. In the last three decades she has worked steadily on television and stage, but has filmed only once – an absurd waste of a robust talent.

Interview date: October 1989.

Was the role of Lucy in *Fanny by Gaslight* in 1944 a turning point for you?

Definitely, I was most excited, but I think it was purely accidental that I got the part. Perhaps Ted Black suggested that I be tested. Perhaps he saw the rushes of something else and thought, well, she's blonde too, why don't we test her?

But it got me noticed. Perhaps I was just a new face popping up. Certainly, you can't mistake Phyllis [Calvert] and me for each other. *Fanny* was one of the better Gainsborough melodramas. It's a good story isn't it? And it has marvellous sets and wonderful clothes. There was enormous skill and effort taken over them. Elizabeth Haffenden, who did the clothes, was a magnificent designer.

What sort of director was Anthony Asquith?

Wonderful. He was the only director who actually introduced members of the cast to each other! He used to

wear this blue boiler-suit and sit like a little pixie under the camera. Unless he got under the camera he couldn't actually see the scene that was being shot. He was always encouraging to his actors. You'd rehearse the scene and he'd say, 'I love the way you do . . .' or 'Do you think this . . . ?' By the time we'd finished he'd turned the whole thing around as he wanted it, but you'd agree every step of the way. Actors are tender plants – you can't pour acid on them and expect them to flower.

Was it exciting working for Gainsborough in those highly successful melodramas?

Oh, yes. Gainsborough was a very good studio – I mean the Lime Grove one. It's always home to me. The other Gainsborough studio at Islington was closed down; the only film I did there was *Miss London Ltd*. It only had one big stage and one minute stage, whereas Lime Grove had five – two big and three small – and it had a friendly family feeling about it.

You made over twenty films during the remainder of the decade, up till 1950. Were you under contract?

I was under contract to Gaumont-British. They also leased me out to several studios, including Ealing, where I was never as happy, because there was an edgy atmosphere (though I loved the films I did, *Champagne Charlie* and *The Loves of Joanna Godden*). It was a seven-year contract. I got £5 a day with a guarantee of fifty-two days for the first year which is approximately £5 a week, so, although I made three films, I didn't make a lot of money. After seven years, I ended up with the magnificent sum of £1,000 a film. After I went into *Caravan*, Gaumont-British and I decided to tear that contract up.

What do you remember of those early Gainsborough films: *2000 Women* and *Madonna of the Seven Moons*?

I remember those very well. Frank Launder did *2000 Women*. He was a timid sort of fellow then. I know Phyllis [Calvert] wanted to play my part and I wanted to play hers, but they wouldn't let us change. And I remember Muriel Aked very well, a lovely actress, and she and Flora Robson had some lovely scenes together. And Betty Jardine – oh, the fight we had! We were black and blue. There were no punches pulled in that. I remember we finished filming the fight late one foggy evening, and Frank said, 'Come on, we'll go down to the pub and I'll buy you both a drink'. We were worn out, and he was very pleased with us.

Jean Kent and Beatrice Varley in David MacDonald's *Good-Time Girl*, 1947

In _Madonna_ you had the small, vivid part of Vittoria, Stewart Granger's jealous mistress.

That's right, with the black curly wig. It was rather fun and I enjoyed it very much. It was all done in the studio. In those days the sets were magnificent. They were all wood, done with heavy plaster work. They say it is expensive to build sets, but, given the time you waste on location, surely it must be as broad as it is long.

Your 'bad-girl' image was confirmed in 1945 with _Waterloo Road_, _The Rake's Progress_ and _The Wicked Lady_.

I always said that, if they opened a script and read 'A girl appears in cami-knickers', they would send for me. But they were good parts. I never wanted to play heroines, they're not my line of country at all. I got the reputation for having sex appeal, and, as you know, no good girl ever has sex appeal. Not in the 1940s anyway. No _good_ girl even now.

The doxy you played in _The Wicked Lady_ is often omitted from cast lists, yet it's one of the truest things in the film.

I think it's because I wasn't cast for it. Valerie White was cast and she did the first scene. When Margaret [Lockwood] breaks into the room and Mason's in the bed with her, that's Valerie with her back to the camera. But she developed appendicitis during the filming, and I was stuffed into a blonde wig and pushed into the part. I got all the splendid close-ups.

By 1948 you were virtually solo-starring in _Good-Time Girl_, _Bond Street_, and _Sleeping Car to Trieste_, all for different companies.

I was being loaned out by the studio. When I signed with Gainsborough, I knew I might be loaned out. At least they paid you – they were forced to. We used to go halves in what they got for us. I made a lot more money than if I was working for them.

I didn't like _Sleeping Car_ and didn't get on very well with the director Paddy Carstairs. You never knew where you were with him. I remember Rona Anderson was in it, her first movie, but apart from that I don't remember enjoying it. I had silly clothes. I wanted to be very French in plain black and a little beret, but I had to wear these silly 'New Look' clothes. I was playing a superspy of some kind. But who was I spying for?

I've seen _Good-Time Girl_ recently and it is impressively hard-hitting. Were you the obvious

Gainsborough star to play Gwen Rawlings?

Presumably, yes. Sydney Box had taken over by then. I enjoyed working with David Macdonald, who was a very good director with actors. He was what I call workman-like. He knew what he wanted. I prefer a director who knows where to put the camera, gets on with the action, says what he wants in that way, and lets me do the acting. He can then tell me whether it's right or wrong. David was excellent in that way.

In Arthur LaBern's book, the balance of Gwen's character is much better, I think. She's very young, it's true, and rather foolish, but a bit of bad lot. The father beats her and so forth, but she isn't quite the wide-eyed little pest she is made out to be in the film. And I thought it was better for being so, because it was the story of an actual girl who _did_ get involved with these two men and the taxi murder. She is a sad character.

All I remember about _Bond Street_ is that I'd had appendicitis, had just come out of hospital, and had to do that fall down the stairs myself because the double wouldn't do it. So when I am dragging myself down those stairs, that's real pain you see!

Did you regard getting _Trottie True_ in 1949 as your biggest break to date?

Yes. The three land-marks, I would say, were _Fanny by Gaslight_, _Good-Time Girl_ and _Trottie True_. I hoped to do more musicals and more comedy. I adored _Trottie_. It's my favourite film. And Harry Waxman was a marvellous cameraman. They weren't good with the music though. I had a battle about that. We were scheduled to start, and I hadn't heard a word about the music, so I rang up whoever was the head of Two Cities. I finally managed to get half the music done, and then I had another argument about the first number. It dissolves from the brown-eyed young Trottie [Dilys Laye] to the hazel-eyed big Trottie, which was hysterical. They wanted me to sing something in a schottische [hums a tune rather like a slow polka]. Carroll Gibbons was doing the music, and he'd written this number, so I said, 'It's a very nice number, but I come from the music halls and I tell you you cannot use a schottische at this point'. So he changed it to 6/8 time. Another thing was that I wanted to prevent them, while I was actually singing the number, from cutting away too much, which they used to be very fond of doing in British films. The whole point of somebody singing the song is for the audience in the cinema, not for the people in the movie. So I had to devise ways to keep moving all the time so they couldn't get the scissors in, particularly during the Marie Lloyd number in the ballroom scene after I'd become the Duchess.

Oh, I like *Trottie*! I remember that scene when Hugh Sinclair says, 'Will you have a cup of tea?' and I say, 'Oh many a gal's been caught with a cup of tea. A bottle of champagne please'. And lovely Philip Stainton, who turns around and says, 'I'm in wool', and I say, 'Oh, does it tickle?'

Was there much competition for the role of Astra in *The Woman in Question*? It seems like an actress's dream role.
I don't know. I remember Puffin [Asquith] taking me out to lunch at the Savoy Grill, telling me about the part, and saying, 'I will be quite frank with you; we originaly wanted Bette Davis'. And I said, 'I am deeply honoured that you feel I could accomplish something that you really wanted Bette Davis for'. And, of course, I accepted with alacrity. The film's a little patchy I think. When I saw it, I was a bit disappointed. It's a *Rashomon* sort of story; you're not really supposed to know what she was like. I thought the nearest to what she was really like was probably the character in the John McCallum episode – the good-hearted, lovable, don't-care-very-much sort of girl. This is the point I started from. To do a character, which is five different versions of one person, is very tricky. It's tricky to get enough difference and for each to be near enough to the others. I thought it was a pity that the Susan Shaw version of the character went over the edge. It wasn't a bit real.

The wife in *The Browning Version* must have been your most unsympathetic role ever. What attracted you to it?
I thought it was a splendid play. I always feel that, even with unsympathetic characters, you should always en-deavour to show why you feel the character is like that. With Millie [Crocker-Harris], you can see why she is exasperated with that man, because he *is* an exasperating character. You can see why she has taken a lover and why the lover does not want the affair to go anywhere, and why he slipped into that relationship, which he shouldn't have done. You can understand everyone's behaviour, and I think that's how one should create the picture. I think Millie is a really fascinating character, but I always said she finished my career because playing a woman who should have been say forty-five, when I was only at that time thirty-two or thirty-three, made people think I was that age. I swear it finished my career in pictures . . .

From 1960, you worked solidly in the theatre for sixteen years. Was this because it offered more interesting opportunities?
I have to admit that I prefer working in the theatre, but then I think most actors do. However, as I get older, I'd love to make another film, if somebody would only ask me. I have a very good agent, but the trouble is I am plagued by a curious costume-picture image from the 40s and 50s.

Was there any role you'd really like to have played?
Yes. I very much wanted to play Alice in *Room at the Top*, and I'd have been very good at it if I may say so. I was the right age, too. They didn't need to bring Simone Signoret over to do it. She's a wonderful actress, but the character was never meant to be a foreigner. It was just this old English thing that only foreigners have sex appeal. They'd forgotten me by that time. They'd forgotten that I was supposed to be the sexy girl in the movies.

Major Barbara, *Love on the Dole*, *Penn of Pennsylvania*, *Hatter's Castle* (1941), *The Day Will Dawn* (1942), *The Life and Death of Colonel Blimp* (1943), *Perfect Strangers* (1945), *I See a Dark Stranger* (1946), *Black Narcissus*, *The Hucksters* (1947), *If Winter Comes* (1948), *Edward My Son*, *Please Believe Me* (1949), *King Solomon's Mines* (1950), *Quo Vadis*, *Thunder in the East* (1951), *The Prisoner of Zenda* (1952), *Julius Caesar*, *Young Bess*, *Dream Wife*, *From Here to Eternity* (1953), *The End of the Affair* (1955), *The King and I*, *The Proud and Profane*, *Tea and Sympathy* (1956), *Heaven Knows, Mr Allison*, *An Affair to Remember* (1957), *Separate Tables*, *Bonjour Tristesse*, *The Journey* (1958), *Count Your Blessings*, *Beloved Infidel* (1959), *The Sundowners*, *The Grass is Greener* (1960), *The Naked Edge*, *The Innocents* (1961), *The Chalk Garden* (1963), *The Night of the Iguana* (1964), *Marriage on the Rocks* (1965), *Eye of the Devil* (1966), *Casino Royale* (1967), *Prudence and the Pill* (1968), *The Arrangement* (1969), *The Assam Garden* (1985).

In 1947 British studios suffered a major loss when Deborah Kerr went to Hollywood and became an international star. Nevertheless, before this time she had established herself as one of the most attractive and incisive actresses in British films, and nearly fifty years later her performances still have a remarkable truthfulness to them. She is very affecting as the daughter who marries out of poverty in *Love on the Dole*, understands the melodramatic needs of Lance Comfort's *Hatter's Castle*, differentiates clearly among the three female protagonists of *Colonel Blimp*, suggests the passion suppressed beneath the nun's habit in Powell's *Black Narcissus*, and is entrancing as the anti-British heroine in Launder and Gilliat's *I See a Dark Stranger*. Hollywood eventually broadened her range, notably in *From Here to Eternity*, but the images she created in those earlier British films remain ineradicably fresh. She returned to the big screen in 1985 with a finely astringent performance as a former memsahib adjusting to the Home Counties in *The Assam Garden*.

Interview date: April 1990.

Unlike most British film actresses of the 1940s, you seem to have been pre-eminently a film star rather than a stage star. Was this a matter of preference?
No, it was purely a matter of chance, as these things tend to be.

Your first film appearance was in *Major Barbara*. How did that come about?
Gabriel Pascal saw me on the stage when I was playing with the Oxford Repertory Company, and chose me for the part of Jenny Hill in *Major Barbara*. Gabby was hell to work with, but he did have great taste and flair.

At barely twenty years old, you starred in three 1941 films: *Love on the Dole*, *Penn of Pennsylvania*, and *Hatter's Castle*. Was someone looking after your career?
I had a very good agent at the time, John Gliddon, and he got me these roles.

Penn of Pennsylvania and Hatter's Castle were both directed by Lance Comfort, a director who I believe is under-rated. What do you remember about him?
I enjoyed working with Lance enormously, and I agree with you that he is very under-rated. He is scarcely heard of today.

Hatter's Castle seems to me an absorbing melodrama. Would you agree that British cinema, unlike American, often seemed shy of melodrama?
Melodrama has never been well-portrayed in British cinema. Our producers always seemed shy of it. I must say that working with Robert Newton in *Hatter's Castle* was a bit nerve racking, but, despite his faults, he was a marvellous actor.

Clifford Evans and Deborah Kerr in John Baxter's *Love on the Dole*, 1941

How did you feel about *Love on the Dole's* depiction of life?

It was an excellent book and an excellent play, and I think they made a very good movie from it. Strangely enough, it was much more appreciated in America than in Britain.

What do you remember of Harold French's *The Day Will Dawn*?

It was really a propaganda piece, done in the guise of a thriller.

How did you come by the splendid triple role in *Colonel Blimp*? And did you find Michael Powell a sympathetic director of actors?

I'd had a small part in Michael Powell's earlier film, *Contraband*, but it was cut from the final print. Then he chose me for the triple role of the heroine in *Colonel Blimp*. Michael really was a brilliant man of the cinema, and I loved working for him on both *Colonel Blimp* and *Black Narcissus*. Although *Black Narcissus* looks like wonderful location shooting, it was all filmed entirely at Pinewood Studios in England.

Was it stimulating to work with Robert Donat in *Perfect Strangers*? And what sort of director did you find Korda?

Robert Donat was a fine actor, and Korda was both a very clever man and an unexpectedly good director.

One of your most charming 40s films is *I See a Dark Stranger*. What do you recall of the Launder-Gilliat team?
I loved the film. Frank Launder and Sidney Gilliat contributed wonderfully British humour in all their work. I found working with them a joy.

You went to Hollywood in 1947 — what were the major differences you found in filming there?
Hollywood has vast studios and dozens of technicians; everything is on a much bigger scale. With very few exceptions, I appreciated all my Hollywood films. They gave me such a wide range of opportunities — romantic dramas, comedies, adventure epics and so on. I have always wanted to play completely different parts, and, if you look at my record, I *have* played just about everything. Two parts I did in a row in *An Affair to Remember* and *Separate Tables* could hardly be more of a contrast.

In 1949, you came back to England for *Edward My Son*. What attracted you to the role of the wife?
It was an excellent and challenging role for an actress, and of course it was a great thrill to be working with Spencer Tracy. I admired him greatly.

Your next British film was Otto Preminger's *Bonjour Tristesse*. How did you find working for him?
Otto was a very clever witty man, but he was certainly difficult to work with. However, when one met him socially, he was delightful and amusing.

How important do you think stars were in building a film industry?
I think they *were* important, but there are no longer the great studio 'star-makers', which is rather sad. I think I was very lucky to be a part of those exciting days.

Who do you regard as the most influential film-makers in your career?
I can only answer that by saying just about everyone I have ever worked with!

What are the highlights of your post-60s career?
The highlight was definitely a British picture I made in 1984 called *The Assam Garden*, and directed by Mary McMurray.

Philip Leacock

Out to Play* (1936), Kew Gardens* (1937), The Londoners* (1939), Island People*, The Story of Wool* (1940), Riders of the New Forest (serial) (1946), Pillar to Post* (1947), Out of True, Life in Her Hands, Festival in London* (1951), The Brave Don't Cry (1952), Appointment in London, The Kidnappers (1953), Escapade (1955), The Spanish Gardener (1956), High Tide at Noon (1957), Innocent Sinners (1958), The Rabbit Trap (1959), Hand in Hand, Let No Man Write My Epitaph, Take a Giant Step (1960), The War Lover, Reach for Glory, 13 West Street (1962), Tamahine (1963), Firecreek (1968), Adam's Woman (1970).
* Documentary.

One of the unexpected successes – critical and commercial – of the 1950s was a small-scale film set in a Nova Scotian forest, with a cast of grandparents, unconventional lovers and two gravely charming little boys who find and hide a baby in the woods. The film, *The Kidnappers*, established Philip Leacock as a sensitive director of children, an impression he confirmed in other films such as *The Spanish Gardener*, *Escapade*, and *Innocent Sinners*. Like many directors of the period, his background was in wartime (and earlier) documentary, and his early fiction films (for example, *The Brave Don't Cry*) skilfully combine the social and the didactic with the expectations of film story-telling. His first Hollywood film, *The Rabbit Trap*, also exemplifies his major strengths as a filmmaker, and he directed a lot of efficient television there, but his best work is arguably to be found in his British films of the 50s. Leacock's was a gentle talent, at its best in recording the minutia of everyday life, and in rooting well-observed human drama in realistic settings.

Interview date: June 1990.

Were you with the Army Kinematograph Unit during the war?
I didn't start off there. I had been in the Army for about a year, doing my training. Carol Reed had been brought into the Army as an instant Captain to do a film called *The New Lot*, written by Eric Ambler and Peter Ustinov. I was the Sergeant whose job it was to show them how to dress properly, and so on, and to be their liaison with the Army itself. This was a film to show people what the Army was like. They re-made it as *The Way Ahead*, a feature film. Later, I was in the AKU for a while; and I was commissioned to direct some interesting stuff on training, although some of it was very routine. After the War, I worked for the Crown Film Unit.

How did you come to be assistant director to Lawrence Huntington on *Mr Perrin and Mr Traill*?
Donald Taylor was one of the producers on *Mr Perrin and Mr Traill* and he put my name up to the actual producer [Alexander Galperson]; they just wanted me to do two weeks of background shooting in Cornwall for the climactic sequence of Marius Goring and David Farrar fighting on a cliff. There was a lot of back projection material, very technical and we ended up staying there about two months. Lawrence Huntington was certainly very nice to me, and very helpful in explaining things to me when I was in Cornwall.

Did you feel you were combining documentary and feature film-making experience in your first films as director *Out of True* and *Life in Her Hands*?
Very much so, yes. *Out of True* was written by my wife's father, Montagu Slater. The Government wanted us to make this film as an answer to *The Snake Pit*, because the mental hospitals had been trying for a long time to break down the image of being 'hell-holes'; this film was meant to allay people's fears about them. We shot the

Dinah Sheridan, Charles Victor and Dirk Bogarde in *Appointment in London*, 1953

whole thing in a mental hospital called 'Nethern' in South London.

On *Life in Her Hands* we were trying to capture the reality of the locations and some of the people were actual hospital people. That was all shot on location at a hospital on the outskirts of London, near Barnet. Even the party scene was for real, partly actors and partly nurses.

The Brave Don't Cry, was made for Group Three, I think.

Yes. Grierson talked to me about doing a film for Group Three, which had Government finance to help young directors. He told me about a coal-mining disaster that had occurred in Ayrshire and gave me some press cuttings of the story; a lot of people had been killed and others trapped. Montagu Slater and I did some research on it and spent a lot of time in Scotland in the actual coalmine.

Montagu particularly felt that we weren't getting the full story, that these guys had been trapped in a situation where they couldn't be got out because the only escape route would have allowed gas to flare up into the mine. During the rescue, they had to get oxygen masks from all over Europe before they had enough equipment for the trapped men. We gave a party to loosen the miners up a bit – they were wonderful dour people who didn't say a great deal. Then somebody started to blurt out what really happened. There were about a hundred of them underground and the official leadership had lost the

men's confidence because they couldn't understand why they weren't being got out. There was a riot situation and the younger guys took over. It was only their energy and anger that got the British Coal Board to make this huge international effort of getting the gas masks to the trapped men. This gave us a core of conflict which worked well. There is no music in the film, other than when the men themselves sing a song. 'Flow Gently Sweet Avon' was recorded by a choir which sounded absolutely terrible, so we won and used our original footage of the men singing. We did some location shooting but very little; it was a very small budget. Group Three was a wonderful idea; all their films were interesting. It's suggested that Group Three were unpopular with the unions, but I don't know if that's true.

Was *Appointment in London* your first big-budget film?

Yes. I was lucky to have Aubrey Baring as producer; he was wonderful to me. Also Dirk Bogarde and I got on extremely well. It was a very hard-working picture, with a lot of night shooting. I was incapable of handing over to a second unit director, out of pride or whatever, so when we were on location I was working two shifts at one point. We got wonderful co-operation for all the planes and so forth.

Was your ability to direct children a key element in your reputation as a British director of the 50s?

Probably. My feeling is that, especially for younger kids, acting is part of their social life, part of playing. Margaret Thompson, who had done a lot of film work with children, was absolutely wonderful and she worked with the kids more than I did. For *The Kidnappers* she found Vincent Winter in Aberdeen, but Jon Whiteley had already done a film. We brought the children in to test for the parts; we did play situations, as we did with the film itself. Vincent couldn't read so he had to be firmly taught lines – he had a memory like a computer. He would do his own lines aloud and then silently mouth everyone else's words!

I was lucky to get Jean Anderson for *The Kidnappers*. The brass wanted a bigger name. In the event, there was some sort of a conflict just before we started shooting; Jean was available so I was able to have her as the grandmother after all.

We filmed the long wide shots of rivers and streams at Glen Affric in Scotland (not Nova Scotia), outside Inverness and made back-projection plates to use in the studio. The interiors were all studio stuff. We searched for places to build the cabin. This was stupid of us because, after all, Pinewood *was* called 'Pinewood'. We finally went out to the back of the studios and built the cabin there! It was certainly the film I enjoyed most.

I think *The Spanish Gardener* is one of the finest films of the 50s. What do you recall of it?

Dirk originally turned it down. I was so upset because we had become good friends during *Appointment in London*. I suggested we get together and talk it through, and eventually it worked out all right. John Bryan was a very good producer; he had been an art director and was one of the few who really dominated the visual look of a picture. The look of *Great Expectations* is very much John's work. On *The Spanish Gardener* John was producer but, nonetheless, he tore practically all of the models to pieces.

Was it the pacifist theme that most interested you about the 1955 film, *Escapade*, again with excellent child actors?

Yes, I liked the irony of it – to be a pacifist you really have to be a fighter. And I liked the children's parts. It was at the time of McCarthyism and Donald Ogden Stewart wrote the script under a pseudonym because he wasn't allowed to have his name on it. I'm sure he wasn't a communist, but the McCarthy mob made it so rough for him that he left the US and came over here.

Your three films in 1956, 57 and 58 – *The Spanish Gardener*, *High Tide at Noon* and *Innocent Sinners* – are all for Rank. Were you under a contract?

I had a seven-year contract with Rank. Michael Balcon was the Chairman of the Board of the Rank film section and they turned *The Kidnappers* down on the script. Balcon said they all liked it, but they didn't think there was a possibility of its being successful. We were absolutely devastated. Some time later I had a phone call on a Saturday morning, asking if I could come in to see Arthur Rank in a couple of hours' time. So, I had a strange interview with this big man with a North Country accent who said he was about to do something he had never done before, and that was to go against the advice of his Board. He said he liked *The Kidnappers* and believed I would do a good job of it. Then he said he had one thing to ask me, and my heart sank; but he only asked me if I would bring in 'the name of the Good Lord' – I think that was the phrase he used.

Was there a lot of location work on *High Tide at Noon* and *Innocent Sinners*? Did you favour location work?

Yes, I think most directors do. *High Tide at Noon* was done at Pinewood but we did do some shooting in Nova Scotia with a few of the cast, mainly footage of the boat landing, stuff like that. Then we did two locations in Cornwall. We had great difficulty getting the boat started and had one of the local fishermen on the boat in the storm scene when the engine broke down. It was a nasty fifteen minutes while this little boat was drifting nearer to the rocks and we couldn't do a damn thing. For *Innocent Sinners* we did quite a bit of location work, although all the interiors were shot on the stage.

Flora Robson was in both of those films and she was a lovely woman. I remember she had supreme contempt for 'method' acting; she would say 'The method I use is *my* method!'. She didn't believe you had to 'feel' it; her job, she said, was to make other people feel it. In one scene she had to be very emotional, crying on the screen. Off the set she was knitting while we were getting ready to shoot, and she began to tell a very long and complicated story. In the middle of the story she was called to do her scene, which she did with tears streaming down her face – absolutely genuine. She finished the scene, still with tears everywhere, and said '. . . and then . . .', and proceeded with the story!

The Pilot is Safe* (1941), *Ordinary People** (co-dir) (1942), *Close Quarters** (1943), *By Sea and Land** (1944), *The Eighth Plague** (1945), *Children on Trial** (1946), *The Woman in the Hall* (1947), *Once a Jolly Swagman* (1948), *The Wooden Horse* (1950), *South of Algiers* (1952), *Turn the Key Softly* (1953), *A Town Like Alice* (1956), *Robbery Under Arms* (1957), *The Captain's Table* (1958), *The Circle of Deception* (1960).
* Documentary.

Like several other British directors of the period (for example, Pat Jackson and Philip Leacock), Jack Lee cut his teeth on documentary film-making, during and immediately after the war. In fact, *Children on Trial*, a documentary focusing on juvenile delinquency, which Lee both wrote and directed, remains his favourite among his films. The influence of these early film-making years is felt in the speedway racing drama, *Once a Jolly Swagman*, which has a very convincing feel for place, both in its use of the New-cross Race Stadium and its evocation of working-class life. He had a big popular success with his next film, *The Wooden Horse*, based on Eric Williams' best-selling account of his wartime escape, and another with *A Town Like Alice*, this time based on Nevil Shute's bestseller. Lee showed a fresh light touch for re-activating familiar comic ingredients in *The Captain's Table* but, after one further film in 1960, he retired to live in Australia.

Interview date: October 1990.

Did you join the Crown Film Unit in 1940?

Yes, the GPO Film Unit changed its name to the Crown Film Unit in 1940, but it was run by the same people. On the first night of the Blitz, Pat Jackson and I decided, as the bombs were falling like mad at about five o'clock, that we would go out and do some filming that night. We were working at our Blackheath studio and were mixing the soundtrack for a film. We filmed all over the East End that night; I fell into the Thames with the camera clutched to my tummy so it wouldn't be damaged; and that was the start of the famous film called *London Can Take It*. Harry Watt liked what we filmed that first night, and sent us out to do more filming every night over the next week or so.

I did about one film a year – it took a lot of time to research and write them as well as make them. My final film for the Unit was *Children on Trial*, which friends say is my best film. It's about a young thief, a juvenile delinquent; it runs for about seventy-five minutes. I wrote and directed it and invited a famous critic, Richard Winnington, to see a rough cut one Saturday morning. I thought if he liked it, he would write a piece about it. He did so, saying it was brilliantly written and directed, which I thought was a bit over the top!

I then went to work with Ian Dalrymple's Wessex Films, one of those semi-independent production companies, like Cineguild, under the Rank umbrella of Independent Producers. Dalrymple was a charming and well-educated man, the shyest man I ever knew. We made a few films, unsuccessful films, and he then set up a company making documentaries under the Marshall Plan. I never worked on any of those because I'd had enough of documentaries.

There was one thing about *Woman in the Hall*, my first film for Wessex, which revolted me. It reminded me of when I was a child and my mother would send me out on begging expeditions because she never had any money. It was a bloody awful novel and a terrible film. It was a rare starring role for Ursula Jeans, and she was a splendid woman. Jean Simmons and that wonderful actor Cecil Parker were also in it, and I learned a lot about comedy delivery and timing from him.

You had a change of pace with your second Wessex film, *Once a Jolly Swagman.* What was your experience of working with Dirk Bogarde?
I liked that film. Dirk, even then, was a splendid actor. He was terrified of motor-bikes and rightly so, because he'd had a terrible accident about which I knew nothing at the time, but he was jolly good. I built part of a speedway track in a field to do some night scenes. We stripped a truck down to the chassis and strapped Dirk onto the back of it. He was tethered by huge elastic bands which forced him down. We drove round that track all night in the dark and I was as frightened as he was. A lot of the film was shot south of the river, and at the Newcross Speedway, which was a bit small but easy to work in.

I enjoyed doing that film because it was physical, there was action and I had good actors like Bill Owen and Bonar Colleano, and Patric Doonan who, sadly, committed suicide when he was quite young. Renee Asherson did her part very well because she wasn't that sort at all. Richard Winnington praised the unsentimental treatment of working-class life – this approach was uncommon in those days. He was working-class himself, as I was. I co-wrote the screenplay with William Rose. We had daily meetings to decide on the next bit.

Did you seek out *The Wooden Horse*, which is one of the great escape stories?
Yes, Ian and I had read it and agreed we should do it. I learned later that Johnny Mills had wanted it, too. We bid more than he did for the rights, so we got it and Eric Williams [author] and I did the screenplay. I expect John would have been very good in it also, probably better than Leo Genn, who was very stolid as an actor. Tony Steel was fine to work with – just a physical type, a young chap who could do certain things, though he didn't have much acting to do in that film.

I enjoyed making it even though a lot of it went over budget. We had to re-shoot certain scenes which weren't good enough. Most of it was made in Germany and I've always enjoyed location work. We had to build a POW camp. There were lots of POW camps still in Germany, but they were mostly occupied by displaced persons waiting for their immigration papers for Australia, America and so forth. There were many reasons for the film going over budget. Firstly there was the weather, but probably a lot of it was my fault, taking too long to

shoot and shooting too much stuff.

There was also indecision on my producer's part about the ending; Ian said we should shoot things in two different ways. The ultimate ending was a perfectly reasonable one, but I was off the film by then. Ian shot it himself. Then I was out of work for a year. *The Wooden Horse* was a great success, but I didn't get any of the profits and my name didn't bring in any work. Just before the end of that year I was offered *South of Algiers*, which was a piece of old hokum, made almost entirely on location. It was quite fun, but it was all cliché stuff, with goodies and baddies and all those spahis riding around chasing bandits.

You made three consecutive films for Rank. Were you under contract?
The first one, *A Town Like Alice*, came about because I had met Joe Janni who liked my work. He was an Italian refugee from Mussolini's fascists who came to Britain in 1938, a splendid man. One day Joe said he was sending me a script he'd just received. I read it that evening and

David Tomlinson and Leo Genn in *The Wooden Horse*, 1950

phoned him to say we should make it. It was *A Town Like Alice*; the script was written by W.P.(Bill) Lipscombe. I then read the novel and realised Lipscombe had very cleverly cut the book in two, because it is, in fact, two stories, the second half being set entirely in Australia. The script made me cry and I knew it would make audiences cry, too.

When Joe and I put this project to Rank they agreed immediately. I worked on the script with Lipscombe first, then with Richard Mason, an old friend. We re-wrote certain scenes and invented a few others. Then we did a budget and went to Malaya and Singapore. I soon realised that if we cast the film in the UK, decided on their exact clothing, and filmed their characteristic ways of walking, we could find a second cast in Malaya and, if we were careful, we could work very close to them on location.

I always had a strong feeling that I made the film twice: first in Malaya because I did a great deal of shooting there; then back at Pinewood, shooting all night with the cast wading through mud. We had to fortify the cast with brandy to keep them going – they were splendid, those women, both in Malaya and in England. I think Virginia McKenna never looked better than when she was covered in mud! She is a marvellous actress and woman. Marie Lohr and Nora Nicholson were both quite old when they did the film, but they didn't mind the arduous work. They were good parts with good scenes for all of them and they were doing work they enjoyed. Only recently I learned from Jean Anderson that Renee Houston hated having to wear those terrible rags, but, by God, she was good at it. Peter Finch was cast because of his Australian connection. He had a small part in *The Wooden Horse*. I don't think we ever considered anyone else for the part.

How did you come to do *Robbery Under Arms*, from another Australian novel, again with Finch?
After the success of *A Town Like Alice*, Rank put Joe Janni and me under contract for two years as a team. I wanted to work with Finch again and I was attracted to Australia. I remembered landing in Darwin in the mid-50s when it was almost a one-horse town. It was fasci-nating for an Englishman, to come out to this extra-ordinary experience, so I wanted to make another film in Australia.

I made a mistake choosing *Robbery Under Arms*. It was a complicated Victorian novel with masses of plots and sub-plots, and too much moralising. However, I went ahead with it and chose the part for Peter Finch, who complained that he was over-shadowed by everyone else and, in a way, he was right. Janni and I weren't happy with the script and would have liked to put it off for another year. But we were under pressure from Rank, so we went ahead with an inadequate script. There are one or two nice scenes in it, but it's too slow and talkie.

Though it has a lot of familiar ingredients, your next film *The Captain's Table* is very fresh and funny.
I thought I'd like to make a comedy, although I didn't know anything about comedy. I said, 'All we need are funny scenes, funny lines, actors who can pull faces, and that's it'. Joe got a lot of marvellous people writing for it – Bryan Forbes, Nicholas Phipps and John Whiting – and they wouldn't let me near the script. I liked Nadia Gray very much indeed. She brought a very different quality to the film, living as she did in Paris. Donald Sinden was very good too; it was a fairly conventional part for him, but when I saw the film again recently I was surprised at just how good he was. And we had some good old ham actors in it, like Reginald Beckwith, camping away like mad.

Why did you stop making films after *Circle of Deception* in 1960?
In a sense, films gave *me* up. I wasn't wanted. I lost my confidence and I think I lost my enthusiasm. The whole face of the industry was changing at that time and I remember seeing a newspaper article referring to me as 'the veteran British film director'. I thought, '*Am* I?' I realised new talent had taken over and that it was un-likely I would make another film. Although I wasn't happy about it, it was something I had to accept. I'd enjoyed my life as a film-maker very much indeed.

Herbert Lom

Zena Pod Krizem (1937), *Mein Kampf My Crimes* (1940), *The Young Mr Pitt* (1941), *Secret Mission, Tomorrow We Live* (1942), *The Dark Tower* (1943), *Hotel Reserve* (1944), *The Seventh Veil, Night Boat to Dublin* (1945), *Appointment with Crime* (1946), *Dual Alibi* (1947), *Snowbound, Good Time Girl, Portrait from Life, The Brass Monkey/Lucky Mascot* (1948), *The Lost People, The Golden Salamander* (1949), *Night and the City, State Secret, The Black Rose, Cage of Gold* (1950), *Hell is Sold Out, Two on the Tiles, Mr Denning Drives North, Whispering Smith Hits London* (1951), *The Ringer, The Net, The Man Who Watched Trains Go By* (1952), *Rough Shoot, The Love Lottery, Star of India* (1953), *Beautiful Stranger* (1954), *The Lady Killers* (1955), *War and Peace* (1956), *Fire Down Below, Hell Drivers, Action of the Tiger* (1957), *Chase a Crooked Shadow, I Accuse! The Roots of Heaven, Intent to Kill, No Trees in the Street, Passport to Shame, The Big Fisherman* (1958), *Northwest Frontier, Third Man on the Mountain* (1959), *I Aim at the Stars, Spartacus* (1960), *Mr Topaze, El Cid, Mysterious Island, The Frightened City* (1961), *The Phantom of the Opera, The Treasure of Silver Lake, Tiara Tahiti* (1962), *The Horse Without a Head* (1963), *A Shot in the Dark* (1964), *Return from the Ashes, Uncle Tom's Cabin* (1965), *Our Man in Marrakesh, Gambit, Die Nibelungen (Whom the Gods Wish to Destroy)* (1966), *Die Nibelungen II, Assignment to Kill, The Karate Killers* (1967), *The Face of Eve, Villa Rides! 99 Women* (1968), *Doppelganger/Journey to the Far Side of the Sun, Mister Jericho* (1969), *Count Dracula, Dorian Gray, Hexen bis aufs blut geqvalt* (1970), *Murders in the Rue Morgue* (1971), *Asylum* (1972), *Dark Places, Mark of the Devil? Blue Blood, And Now the Screaming Starts* (1973), *The Return of the Pink Panther, Death in Persepolis, And Then There Were None* (1974), *The Pink Panther Strikes Again* (1976), *Charleston* (1977), *Revenge of the Pink Panther* (1978), *The Lady Vanishes, The Man with Bogart's Face* (1979), *Hopscotch* (1980), *Trail of the Pink Panther* (1982), *Curse of the Pink Panther, The Dead Zone* (1983), *Memed My Hawk* (1984), *King Solomon's Mines* (1985), *Whoops Apocalypse, Going Bananas* (1986), *Coast of Skeletons, The Master of Dragonard Hill* (1987), *River of Death, Death on Safari* (1988), *The Pope Must Die* (1991).

Although Herbert Lom rightly complains of being stereotyped as 'sinister foreigner' in British cinema, he was also one of its busiest actors throughout the 1940s and 50s. Indeed, after 1960, he scarcely noticed the decline of the British film industry because he was filming all over the world. Despite difficulties of typecasting, he was memorably sympathetic as the psychiatrist in *The Seventh Veil*, a rare romantic hero in *Hell is Sold Out*, a likable philan-derer in *The Net*, comically menacing in *The Lady Killers*, and a striking presence in such superior melodramas as *Good-Time Girl, Chase a Crooked Shadow* and *Hell Drivers*. His career took a new turn with the 'Pink Panther' films and, fifty-odd years after its start, it is still going strong.

Interview date: June 1991.

You seemed to have settled quickly into British films in the early 40s. How did this come about?
Carol Reed was looking for an unknown person to play Napoleon in a film called *The Young Mr Pitt*. He interviewed me and gave me the small part. I got the interview through my agent, Christopher Mann, who was married to the concert pianist, Eileen Joyce. I met her later when she played the piano on the soundtrack for Ann Todd in *The Seventh Veil*. I was thrilled to be chosen by Carol Reed. He was a charming man.

After several entertaining films in the early 40s, did you regard your success in *The Seventh Veil* as a turning point?
Yes, but for British films as well as my career. The film took psychiatry seriously, but in the most popular sense, of course. No girl would have chosen a sadistic man who beat her with a stick while she practised the piano! But

the sadist was James Mason and so psychiatry was 'popularised' to suit the star. The psychiatrist I played was meant to be years older than I was then, but the make-up people put black lines under my eyes and greyed my hair. I was meant to present a very sympathetic image of psychiatry as a form of treatment. I think the romantic use of classical music helped the film's popularity. But, really, it owed everything to Sydney and Muriel Box, who were the creative team behind it. James Mason was also becoming a very big star.

You made four films in 1948. Did you have much choice of roles then?
Not at all. I had a three- or four-picture deal with Gainsborough Studios, and I made films like *Snowbound* and *Good-Time Girl*. David Macdonald directed them, but I don't remember much about him except that he looked like Ronald Colman and I got on very well with him.

Were you happy with the suave villain image you had at this time?
I was a foreigner and in English eyes all foreigners are villains! I did have one romantic role in a film called *Hell is Sold Out*, with Mai Zetterling, who was then a budding star. This was directed by a very nice man, Michael Anderson, who went on to do big films. The newspapers often compared me with Charles Boyer, and, in the early 50s, that might have come about, but not in England.

I'd been signed to a seven-year contract with 20th Century-Fox in Hollywood, when the US refused me an entry visa. No reason was given, which meant it was clearly political – I was a victim of the anti-communist fever running at that time in the US. My political inclinations were certainly leftist, but I had never been a member of the Communist Party. However, I was a Czech and, as my parents were still in Czechoslovakia, I had followed the war news keenly and had been intensely interested in the role of the Russians in expelling the Nazis. So I was not as anti-Russian as I might have been, or as Hollywood would have liked me to be. One of life's ironies is that, some years after the war, I wanted to return to Czechoslovakia and was refused a visa by the Communists. Eventually, I was able to get my parents to England.

What do you recall of the three films you made at Ealing in the early 50s – *Cape of Gold* (1950),

Cecil Parker, Peter Sellers, Danny Green, Herbert Lom and Alec Guinness in Alexander Mackendrick's *The Ladykillers*, 1955

The Love Match (1953) and The Ladykillers (1955)?

I don't really remember the first two, except that David Niven played a film star in *The Love Lottery*. I do remember *The Ladykillers*, which we all enjoyed making. The writer, Bill Rose, told me he had dreamt the story one night and written it the next morning. Katie Johnson, I remember, was a very charming old lady, who was brought out of retirement for the part. She was a great success in the film and then, sadly, died shortly after.

What was your experience of working with imported Hollywood players in the 50s?

You need to remember that it was cheap to make films in Britain then and a lot of American companies took advantage of this. When the pound recovered in the late 60s, the Americans pulled out. As for the Americans I played with, I particularly liked Anne Baxter, a beautiful actress and a beautiful woman, with whom I did *Chase a Crooked Shadow*. Then there was *Rough Shoot* with Joel McCrea and Evelyn Keyes. McCrea did not enjoy being called an actor, but there was an odd mixture of modesty and pride when he'd say, 'I'm not an actor, I'm Joel McCrea!'. I remember the director [Robert Parrish] saying to him, 'When Artur Rubinstein plays the piano, he's plays high and low notes, soft and loud notes. He's looking for the right note'. McCrea replied, 'Well, I found the right note a long time ago and I've stuck with it'. The leading lady, Evelyn Keyes, had played Scarlett O'Hara's sister in *Gone with the Wind*. I thought she was very attractive, entertaining and intelligent, but she was much under-used.

In a film as tough and vigorous as *Hell Drivers*, which you made for Cy Endfield in 1957, is there an American influence at work?

Yes, in the dramatic tempo and vigour. That was a very popular film that often crops up on television. It's exciting, has a good script and a strong cast, with actors like Stanley Baker, Patrick McGoohan and Sean Connery in a bit-part. It worked very well, but Cy Endfield was a rather unhappy character, who didn't fit too well in English society.

You played Napoleon again for King Vidor in *War and Peace*.

I enjoyed working for King Vidor and doing Napoleon again after all those years. But we had two directors making this huge epic. Mario Soldati was the Italian director and Vidor the American, and the two could never agree on anything! I was criticised in the French press for portraying a mean and villainous Napoleon, which is how Tolstoy presents Napoleon. For the French he is always 'The Emperor', and my performance didn't fit their image of him.

Would you choose a film on the basis of its director?

Yes, I would certainly choose a film if it was to be made by a director I respected, but I'd be even more likely to choose one on the basis of the script. When I look back at all the parts I've played, I think I was most often attracted by what I thought they would teach me. The parts I really loved taught me what it was like to be a Harley Street psychiatrist, or a disillusioned emperor, or the victim of a concentration camp, or a lunatic police inspector. I'm attracted to scripts that offer me roles which take me out of my own skin and into other lives.

As for directors, the kind I don't like is the one who comes to me before a take and says, 'Now, Herbert, give me your best'. Often people who've been actors before they become directors are especially good to work with. They know what an actor suffers; they speak his language; they *like* actors. I am thinking of people like Carol Reed or Harold French [for whom Lom made *Secret Mission*, *The Man Who Watched Trains Go By*] who used to address his cast as 'My darlings'. David Lean was a great director in many ways, but I think he was a little afraid of actors. He didn't quite know how to tackle them.

Was your involvement in the 'Pink Panther' movies a major highlight of your career?

Oh, certainly. I was badly typecast in British films and it needed an American – Blake Edwards – to take me away from endless villainous roles, and into the comedy of the 'Pink Panther' films. I loved playing the part of the dithering lunatic of a police inspector. I think people *like* to see the police in trouble; they enjoy seeing Inspector Dreyfus reduced to an utter twitching wreck.

In recent years has it been increasingly difficult to maintain an interesting career in Britain?

I find it impossible to maintain an interesting career in Britain. Mind you, for as long as I can remember British films have been hovering on the brink of death, so perhaps it is not really so different today. Certainly in recent decades I have filmed more often all over the place than in Britain.

Virginia McKenna

The Second Mrs Tanqueray, Father's Doing Fine (1952), The Oracle, The Cruel Sea (1953), Simba, The Ship That Died of Shame (1955), A Town Like Alice (1956), The Smallest Show on Earth, The Barretts of Wimpole Street (1957), Carve Her Name with Pride, Passionate Summer (1958), The Wreck of the Mary Deare (1959), Two Living, One Dead (1961), Born Free (1965), The Lions are Free (1967), Ring of Bright Water, An Elephant Called Slowly (1969), Waterloo (1970), The Lion at World's End (1971), Swallows and Amazons (1974), Holocaust 2000, The Disappearance (1977).

After three forgettable films, Virginia McKenna appeared in *The Cruel Sea* in 1953 and for the rest of the decade became Britain's top female star. Her success in the 1950s is the more striking since the decade was so male-dominated and since the war films, in which she established herself, were notoriously short of rewarding roles for women. Her role in *The Cruel Sea* was followed by a similarly small but memorable role in the Dearden-Relph film, *The Ship That Died of Shame*. The films for which she is perhaps best remembered are those two accounts of heroic women – *A Town Like Alice* and *Carve Her Name with Pride*. In these two extremely arduous roles, she subjugated her delicate beauty and apparent fragility to the unglamorous rigours required of her, and scored major successes. Since 1960, she has been most closely associated with her role as Joy Adamson (opposite her husband Bill Travers) in *Born Free*, and she and Travers have worked together on several films reflecting their interest in and concern for wild life.

Interview date: October 1989.

You are one of the very few British film actresses who became a star in the 1950s. Was there a shortage of good roles for women?

That's traditional, I think. I was lucky because, at the beginning of the 50s, they started to make those wonderful war stories, starting with *The Cruel Sea*, and going on to *A Town Like Alice* and *Carve Her Name with Pride*. I just happened to arrive at the right moment and had the kind of very English looks or personality which fitted into that slot. At the time, Britain was wanting to look back, and showing the courage and struggles that people had had to go through was a very pertinent thing.

You became a star in tough roles for women, showing that a woman could be just as brave and as enduring as a man. Were you aware of this kind of image being built up?

No, I never thought of it like that. I *do* think there are women who are just as brave as men, though they usually face quite different kinds of problems and challenges. I became very close friends with Odette during the making of *Carve Her Name with Pride*, because she was our technical adviser. She was living proof of a woman who had suffered enormously – torture, solitary confinement, things which are probably almost impossible for us to imagine coping with. Not many films had been made about women during war so, until that time, women hadn't had the same opportunity as men to show other dimensions of their nature. But although those women were enormously courageous and tough, I always tried to show where they were vulnerable, to make them whole people.

Were you being as carefully groomed as you might have been in Hollywood?

Oh, no. I never went to Rank's Charm School or anything like that. I went into Rep for six months in Dundee, did two plays in London for Tennent's, did *The Second Mrs Tanqueray* for Dallas Bower, did some other films and television, then went back to the theatre. I had a very good agent who put me up for things, some of which I got, some of which I didn't. I was offered a Hollywood contract but I didn't take it, because I didn't want to be a groomed, Hollywood-type young actress, cast in roles for which I didn't much feel anything.

What sort of contract(s) were you under?
My only film contract was with Rank; I had to sign it in order to do *A Town Like Alice*. It was for five films; I did that one, *Carve Her Name with Pride* and *Passionate Summer*. I was pregnant when I did the last one, so that was the end of that for a bit. Then they asked me to do a film I didn't want to do, and then, when they asked me to do a further film, I was having my next child, so I think they gave up on me and released me from my contract. At one time I was leased by Rank to do *The Smallest Show on Earth*. They charged a lot of money for me to do it, but I was only paid my contract money.

***The Cruel Sea* really brought you to public notice. Did you enjoy working at Ealing?**
Oh, I loved it. I didn't have a very big part but, as it was virtually the only woman's part in the film, it was a much sought after part. People always remember that film, and they remember me – I think it was the WREN's hat, which was attractive. Everyone seems to remember that! It was the first time I had a screen kiss! I was very nervous and it's quite difficult at first. Later on, you learn not to take any notice of the people standing around looking at you. It was Donald Sinden's first film, too, and he was very jolly and nice. My character was very British and a bit 'stiff-upper-lip'.

After a season at the Old Vic, you returned in Brian Desmond Hurst's *Simba*. Why were there so many of these outpost-of-Empire films in the 50s?
Perhaps it was the need for adventure, standing up against other cultures or environments which seemed harsh – pitting ourselves against unknown forces and emerging again as courageous and brave. Also it was the beginning of filming in other lands, which has increased as the years have gone by. Africa had its moment when practically every film you saw seemed to have been shot in Kenya.
   I got on extremely well with Brian Desmond Hurst

and, of course, Dirk Bogarde was the leading man in that film, and he was so sensitive and kind and helpful. He was much more experienced than I was and was very supportive when we were rehearsing. I've never met anyone who *hasn't* liked working with Dirk. He was the top male star in Britain then and he developed into such an incredible character actor.
   I think *Simba* was ideologically fairly black-and-white – an unfortunate term! I think it was rather 'we were the victims of this devastatingly cruel group of people who wanted to massacre us all'. In reality, many more Africans than British were killed by the Mau Mau. It was just a story of this one family and what happened to them; and I played the daughter. Dirk and I didn't go on location, we did our filming at Pinewood. They did the location scenes with doubles. They dressed my double in a scarlet dress for the scene in which I discovered my parents killed, and that seemed all wrong.

You won awards for your next role, as Jean in *A Town Like Alice*. Was this the film that really established your image with film-goers?
Probably. Again, we never went away, we did it all in the studio! There was a second unit, which did a little bit in Alice Springs and all the jungle stuff. We tramped through the woods at Burnham Beeches in the freezing cold with glycerine sprayed on our faces! It was quite nasty because we were wading through a swamp full of tins and the things that people just chuck, and we were falling all over ourselves and absolutely freezing. When we came off we were quickly wrapped in blankets and given brandy.
   The film was a great success and Peter Finch was superb in it. He was one of the most imaginative and truly creative actors I think we ever had here. I got such a lot from working with him. We would sit and rehearse our scenes quietly together and it was wonderful. There are people who don't like to rehearse at all, but I find it important to rehearse first, and then hope that the first take is the one. Jack Lee, the director, was a very creative person, very quick, and there was a cast full of marvellous actresses – Marie Lohr, Renee Houston, Jean Anderson, and Maureen Swanson. Making that film was a happy experience; I don't think we had anyone who was difficult.

***The Smallest Show on Earth* was your second film for Basil Dearden, who had also done *The Ship That Died of Shame*. How would you describe him as a director of actors?**

He was quite low-key in his advice. He was very help-ful, but he left you a lot of freedom; I think he liked actors – some directors don't. *The Smallest Show on Earth* was a lightweight sort of comedy, and was the film I had the most fun making. What with Margaret Ruther-ford, Peter Sellers, Bernard Miles, Leslie Phillips – and of course, my husband Bill, although he wasn't my hus-band then - it was tremendous fun. People were so amusing in their scenes. We only managed to stop our-selves from laughing with difficulty.

Having starred in several films, what attracted you to the secondary role in *The Barretts of Wimpole Street*?
The leading role had already been cast to Jennifer Jones, but I think Henrietta is a wonderful part, almost better than Elizabeth Barrett. There is a defiance and grit about Henrietta which I found very interesting – stand-ing up against authority, madly in love, defying every-thing. That is more interesting than lying on a chaise longue! I enjoyed playing her very much. In a way the star system is more evident on an American film. Jen-nifer sat slightly apart, but she was always charming to talk to. If she was a little detached, that was the back-ground of American stars. We don't have a star system in that way.

How did you prepare yourself to play the role of Violette Szabo in *Carve Her Name with Pride*?
I read the book, of course. I also went to a gymnasium in London and learned judo and how to shoot a Sten gun; I learned parachute jumping, and, of course, I talked to Odette. She told me a lot of stories about prison camp. I also met people who had known Violette in the coding office, including the man who had written her code poem, and I did quite a lot of research. It's one of the films I'm proudest of – not because of what *I* did, but because it told the story of this extraordinary person who represents so many others whose stories have not been told. The courage of women who work behind enemy lines, the terror they must feel on a day-to-day basis, risking their lives and risking never seeing their families again. All that became a real experience for me which affected me very deeply.

Two Living, One Dead is one of the most mysterious films – directed by Anthony Asquith and with well-known stars – and virtually unseen.
We went to Sweden to make it and it was really fascinat-ing. Asquith was a superb director – he looked like a

Peter Finch and McKenna in *A Town Like Alice*, 1956

brilliant pixie – and I think it's an excellent picture. But when it was shown to the distributors they said it had no sex and no violence, and they refused to handle it. It was never seen, except perhaps at two o'clock in the morning on television. Patrick McGoohan was in it and Bill, my husband, and Alf Kjellin and Dorothy Alison. It's about the victims of a robbery in a post office, about the Post-master who is accused of collusion with the robbers and how it ruins his life. It was very well done.

After 1960, you filmed much less frequently. Did you find fewer congenial roles or did your interests after *Born Free* change more to wild life matters?
The main reason was that I started to have a family. I had my first child in 1958, and others in 1960, 1963 and 1967. By the time we had filmed *Born Free* and come back, it had taken over a year out of the 60s. Playing a real person, who was not only alive, but there during much of the filming, made it a unique experience. The relationship that developed between Bill and me and the lions sowed the seeds of the work that Bill and I do today in our charity, Zoo Check, now renamed The Born Free Foundation (of which Zoo Check, Elefriends and Into the Blue are projects).

Lord Bernard Miles

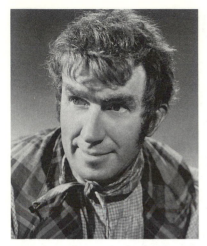

Channel Crossing (1933), *The Love Test* (1934), *Late Extra*, *Twelve Good Men*, *Crown vs Stevens*, *Midnight at Madame Tussaud's* (1935), *Kew Gardens** (narrator) (1937), *The Citadel*, *The Challenge*, *13 Men and a Gun*, *Convict 99*, *The Rebel Son* (1938), *Q Planes*, *The Four Feathers*, *The Spy in Black*, *The Lion Has Wings*, *Band Wagon*, *The Stars Look Down* (1939), *Pastor Hall*, *Dawn Guards**, *Sea Cadets**, *Contraband* (1940), *Freedom Radio*, *This Was Paris*, *Quiet Wedding*, *Home Guard**, *The Common Touch*, *The Big Blockade* (1941), *One of Our Aircraft is Missing*, *The Day Will Dawn*, *In Which We Serve*, *The First of the Few*, *The Goose Steps Out* (1942), *Tunisian Victory* (narrator) (1943), *Tawny Pipit*, *Two Feathers** (1944), *Carnival*, *Great Expectations* (1946), *Nicholas Nickleby*, *Fame is the Spur* (1947), *The Guinea Pig* (1948), *Bernard Miles on Gun Dogs** (1949), *Chance of a Lifetime* (1950), *The Magic Box* (1950), *River Ships** (narrator), *Never Let Me Go* (1953), *Moby Dick*, *Tiger in the Smoke*, *The Man Who Knew Too Much*, *Zarak* (1956), *Fortune is a Woman*, *The Smallest Show on Earth*, *St Joan* (1957), *Tom Thumb*, *The Vision of William Blake** (narrator) (1958), *Sapphire* (1959), *A Flourish of Tubes** (1961), *Heaven's Above!* (1963), *The Specialist** (1966), *Baby Love* (1968), *Run Wild, Run Free* (1969).

* Documentary and/or short film.

Bernard Miles' great strength as an actor was his capacity to suggest simplicity and goodness without weakness. This screen *persona* was established in the film *In Which We Serve*, in which he is the incarnation of working-class stoicism, and was memorably clinched in his roles as Joe Gargery in *Great Expectations*. In 1956 he appeared in two films which made use of and subverted the kindly Miles image: *Tiger in the Smoke*, an often-chilling thriller, and Hitchcock's re-make of *The Man Who Knew Too Much*, in which

Miles' benign *persona* makes the revelation of his villainy the more shocking. Perhaps as a result, in later films, such as *Sapphire*, one is led to wonder whether the kindly surface hides slyness or something more dangerous. The two films he directed – *The Tawny Pipit* and *Chance of a Lifetime* evoke him and their period vividly in their visions of cross-class consensual activity.

Interview date: July 1990.

You made a great many films during the 30s. What do you remember of working with people like Michael Powell?

Micky was lovely; I made *The Love Test* for him when he was doing quota quickies. He was rising through the ranks as I was making my own way and we did several films together. I enjoyed working with him. He used to come to our home, a little country cottage, and loved our food! I used to cycle twenty-five miles to the studio each day and twenty-five miles back. I met Del Giudice then, too; he was a true genius who had lived an outrageous life. Two Cities was really Del Giudice's creation - and he was responsible for *In Which We Serve*.

What do you remember of this film which really established you as a film star?

Having spent wonderful times with the Mediterranean Fleet, Noel Coward decided he would like to make a

naval film. Dickie Mountbatten felt that it was high time a film was made about the Navy and hit on the idea of a film about a destroyer. He then fed the information to Noel who did the script. Dickie Mountbatten sold the idea to the King, then he came to see Del Giudice with two Royal Marines in full uniform. It was financed by a great man, the Jewish carpet merchant, Sassoon. When Sassoon sent him the cheque, in one stroke Del Giudice was the only free man in the industry, the only man with £195,000 in his pocket and he owned *In Which We Serve*. He was a great impresario. Dickie Mountbatten himself suggested me for the part I played – Kath Harrison and I were a real working-class couple.

Did the two films you made for the Boultings, *The Guinea Pig* and *Fame is the Spur*, appeal to your Socialist instincts?

Yes, they did. *Fame is the Spur* was said to be based on

Josephine Wilson and Bernard Miles in *Chance of a Lifetime*, 1950

Ramsay Macdonald's career. The film didn't do very well; Michael Redgrave wasn't a popular star and it wasn't a sympathetic role, but Rosamund John was wonderful in it.

I did some of the writing for *The Guinea Pig* with Warren Chetham-Strode – a difficult man who didn't want his play altered. I wrote some lovely things which the Boultings had to force him to accept. Dickie Attenborough was very good in it. He was also wonderful in *In Which We Serve*. His part in that was modelled on a young sailor on the *Kelly* which was sunk at Crete. He was stationed below decks, loading shells, when he heard dive-bombers overhead and ran away.

How did you come to direct *Tawny Pipit* and *Chance of a Lifetime*?

I directed *Tawny Pipit* for Two Cities. Del Giudice was asked by Dickie Mountbatten and others to make a film about the true nature of the British people. Del asked me

to think up a story and said he would get the money from Arthur Rank. I lived near Julian Huxley, the great biologist; and he suggested that, in the teeth of all the people making war films like *San Demetrio, London*, I should make a film about something which was then happening in the ornithological world. A bird, the Tawny Pipit, had been sighted in Norfolk which had never been seen in Britain before. He put me on to a publican in Norwich, Jim Vincent, who had seen the original nest. Well, he didn't want to show us where it was, so we had to get Julian Huxley to talk to him. It was a charming film, I think. When the Americans first saw it, they dumped it in a cupboard for two years but it was finally shown and got the greatest notices.

I didn't know anything about filming really; I had a good cameraman and knew the cutters were good. Charles Saunders was really the cutter, but I felt that he should be given credit as co-director because he put the whole thing together as a coherent film. We had Rosamund John, Lucy Mannheim, a German refugee and a fine actress, who married Marius Goring, and Jean Gillie who was absolutely gorgeous; she died a few years later.

Del liked the film very much and asked me to do another for him. By that time I had become a sort of socialist; I'd met Ernie Bevin, Stafford Cripps, all of whom backed Del Giudice. I was very attracted to the idea of co-operation between management and workers; that was my kind of Socialism.

A few years later, I came up with the story for *Chance of a Lifetime*. I got the idea of the one-way plough from the great industrialist, Harry Ferguson, who actually manufactured and sold this implement. The plough is really the star of the film. Basil Radford played the boss of the factory and he was a wonderful actor - he could only do one thing, but he did it better than anyone else. Del knew that Arthur Rank, being a rich Methodist Tory, wouldn't like the film; so he set about winning Stafford Cripps, Bevin and others.

When we arranged the showing it was seen by half the Labour Party. Anthony Crossland was there, and Sir John Reith, too. I stood in the doorway waiting for them to come out and Reith, the Scottish head of the BBC, said 'Great job, you should be proud of it'. Then Crossland came up to me and said 'Bloody marvellous! And you don't mention the word "Socialism" – you're a clever bugger!'. You see, I had a conceit that I could 'speak for England'. Churchill had used that phrase in a speech as Prime Minister and I didn't see why I shouldn't borrow it! So I was impudent enough to make the films 'speak for England'.

Did you enjoy playing Joe Gargery in *Great Expectations*?

I got on very well with David Lean. I fell foul of him once, though, because, when Joe Gargery meets Pip and Herbert in London and is so struck with the importance of the meeting, he is supposed to put his new top hat on the mantelpiece. However, the mantelpiece was very narrow and I realised I couldn't do the shot. I was very shy of David then, so I went on with the first take and of course the hat fell off. David was disappointed because it would have been such a good shot, so I asked if I could do it the way I had the first time, which was to catch the hat each time it fell off the mantelpiece. Francis L. Sullivan as Jaggers was wonderful, a great presence. Martita Hunt was a flamboyant character off-screen as well as on; she had taken Alec Guinness under her wing. All those scenes with the boy, Tony Wager, were done in North Kent on the river, near the marsh country. We stayed in Gravesend when we were doing all that stuff.

Why do you think it was such a success?

I think the moralities had changed. Pip is awful, really, because he lets Joe and Magwitch down. John Mills was so good in it, he's such a great technician and a lovely human being. David Lean did a marvellous job with the script, given that he was a non-reader. I didn't steep myself in the book to play the part, but I knew my Dickens.

I also played Newman Noggs in Cavalcanti's film of *Nicholas Nickleby*, which we made at Ealing. Cavalcanti was lovely to work, with but the crew played bad tricks on him. He had one or two altercations with the electricians at the time when the trade unions were very strong. I was doing a scene one day and there was a book or something lying on the floor of the set. Cav called to Jack Martin, the First Assistant in charge of the shot, and said we had to get rid of it. Jack replied that we couldn't touch it because there were no Props people available and if anyone else touched it there'd be a strike. They had to send a car to Wembley to fetch a Props man to move the thing, while shooting just stopped.

I remember Cedric Hardwicke in that film. He decided at the outset of his career that he couldn't play romantic leads, and that he would have to specialise as a character actor.

What do you recall of working for John Huston on *Moby Dick* in the mid-5Os?

When the sun wasn't shining we would all meet on the deck of the *Pequod* – Huston, Richard Basehart, Greg Peck, Leo Genn and I – and we would play poker until the sun came out and we could start filming again. Greg was usually given 'handsome' parts and had a lovely light comic touch, but he was marvellous in *Moby Dick*, such a tragic part. He was so modest, an absolutely lovely man. I kept in touch with Huston until he died.

I was there when Orson Welles did his great preaching scene. He came on to the stage and Huston called for quiet. He told us that he, Huston, would leave the stage, and gave the impression that Welles was such a great actor, we were privileged to have him there. Orson, however, didn't like Huston very much, and used to give him orders because he was so used to directing himself. John always spoke softly, but he was a bit cruel and liked to let the actors suffer a bit.

Sir John Mills

Words and Music, The Midshipmaid (1932), *Britannia of Billingsgate, The Ghost Camera* (1933), *The River Wolves, A Political Party, The Lash, Those Were the Days, Blind Justice, Doctor's Orders* (1934), *Royal Cavalcade, Forever England/Brown on Resolution, Car of Dreams, Charing Cross Road* (1935), *First Offence, Tudor Rose* (1936), *OHMS, The Green Cockatoo* (1937), *Goodbye Mr Chips* (1939), *Old Bill and Son* (1940), *All Hands** (1940), *Cottage to Let, The Black Sheep of Whitehall* (1941), *The Big Blockade, The Young Mr Pitt, In Which We Serve* (1942), *We Dive at Dawn* (1943), *This Happy Breed, Victory Wedding*, Waterloo Road* (1944), *The Way to the Stars, The Sky's the Limit*, Total War in Britain** (narrator) (1945), *Land of Promise** (voice only), *Great Expectations* (1946), *So Well Remembered, The October Man* (1947), *Scott of the Antarctic* (1948), *The History of Mr Polly* (+ prod), *The Rocking Horse Winner* (+ prod), *Friend of the Family** (narrator), *The Flying Skyscraper** (narrator) (1949), *Morning Departure* (1950), *Mr Denning Drives North* (1951), *The Gentle Gunman, The Long Memory* (1952), *Hobson's Choice, The Colditz Story* (1954), *The End of the Affair, Above Us the Waves, Escapade* (1955), *It's Great to be Young, War and Peace, The Baby and the Battleship, Around the World in 80 Days, Town on Trial!, The Vicious Circle* (1956), *Dunkirk, Ice Cold in Alex, I Was Monty's Double* (1958), *Tiger Bay, Summer of the 17th Doll* (1959), *Tunes of Glory* (1960), *The Swiss Family Robinson, The Singer Not the Song, Flame in the Streets* (1961), *The Valiant, Tiara Tahiti* (1962), *The Chalk Garden* (1963), *The Truth About Spring* (1964), *Operation Crossbow, King Rat* (1965), *Sky West and Crooked* (dir, prod), *The Wrong Box, The Family Way* (1966), *Chuka, Africa-Texas Style!* (1967), *Lady Hamilton, A Black Veil for Lisa, Oh! What a Lovely War* (1968), *Run Wild, Run Free, Adam's Woman* (1969), *Ryan's Daughter* (1970), *Dulcima* (1971), *Young Winston, Lady Caroline Lamb* (1972), *Oklahoma Crude* (1973), *The 'Human' Factor* (1975), *A Choice of Weapons* (1976), *The Devil's Advocate* (1977), *The Big Sleep, The 39 Steps* (1978), *Zulu Dawn, Quatermass* (1979), *Gandhi* (1982), *Sahara* (1984), *Who's That Girl?* (1987).

* Documentary or short film.

A star of British films for nearly fifty years, John Mills has had one of the longest careers in British cinema. He has made almost one hundred films for the screen, and the range is as impressive as the number. During the 40s he was much associated with brave servicemen roles, but, even in these, there is a surprising range: he is as convincing below decks in *In Which We Serve* as when playing the RAF Officer in *The Way to the Stars*; and he is a persuasive villain in *Cottage to Let*. His graceful and intelligent playing as Pip holds together the episodes of *Great Expectations* in which a cast of superb grotesques does its appointed turns. He is a different kind of upwardly mobile hero

in *Hobson's Choice* in which his quietly dogged Willie Mossop is a match for the pyrotechnics of Charles Laughton, and gave one of his finest performances as the neurotic officer in *Tunes of Glory*. He filmed regularly throughout the next two decades, winning an Oscar for his role in *Ryan's Daughter* in 1971. In 1949 he produced two films – *The History of Mr Polly* and *The Rocking Horse Winner* – which, unsuccessful in their day, now hold up very well.

Interview date: July 1990.

Your long career in cinema started in 1932, but it was the 40s that established you as a major star. You worked several times with Anthony [Puffin] Asquith. How did you find him as a director?

Wonderful, very sympathetic and totally charming. He loved actors, loved movies. I made a film called *The Way*

to the Stars with him. One very hot day we were doing the famous John Pudney poem ["Johnny-in-the-clouds"] when Puffin said he wanted to do the whole thing in one long tracking shot with no cut. So I started off with Take One and it seemed to go all right. I had tears in my eyes. I got to the end of it, but nobody said 'Cut', so I waited; then looked around and there was Puffin, cross-legged, like a little Buddha, sitting underneath the camera fast asleep! When he woke up he said, 'Wonderful! Print it!'.

My first film for Puffin was *Cottage to Let* and I needed this badly because I'd just come out of the Army and was very hard up. Any job would have done, but I loved playing the villain. I was remembered from before the war as a hero and I was attacked by the fans for 'letting down the country' and all that stuff. It had a very good cast – Alastair Sim, George Cole and so on.

'Your next Asquith film, *We Dive at Dawn* was made at Gainsborough, as was *Waterloo Road*. What do you recall of that studio?

It was a nice little studio. I remember *Waterloo Road* very well because that was Sidney Gilliat's first picture. The great fight with Stewart Granger was interesting. When I saw Sidney's script it had the hero and the villain not meeting until the very end of the movie, running parallel to one another throughout the film. They were to meet at the very end and I (the hero) was to knock him out and that was to be it. I told Sidney that people would expect a major fight. Well, Granger and I rehearsed for ten days. He was a very good boxer and I'd done quite a lot, too, so it was a really good fight. I think it was a damn good movie. Almost all of it was made in Gainsborough's Islington studio, except the bit where I'm running across live railway lines!

How do you feel about your third Asquith film, *The Way to the Stars*?

I saw it recently on television and it's like watching a piece of history now. I don't like watching my films because I'm much too critical of them, but I thought this one had great reality. It was very nostalgic and was helped very much by being in black-and-white. At the time we hoped it would help Anglo-American relations. I talked a lot about that to Terry Rattigan [screenwriter] and to Tolly de Grunwald who produced it, and we felt we had something there which might be considered important later on. The main thing during the making of it was, 'Is it entertaining?' and that's always been my yardstick. I don't like speaking from the pulpit. If you have a message it should be packaged in a chocolate wrapper. I think *The Way to the Stars* is an entertaining movie *and* very much a movie for peacetime.

You made *The Young Mr Pitt* for Carol Reed in 1942. Did you feel it was a film about 40s England as much as an historical film?

I didn't think about that aspect of it. All I was worried about was my wig and the coat! I went into that film at the last moment because Carol hadn't got anyone for it, and I needed the job. Carol cast me as Wilberforce and there were no clothes. I was fitted out on the morning I played the scene in the House of Commons! Carol was one of the best directors I ever worked with. He had an uncanny sense of saying 'yes' at the right moment and spotting anything that was slightly untrue. He loved actors and was a good actor himself.

How did you come to be involved in *In Which We Serve*?

Noel [Coward] wrote the part of Shorty Blake for me because he knew I needed the work. I owe him so much. There were some terrific scenes, such as the one with Bernard Miles and the telegram, and the scenes with Kay Walsh – all that stuff was handled beautifully. Kay's great strength is her reality. I did *This Happy Breed* with her too. You can hardly believe she is acting; when the cameras turned over she just *did* it.

There was also, of course, the fun of working with David Lean for the first time. Essentially, he directed the picture even though he and Noel are credited as co-directors. Part of Noel's genius was that he could judge when to leave things to someone else, as he did with David. He knew David was a brilliant technician and, of course, Carol Reed had suggested David for the directing, so he just left the whole thing to David (including the direction of Noel's own performance). They got on like a house on fire. David has a reputation for not liking actors and not getting on with them, but I can't join that club. We started together with *In Which We Serve* and went on to make four or five other pictures together. The thing about working with David Lean is this: I don't care if I wait a year, I know that the set-up for each shot will be the best set-up I could possibly have. I waited a year for him in Ireland [*Ryan's Daughter*] and it was well worth it – I got an Oscar out of it! David is the best editor in the world, bar none. He is also a great story-teller. Anyone who can take a book of the length of *Great Expectations* and do such a masterful job on a script which keeps the story – well . . .! I firmly believe that you must cut any scene that doesn't promote either the character or the story – you have to be ruthless. David's films have always held their story line.

In Which We Serve was a very arduous film to make, physically, with lots of time spent in cold water in the tank. We were in that tank for nearly two weeks and it was absolutely filthy by the time we finished.

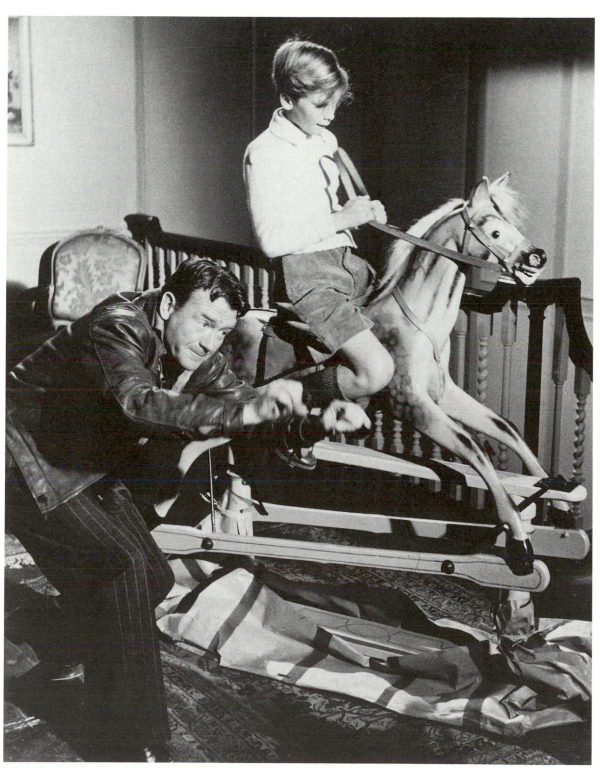

John Mills and John Howard Davies in Anthony Pelissier's *The Rocking Horse Winner*, 1949

Did you feel at the time that *Great Expectations* was something special?

Yes, I thought so half-way through when we were shooting the river scenes with the paddle-steamer. When I saw those rushes I thought they were sensational, and I loved the script. I felt the film was going to be a very big success, but what I didn't know was that it would turn out to be David's best picture, in spite of all his bigger films later on. I remember David saying he wanted me to play a part which could be seen as a coat-hanger for the other great characters. He said he needed someone with a lot of drive for Pip, otherwise the whole thing would collapse. The picture couldn't succeed on the other characters, *they* had to succeed on Pip. Where I think David was so clever was to use the voice-over commentary that I did. That enabled us to cover chunks of the story in a couple of lines. Pip avoided the coat-hanger effect and avoided being too much smothered by the others. In other words, Pip emerged as a good leading man's role. I loved playing with all those great grotesque characters; the actors and actresses themselves were such wonderful characters to act with – Francis L. Sullivan, for instance, as Jaggers. And there has never been a better Miss Havisham than Martita Hunt, ever.

If I remember any scene particularly it is the one in which Miss Havisham catches fire. This was very difficult to stage because we only had one take; the long table which David had set up for the wedding feast, with the cake and the mice and cobwebs, had taken Props two days to do. Luckily, we got it in one take. The business of Miss Havisham seeming to be on fire was done with padding soaked in methylated spirits. It was a brilliantly shot scene. It could have been very dangerous, but we had very good Props and Special Effects people.

What do you think of the rather upbeat ending of *Great Expectations* – you and Valerie Hobson running down the path together?

David wanted a happier ending. I liked it because there had been so much tragedy and heartbreak throughout the story that it was nice to send the audience off feeling it was all right in the end. It could have been a touch of post-war optimism also – David didn't want people to go out feeling sad.

Do you remember Anthony Wager who played young Pip?

Yes, I worked with him quite a bit and he was very good. We did a couple of things like getting him to do particu-

lar hand movements which I repeated later on, so that we'd seem like the same character.

You worked for a number of different companies throughout the 40s and 50s. What kinds of contracts did you have?

For about twelve years I was under contract to Rank, to act, direct and produce; the other contracts were just one-off picture deals. It was a very enjoyable way to work: often I'd be two weeks into a film before I even signed a deal. You'd say you liked the idea, shake hands and start shooting! Today, it's endless lawyers, agents, and contracts. It was a very happy time then to make movies.

Did producing add greatly to your worries on *The History of Mr Polly* and *The Rocking Horse Winner*?

I don't think I worried enough! I wasn't a very good producer because I was always dying to get on the floor and didn't really like the office work. However, I wanted to make those two movies which people were shying away from them because they weren't run-of-the-mill. Now I'm rather proud of them. At the time, *Mr Polly* didn't succeed because I was a blue-eyed hero up to then and the audiences hated seeing me as a little, wizened chap with smarmed hair and a moustache, being a henpecked husband. But I wanted to do it. I thought *The Rocking Horse Winner* was a wonderful story, so I also wanted to do that, too. I'm not ashamed of doing either of those films, but they weren't hits with the public. Anthony Pelissier [director] was a great friend of mine and very talented. I gave him his start with those two films.

A nice thing about it all was that, when I said I wanted to do these films they didn't oversee us, didn't come to see it until the cut version was available. Rank was a very nice, honest man who didn't know anything about movies. He came to my dressing-room during *Great Expectations* and said he would like me to sign a contract; he didn't want to go through an agent, just for me to take a pencil and write my own deal. I couldn't believe it! I called my agent and we wrote a deal together; we didn't ask for the earth, but it was a wonderful deal and almost immediately Rank allowed me to make those two seemingly non-commercial films. I was *very* fond of Arthur Rank.

What drew you to *Scott of the Antarctic*?

I had been a schoolboy admirer of Scott. When I heard

Micky Balcon was doing the film I rang him up and asked if I could play the part of Scott. It was one of the best experiences of my career. The whole unit got carried away with the Scott story, partly because we shot it in continuity. We shot in hair-raising conditions, at the top of the Finse Glacier, for instance, and, at one stage, the cameraman was sent home with very bad frostbite. The location work had such reality and we actually *did* all the stunts ourselves, some of them quite dangerous. The continuity aspect of it was important emotionally – and also from the point of view of our beards!

You did several films in the 50s for Roy Ward Baker. What do you recall of *The October Man*, *Morning Departure* and – one I haven't seen – *The Singer Not The Song*?

The October Man was Roy's first film. I've worked with quite a few first-time directors. He was a very intelligent, very nice man, and it was a good tense little picture. *Morning Departure* was rather good, too. It was the story of the *Truculent*, the ship which went down just before we were due to start shooting the movie. In the circumstances, we thought we wouldn't be able to make the film, so we sent the script to the Admiralty, who said to go ahead because the script was uplifting rather than depressing. So we made it, and I received about twenty-five letters from the relatives of boys lost on the *Truculent*, saying how glad they were we had made the film.

But *The Singer Not the Song* – you haven't seen it? Oh, you haven't lived! That was one that went wrong. I had better be careful what I say. Originally, it was to have been played with me and Brando, and you couldn't have two more different people than Bogarde and Brando. They are chalk and cheese! When Brando turned the film down, Dirk, who was under contract to Rank at the time, was asked to play it and he agreed. But he wasn't happy with the film, nor was Roy.

What do you remember of working with Charles Laughton in *Hobson's Choice*?

Charles was a unique, enormously gifted actor, capable of suddenly doing the most exciting things. I always admired him very much, ever since seeing him in *Henry VIII*. He was a weird one, talking in rather a high-falutin' way when we were rehearsing. I loved working with him, although David Lean was rather in awe of him, because he was the first international star David had worked with. And Willie Mossop was a wonderful part for me – he was an unglamorous chap, but he was a hero. It was the performance I have enjoyed most.

You made a lot of war films in the 1950s. Why do you think, a decade after the war, British films were so preoccupied with it?

I suspect people saw the war as rather heroic, exciting and romantic; and we were still going through a certain degree of austerity. *Ice Cold in Alex* was a tremendously exciting picture to make and Lee-Thompson was a wonderful director. He could make a scene out of nothing. The minefield sequence, for instance, was two lines in the script, yet it took four days to shoot and was one of the best sequences in the film; most of it was put in on the spur of the moment by Lee-Thompson. It was 110 degrees in the shade, I remember. I was so disappointed in my love scene with Sylvia Syms. Up to then, I had made love to virtually nothing but submarines and destroyers and this was my big chance, and most of it was cut! A good actress, Sylvia.

Would you agree that *Tunes of Glory* gave you one of the best parts of your career?

It did, definitely. What attracted me to the film was the super script. It was a toss-up to begin with, which part Alec Guinness would play and which part I would do. I was originally intended to play Jock, but I preferred the part I did in the end, even though it was frightfully difficult. I've been asked a hundred times how I did the quivering eye bit – and I will not tell you, either! I had been produced and photographed by Ronnie Neame before, but this was the first time he had directed me. He said, 'I'll tell you one thing to make you feel confident: if you produce a moment of magic, I promise to be in the right place to get it'. An actor can't ask more than that.

Ronald Neame

As cinematographer or co-cinematographer:

Blackmail (assistant c) (1929), *Happy* (co) (1933), *Girls Will Be Boys* (1934), *Drake of England* (co), *Honours Easy, Invitation to the Waltz* (1935), *A Star Fell from Heaven, The Crimes of Stephen Hawke, King of the Castle, Once in a Million, Radio Lover* (1936), *Against the Tide, Café Colette, Strange Experiment, Brief Ecstasy* (co), *The Londonderry Air, Catch as Catch Can, Feather Your Nest, Member of the Jury, There Was a Young Man* (1937), *The Ware Case, The Gaunt Stranger, Who Goes Next?, I See Ice* (co), *It's in the Air* (co), *Murder in the Family, Penny Paradise* (co), *Second Thoughts* (1938), *Cheers Boy Cheer* (co), *Young Man's Fancy* (co), *Come On George* (co), *The Four Just Men, Let George Do It* (co), *Let's Be Famous* (co), *Trouble Brewing* (1939), *Major Barbara, Return to Yesterday* (co) (1940), *In Which We Serve* (1942), *This Happy Breed* (+co-sc) (1944), *Blithe Spirit* (1945).

As director, unless otherwise indicated:

Brief Encounter (co-prod) (1945), *Great Expectations* (co-prod, co-sc) (1946), *Take My Life* (1947), *Oliver Twist* (prod) (1948), *The Passionate Friends* (prod) (1949), *The Golden Salamander* (+co-prod) (1950), *The Magic Box* (prod) (1951), *The Card* (1952), *The Million Pound Note* (1953), *The Man Who Never Was* (1956), *The Seventh Sin* (1957), *Windom's Way* (1958), *The Horse's Mouth* (1959), *Tunes of Glory* (1960), *Escape to Zahrain* (+prod) (1961), *I Could Go on Singing* (1962), *The Chalk Garden* (1963), *Mister Moses* (1964), *A Man Could Get Killed* (co-dir), *Gambit* (1966), *Prudence and the Pill* (co-dir) (1968), *The Prime of Miss Jean Brodie* (1969), *Scrooge* (1970), *The Poseidon Adventure* (1972), *The Odessa File* (1975), *Meteor* (1979), *Hopscotch* (1980), *First Monday in October* (1981), *Foreign Body* (1986).

Ronald Neame is the most distinguished of those British directors who began their careers as cameramen. Son of actress Ivy Close and a successful photographer, he shot more than thirty films in the 1930s, many of them 'quota quickies', hitting the big-time with *Major Barbara* in 1940. This began his very fruitful collaboration with David Lean, culminating in his co-producing films, such as *Great Expectations*, associated with the major prestige period of British cinema. His first film as director was the excellent, unpretentious thriller, *Take My Life*, and, during the ensuing decades, he made a number of first-class entertainments, filming on both sides of the Atlantic. *The Card*, a charming adaptation from Arnold Ben-

nett, is the first of several excellent films Neame made with Alec Guinness, including *The Horse's Mouth*, in which Guinness played anarchic artist Gulley Jimson, and *Tunes of Glory*, with its fine co-starring performances from Guinness and John Mills. Neame also elicited one of Judy Garland's best performances in *I Could Go on Singing* and an Oscar-winning display from Maggie Smith in *The Prime of Miss Jean Brodie*. He is a very sympathetic director of actors and a craftsman of the kind British cinema now badly needs.

Interview date: October 1989.

After working on so many 30s films, how did you come to photograph *Major Barbara* in 1940?

At Ealing I'd worked on a lot of Michael Balcon pictures as a cameraman. My opportunity came when I was phoned by Gabriel Pascal. I'd worked for him on a 'quota quickie' and he wanted me to photograph a test of the star of his new film – Wendy Hiller. Gabby was away on location on *Major Barbara* and the young editor in charge of directing this test was David Lean, who really

directed *Major Barbara*, though Gabby has the credit. For the first time I was photographing a really important picture. David and I became close friends, and we then worked together on Michael Powell's *One of Our Aircraft is Missing*.

Around this time an Italian, called Filippo Del Giudice, decided that he wanted to put British films on the map, and asked Noel Coward if he would make a film about the British war effort. Noel was a bit lukewarm about the idea. He didn't have anything particularly in mind. Then, when he was chatting with his friend, Lord Louis Mountbatten, they got talking about Mountbatten's ship the *Kelly*, a destroyer that had been sunk by the Germans in the Mediterranean. Noel suddenly thought, 'I'll make the story of the *Kelly*. So he got back to Filippo and said, 'I'll make a film for you; I don't know a great deal about directing films, but I *want* to direct it. And I must have around me professional people I admire', and he went to see a lot of films. Amongst these was *Major Barbara*. As a result of seeing this, Noel invited David Lean, me and Tony Havelock-Allan to work on *In Which We Serve*. Later, Noel asked us to come to his studio so that he could read us the script of the film that he had written, and David, Tony and I sat down, in front of a big roaring fire and had a nice large drink. Noel said, 'I will now read you my story', and, for the next four hours, he did just that. There were some wonderful things in the story, but, if it was put on the screen in the way it had been written, it would have run for four hours. So we said, 'Can we take the screenplay and analyse it a bit?' David's idea was that we should take the best things from the Coward screenplay and drop the rest. We would then link the scripts together and make a full story with the shipwrecked crew clinging around a raft in the water, and flashing back to what they were before they found themselves there. I think we got a pretty good script out of it and a very good cast, mainly because of Noel's influence.

Again because of Noel's influence, we got enormous support from Lord Mountbatten and the British Navy. However, at the time we had great opposition from officialdom in England, from the Ministry of Information, and so on. They said this was a very bad film to make, because it showed a British ship being sunk by the Germans and this was not the kind of film to present when we were hoping to win a war. But Mountbatten, who was very powerful, overcame that opposition.

In Which We Serve had a strange history because Del Giudice was a pirate – I mean one of those men who were determined to get their film made no matter what they had to do, no matter how many ships they had to sink – and I'm inclined to get Del mixed up with Gabriel Pascal because they were so similar. Anyway, *In Which We Serve* was Del's baby and he gave this party to which everybody was invited and announced the commencement of the film that we'd already been shooting for about ten days at Denham. A bit later, Del came to David, Tony and me and said, 'Don't tell Noel, but I have something terrible to tell you. We have no money.

The whole thing has been done on credit. The studios have built everything till now without getting any money. Outside of the few salaries that I have paid there is nothing. But', he said, 'we have one hope that might enable us to continue. We've shot ten days. David, can you, over this weekend, cut the first twenty minutes that we have shot and get it into some kind of shape that can be shown?' David said, 'Yes, I think I can do that'. Del said, 'Well, Sam Smith, who is the head of British Lion film distributors, has promised to come and see the film on Monday. I hope he will like the material and that we'll get the guarantee', and that's what happened!

You went on to be the cameraman on *Blithe Spirit*?
After *In Which We Serve*, Noel became very enamoured of our little crew, and said, 'I have a lot of material, why don't you film some more of it?' So, we made *This Happy Breed* which is the first film I photographed in colour, using it to make drab rather than bright colours. We wanted to use colour in a new way and I think we did that successfully. *This Happy Breed* was a key film. And then came *Blithe Spirit* which was a tremendous challenge for a cameraman, because this ghost lady, played by Kay Hammond, was in a grey tulle dress with completely grey make-up and she had to be lit with a green light to create the ghostly illusion. This green light had to follow her everywhere. The problem was keeping it off the other actors, and it was even more difficult when she walked behind them. However, we achieved a good result and I must say I think *Blithe Spirit* holds up today, whereas *This Happy Breed* doesn't. I don't think *In Which We Serve* holds up any longer. Last time I saw it, I felt, well, it's sort of gone.

Some of the upper-class stuff in *In Which We Serve* is a bit excruciating, but the rest isn't – Bernard Miles and co.
Yes, their side of it, the lower deck, stands up. One of our problems was that we had two advisers. We had a lower-deck adviser, an AB (Able-bodied Seaman) who had been Mountbatten's batman during the time of the *Kelly*. And we had a lieutenant in charge of the upper-deck routine and behaviour. They regarded themselves as the technical advisers and they could never agree about anything. Sometimes we got into such trouble that we would get on to the Admiralty just to get their opinion. After *In Which We Serve*, we did *This Happy Breed* and *Blithe Spirit*, and then the war was coming to an end, and Uncle Arthur [Rank], came along.

What were your relations with Rank and Cineguild?

After *Blithe Spirit* we formed Cineguild and Noel was very sarcastic about it. He wanted us to go on making Noel Coward projects and we wanted – Tony, David and I – to form our own little company because we didn't always want to make Coward stuff. Noel was never part of Cineguild, which became part of Independent Producers which was totally owned by Rank. Arthur was a wonderful man. He said to us, 'Make me some good films and leave the rest to me'. First of all, in 1944, he sent me to America for six weeks. He wanted me to look at the American studios and see what we had to do to bring ourselves up-to-date so that we could compete. At that time he was wooing 20th Century-Fox. When I came back from America, having loved it, I was convinced I could make a film that American audiences would like and accept. I told Arthur I would prefer to produce it. I was a good cameraman and I was still very young, but I thought I *could* become a producer. Arthur said, 'I don't see why you shouldn't, so what do you want do?' I said I would like to ask David Lean if he would direct if I produced a film, and he said, 'Go ahead, Ronnie. Tell me what you want to make'. So I asked David if he would direct *Great Expectations*. I can remember David and I walking around the studios and David saying, 'You're one of the top cameramen in the country and it's true I've directed, but are you sure this is good idea?' I said, 'In my opinion, David, you're going to be one of the great directors and it would be an honour for me to produce a film if you'd direct it'. As a result of all this, we made *Great Expectations*. The American market liked it very much, but of course it was still an art-house film as all ours were. There were several others that were all acclaimed as highly successful films, but we were spending too much money. *Great Expectations* only cost about £375,000, but it was too much for what we were receiving back. We needed a world market and we needed America. Then Arthur, with his tremendous enthusiasm, began to get the Rank Organisation into financial difficulties. Eventually, the Independent Producers – Cineguild, Wessex Films, and so on – were shut down.

John Davis, Rank's right-hand man, said we must stop making films for a while, which was not such a silly move because, the moment we stopped making films, the outlay also stopped. Davis was more interested in diversifying the Rank Organisation. He reduced the overdraft in twelve months, but stopped the making of films and started selling the property. A little later he realised that, because Rank owned 600 theatres, the company needed a product for those theatres, even if it was only to bargain with how much they were charging the Americans for their films. We needed films, so they formed another company at Pinewood where I worked under an American called Earl St John who was Executive Producer. We started again as if we were independently making pictures for Rank, but under much tighter control. By that time David had long since left and gone to Korda, but I went back with John Bryan who was one of the greatest set designers in the world. He did the Dickens films and the sets for *The Horse's Mouth*. After that, we parted company in a friendly way, but *The Card*, with Alec Guinness, was the first picture we made when I went back.

So, after we made *Great Expectations*, *Oliver Twist* and *The Passionate Friends*, which David directed, Cineguild broke up. By that time David was becoming more and more important as a director and really didn't need a producer. I would've been so overshadowed by David that it was better that we part. However, I'd decided I would like to direct and indeed I had started to direct before Rank collapsed. After we made *Oliver Twist*, Arthur once again gave me full support and I made my first film, *Take My Life* in 1947. It was a thriller with Tam [Hugh] Williams, Greta Gynt, and Rosalie Crutchley in her first film. Then, after that, came *The Golden Salamander* with little Anouk Aimée and Trevor Howard.

Did you film *The Golden Salamander* on location?

Yes, we went to North Africa. Some films should be made in studios; but I think that, if a film fits being shot on location in North Africa with mud huts, that's where it should be shot. I had directed two films with the Rank people before Arthur moved out, and I then went back, but I've forgotten the order of the films

I think the order was *Great Expectations, Take My Life, Oliver Twist, The Golden Salamander, The Card* . . .

The Card was not Cineguild. That was for the new regime, British Film Makers. This was the Rank Organisation under the auspices of John Davis, and the film was made at Pinewood. A man called Robert Clark was the boss of Elstree Studios which owned *The Card*, but had done nothing with it. They had an option which ran out, and I went to the Arnold Bennett estate and bought it because I thought it was a perfect Guinness part. I sent the book to Guinness, he read it and said, 'Yes, I'll do this one'. We brought in Eric Ambler who did the

Alec Guinness and Kay Walsh in *Tunes of Glory*, 1960

screenplay of *The Card* and it was one of the happiest pictures I worked on. We had a superb cast – Alec, Valerie Hobson, Glynis Johns, Edward Chapman, Veronica Turleigh . . . they all just fell into place, all wanted to do it. They loved the idea of working with Alec and it was a very good script.

Your next two films had American stars, Gregory Peck in *The Million Pound Note* and Clifton Webb in *The Man Who Never Was*? Was this casting a matter of economic strategy?
Not entirely. I think it was John Bryan who, shortly after we finished *The Card*, read a short story by Mark Twain called *The Million Pound Note*, and we got a girl called

Jill Craigie [who later directed several films] to come in and write the screenplay. She turned this short story into a full-length film and I think she did it very well. We wanted Dinah Sheridan for the female lead, but she'd stopped acting by then. We were in desperate straits because we just couldn't find a girl. Greg came in because it's an American part. We owed that to John Davis because, by then, he had built up a relationship with the people who were running United Artists. They said they would put up the money for Greg Peck, if he would do it. Greg wanted to make a picture in England, took a liking to the story, and his salary on it was £75,000, which was a very reasonable sum for Greg. So that's what came after *The Card*.

What about *The Man Who Never Was*? Clifton Webb and Gloria Grahame seemed a curious pairing.

That was purely 20th Century-Fox. Darryl Zanuck's son-in-law, André Hakim, came over to England to produce a film and brought this story, a true story. I mean it was factual, and I was what is laughingly known as a 'hot' director at that time, and André asked me if I would direct it. I liked the idea and we got in Nigel Balchin, who knew a lot about that particular aspect of the war because he had been in Intelligence himself, and so we got rather a good script. This went back to Zanuck who said, 'Well, this is fine but I've got to have names. I have Clifton Webb under long-term contract, and I suggest that he could play a British Officer and get away with it'. Well, he *was* a name and I took a liking to him, and Gloria Grahame was, I guess, another of Zanuck's suggestions. I don't know whether the character was originally American, but it wasn't dishonest to use an American in that part and we cast her as a useful second name. I thought she was very good, but she got bad reviews for it. That again was a very happy film and it was very interesting going to Spain where 'the man who never was' was buried under the name of the naval officer.

Your next film, *The Seventh Sin* for MGM, was I think your first strictly American film.

I was given me the opportunity of directing a film in Hollywood and I jumped at it without really considering whether the film was any good or not. It was a dreadful script, based on a Somerset Maugham novel, and it was a desperately unhappy venture. In fact, it became quite clear, once I started shooting in the studio, that it was going to be disastrous for me. The management of the studio was just changing, and I became very insecure indeed. Anybody else can show insecurity, but not the director. I knew I would never be able to finish the picture. I had never been in such a state in all my life. Eventually Vincente Minnelli finished the film. He didn't want a credit on it; neither did I, but I had to take it. The reason I am telling you this story is to show that there are some bad things that can happen, but wonderful things can happen as a result. When I got home that night, convinced that my career was at an end, the phone rang. A voice said, 'This is George Cukor. I am phoning because I imagine you're feeling pretty low this evening, aren't you?' and I said, 'That's putting it mildly'. He said, 'Well the reason I am phoning is I want to tell you that it is not going to make any difference to

your career. It will not do any damage at all, and you must not worry. I speak with authority because I was the director who was thrown off *Gone with the Wind*'.

You went back England to make *Windom's Way* after that?

Immediately after that, John Bryan, who had been my partner, rang and said, 'I read in *Variety* that you left the picture. How about coming back and making *Windom's Way*?' which he was going to produce with Peter Finch. It was not a successful picture, I'm afraid. It fell between two stools, neither politically profound nor exciting enough as an action film. John just liked the book very much and I would have directed anything to get back to the studios again.

Did you work with James Kennaway on the screenplay for *Tunes of Glory*?

Yes. We did the screenplay together. I firmly believe that the best director is the writer-director because then you have one man who both creates the material and directs it, but that's not always practical, because sometimes a writer is not a good director and vice versa. The next best thing is to have a director and a writer who work so closely together that they are like one man. That's the way I work with writers.

Tunes of Glory seems like a film that would make a good stage play . . .

Yes, and funnily enough, I was asked, by an American called Doolittle, who has a theatre in Los Angeles, if I would turn it into a play and direct it. I would have liked to, but I am afraid of the theatre. I am scared of television, too, because I'm convinced they'd fire me after the fourth day for being two days behind schedule!

The Horse's Mouth and *Tunes of Glory* were both financed by a man whose name I've forgotten. He was a partner of Alexander Korda's and he inherited London Films' contracts when Korda died. One of the contracts was a three-picture deal with Alec Guinness who still had two to do for (I think) £12,000 each.

Did *Tunes of Glory* and *The Horse's Mouth* do well in America?

They did very well, in terms of kudos. People in America today always say, 'I loved your film *Tunes of Glory*'. Everybody saw *Tunes of Glory*, but they saw it on television. This raises another point which is interesting about this particular period. Arthur Rank did everything on God's earth to try to get British films on to the American market, but he failed. Then, American television just didn't have enough material to fill the hours on air. They were frantic for material and among the cheap material they could lay their hands on were old British films. And so, through television, British films became understood and appreciated by Americans. What Arthur had tried so hard to do for so many years happened automatically.

What do you see as the major strengths and weaknesses of British cinema during the period we have been talking about?

There was too much emphasis on 'this is a *British* film'. The most guilty person re this was Michael Balcon who was very parochial in his thinking, although he did make some lovely films. At one time, Michael wanted a title at the end of each film reading, 'This is a British film', and the last thing the Americans wanted was British films. When I was making *Tunes of Glory*, it didn't concern me in the least whether the film would be successful in America because it was a wholly British scene. Now, before I make a film, my first thought is, 'Will this be for a mass American audience?' and we fall between two stools. We are trying in England, except there's practically no industry anyway now, to make films that will appeal to the world market and we can't. We don't know how to do it.

Song of the People*, The Way to the Stars, Perfect Strangers (1945), *School for Secrets, Daybreak* (1946), *Dancing with Crime, When the Bough Breaks, Easy Money* (1947), *Trouble in the Air, My Brother's Keeper, The Weaker Sex, Once a Jolly Swagman* (1948), *Trottie True, Diamond City, The Girl Who Couldn't Quite* (1949), *Hotel Sahara* (1951), *The Story of Robin Hood and His Merrie Men, There Was a Young Lady* (1952), *The Square Ring, A Day to Remember, Thought to Kill* (1953), *The Rainbow Jacket* (1954), *The Ship that Died of Shame* (1955), *Not So Dusty* (1956), *Davy* (1957), *Carve Her Name with Pride, Carry on Sergeant* (1958), *Carry on Nurse, The Shakedown* (1959), *The Hellfire Club, On the Fiddle, Carry on Regardless* (1961), *Carry on Cabby* (1963), *The Secret of Blood Island* (1964), *Georgy Girl, The Fighting Prince of Donegal* (1966), *Headline Hunters* (1968), *Mischief* (1969), *Kadoyng* (1972), *O Lucky Man!* (1973), *In Celebration* (1974), *Smurfs and the Magic Flute* (1975), *The Comeback* (1977), *Laughterhouse* (1984).
* Documentary.

Bill Owen came to notice as a cheerful sergeant in his first film, Anthony Asquith's *The Way to the Stars*. As he says, he never got to play a rank higher than sergeant and most of his characters were called Fred or Alf. Within the middle-class limitations of British cinema, Owen had a very busy career, bringing effortless credibility and authority to such roles as the Australian speedway driver down on his luck in *Once a Jolly Swagman*, and as Jean Kent's music hall partner in *Trottie True* (he could sing and dance, too). He had a good run of films at Ealing, where he credits the Basil Dearden-Michael Relph combination with understanding and using his talents. His best opportunity came in 1974 when he played the father in *In Celebration*, directed by Lindsay Anderson for whom he has worked several times on the stage. He has done notable work in the theatre, including *As You Like It* with Katharine Hepburn and as Albert Finney's father in *Luther*. In television, he has appeared for over nineteen years in the hugely popular series, *The Last of the Summer Wine*.

Interview date: November 1990.

Before the War, you'd been an Entertainments Manager at Warner's Holiday camp and worked for the left-wing Unity Theatre. Did you have any film involvement then?
Through my work at the Unity Theatre, whose members included H.G. Wells, O'Casey and Paul Robeson, I had been involved, before the war, with the Crown Film Unit and done documentaries. So, I had tasted film-making quite early on. I appeared for odd moments in documentary films, as a worker in a line, for instance. The Crown Film Unit used to come to the Unity Theatre quite often to cast people for film work. When I was released from the Pioneer Corps in 1943, I went straight back to Unity. There I was discovered in a revue by David Henley of the Myron Selznick agency, and he offered to take me on. My first job was a part in *The Way to the Stars*, which was a good film to start with. It was one of those performances that I would give over and over in many films.

Anybody who knew his business jumped from one film to another in those days. The industry was enormous.

British cinema, then, seems to have been primarily middle-class. When you were in *The Way to the Stars*, were you aware you were playing 'the working-class character'?
Of course. I played one of the few characters of that type in the film. I was a sergeant and I never played anything higher. Apart from the two extraordinary characters that I played in the stage musicals, *The Threepenny Opera* and *The Mikado*, my roles were all working-class. That was my compartment in those days.

Is it true your name was changed because Rowbotham wasn't considered actorish enough?
After I signed my Rank film contract with Sydney Box the American distributor said that the name Bill Row-

botham (my real name, with which I had scored quite well both on stage and in films) could have 'an adverse marketable effect'. After a great deal of pressure, I agreed to use two of my Christian names and became Bill Owen. I did several films under that Rank contract including *When the Bough Breaks*, *Easy Money* and *Once a Jolly Swagman*. *When the Bough Breaks* was not a good piece of casting. If ever there was a film I should not have been launched in, that was it. I played the leading role with a very beautiful and popular actress called Patricia Roc. Then I went to America for about a year for *As You Like It*, with Katharine Hepburn. When I returned my contract was not renewed. I didn't do much of anything then, except some good work at the Unity.

Do you remember the gloomy-sounding melodrama, *Daybreak*, directed by Compton Bennett, and the thriller, *Dancing with Crime*?
The part I had in *Dancing with Crime* was perfect for me – a sharp young spiv, a real Cagney character. I was shot in the first reel and the critics took note. The next time such a part occurred, in which I could really exploit my character, was with Basil Dearden, who filmed the play I'd done, *The Square Ring*. With more parts, like these, I could have been made into a name at the box-office, but such films weren't being made. I remember very little about *Daybreak*, other than the care taken by Eric Portman to put me at my ease.

Did you enjoy your song-and-dance role in *Trottie True*?
This was the kind of role I could play. I was part of a knockabout vaudeville act, the other members being Hattie Jacques and Jean Kent. Jean provided the glamour and I, as the little working-class comic, was hopelessly in love with her. But with a name like Joe Jugg, what chance did I stand? It should have been a real musical of course . . .

What about Jack Lee, who directed you in *Once a Jolly Swagman*?
I liked him and it wasn't a bad part either. I played an Australian has-been dirt-track star, on the skids and drinking a lot.

What do you recall of Ken Annakin's comedy, *Hotel Sahara*?
The story, which was set in the midst of the Sahara desert, was made entirely in a studio at Pinewood! Ken Annakin concentrated on his actors, and what an excel-

lent team he had! I think it is one of the best films he ever made, and I had the impression he felt very comfortable directing it.

Do you think I over-stress the director's function?
I prefer working with a director who concerns himself more with what his actors are doing in front of the camera rather than with the effect of the angle at which he is photographing them. I remember Silvio Narizzano, the young Canadian director who did *Georgy Girl* – I remember his sharpness and how he cared about the actors and their roles.)

I was in at least one of those Pinewood films that used the experimental technique of Independent Frame. It starred Michael Redgrave and was written and directed by Noel Coward. It was called *The Astonished Heart*, and Michael and I had a ball on my one scene. Then I picked up the paper a few days later to read that Michael had walked off the film. I got a phone call to come back to the studio; Noel Coward had taken over; he'd written it, was acting in it, and was now directing it! I reshot my

Bill Owen and Renee Asherson in Jack Lee's *Once a Jolly Swagman*, 1948

scene with Noel in half a day; it had taken nearly a week with Michael. I went to see the film and I wasn't in it at all; Noel had cut the whole scene.

Did you have a contract with Ealing when you made *The Square Ring* in 1953?
I didn't have a contract there. Working at Ealing was like working in a family atmosphere. It was a very compact studio which, under the guiding hand of Michael Balcon, had become one of the most prestigious production companies in the country. The four films in which I appeared, all made by Michael Relph and Basil Dearden, gave me leading roles and fitted me like a glove – the lightweight boxer in *The Square Ring*, the warned-off jockey in *The Rainbow Jacket*, the member of the music hall act in *Davy* and the bo'sun in *The Ship That Died of Shame*. Basil was the only person who seemed concerned to find the right 'lane' for me to travel in.

The Ship That Died of Shame now looks like a key film of its time. Did you feel the ship's story was a metaphor for post-war England?
You may be right about that, but I don't remember much about it, except the extreme discomfort of filming at sea. Above all, I remember the feeling of security that came with the making of those films. Here were a couple of film-makers who seemed to understand what I was about.

Did you feel you were getting a satisfying range of roles in the 50s?
I certainly knew and felt that I was capable of better things, but what actor doesn't?

How did you get involved in the 'Carry On' films at the end of the decade?
I only did about four, I think, but was certainly in the most important one, *Carry On Nurse*. I think the reason I was dropped might have been that the people in the regular company were more suited; people like Kenneth Williams were such definite types.

You filmed less often in the 60s and early 70s. Were there fewer congenial film roles on offer or did you find more interesting opportunities on stage?
I suppose I was symptomatic of a fading industry which is now almost non-existent in this country. I wasn't being offered parts because films weren't being made. I think if I'd been a young actor at the Royal Court, then, things would have been entirely different. I did work at the Royal Court, but as a much older actor. And, although I say it myself, I was able to do so many things: I was able to sing, dance, do a music hall act, anything, so that my spectrum was very wide. Whether I did these things well or not is another thing, of course, but the fact is that I could do them. I did some interesting things in the theatre during that time.

What do you regard as your most satisfying film work in the post-50s period?
The one major film I made was Lindsay Anderson's film version of *In Celebration* by David Storey. Lindsay first directed it as a play at the Royal Court Theatre, with the same cast. It was a milestone for me because I was virtually finished in the profession until Lindsay came along, picked me up, and dusted me off.

Muriel Pavlow

Sing as We Go (1934), *Romance in Flanders* (1937), *Quiet Wedding* (1941), *Night Boat to Dublin* (1946), *The Shop at Sly Corner* (1947), *Out of True* (1951), *It Started in Paradise* (1952), *The Net*, *Malta Story* (1953), *Doctor in the House*, *Conflict of Wings*, *Forever My Heart* (1954), *Simon and Laura* (1955), *Eyewitness*, *Reach for the Sky*, *Tiger in the Smoke* (1956), *Doctor at Large* (1957), *Rooney* (1958), *Whirlpool* (1959), *Murder She Said* (1961).

Muriel Pavlow belongs so firmly to British cinema of the 1950s that one is startled to find that she has been in films since the 1930s, starting as a child with a bit-role in a Gracie Fields film. Because she was always acting on the stage, her screen career seems to start several times: first with Asquith's immaculate version of *Quiet Wedding*; second, opposite legendary roisterer, Robert Newton in *Night Boat to Dublin*; and third, when her run really begins, in the early 1950s. If she was never asked to do anything wildly at odds with her established *persona*, she appeared in a wider range of roles and genres than might be supposed.

Her normality and responsiveness to those around her are easy to undervalue when, in fact, they are very important to the balance of such comedies as *Doctor in the House* and *Simon and Laura*. She was also an attractive heroine in such thrillers as *Eyewitness* and *Tiger in the Smoke* and war films such as her own favourites, *Malta Story* and *Reach for the Sky*. After 1960, she and her late husband, Derek Farr, worked a great deal on the stage and in television.

Interview date: July 1990.

Do you think of yourself as primarily a stage star who made some films or a film star who often worked on stage?

I think of myself as a stage actress because I began in the theatre when I was fourteen. It wasn't until the beginning of the 50s that I suddenly got a little run of films. I never considered myself a 'film star'; I just suddenly got an extraordinary run of exciting things to do.

Did you play the part of Miranda in *Quiet Wedding* on the stage?

No, Glynis Johns played it on the stage, but I think she was unavailable, so the part fell to me. That was how I first met Derek [Farr], who was starring in it with Margaret Lockwood. I saw it recently and it's typical of English comedies of the time. I remember working with the director Anthony Asquith. He was a charming, slightly 'pixie' character, so gentle in his direction, yet

he knew exactly what he wanted from his actors and usually got it.

Five years later you returned to the screen as leading lady to Robert Newton in *Night Boat to Dublin*. Was this a daunting experience?

I was extraordinarily naive! This was around 1945 and I must have been the only person working in the British film industry who didn't realise that Robert Newton had a drink problem! One morning I was called for 8 o'clock as usual and there was a long pause while I waited in my dressing room. Only much later did I realise that poor Bob had been in no fit condition to work when he arrived at the studio that morning. I remember him as being very charming, but I just didn't realise he had a problem. Everyone treated him as if he were made of eggshells, so not to upset him in any way. In his best roles, he was sheer magnetism on the screen.

What do you remember of Lawrence Huntington as a director?

I remember him well because it was my first film role of any importance. I was very lucky to have him directing me. He wasn't a brilliant director, but he knew his job and was very workmanlike, very professional, with a good understanding of actors. He just rather faded away, I'm afraid; he was a dear man.

The only other film you made in the 40s was *The Shop at Sly Corner*, based on the stage play.

What I remember about that film was that I fell in love during the making of it. I was having costume fittings and still didn't know who was to be my leading man. One day the producer's wife came up to me and announced that it was to be Derek Farr. The first scene we had was the one where my character comes in, sees him, throws herself into his arms and kisses him – and that did it! We announced our engagement in September 1946, and married in January 1947.

I saw the film on television a few weeks ago, and was amazed at how well it stood up. The set-up of some of the scenes was a little mannered, which perhaps came from its having been a stage play. It had a very good cast, including Oscar Homolka. He would always upstage me and I gave up after the first day's work! I knew that if I tried to fight this experienced actor on that score I would come off the worse. After that, I just enjoyed working with him. He was a 'cuddly bear' sort of man, but he had a very penetrating glance. Nothing escaped him. George King, the director, was very easy-going, but he kept his eye on the budget.

Robert Newton and Muriel Pavlow in Lawrence Huntington's *Night Boat to Dublin*, 1946

You made at least one film per year throughout the 50s. Was this a good time to be getting a film career going?

I met Lawrence Huntington again when I had just done the first of my 50s films. He asked what I was doing and I told him, saying that the studio felt the film I had just made would be good for me. 'Ah my dear', he said, 'I'm afraid it's too late!'. He said that the film business was going downhill. But to me, making films during the 50s was super and I have always been glad that my turn came then. It was the last carefree period of British film-making.

What do you recall of a semi-documentary called *Out of True* for director Philip Leacock?

It was about mental breakdowns and we filmed it in a mental hospital south of London; it was very interesting and, for me, very worthwhile because from that film I got *It Started in Paradise*, which started my whole run. There were a lot of 'backstage' problems on *It Started in Paradise*. It was about the world of *haute couture* and they engaged a nice young woman who had produced some fine designs, but she had no experience of dressing films. About a third of the way through it became apparent that what she was doing was a disaster; so another designer was brought in to finish off the film, and, from then on, we all began to look rather smarter. The story was fairly 'Peg's Paper'; still, it was a very lucky film for me. Compton Bennett had considerable success directing in Hollywood, but he didn't whip us along as he should have done in this one.

You then did *The Net*, again directed by Anthony Asquith.

Yes, it wasn't my best part, but it had a bit of bite and it was nice to be part of the leading quartet with James Donald, Phyllis Calvert and Herbert Lom, also the young actor Patric Doonan. We were all sitting around the lunch table one day, laughing about the progress or otherwise of our careers; someone asked if we would be players of whom people would say, 'Whatever became of so-and-so?', and, about a year later, poor Patric committed suicide. That lunchtime conversation haunted me after that.

What do you remember of working with Brian Desmond Hurst on *Malta Story*?

Oh, I thought he was very talented and I liked his direction, but he was inclined to get a bit bored with a project. Towards the end of the film you could see that

his interest was waning. The whole cast went to Malta for the exteriors and night shootings, and the studio work was done at Pinewood. The film remains a highlight for me, even though it wasn't successful, because of the experience of working with Alec Guinness. I played a Maltese girl who became Alec's girlfriend. It was a moving part and I loved playing it.

I suppose *Doctor in the House* was your most commercially successful film? Was it fun to make?

Oh, yes, it was fantastic – my first experience of being in a genuine hit. And making it – oh, we had such fun! And that marvellous director of comedy, Ralph Thomas, was so easy-going and relaxed. For instance, I had to say a very long medical word when I was giving Dirk directions on how to reach a certain department; Ralph said to me, 'Don't worry darling, you won't get it first time but it's all right, we've plenty of time'. Later one of the 'sparks' came up with a great bouquet of flowers for me because I did manage it in one take! If you're surrounded by people like Dirk, Kenneth More, Donald Sinden, Donald Houston and so on, it can't fail to be fun. It was the first of that series and it was the best, I think. When I read the script I laughed, and said to Derek how lucky I was to be in this lovely comedy but we had no idea it would take off in the way it did.

Then Dirk did *Doctor at Sea* with Brigitte Bardot, followed by *Doctor at Large* with me in it again (and Derek playing a Harley Street smoothie). That was fun, too, but it didn't have the freshness of the first one, which has all the right ingredients: the balance of casting was right and, as we say, the soufflé rose. Of course, Nicholas Phipps who did the screenplay was one of the great comedy writers of the 50s, a very witty man.

Do you remember making *Conflict of Wings* for Group 3?

Yes, with the exception of a few interiors at Beaconsfield, we made it all on the Norfolk Broads. I had to drive one of those little power boats and it went quite well. That was a happy film, too. John Eldridge, the director, had a background in documentary films, but his career was hampered by bad health. I doubt if he made any more films after that.

Your co-star, John Gregson, starred with you again four years later in *Rooney*. Did you work well together?

Yes, I think we did. He, too, was very easy-going and relaxed and, if your co-star is relaxed, then you are too.

It was a sweet 'Cinderella' story, really. It was directed by George Pollock who was a first assistant for many years. He then directed some minor films and finally began to be given the big films, including the Miss Marples with Margaret Rutherford. Barry Fitzgerald was in *Rooney*, and he was an old darling. We were all very protective of him, because he really was very old at that stage. We worried that we might be tiring him or whatever, but he was fine.

How did you find working with a woman director – Muriel Box – on *Simon and Laura* and *Eyewitness*?
She was a fine director [she died in 1991] and a charming woman with great knowledge of film-making. We got on very well, but I think I respond better to a male director. Somehow I am more stimulated by a male director to bring out my best.

Simon and Laura was a Rank film; I wasn't under contract then, but I could have been described at that time as 'the flavour of the month'. I only went under contract for the last two films I made for Rank; it was supposed to be three films but I foolishly turned down one called *The Gypsy and the Gentleman* – foolishly because, although it was a rubbishy film, it was directed by Joseph Losey. I think Kay Kendall and Peter Finch were delightfully cast in *Simon and Laura* and Ian Carmichael was *very* good, too.

As for *Eyewitness*, I can't remember much about it except that I started off with a good scene with Michael Craig, from which I stormed out, witnessed the hold-up which Donald Sinden was carrying out, was then promptly knocked down by a bus and spent the rest of the film in a hospital bed looking like a cross between an advertisement for Elizabeth Arden and a nun! I just lay there, in the worst-guarded hospital of all time!

How did you come to play Thelma in *Reach for the Sky*?
I really fought for that part as Douglas Bader's wife. In 1954 I read a book called *Reach for the Sky*; I phoned my agent and told him that if ever a film was to be made of the book, I wanted to play Thelma. About a year later, I met Danny Angel [producer] and Lewis Gilbert [director] and asked them to let me test. Lewis was rather keen that I should play Brace, the nurse, but I couldn't see it. So I tested and got the part of Thelma. I recently attended a Royal Première of the film at the Cannon Theatre in Shaftesbury Avenue. It was to tie in with the fiftieth anniversary of the Battle of Britain. For the first time since around 1957 I saw the film again on the big screen and it was a marvellous print. I suddenly felt rather proud to have been associated with it.

Your next film seems to me a genuinely scary thriller, *Tiger in the Smoke*. Had you read Margery Allingham's novel?
Yes, I was a great fan of Margery Allingham. I was delighted when I got the part but the film didn't quite come off. Unfortunately, I don't think Tony Wright was sinister enough and I would have liked to see him and Donald Sinden reverse their roles. Tony had too much charm for the villain; he was too relaxed almost.

Do you hope to film again?
Yes, but I'm realistic about my chances. I'm lucky to be able to look back on *Malta Story*, *Reach for the Sky* and *Doctor in the House* – three wonderful films in which to be involved.

Little Friend (1934), *The Man Who Knew Too Much*, *Tudor Rose* (1936), *Young and Innocent* (1937), *Cheers Boys Cheer* (1939), *Pastor Hall* (1940), *Spring Meeting*, *Banana Ridge* (1941), *Next of Kin* (1942), *Yellow Canary* (1943), *Out of Chaos**, *Man of Science** (1944), *This Man Is Mine* (1946), *Green Fingers* (1947), *The Three Weird Sisters* , *Counterblast* (1948).
* Documentaries.

Lady Jane Grey was nine days a queen, but her name resonates through British history with an insistent sweetness and innocence at odds with the brevity of her place in the story. It is tempting to see a parallel with Nova Pilbeam, who played her unforgettably in the 1936 film, *Tudor Rose*. Nova Pilbeam's name, too, echoes through British cinema history with an insistence at odds with her comparatively few films. During the 1930s she was undoubtedly Britain's most celebrated child and teenage star, holding her own in such formidable adult company as Matheson Lang in *Little Friend*, Leslie Banks and Peter Lorre in Hitchcock's original *The Man Who Knew Too Much*; and Cedric Hardwicke and Sybil Thorndyke in *Tudor Rose*. If her nine films of the 40s never gave her such opportunities again, she was never less than charming and intelligent. She particularly relished her bitchy role in *Green Fingers* in 1947, but a year later she vanished from British films. However, her name, beauty, and talent remain in the annals and the memory.

Interview date: June 1990.

Although you made most of your films in the 40s, I'd like ask you about several of your 30s films. Did Hitchcock cast you as the kidnapped daughter in *The Man Who Knew Too Much* on the basis of seeing you in *Little Friend*?
I don't know, but the film was for Gaumont-British to whom I went under contract after *Little Friend*. I assume they would have done the casting. It was a very long contract – six or seven years, which was pretty outrageous. It prevented me from being in the theatre as much as I would have liked.

What are your recollections of *The Man Who Knew Too Much*?
A lot of it was set in Switzerland; I don't know if the others went on location, but I certainly didn't. My part was all made at Gaumont-British. I've heard people who worked with Hitch say that it was not the most exhilarating experience, and, though I was only about fifteen, I felt something of that. Hitch had everything in his head before he went near the set; therefore one was rather moved around and manipulated but, having said that, I liked him very much. For instance, in *Young and Innocent* there was a dog that both Hitch and I adored; there came a time when we had finished the sequences with the dog and he was supposed to go back. We were both so upset that Hitch decided to write him another sequence, so we kept him for another five or six days!

Did you enjoy making *Young and Innocent* for him?
Very much. We did a lot in the country and I enjoyed that. My first husband [Penrose Tennyson] was Hitchcock's assistant director and he was on that film, too. I think it was quite the sunniest film I was involved with. We didn't use doubles. I did that scene in the mine myself, and it was my husband-to be, Pen's, hand holding me up as I dangled there. I was terrified! But Hitch had this quirky sense of humour and made that scene go on and on, so that I thought my arm would come out of

its socket. My daughter had never seen the film until it came to a little cinema in Camden Town recently and she insisted on going to see it. I hate to watch my films, but I took a large sip of gin beforehand and we went. What amazed me was that, firstly, the cinema was full and, secondly, it was full of young people. I would have thought *Young and Innocent* was a very dated film, yet they seemed to find it fascinating. I don't remember the details of how that great tracking shot at the end was done, but I know it went on and on and everyone had to know exactly when to move – it was done like a military manoeuvre.

I think Hitchcock's early films were lovely – things like *The Thirty-Nine Steps* and *The Lady Vanishes*. He was a wonderful director and was charming, though he had a really wicked wit.

You were the star of *Tudor Rose* at the age of sixteen. Did it seem a big responsibility?
I must have been very excited at the time; it was certainly a wonderful part. I knew about Lady Jane Grey and thought the script was extremely good. I was very overpowered by the names in the cast list – Cedric Hardwicke, Sibyl Thorndike, all those great people. I felt very supported by them, but I was also scared, as you can imagine. Robert Stevenson [director] was very supportive of me and I liked him very much. He was married to Anna Lee who was so beautiful! Oh, and I do remember John Mills, who was very young also, and we both rather held each other up. Martita Hunt played my mother in the film and she was as great an eccentric off the screen as she was on it. She was a highly intelligent and witty woman.

I can remember doing the close-up for the final scene in the Tower, when the cannon goes off, meaning that Jane has been beheaded. In order to make the noise of the cannon they used a gong, and I can recall having a great desire to have hysterics. It seemed such an extraordinary noise to make! I haven't seen the remake [*Lady Jane*] but I read some reviews which suggested she was played as a much more headstrong character. I would have found it very difficult to play her that way because I'm sure, as a young girl brought up in Tudor times, she would have done as she was told.

You made two films in 1941 directed by Walter Mycroft, *Spring Meeting* and *Banana Ridge*. Do you remember him?
He did a number of films, but he isn't much heard about for some reason. He was a rather unobtrusive director,

but I do remember *Spring Meeting* with Michael Wilding; that was lovely. It had been a famous play and was quite amusing. I think *Banana Ridge* must have been based on a stage farce; that was with [Alfred] Drayton and [Robertson] Hare. They were very funny as comedians but, like most comedians, they weren't at all funny off the set. Hare and Drayton were such a physical contrast to each other – and in every other way, too. Alfred Drayton was rather an obsessive, dogmatic character, whereas Robertson Hare was very gentle and charming. And Isabel Jeans was in it, too, and she had tremendous style. I have memories of her being wonderfully dressed, very chic.

What do you remember of the Ealing film, *The Next of Kin*?
We went on location for that, somewhere in the South-West. It had a very interesting director, Thorold Dickinson. It was intended as a propaganda film, but it went a little beyond that and was a good film in its own right. I imagine it was through the Ministry of Information, but it was Micky Balcon's studio and I think Thorold was under contract to Micky. I did several films at Ealing and was very fond of Ealing and of Micky. My husband, Pen, was also under contract to him. We had plans to work together in the future, but he was killed in the war two years after we were married. I think *Next of Kin* stands up well and, even during the making of it, I thought it was a very interesting film. And Thorold was a very warm person. I like someone who gives me room to move, but at the same time is open to discussion.

Do you recall *Pastor Hall* made before the War but, because of its anti-German sentiments, not released until 1940?
I have little recollection of it, other than that the cast included Wilfred Lawson, and that it was directed by Roy Boulting, who is a very interesting intelligent man. I did think it was an interesting script and very prophetic.

You played Anna Neagle's sister in *Yellow Canary*. Did you enjoy working with the Wilcoxes?
Anna and Herbert were lovely to work with. I didn't spend much time with them because I only had a couple of scenes with Anna, including a breakfast scene with Marjorie Fielding as our mother. Anna and I looked rather alike, I think; we could both see the resemblance. Again, this was pretty much a propaganda film.

Stephen Murray and Nova Pilbeam in *The Next of Kin*, 1942

You are listed in one reference as having made two films in 1944, *Out of Chaos* and *Man of Science*, which I haven't been able to trace. Were they documentaries?

Man of Science could have been a short film about Faraday. I don't recall the other one. The film I do remember and very much enjoyed doing, utterly unlike anything I had done before, was called *Green Fingers*. I don't think it was a particularly good film, but I simply loved playing in it. I played a bitch, coming between Robert Beatty and Carol Raye, and that was fun. I suppose the film was fairly controversial in its day, being about osteopathy which was not recognised then.

Those films all had very strong casts . . .

England has always had the most wonderful reservoir of character actors, and that is still true. We were never very good at making stars, although I suppose you could say I was made into a star in the 30s, but not by Hollywood standards. After I made *Tudor Rose*, nothing happened for something like eighteen months. I longed to do something in the theatre, but I wasn't allowed. Then Hitchcock wanted me to go to Hollywood to test for *Rebecca*, but my name meant nothing over there. *Tudor Rose* played at the Roxy in New York, but beyond that I think it was only showed in the art houses. I don't know if I would have been allowed to go to Hollywood – I suppose Selznick would have had the last word on it.

Your last two films represent a complete break in that they were both crime films.

Yes, one of them was very interesting. It was called *Three Weird Sisters*, a sort of Gothic horror job, and it had a script by Dylan Thomas. They found it difficult to get him to finish a scene, because, by then, he was well on to the bottle! It didn't work, but it was an interesting film. Mary Merrall was in that, as were Nancy Price and Mary Clare, and they were formidable! Daniel Birt, the director and I got on very well. He was very amusing. We did some of the filming in a Welsh mining district. Time draws a veil over the making of it – but nobody got on with anybody, except Dan in the middle who was lovely and made it all possible for everyone! He was highly intelligent with wide interests.

The second of those crime films was *Counterblast*. What do you remember of that?

That was Robert Beatty again. We'd been together in *Green Fingers*. And Mervyn Johns and Margaretta Scott, who was lovely. It was something about laboratories and rats in cages, that's all I remember. I've obviously blocked it out!

In the 40s, were you able to choose your roles?

What I really wanted to do in the 40s was the theatre and I did do quite a bit. The films I made were mostly not very good and I didn't particularly like the business of filming. My first husband was in the profession and, had he not been killed, I might have stayed in it.

As producer or associate producer, unless otherwise indicated:
Everything Happens to Me (co-designer), *Many Tanks, Mr. Atkins* (co-des), *Mr. Satan* (co-des) (1938), *They Drive by Night* (1939), *The Bells Go Down* (art director) (1943), *Halfway House* (art dir), *They Came to a City* (art dir), *Champagne Charlie* (art dir) (1944), *Dead of Night* (art dir) (1945), *The Captive Heart* (+ art dir) (1946), *Nicholas Nickleby* (art dir), *Frieda* (1947), *Saraband for Dead Lovers* (+ art dir) (1948), *Kind Hearts and Coronets, Train of Events* (1949), *The Blue Lamp, Cage of Gold* (1950), *Pool of London* (1951), *I Believe in You* (+ co-sc) (1952), *The Square Ring* (1953), *The Rainbow Jacket* (1954), *Out of the Clouds* (+ co-sc) (1955), *The Ship That Died of Shame* (+ co-sc) (1955), *Who Done It?* (1956), *The Smallest Show on Earth, Davy* (dir) (1957), *Rockets Galore* (dir), *Violent Playground* (1958), *Sapphire, Desert Mice* (dir) (1959), *The League of Gentlemen, Man in the Moon* (+ co-sc) (1960), *The Secret Partner, Victim* (1961), *All Night Long* (+ des), *Life for Ruth* (1962), *The Mind Benders, A Place to Go* (+ co-sc), *Woman of Straw* (+ co-sc) (1963), *Masquerade* (+ co-sc) (1964), *The Assassination Bureau* (+co-sc) (1969), *The Man Who Haunted Himself* (+ co-sc) (1970), *Scum* (co-exec) (1979), *An Unsuitable Job for a Woman* (co-exec) (1981), *Heavenly Pursuits* (1985), *The Torrents of Spring* (prod cons) (1988).

Michael Relph's more than fifty-year career, as producer, director, screenwriter and art director, has given him a very comprehensive grasp of British cinema. He began as an assistant art director at Gaumont-British, and became a notable set designer and art director at Ealing on such handsome films as *Dead of Night*, *Nicholas Nickleby*, and *Saraband for Dead Lovers*. The central and most enduring element of his career was his long partnership with director Basil Dearden in which their capacities fruitfully complemented each other. Relph has an unpretentious approach to film-making. He and Dearden, he says, loved making films and weren't prepared to wait around for the ideal project to turn up. Nevertheless, they made a large number of impressive films – often films which contrived to *say* something within their genre frameworks, including such titles as *The Blue Lamp*, *The Ship That Died of Shame*, *Sapphire*, *Victim*, and *The League of Gentlemen*. Those five films reflect a good deal of post-war British life and attitudes, and are all accomplished entertainments.

Interview date: October 1989.

Yours is one of the longest and most varied careers in British cinema. Were you always wanting to direct or produce, and moving consciously towards this?

No, not until I went to Ealing as art director. I had actually started as an apprentice with Michael Balcon at Gaumont-British Studios. He was a friend of my family, so there was a spot of nepotism involved. After a brief episode as art director at Warner Brothers, I was very pleased to end up at Ealing, because Balcon had a reputation for promoting people from the ranks, as it were, and this encouraged me towards producing. We were turned into director/producer teams and, though Mick had the final word on everything, the origination and development of projects was up to those teams.

The directors got their credits whereas the producers didn't because of the conflict with Balcon's own credit. Eventually, although our function didn't change in any way – I suppose Mick just got a little older and more secure – he allowed the credits to read 'A Michael Balcon Production (full screen), Produced by Michael Relph (or whoever – also full screen)'.

In the mid-40s you were set designer and art director on three Ealing films directed by Alberto Cavalcanti — *Champagne Charlie*, *Dead of Night* and *Nicholas Nickleby*. What are your recollections of that period and of Cavalcanti?

Balcon was searching for some more realistic roots to put down because of the war situation. He brought Cavalcanti and Harry Watt over from the Crown Film Unit. Cavalcanti, in particular, became the sort of *éminence grise* of the studio and had tremendous influence with Balcon. Cavalcanti was very anxious first of all to get more documentary realism into our film-making, and he also played power politics with everybody. My ultimate partner, Basil Dearden, had been there before Balcon's time and I had worked (as art director) with Basil who was directing a film called *Halfway House*, which Cavalcanti produced. He thought I was a good influence on Basil – that I was able to direct his amazing technical skills into the right channels. So Cavalcanti suggested to Balcon that he should team Basil and myself, and I think it was a very good arrangement. Basil was a very easy person to work with and I was able to convey any creative ideas I had through him. We complemented each other, and also loved making films. I made all my Ealing films with him, except for *Kind Hearts and Coronets*, directed by Robert Hamer. Some people at Ealing were inclined to make a film every three years or so, waiting for the perfect subject for their reputations. But we had a big staff working there and we had to keep the studio going. Basil and I were always stepping in with some subject or other. It mightn't have been the one subject in the world that we really wanted to make, but it kept the studio working.

How did you divide the co-producing activities?

It was always a problem really because the system was a bit unfair as far as I was concerned. Being an equal partner with Basil in all our projects, I wasn't getting the same sort of credit, so he very generously agreed to share. We took various forms of credit, rather as Powell and Pressburger did. We might, for instance, take a joint credit as 'Produced, Directed and Designed by . . .' even though, of course, I did all the designing and he did all the directing. But, because we were jointly responsible for the production, this conveyed more of the partnership.

You are credited as co-director on *The Gentle Gunman, The Square Ring, Out of the Clouds* and *The Ship That Died of Shame* and, in some cases, you also co-produced and co-wrote.

It was all part of the attempt to get an expression for the very close creative partnership we had, which wasn't really reflected by pigeon-holing our activities. It was generous of Dearden, because the director's credit is sacrosanct anyway, but I think the joint credits really reflected the fact that we had a joint creative responsibility for the films.

When we were doing a film, we would usually both be on the studio floor together. I use the simile of saying that the director is like a tactical commander and the producer is more of a strategic commander. In other words, the producer stands a little further back from it, thereby keeping a better perspective. I didn't go down on to the floor and intervene between director and actors, but I spent a good deal of time there, albeit in a behind-the-scenes, low-key position. If I saw something that I thought was wrong in the way that a scene was being mapped out, or to which I thought I could contribute, I would speak to Basil on the quiet and he would either agree or not, as the case may be. But I was very careful not to intervene publicly, so that he had total control of the studio floor which is very important for a director.

Basil agreed to my directing occasionally – *Davy, Rockets Galore* – but it always boiled down to my getting the subjects on which he wasn't particularly keen. And I am not really temperamentally cut out to be a director. A director has to have a tremendous amount of patience and the ability to make detailed pains, and I find that very difficult to do. I get impatient and start to cut corners. I am much more at home being a producer.

Would you say that there are continuing themes and interests running through the films you either directed or produced?

There were certain things, in the sense that we felt it wasn't worthwhile unless the film had something to say other than just tell an entertaining story. We were always looking for themes that had some social significance, and a lot of our films have that element. It was a conscious policy to tackle important social issues in the framework of an entertainment film. If you get too serious, of course, it limits your audience, so we tried to wrap up a theme in an entertaining form, as an exciting thriller or whatever. *Sapphire*, for instance, was a taut thriller about something very topical, although it looks dated now because of the changes in race relations since then, but it was a good film at the time. It was very successful in America. We had a writer team of Janet Green and John McCormack who wrote *Victim*. And Janet, who was a very clever thriller writer and a playwright and novelist, also wrote *Sapphire*. We had a very close partnership with both Janet and John, and they turned out some good scripts for us.

I Believe in You, a film we made at Ealing, was much more episodic. It was essentially a comedy, written by Sewell Stokes, a 'gent', whose spare-time hobby was working as a probation officer, and the story was autobiographical. The nub of the comedy arose out of the fact that the central character was a bit of a fish out of water, but it was also a very moving little film. I really enjoyed it, although it didn't have a very high voltage. My father played in it, as the probation officer, with Cecil Parker and Celia Johnson. It was also Joan Collins' first film.

Did you see *The Ship That Died of Shame* as a critique of post-war British society as well as being a thriller?
Yes, we did. In a sense, the ship represented what people had done with the country that they had inherited after the war. It was a sort of allegory, and it's probably a better film than one thought at the time. It came from a short story by [Nicholas] Monsarrat and we were immediately attracted to it. The film emerged during a newspaper strike, so we didn't see any proper reviews of it. Reviews were the only way we could ever tell whether our films were any good, because we never saw any returns.

Was there a good creative atmosphere at Ealing in the 40s?
Oh, it was marvellous because we didn't have to think about what I consider to be the more boring aspects of production, such as distribution and financing. We had to be practical and keep to budgets and schedules, but we didn't have to go into the marketplace and raise the money. In a way, it was almost like working for the BBC. We really did sit around discussing projects, usually in the pub of an evening; that was the way most of the script conferences went on.

Peter Bull and Françoise Rosay in *Saraband for Dead Lovers*, 1948

I am very interested in your film, *Saraband for Dead Lovers* which I have not been able to see.
It was a magnificent-looking film, but it wasn't a success at the time. We were trying to get away from the Gainsborough-type romantic costume picture which was totally unreal, and to do a serious historical epic. The public probably wasn't ready for it and it also ended up being a bit heavy. It certainly had a very good cast – Stewart Granger, Joan Greenwood, Flora Robson and Françoise Rosay. I was very pleased to get an Oscar nomination for the set design – there were only two of us nominated: Cedric Gibbons of MGM and myself, and unfortunately he won! It was Ealing's first colour film, shot on three-strip Technicolour, and was very expensive for those days.

When did you finish at Ealing?
More or less when Ealing finished. The studio had been sold and we moved over to the MGM studio at Elstree, where we were never very happy. I think the whole seam of Ealing films had rather run out by that time. I directed one film called *Davy* with Harry Secombe which wasn't very good. It was written by Bill Rose who had written some of the big Ealing films such as *The Ladykillers*, but *Davy* wasn't one of his best. He had another subject on which we had always been very keen and which, for some reason, Balcon wouldn't do. That was *The Smallest Show on Earth*, about a couple inheriting a run-down cinema. I thought it would make an enchanting film, so, given that we could see the end of Ealing coming, we took the umbrella, as it were, of doing it for Frank Launder and Sidney Gilliat's company.

In 1958 did you set up your own company to make *Rockets Galore*?
No, that was for Rank. We made *The Smallest Show on Earth* and were then given a contract with Rank at Pinewood. We then made *Violent Playground* and *Rockets Galore*, which wasn't a great success. It was rather a silly thing to do – to make a sequel to *Whisky Galore!*. We were with Rank for quite a long time and made some successful films such as *Sapphire*. Then we formed a company with Dickie Attenborough, Bryan Forbes and Jack Hawkins – Allied Filmmakers – which was a sort of mock distribution company, funded by Rank. It was quite a nice arrangement, in fact, but it all fell apart because everyone wanted to go their own ways. However, we made some very successful films for it, such as *Victim* and the first one, *League of Gentlemen*.

Rank did the actual physical work of distribution, but Allied had a small override on the commission. It was the only way that anyone could make any money out of films. Everybody was trying to be independent and have the necessary freedom. One way of channelling money into production (which Rank and other distribution companies tried) was this strategy of forming groups of independent producers. If a film was financed by Rank, then we used Rank studios, distribution, labs and so on – it was to all intents and purposes a Rank picture and probably made at Pinewood, where we worked for about fifteen years.

When we worked for British Lion we shot at Shepperton, and when we made *The Mind Benders* for Anglo-Amalgamated we had to work at Elstree. In other words, the people who put up the money dictated which studios you used.

***Victim* was surely a very courageous film to make in 1961.**
I was rather surprised that Dirk [Bogarde] agreed to do it. He was famous as a matinée idol and we didn't think that he would take the risk of playing a part which suggested homosexuality. I think he was very courageous to do it and so was Rank, because Dirk was one of their biggest assets. It was a tremendous challenge to any actor, but, in fact, it did Dirk's career a lot of good; it was a very wise step for him, but, at the time, it could very well not have been. It was good for us, too.

How did you view the 'new wave' of social realist film-making that came in with *Room at the Top* at the end of the 50s?
We welcomed it tremendously because that was what we had been trying to do, although by that time we were a bit old-fashioned, really. We made one film in that sort of mould, but it came at the end of the cycle and was very unsuccessful. It was called *A Place to Go* with Rita Tushingham and Mike Sarne. Looking at it now, it doesn't look so different from all those other 'kitchen-sink' films, but it came too late. Those films made everyone feel that film-makers were really dealing with life as it was.

Do you agree that the 40s and 50s seem to constitute a boom period in British cinema history?
I do think so. It was certainly the best time to be working in the industry. To my mind, that period produced much more benign working conditions. But, of course, it coincided with the mass audiences which then fell away.

Now it is more of a struggle. The real difficulty is that we are now quite unprotected by any sort of legislation and we just have to compete, in a totally unequal struggle, with the American product. They make films costing $30m or $40m and we have to compete with little films that cost maybe $3m. We can't do that and I think the fact that we have to make do with shoestring budgets is making our films very parochial. Certainly the British market is no longer strong enough to support films which don't penetrate the American market, so it is the crucial factor in every case.

What is your attitude to the way that the Government and its instruments have intervened in the British film industry?
Well, they have always tried to redress the imbalance between us and the American industry, and I think Harold Wilson's measures – the National Film Finance Corporation and the Eady Levy – went a long way towards helping the industry to survive. But *his* Government did want to see the survival of the industry. Now, whether it is because the Government doesn't like the sort of subjects that are being made; or whether it is simply an ideological refusal to interfere in the market, I don't know. The Conservative Party appears to have no interest in films at all or, if there is any interest, I think it is an antagonistic one.

How would you respond to criticisms that British cinema has been too literary, too class-bound and too tied to the theatre?

I think they are perfectly true criticisms. The country is, of course, class-bound and, insofar as British film reflects life in this country, then class is sure to come into films as an element. Ealing films were very middle-class, really; it was a middle-class business at that time. As for being too literary, we obviously have a great literary tradition which seeks some sort of expression. Another thing is that to be utterly physical on the scale of *Indiana Jones* requires an enormous amount of money. So, if we are going to rely on physical excitement we are talking about making very expensive films. Perhaps this need to find interesting subjects which don't require enormous costs has forced British film-makers back into the literary mould.

I think that, while British acting has benefited from the contact with the theatre, it definitely worked against the cinema in the 30s and 40s. When you consider the realism that people like Cagney were bringing to the cinema at that time, the upper- or middle class stage acting then looked ridiculous on film. My father was a distinguished stage actor and he always said that British stage acting was an absolute killer as far as film was concerned. British stage acting in the 30s and 40s was almost totally middle-class and was just not transferable to the screen. It was, I think, a great disadvantage that the theatre and the film industry were situated in such close proximity to each other. It was good for actors, but a great obstacle to the film industry; it meant that we were using people from a very narrow spectrum. All those new regional people who came in with the 'kitchen-sink' era were revolutionary, a real shot in the arm.

Margaretta Scott

The Private life of Don Juan, Dirty Work (1934), *Peg of Old Drury* (1935), *Things to Come* (1936), *Action for Slander, Return of the Scarlet Pimpernel* (1937), *The Girl in the News* (1940), *Quiet Wedding, Atlantic Ferry* (1941), *Sabotage at Sea* (1942), *Fanny by Gaslight* (1944), *The Man from Morocco* (1945), *Mrs Fitzherbert* (1947), *The Idol of Paris, The First Gentleman, Counterblast, Calling Paul Temple, The Story of Shirley Yorke* (1948), *Landfall* (1949), *Where's Charley?* (1952), *The Last Man to Hang, Town on Trial!* (1956), *The Scamp* (1957), *A Woman Possessed* (1958), *An Honourable Murder* (1960), *Crescendo* (1969), *Percy* (1971).

One of the pleasures of British television in the last decade or so has been the glimpses it gives of British players no longer active in cinema films. Margaretta Scott, regularly seen as the benevolent upper-class Mrs Pumphrey in *All Creatures Great and Small*, has appeared in television since its early days at the Alexandra Palace, but, regrettably, in no feature film since 1970. That she has forgotten many of the films she made can be explained partly by the fact that too many of them were indeed unworthy of her and partly because the stage was always her first love. However, she does remember – and was memorable in – those films which gave her real opportunities: *Things to Come, Quiet Wedding, Fanny by Gaslight*, and *The Man from Morocco*. Her striking, dark beauty and sure sense of style made her a vivid presence in these films. As Alicia in *Fanny by Gaslight*, lovelessly married to Stuart Lindsell's gentle politician and conducting an affair with the sadistic rake played by James Mason, she created a potent figure of cold-hearted, humanly believable selfishness; and she was a gracious heroine when Anton Walbrook offered her the chance in *The Man from Morocco*.

Interview date: June 1990.

Among your 30s films *Things to Come* particularly interests me. Did you feel, then, that this was a landmark film?

Not as much as it became. It was a great adventure, but I was a bit young to really enjoy all the people I met; and I never got to know Korda well. It was also the first time I worked with wonderful Ralph Richardson, and Raymond Massey. I am shown on the cast list of *Things to Come* as playing both Roxanne and Rowena, but Rowena was cut. I was supposed to be in the future sequences (in the white outfits) as Raymond Massey's wife. I had been Ralph's 'moll' in the earlier sequences. In the future sequences I was going to be Raymond's wife and our daughter (Pearl Argyle) was going to be sent to the moon. I played quite a few scenes for it, but they were never used – I think it was a question of time, not because we were bad!

The film was all done at Denham, and the huge open lot which we used for the City Square was known as that for years afterwards. I remember William Cameron Menzies, the director, very well; he was a delightful person to be with and frightfully good. I think Menzies and Korda worked very much as a team and the back-up people were terrific. Korda's brother, Vincent, did the art direction, and he was responsible for the design of the sets. The music was by Arthur Bliss, and Georges Périnal was, of course, the cameraman. I didn't have much to compare with then, but Georges really was wonderful at photographing women.

Some of the costumes were designed by the Marchioness of Queensberry. I remember that she designed the most elaborate costume for me as the future woman, Rowena. Korda didn't like the costume when I went on the set to show it to him, and chose a very simple white costume from one of the extras for me instead. Korda certainly had an eye for talent because so many of the cast became very big names afterwards. What I find remarkable about the film is that we actually made it about five years before the war, yet all those scenes of London under the Blitz and, so on, were so nearly right – very prophetic.

You made three films in a row for London Films – *Things to Come*, *Action for Slander* and *Return of the Scarlet Pimpernel*. Did you have a contract with Korda?
I was under contract, although I don't recall for how long. I suppose I was under contract to London Films, but Korda *was* the studio, which was at Denham. All those people in *Action for Slander* – Ronald Squire, Ann Todd and Clive Brook – were really theatre actors. The reason those films were so good was that the people in them had a grounding in the theatre.

***Return of the Scarlet Pimpernel* stars Barry K. Barnes, a largely forgotten actor.**
Because I was under a Korda contract I did tests with the other actors; one of those being tested for the part of Sir Peter Blakeney was Rex Harrison. He didn't get the part though – Barry K. Barnes did. You couldn't get two people more unalike. It wasn't a very good film, and was very overshadowed by the original with Leslie Howard. Also, it was made by a rather tough German director, Hans Schwartz, who was a bit of a bully. I remember him telling me to cry in a scene. He shouted at me and I went very uptight, not a tear in sight.

***Quiet Wedding* still seems a charming film. What do you recollect of it?**
That was Anthony Asquith's film, and we did it during the war. I had been in the play, although not in London. When the war came I wanted to go overseas with ENSA and toured North Africa in *Quiet Wedding* with most of the original cast. In fact, I did the play after I did the film, in the same role of Marcia. There were some wonderful people in the film, including Athene Seyler; it really was a happy company. I remember there was a bomb warning while we were on the set making the film; a friend, a Colonel in the Army, had come round to watch the film being made and I remember him commanding loudly, 'On the floor. Down everyone!'. I was wearing this beautiful nightie and only crouched on the floor; I wouldn't dream of lying on the floor in it. It was very sad because one of the crew, a young electrician, was fatally hit by a piece of shrapnel. The film was a huge success. We made it at Shepperton and it was produced by Paul Soskin, a very elegant, beautifully turned-out man.

How did you come to play Alicia in *Fanny by Gaslight*?
Oh, that was a lovely film, made for Gainsborough at Shepherd's Bush. I can't remember how I got the part, but I wasn't under contract. I know I wasn't tested for it. The only contract I ever had was with Korda. We had beautiful sets and costumes, and Arthur Crabtree, the cameraman, lit us beautifully. I liked that part very much; she was rather a bad lot, but humanly so.

And of course Anthony Asquith, always known as Puffin, was the most wonderful director. He was very gentle; he would ask you to do something and you might say, 'I don't think I can do that', and he would say, 'I'm so sorry, but I'm afraid you must'. He was quite firm but with such charm. *Fanny* had a wonderful cast – when there is a director whom everybody loves everybody wants to be in a film. Puffin always wore trousers that were a bit too short, sort of cut-down dungarees; I remember him having a party with the crew. He was rather precious and one would have thought that the lads mightn't have gone to the party, but they adored him. As a director he was very sympathetic. Really, I liked all my directors except the German one, who was a bully.

Anton Walbrook and Margaretta Scott in Max Greene's *The Man from Morocco*, 1945

The Man from Morocco was a slightly curious project for 1945 in the way that it goes back to the International Brigade in 1939.

The Man from Morocco was a great experience for me because it was Anton Walbrook himself who asked me to do it – or persuaded the powers-that-be to invite me to do it. We had played together in the theatre in *Watch on the Rhine*, and Anton had told me about this film that he wanted me to do. They made a test for it and he took infinite care over the test. He got Stanley Hall, the make-up artist, to stay the night in my flat so that he could make me up early.

Then I went overseas with *Quiet Wedding*, but left this about a fortnight early in order to start the film. I got back on the day I had promised, sad to be leaving my chums behind, and Anton came to lunch looking very grey in the face. He said 'Peggy I'm sorry, it's not going to happen'. I think he told me that they wanted someone else in the part. Naturally, between the disappointment and having left what I was enjoying, I was shattered. Then, about a week later Anton came to lunch again, much more up-beat and saying, 'Peggy, you are doing it!' I think he really held out for me to play the part and it was a lovely experience. I know Anton was very keen on the project, but as to whether it was his idea or Mutz Greenbaum's [Max Greene, director] I can't tell you. I am sure Anton would have given advice to Max about directing and Max would have given advice to whoever was photographing it. I do remember that Anton always insisted on being shot from his right profile, which was also the side I needed to be photographed, so there was a great deal of over-the-shoulder acting! The film wasn't a huge success, but I certainly enjoyed it.

What do you recall of *The Idol of Paris* which seems to have caused a scandal at the time, partly because of the two whip-cracking heroines, Christine Norden and Beryl Baxter?

I can remember I was playing the Empress Eugenie (with Kenneth Kent), and I was making a tremendous exit when the door handle came off in my hand! I have completely forgotten the duel with whips. I can remember Christine Norden, but not Beryl Baxter, and I recall the director, Leslie Arliss, as being very nice.

In 1948, after your long run on the stage in *The Hasty Heart*, you made five films including two directed by Maclean Rogers and starring Dinah Sheridan – *Calling Paul Temple* and *The Story of Shirley Yorke* . . .

Oh, yes, Dinah is a wonderful lady. My husband [John Wooldridge] wrote a film called *Appointment in London* about the Bomber Command; he wrote a lovely part for me as a WAF officer, but Susi [Susan Wooldridge] decided to arrive and they couldn't very well have a pregnant WAF officer! So Dinah did the part most beautifully. John wrote the music for it, too, because he was a film composer as well. Those two Maclean Rogers films were made very quickly; I don't remember anything of them.

Do you recall the musical version of *Charley's Aunt* called *Where's Charley?*

I know I enjoyed it very much indeed. Ray Bolger was delightful. I can remember him dancing and being great fun but, apart from that, I can't recall anything about it – or about those others I did in the 50s, *Town on Trial!*, *Landfall*, and so on.

Did you feel that there weren't many congenial roles in films for women after the 50s?

I just wasn't asked. I don't remember turning any films down. I have been very busy with television since the early Alexandra Palace days, which were often quite exciting. My theatrical experience backed me up, because television went out live and, if you made any boo-boos, you had to get out of them. There was one memorable time when we were doing *The Merchant of Venice* in 1947 with me playing Portia. There was a splendid black actor, Robert Adams, playing the Prince of Morocco, which was memorable in itself, because he was the first black British actor to play in Shakespeare. The scene came where the Prince of Morocco meets Portia and he fluffed a line, then fell in a dead faint at my feet. I was left saying 'Help, ho! The Prince!' and so on. There were always surprises.

Dinah Sheridan

I Give My Heart (1935), *As You Like It* (as dancer), *Irish and Proud of It* (1936), *Landslide*, *Father Steps Out*, *Behind Your Back* (1937), *Merely Mr Hawkins* (1938), *Full Speed Ahead* (1939), *Salute John Citizen* (1942), *Get Cracking* (1943), *29 Acacia Avenue*, *For You Alone*, *Murder in Reverse* (1945), *The Hills of Donegal* (1947), *Calling Paul Temple* (1948), *Dark Secret*, *The Story of Shirley Yorke*, *The Huggetts Abroad* (1949), *No Trace*, *Paul Temple's Triumph*, *Blackout* (1950), *Where No Vultures Fly* (1951), *The Sound Barrier* (1952), *Appointment in London*, *The Story of Gilbert and Sullivan*, *Genevieve* (1953), *The Railway Children* (1971), *The Mirror Crack'd* (1980).

Watching Dinah Sheridan in TV's *Don't Wait Up* in 1990, it is hard to believe that nearly forty years have passed since *Genevieve* appeared. She seems scarcely changed: she has the same graceful touch with comedy, the same wry charm, and treats the men around her with the same good-humoured exasperation. The other surprising thing is that the continuing affection she has inspired in film-goers is based on such a small number of films as a top star. After fifteen years of taking whatever came along – including George Formby, 'Paul Temple', and 'The Huggetts' – she finally found major British stardom in 1951 in Eal-

ing's African adventure, *Where No Vultures Fly*. Two years later, after the success of *Genevieve*, she remarried and retired from the screen until 1971. When she did return as Mother in Jeffries' fond adaptation of *The Railway Children*, it was enough to make you weep for what British films had been missing. In the early 50s, she was perhaps the most attractive female star in British films; all these years later one hopes she will not be allowed to retire again.

Interview date: September 1989.

After eight films in the 30s, you began your 40s career with *Salute John Citizen* and *Get Cracking*. How did you come to be involved in these?
When war broke out we were all conscripted. I was Chief Ambulance Driver for Welwyn Garden City, and I also became secretary to the local Surveyor and Sanitary Inspector. Then after I had been doing this for about two years, I got a call to go and see George Formby for *Get Cracking*. I walked into the office at Denham and there was no Formby, no director; only Mrs Formby sitting behind a desk. She looked at me and asked immediately if I was married; I said, 'Yes', and she asked, 'How long?' I said, 'Three months', and she said, 'You'll do'. From then on, if I was on call, she was also on call! She would not let George go anywhere near the leading lady. From a comedy point of view I learned a lot. But I felt so sorry for George! Everyone seemed to work with him at some stage, and people were always saying that if you played opposite George you went on to better things.

Salute John Citizen **was an 'A' film directed by Maurice Elvey. Were there clear distinctions between 'A' and 'B' productions?**
In a way, yes, because you went to a different studio and there was a different set-up. When I married Jimmy Hanley he had been invalided out of the Army, and had got a Rank contract. In films like *Salute John Citizen* and *Acacia Avenue*, we were cast as a team – then I started having children and Jimmy went on filming. But if I was offered a job I had to take it.

Were directors like Montgomery Tully and Maclean Rogers helpful to you?
Oh, yes. I was very happy making *Murder in Reverse* with Montgomery Tully – he looked like a bank teller, but on the set he suddenly came to life. Maclean Rogers was a good 'B' picture director; he churned them out. I did a lot of 'B' pictures for Mac at Butchers Films, and elsewhere. Later, I worked for Mac in *Dark Secret* and

also *The Story of Shirley Yorke*, which was better than most. I was very lucky to get that part, and it gave me my first meaty romantic lead. It was written by A.R. Rawlinson, the ex-Attorney-General's father.

What was your experience of Denis and Mabel Constanduros in relation to *29 Acacia Avenue* and *The Huggetts Abroad*?

I never met the Constanduroses, mother and son, who wrote the play, *Acacia Avenue*. We did a lot of the interiors for that film at Riverside Studios, Hammersmith. During indoor filming one of the lights fell off the gantry and everything was chaos. That was the result of the first V-2, which had dropped in nearby Chiswick, so you can date it from that. Henry Cass, who directed the film, was a dedicated Moral Rearmament enthusiast, and was desperately trying to convert everyone.

What about Ken Annakin, director of *The Huggetts Abroad*?

Now there was a good director. He was a nice, inventive man who deserved to go further. The 'Huggett' films started with *Holiday Camp* and my son, aged one, was in it with his father. Jack Warner and Kathleen Harrison were a wonderful couple and the *Holiday Camp* family was so successful that they became 'The Huggetts' and were very cleverly whipped up by the Constanduros team. I replaced Jane Hylton in the third of them. Jane was ill and Jimmy rang me from Islington Studios to tell me that I was starting work the next day. It meant making quick arrangements for two small children, and having my hair considerably lopped off.

Your years as a top star occurred in the early 50s, starting with *Where No Vultures Fly*.

Yes, suddenly in 1949 my career took off. I was flown out to Africa, which wasn't easy, of course, with two very small children and home troubles. However, suitable arrangements were made, and that was really the beginning for me. *Where No Vultures Fly* was the Royal Film of 1951, and it led to the four films that I made in 1952 – *The Sound Barrier*, *The Story of Gilbert and Sullivan*, *Appointment in London* and *Genevieve*. While *Genevieve* was waiting to come out, I married the man who was, at that time, the Managing Director [John Davis] of the Rank Organisation, and agreed to give up my career. It was only subsequently, when I went to Hollywood, that I learnt of some of the roles I'd missed as a result, in big films like *The Court Jester* and *The Million Pound Note*. But there's no point in looking back and feeling bitter.

How did you come to be in *Where No Vultures Fly*?

I wish I knew! There was a sudden offer on the telephone; I made arrangements for my children and flew over to Kenya within two weeks – with misgivings. But I had had no other offer – it had to be accepted, and the film proving so popular was the turn of fortunes I needed. When I went to try on the clothes, the wardrobe mistress said 'Oh, you're not the same size as the other lady, are you?' I asked what other lady, and she implied someone had dropped out or was fired – I still don't know who it was; but that's why the whole thing was so rushed.

What was your experience of working with Harry Watt?

Harry was a large bear of a man who should have been tied to a tree and not allowed to come to civilisation. He made very good films, but his idea of filming was that, if he got a good shot of you dying and a jolly good shot of the blood, he'd change the script. I loved being in Africa, even though it was under terribly primitive conditions; I was ready for a change and it did me good.

After four months Michael Balcon sent out Hal Mason, his Production Manager, to ask us to stay an extra two months because they had got a better picture than they had expected. They wanted some more good shots with animals. I think it was the first film that did not disguise the animals with back projection; we were actually with them. For instance, there was a scene with a rhino charging the truck that we were in; off we went to look for a rhino that would like to charge us. We found one sitting under a yellow thorn bush, very tired and hot and not wanting to be disturbed. The white hunter driving the truck stopped, got out, made rhino-mating noises, and the rhino began to think that perhaps it was worth getting up! He finally charged; the truck was parked at right angles to him. The white hunter got back into the truck, tried to start it, but it stalled. Fortunately, the rhino must have realised we were an immovable object. He planted his feet and literally braked before hitting us, but he sprayed us with dust all the same. By now he was really mad. We did that sequence four more times; the animal was right beside me as we accelerated away, and I could have touched him. All Harry wanted to know was had they got the shots, not were we all right!

You followed *Where No Vultures Fly* with *The Sound Barrier*. Did you feel this was a good role for you, even though it was a secondary one?

John Gregson, Joyce Grenfell and Dinah Sheridan in Henry Cornelius's *Genevieve*, 1953

It was wonderful, because, apart from the leading lady, Ann Todd, I was the only other female and thrilled to get the part. I went to see David Lean and Bill O'Bryen [in charge of production for London Films], and they offered me the part. It was a marvellous part, but I have to tell you that a lot of me ended up on the cutting-room floor. I didn't mind being secondary to Ann Todd; what I wanted was to be directed by David Lean, who was wonderful with actors; he somehow brought the best out in you. He praised and criticised at the right time.

Were you in a position to choose roles by then?
No, I don't think I was ever in that position. I had two children to support. *The Story of Gilbert and Sullivan* came along and I was sent to Shepperton to audition for Mrs D'Oyley Carte. Eileen Herlie got the part, but they rang to ask if I would play Sullivan's girlfriend instead. I was much happier in that role, though it was quite small. The film was a big popular success. During the making of it, Maurice Evans asked me if I would go to New York and do a play – *Dial M For Murder* – with him, but I couldn't because of the children.

Then I went on to play opposite Dirk Bogarde in *Appointment in London*, which was marvellous. He's a terribly nice man and a brilliant film actor. I felt it was an honour to work with him. It was a well-written, stirring account of wartime flying and I was proud to be in it. While doing *Appointment in London*, I had three scripts poked through the letterbox. One was a fairly ordinary 'B' picture about a race course, to star Nigel Patrick [*Grand National Night*]; one was about women police [*Street Corner*]. Both could have been mine by saying yes. The third, which was not mine by any means, was *Genevieve*. I quickly said no to the racetrack and the policewomen, and went to a restaurant called 'The Vendome', to meet Henry Cornelius producer/ director of *Genevieve*. I squeezed into a window seat, and when Henry Cornelius finally came in he said in a loud voice, 'I see you're sitting with your back to the light because you know you're too old for this part'. It was not a charming start, and that sort of thing continued all the way through the film. He was not a character I would have enjoyed working for again. After the near-fatal lunch with Henry Cornelius, Bill Rose [screenwriter] came in and we had a few glasses of wine. I must have relaxed and been funny because I was offered the role.

Before the lunch, I'd talked to Dirk when we were out on location somewhere near Shepperton Studios. I told him about the three scripts and he told me to take *Genevieve* if I were offered it. He had turned it down because he didn't want to do comedy again. They didn't want Kenneth More, they wanted Guy Middleton; they wanted Dirk instead of John Gregson, Claire Bloom instead of me and I can't remember who they wanted instead of Kay Kendall. But we all got on so well together and it worked. Ninety per cent of the credit must go to Bill Rose, a wonderful writer.

What lured you back to do *The Railway Children* in 1970?

Lionel Jeffries. He phoned and asked if I had read it or seen it on television. I had read it years ago. He asked me to meet him for lunch. I had my fingers crossed under the table the whole time, hoping he would make a firm offer. We were already on the set when Lionel confessed that he had also had his fingers crossed, hoping I would agree to do it! We had lunch and discussed the film, but there was no definite offer made at the time. From *Where No Vultures Fly* to *The Railway Children* was eighteen years – and almost another eighteen years to *The Mirror Crack'd*. We made the film in Yorkshire and it was the most wonderful, joyous time I ever had in making a film. Lionel, being such a very good actor himself, was an excellent director for actors.

Do you think British cinema ever competed satisfactorily with American films?

No, because we didn't – and don't – have the money here to make big things. Britain has never really gone in for making stars, whereas look at America, with Bette Davis, Hepburn and so on – they made stars and had the money to do it. In Britain it's all very 'genteel', unsophisticated, and made on a shoestring. It always seems that British cinema doesn't have enough money to tie its stars down, so they go off and work somewhere else.

Donald Sinden

Portrait from Life (1948), *The Cruel Sea* (1952), *Mogambo, A Day to Remember, You Know What Sailors Are* (1953), *Doctor in the House, The Beachcomber, Mad About Men, Simba* (1954), *Above Us the Waves, An Alligator Named Daisy, Josephine and Men* (1955), *The Black Tent, Eyewitness, Tiger in the Smoke, Doctor at Large* (1956), *Rockets Galore, The Captain's Table* (1958), *Operation Bullshine* (1959), *Your Money or Your Wife, The Siege of Sidney Street* (1960), *Twice Round the Daffodils, Mix Me a Person* (1962), *Decline and Fall* (1968), *Villain* (1971), *Rentadick, Father Dear Father* (1972), *The National Health, The Day of the Jackal* (1973), *Island at the Top of the World* (1974), *That Lucky Touch* (1975).

Donald Sinden was a star in *The Cruel Sea* (virtually his first film) and remained so in the twenty-two films he made in the decade that followed. In his own opinion, he never again had such a good role as that of Lockhart, Jack Hawkins' second-in-command, in *The Cruel Sea*, but, during his years with Rank, he was kept very busy, making three or four films a year. His screen *personae* were usually those of dependable young officer or of irrepressible lady-killer. If Lockhart initiated the former strain, it was his medical student Benskin in *Doctor in the House*, which launched the latter. Just once he was allowed to be a

dangerous thug (in *Eyewitness*), and, on the other side of the law, he played the aristocratic detective Campion in *Tiger in the Smoke*. In the 50s, he worked five times with director Ralph Thomas in popular entertainments which established Sinden as a reliable Pinewood star. He has built a substantial stage reputation in classical roles; his inimitable voice and comic timing have enlivened several television series; and he is the author of two entertaining volumes of autobiography.

Interview date: September 1989.

Were the 50s a good time to come into films in Britain?

No, it was the wrong time. Just before then the large studios had had their own stables of actors under contract – there was the Charm School for the Rank Organisation, ABPC had its own contract players, MGM-British had its lot – and they all tried to copy the Hollywood pattern. Of course, they couldn't do it. Rank still had a large stable of actors – the largest it had in any one year when I was there was fifty-one under contract. One fondly imagined that Rank was looking after one's interests; not at all, they were looking after themselves. So, when a script arrived on my table, I thought, 'They, in their wisdom, have chosen me, of all people, to be in this film!' But what it meant was that six other actors had turned it down already. They didn't 'build' stars the way that Hollywood studios did. English actors are always first and foremost theatre actors. 'Films' are what you do for money, 'art' is in the theatre.

How secure was the British film industry in the 50s?

Secure? We were seeing the run-down at that time. Each year heads rolled. One of the most hideous experiences each year was the Rank Organisation's Christmas Dinner, given at the Dorchester or wherever, for contract artistes, directors and producers. J. Arthur Rank didn't involve himself in the actual business of making films; but this dinner was his celebration. You knew as soon as you arrived how you stood. The Managing Director, was at one end of a large table and the nearer you were to him, the more 'in' you were. If you were at the other end of the table you weren't going to last another year! I spent eight years half-way up the table, which was a safe place to be! Mine was a seven-year contract, renewable on their part (never on mine), and I did eight years because, in the middle of it, I did a play which ran for a year. My contract bought me two houses – one in London and one in the country, so I can't grumble. I would have had to work a long time in the theatre to do that.

You began at Ealing with *The Cruel Sea*, but spent most of the decade at Pinewood. Were there significant working differences between the two studios?

Not really. We worked with the same directors, the same cameramen. In my time at Pinewood, they were making sixteen feature films a year. There was something happening on every stage, so it was more of a 'factory' than Ealing. I think more particular care went into each individual film at Ealing, but Rank distributed Ealing films as well, which was how my contract came about. When Ealing cast me for *The Cruel Sea*, it was distributed by Rank and my contract with Ealing contained a clause that Rank had the right to put me under contract if they wanted to. It was all the same organisation with different pockets.

At Pinewood, I was under contract to Rank and had the right to turn a script down, although they didn't like it if you did. If you turned down two, what a pity, because your contract wouldn't be renewed next year! So you went along with it. Also, for individual producers working under the Rank banner – say, Betty Box or Joe Janni – we were cheaper than having an actor from outside. If they used a contract artiste for a film, they paid the other 'pocket' half that actor's annual salary. That was cheaper than any other actor because there was no daily or monthly rate, or even a picture rate.

You started as a star and never had to serve an apprenticeship, did you?

True, but I don't think I ever had another film as good as *The Cruel Sea*. We were very well looked after, but we worked for our living. Being contract artistes, every Saturday throughout the summer months we were sent off to do 'public appearances', such as opening garden fetes. Every week there would be a film première which we were expected to attend: the Rank Organisation would send a Rolls Royce to the door, pick us up in our dinner jackets or evening dresses, and whisk us off to the cinema where the floodlights would be on and the movie cameras working. In that way, Rank gave me a valuable name, which I wouldn't otherwise have had.

The names which recur most throughout your 50s films are Betty Box and Ralph Thomas. How influential were they in your career?

My third film for Betty and Ralph was *A Day to Remember*, but, sadly, no one has a copy of it. I got on very well

with them and they found lots of things for me to do. I worked more for Betty than for any other single producer. In those days the producer and director were part of a team, and they tended to cast jointly. The director would do the work on the floor and the producer would do the office work. Of course, the film industry is a director's medium whereas the theatre is an actor's medium. Ralph had a great sense of humour and an ability to get on very well with his cast. There was a great enjoyment in being on the set with him, for, say, *Doctor in the House*, every day. You looked forward to going in each morning. We were always encouraged to enjoy ourselves – to find enjoyment in our work.

There was a real sense of camaraderie?

Oh, yes. We all knew each other and would go to each others' sets and have lunch together at the restaurant. That restaurant was great fun, not a hierarchical thing at all. When American actors came over we could not understand their hierarchy. An exception was Anne Baxter, who was very unAmerican in that she joined in with everyone else when she came here to do *Mix Me a Person*. Our salaries were laughable compared with the Americans'. When we came to London in 1953 for the studio work on *Mogambo*, Clark Gable was receiving £750 a week apart from his salary – I don't know what that was – as his living expenses. I was being paid £50 a week! However you look at it, there is a discrepancy!

Were you satisfied with the range of roles you got in the 50s?

Donald Sinden and Jack Hawkins in *The Cruel Sea*, 1952

It was a stable. Dirk Bogarde was the most successful member of that stable, and I was inclined to get the 'Bogarde parts' that Dirk didn't want. He was able to do the more dramatic stuff, which I would dearly love to have done, such as *A Tale of Two Cities*. Kenneth More had done the Douglas Bader film, *Reach For the Sky*, so he was getting that sort of thing. Then there was the *Doctor in the House* sort of character which, if you like, I invented – the chap after all the girls – and I grew a moustache for it. Suddenly, all they wanted me to do was to wear a moustache and be funny, in every film, which was frustrating.

Brian Desmond Hurst [director] and Peter de Sarigny [producer] had got a marvellous script about the Mau Mau and had gone to Kenya to shoot miles of footage, *without having cast the film*. The title was *Simba*. I was doing a film called *Josephine and Men* and the producer wanted my hair high-lit with blond for it. I came into the restaurant one day and Peter de Sarigny saw me. 'Good God!' he said. 'Would you have that done all over?' I agreed, and had my hair dyed blond all over to play the part. Previously, they had never thought of the possibility of me dyeing my hair. All I was expected to be was a dark-haired young actor after the girls.

What do you remember of working with Roy Baker, director of *Tiger in the Smoke*?

Margery Allingham wrote it and I believe that she was rather disappointed in the film. On the whole, I prefer to be left alone by a director, because, whichever way you look at it, all actors work on some form of Stanislavsky method of getting themselves into a character. So you have an initial discussion with the director as to what sort of character you are going to play and then get on with it. John Ford, for instance, was not at all interested in actors.

What do you recall of *The Captain's Table* for Jack Lee?

Jack now lives in Australia; he is the brother of Laurie Lee. *The Captain's Table* was very light and funny. In the Pinewood restaurant one day, Joe Janni, the producer, told me about this terrific script which meant three months' location work cruising around the Greek islands. I said 'Count me in!' I didn't even want to read it! Then, three weeks before shooting was to start, Joe phoned to let me know that the budget wouldn't stretch to the Greek islands and we would be cruising around the Channel Islands instead. Ten days before shooting started I went for a costume fitting and the wardrobe man told me that they were doing it at Tilbury Docks. So we spent three months on this bloody liner, tied up at the docks! We would shoot out to sea on one side, then, when they wanted the reverse shots, they turned the liner around!

You worked with Basil Dearden and Michael Relph on *Rockets Galore*. How did you find that?

They always worked as a team and were always there on location or wherever we were. *Whisky Galore!* was based on a true story, whereas *Rockets Galore*, not such a good film, was based on an invented story.

I'm amazed at the richness of the casts in British films of that time – Raymond Huntley, Dora Bryan, Maurice Denham and so on – often in tiny roles.

Yes, England has produced marvellous character actors over the years but very few romantic leading men, of which the Americans have many. Our strength has always been in the character actor field. The difficulty has always been to find two people to play the leads and bring the customers in.

Did you enjoy working with Fred Zinnemann in *Day of the Jackal*?

Yes, indeed, Fred was wonderful. He loved actors and knew a great deal about the theatre, which a lot of film people do not. I remember before we started shooting *The Cruel Sea* I had lunch with the director, Charles Frend and I started analysing my character. Charlie looked at me goggle-eyed. 'We've not cast you for the villain,' he said. 'Just play yourself!' I said, 'What *is* myself? I'm an actor – all I do is play other people!' Now *Fred* and I would have little chats, with him saying things like, 'Too theatrical, too theatrical'. He would cut acting down to nothing, and it's true, the best screen acting *is* doing nothing. The camera does, as people say, fall in love. It's not a matter of acting ability at all.

Sylvia Syms

My Teenage Daughter (1956), *No Time for Tears*, *Woman in a Dressing Gown*, *The Birthday Present* (1957), *The Moonraker*, *Ice Cold in Alex*, *Bachelor of Hearts* (1958), *No Trees in the Street*, *Ferry to Hong Kong*, *Expresso Bongo* (1959), *Conspiracy of Hearts*, *The Virgins of Rome*, *The World of Suzie Wong* (1960), *Flame in the Streets*, *Victim* (1961), *The Quare Fellow*, *The Punch and Judy Man* (1962), *The World Ten Times Over* (1963), *East of Sudan* (1964), *Operation Crossbow*, *The Big Job* (1965), *Danger Route* (1967), *Hostile Witness*, *The Desperadoes* (1968), *Run Wild Run Free* (1969), *Asylum* (1972), *The Tamarind Seed* (1974), *Give Us Tomorrow* (1978), *There Goes the Bride* (1979), *There Goes Tomorrow* (1980), *Absolute Beginners* (1986), *A Chorus of Disapproval* (1988), *Shirley Valentine* (1989), *Smiling Through* (1992).

From the first, Sylvia Syms had starring roles: she was never one of that unhappy species, the British film starlet, and nowadays when she plays even a quite small role, such as the Headmistress in *Shirley Valentine*, she invests it with a star's authority. As she says, she was lucky – in a male-dominated cinema particularly – to get a series of strong women's roles. After being launched by the Wilcoxes in *My Teenage Daughter* and *No Time for Tears*, she worked for several of the most interesting directors then working in British cinema, including Roy Baker, Basil Dear-

den and Pat Jackson. Above all, she was associated with J. Lee-Thompson for whom she had three of her best roles: as the 'other woman' in *Woman in a Dressing Gown*, as the army nurse in the excellent war film, *Ice Cold in Alex*, and in the film version of Ted Willis' play *No Trees in the Street*. In different vein, she was a charming heroine in David MacDonald's swashbuckler, *The Moonraker* and caught the satirical, acrid mood of Val Guest's *Expresso Bongo*.

Interview date: July 1991.

You must have been almost the last star to be created in the 1950s.

I certainly wasn't 'created' in the sense that people nursed my career or guided me nicely. The only person who nursed me was Herbert Wilcox, who saw me in a television play, interviewed me and gave me the leading part in a film called *My Teenage Daughter* opposite his wife, Anna Neagle. However, I then did a very stupid thing. I accepted a contract that a charming man called Robert Lennard, who discovered lots of people, offered me with ABPC [Associated British Pictures Corporation]. The idea that anybody would pay me £30 a week to work was beyond my wildest dreams! Ben Lyon, with whom I had been in a television play, had warned me not to sign any British contracts. He said he wanted me to meet some people from 20th Century-Fox. However, I was so frightened by the idea of going away from home, I signed my ABPC contract. The film with Herbert Wilcox then came out and I was, as they say, an overnight sensation, and I had saddled myself with a seven-year

contract, the options of which were all on ABPC's side. As a result, I did my first four starring roles for £30 a week – films like *Ice Cold in Alex*, *No Trees in the Street* – and I genuinely thought they were being kind to me because they gave me these big parts.

What do you remember of playing Anna Neagle's rebellious daughter in *My Teenage Daughter*?

I was crashingly ignorant and very young, and Anna and Herbert cosseted me and spoiled me. They made the part bigger as we went along, but I was unaware of what they were doing for me because I had no criterion against which to measure it. When the film was ready, I remember Anna saying I would have equal billing above the title, but I had no idea what they were giving me. Their generosity was incredible. They didn't pay me much, but it was more than I was paid for my subsequent films. I had a car every day and my meals served in my room at Shepperton, so that I could rest during lunch-times.

Anna Neagle also starred in your next film, _No Time for Tears_. What was the essence of her enduring popularity?

People just liked her. I can't say that I have often seen her do great performances, although when I was very young I adored her in a film about Nell Gwyn. When she did _Odette_, people believed it. If you played a war hero today as they really were then, nobody would believe in the character. They really did behave impeccably; and they didn't even use bad language when they were being tortured by the Gestapo!

Woman in a Dressing Gown was the first of your three films for J. Lee-Thompson. Did you enjoy working with him?

Yes, he's a strange man, lives in Hollywood now, but he was a good director. One of the clever things about Lee and Ted [Willis] is that they got the right people for the right parts in _Woman in a Dressing Gown_. It was important that my part should be played as a respectable girl who inadvertently falls in love. When I was playing the part, hero-worshipping Anthony Quayle as I did, it seemed to me absurd that any wife could behave as Yvonne Mitchell's character did in the film. My part, however, was very close to me, because one of my problems was that, as well as being a gifted actress, I thought it was my bounden duty to be a gifted housewife. This was to the detriment of my work because the two things were always conflicting. So I lived that part!

What do you think about _Conspiracy of Hearts_ which you made for the Ralph Thomas-Betty Box team?

Conspiracy of Hearts was one of my happiest films. I've never worked with a producer who got the small things so right as Betty did. We filmed at Certoza, near Florence, although the interiors were done at Pinewood. It was based on a true incident and was really very moving. It was even more moving when we were making it because Yvonne was Jewish. It was quite successful and I won an award for it, a huge eagle, for being the most popular actress in Spain. Later, Ralph gave me a part in _The Big Job_, which was a very funny film. I think Barbara Windsor must have been busy, so they talked me into playing a tarty sort of role that I wasn't often allowed to do.

Pat Jackson told me that _The Birthday Present_ is the only one of his later films that he is pleased with. What do you remember of it?

I had worked with Tony Britton before on stage. He was a very 'hot property' at the time because he had just played Romeo opposite Virginia McKenna on television. I very much liked Pat Jackson – he is a very nice, gentle man. I was still working for ABPC, so I was literally going from one studio to the other. I was making three or four pictures a year. I was initially under a seven-year contract which went on for ten years; I wasn't happy with the contract, but I had poor advice and knew nothing. For the last three years they did pay me a decent salary and loaned me the money to buy my house, which I paid back within one year just by doing loan-outs.

How much choice did you have about your roles?

None – I just did what I was told. Sometimes I would fight for something, such as _Expresso Bongo_. That was rather well-done and was a happy picture, too, because Larry Harvey was delightful. I had just had major abdominal surgery and I can't tell you how carefully he looked after me; he would even check my make-up before a close-up because he knew how casual I was about those things. He was adorable and so was Cliff Richard. I think the film was ahead of its time because it was such a sharp and witty send-up of the pop scene.

Ice Cold in Alex, _The Moonraker_ and _Bachelor of Hearts_ all came out in 1958. What do you remember of making the very successful _Ice Cold in Alex_?

It was very arduous. We filmed it in the Libyan desert and there was another film being made there at the same time, which had the most wonderful facilities compared to ours. We were in a hotel in Tripoli for a while and used to travel to the location each day, moved by the British Army. The men were under canvas and the women were in stone sheds inside a ruined Italian fort. It was very difficult for me, being so young, and would have been impossible if the men in the cast had not been like Dutch uncles to me.

We didn't need to do much 'acting' – we were cranking the engine and driving the thing in the most appalling conditions – we just _became_ those people. We were either very hot or very cold. As for the love scenes, I don't recall them as being particularly daring, but they certainly caused a lot of trouble at the time! They had to cut one close-up of what looked like an exposed bosom. In fact, all John had done was undo some buttons – I still had a bra on.

I enjoyed _The Moonraker_ . . .

Harry Andrews, Anthony Quayle, Sylvia Syms and John Mills in J. Lee Thompson's *Ice Cold in Alex*, 1958

Yes, for its time it's quite sweet, isn't it? At least the costume looked right for the period. I had correct hair styling, covered with a modest lace cap, and the costumes were authentic. I liked working with George Baker, who was also a contract player. They saw him only as a tall leading man who could 'swashbuckle', whereas he subsequently proved what a great character actor he is. And, of course, Max Greene always made me look beautiful.

I remember *Bachelor of Hearts* very clearly because that was done on location in Cambridge, which surely beats the Libyan desert. Hardy Kruger was adorable, a very nice man. It was a most enjoyable funny film to be on, and Geoff Unsworth, the cameraman, made me look stunning, too.

You certainly had the best cameramen, including Christopher Challis, who photographed you in *Flame in the Streets*. What do you recall of that?

It was quite controversial in its day [1958], dealing as it did with race relations. Certainly there hadn't been another British film made with anyone as black as Johnny Sekka, who was blue-black. He was from Senegal. I had the greatest respect for the director, Roy Baker. I've always considered him an underrated director. He was marvellous with that subject and I loved working with him. He was tough on the set but I thought he was very sensitive. All his films are entertaining, and he really had class.

What are your recollections of *Victim*, the first commercial film to deal openly with homosexuality?

I have very strong recollections of it. And Dirk's book is

very honest about it. He says they offered my part to a lot of people, but nobody was interested in playing the wife. I certainly wasn't the first choice. I remember reading the script when I was five months pregnant. I was very involved in politics, then, and thought this was an important film to do.

Later, someone asked me how could a woman be in love, and go to bed with someone, without knowing that he was a homosexual. But, in those days, women of a certain class were very innocent, and a wife's knowledge of sex would be limited. The character, in the film, may have had her suspicions, but I think that it was perfectly possible for her to love Dirk's character and have a reasonably happy marriage. I remember very little about performances, as a rule, because I live the part at the time and then put it aside. But I do remember that there was one scene when I felt that, if that situation had happened to me, I would have been much less inhibited in my response. I remember having to actually talk myself into being the judge's daughter who would not be able to be uninhibited. When I first saw the film I was very worried about that scene – the scene in which she says to him, 'Well, you obviously wanted it'. I was worried that I had not brought out the 'big guns'. Only later could I appreciate that I was actually being truthful to the character – that woman could only react in a certain way, still being terribly polite, so that the pain had to be shown through the fact that she *can't* scream and yell. I wanted to scream but if she had been able to do that, then she wouldn't have been the person he married. Dirk brought to his part, in *Victim*, the enormous restraint of a person who had lived his life knowing something about himself which he had refused to acknowledge was true. My part wasn't very long, but I always remember that film for how Dirk worked, when it was not his close-up, to help me with my reactions.

What lured you back to the big screen again in the late 80s?
Nobody asked me before that. There was plenty of stage and television work, and, in thirty-five years, I've never been out of work for longer than six months. But, even with all those films I did, I've never earned a lot of money. It's a case of doing whatever you're asked to do.

Ralph Thomas

Once Upon a Dream, Helter Skelter, Traveller's Joy (1949), *The Clouded Yellow* (1950), *Appointment with Venus* (1951), *The Venetian Bird* (1952), *The Dog and the Diamonds, A Day to Remember* (1953), *Doctor in the House, Mad About Men* (1954), *Doctor at Sea, Above Us the Waves* (1955), *The Iron Petticoat, Checkpoint* (1956), *Doctor at Large, Campbell's Kingdom* (1957), *A Tale of Two Cities, The Wind Cannot Read* (1958), *The 39 Steps, Upstairs and Downstairs* (1959), *Conspiracy of Hearts, Doctor in Love* (1960), *No Love for Johnnie, No, My Darling Daughter* (1961), *A Pair of Briefs, The Wild and the Willing* (1962), *Doctor in Distress, Hot Enough for June* (1963), *The High Bright Sun* (1964), *Doctor in Clover* (1965), *Deadlier Than the Male* (1966), *Nobody Runs Forever, Some Girls Do* (1968), *Doctor in Trouble, Percy* (1970), *The Quest for Love* (1971), *It's a 2'6" World Above the Ground/The Love Ban* (1972), *Percy's Progress* (1974), *A Nightingale Sang in Berkeley Square* (1979).

Ralph Thomas is entirely unpretentious about his film-directing career. The facts are that he is, perhaps, the most representative British director of the 1950s; that he was enormously prolific; and that several of his films are a good deal more accomplished than his modest self appraisal suggests. He made war films, series comedies (the 'Doctor' films), literary adaptations and exotically-set romantic adventures, all staples of 50s British cinema. He was prolific: he made nearly twenty films in the decade, making two films per year from 1953-63, mostly in collaboration with producer Betty Box. He was accomplished: *Doctor in the House* remains one of the most beguiling entertainments of the 50s, in which high good humour is mixed with enough reality to keep it coherent and credible; and *No Love for Johnnie* was an unusually sharp, cynical look at a corrupt politician. Ralph Thomas is the kind of director on whom film industries are – or, at least, *were* – based: that is to say he wanted to tell on film stories that audiences would want to watch, and he was able to gratify himself as well with the occasional more personal project.

Interview date: June 1990.

You were an assistant editor in the 30s and a maker of trailers in the 40s. What kind of training did this provide for someone who wanted to direct?

Making trailers was enormously useful because, having been in the cutting-rooms for quite a while, I had learned a lot about technique, about how the various directors operated. It also taught me a great deal of discipline about brevity in story-telling.

Looking back, the late 40s and early 50s seem like a boom period in British cinema. How did it feel then?

Enormously exciting and invigorating. We knew we were not always doing very creative work, but there was a chance to gain experience, and this wasn't going to last. My boss was Sydney Box. You were quite likely to finish shooting on Friday, plan to go into the cutting-rooms on

Monday to look over your stuff and get your cut ready, then go for a drink, and you'd be given another script and be told, 'The sets are standing and you start on Monday – this is the cast'! It wasn't necessarily good and we didn't get a lot of money, but it was regular!

How did you come to direct *Helter Skelter* which is quite unlike mainstream British comedy?

Again, it was one of those 'Friday night pictures'. I didn't particularly want to make comedies, but I said that I'd enormously admired a crazy American picture called *Hellzapoppin!*. We cast it well and enjoyed making it, although I never quite understood the story-line! Funnily enough, it has become a sort of cult picture in odd places. One of the scenes in *Helter Skelter* caused a great deal of embarrassment to produce. It required the heating to go wrong, the air conditioning in the hotel foyer not to work, and the reception desk had to shiver

---

209

and shake a little. So we got the special effects men to make a mould of what the desk would be. They filled it with aspic until it seemed firm and then they painted it to look like a real desk. If you blew a wind machine on it, it would shake and look rather splendid. So we switched on the fan without realising that, by this time, the fan was heated. The heat started to melt the jelly, so that instead of just shaking, it literally shrank and melted and the whole of the floor was covered with this jelly. People's feet were stuck in it; we couldn't track the camera; it was an hilarious scene.

Would you say you were a very representative British film director of the 50s, in the kinds of films you made, the people you worked with and the sort of success you had?

I was a sort of journeyman picture-maker who was generally happy to make anything I felt to be half-way respectable. So my volume of work was enormous; I had a lot of energy and made all kinds of pictures. If you make all kinds, you score a hit sometimes. I made thrillers, comedies, love stories, war stories, one or two adventure things. Some film-makers have a lot of talent and genius; others simply have a lot of energy. I'm afraid I belong in the latter category! There were lots of us, then, doing a great deal of work. With hindsight, some of it was more respectable than we thought it was at the time.

You made many films with Betty Box as producer. How did this association come about?

She's a smashing producer, a very bright woman, and she had very good story taste. I started working with her when I made a trailer for a picture called *Miranda*, about a mermaid. It was a rather funny trailer and it obviously helped to sell the picture. Anyway, I then met Betty and we had ideas in common. I didn't see her again until there was a slump and they had to shut down Shepherd's Bush Studios, where I was working. I then went to Pinewood to do *The Clouded Yellow*, and she came over and produced that with me. After that, we made twenty or so pictures together and remained great friends. Betty mortgaged her house to keep *The Clouded Yellow* afloat until the financial problems in our business sorted themselves out. It was a brave thing for her to do and she didn't tell me until the picture was finished. I'm rather proud of that film: Jean Simmons was lovely in it, so was Trevor Howard. It was a very good movie. And Sonia Dresdel was very good value for money – they don't make them like that any more. Wonderful bravura.

I also associate you closely with Dirk Bogarde. How would you describe that working relationship?

Dirk was a very serious splendid young actor and a wonderful-looking fellow. When we made *Doctor in the House* we decided we didn't want to use actors who were professional funny men. We would cast the best actors we could get, actors we'd have cast if it was going to be a straight dramatic story about medicine. So we cast Dirk, Kenneth More, Kay Kendall, people who were bright, 'hot' and good. Not one of them ever did anything because they wanted to make it *funny*. They played it within a very strict, tight limit of believability. Dirk was able to do that, he got away with it and it stopped him from being just another bright, good-looking leading man and made him a star.

We worked together for, I suppose, ten or twelve years and then he moved on to become a more Continental actor. He did several, though not all, of the 'Doctor' films. He played Sidney Carton in *A Tale of Two Cities* – he was marvellous in it and it's become a sort of school classic all around the world. He was very good, as a rather tortured young officer, in *The Wind Cannot Read*, a romantic picture we shot in India. He was splendid in another mad comedy called *Hot Enough for June*, which was based on a very good book called *The Night of Wenceslas* by Lionel Davidson. It was a sort of send-up of the early James Bond pictures. Dirk did that totally differently and very well. He was a pleasure to work with because he always produced more than you asked of him. He is a great contributor. Like other actors, he could be difficult. The only way you could persuade him that what he wanted to do was wrong was to let him do it – the terrible thing was that it very often proved him to be right!

***Doctor in the House* was your first major commercial success, wasn't it?**

Yes. It was a ridiculously big success and, in a way, it doesn't really do your career any good to have such a big success early on. I remember the night it opened, at the British Film Awards; it brought the house down. It was a very cool, professional audience who had gone there to be seen, to get awards and to watch other people get awards, but they absolutely loved it. We knew, then, that it had worked.

It opened to the public the next day and we went down to watch the huge crowds queuing in Leicester Square to see it. We went to a party that night and the Chief Executive of the Rank Organisation said, 'I feel sorry for

Dirk Bogarde, Cecil Parker, Dorothy Tutin and Athene Seyler in Ralph Thomas's *A Tale of Two Cities*, 1958

you, Ralph. You've made a picture which is going to be a classic. It's going to be enormously successful commercially. It's going to make you reasonably well off, and it's going to start you off with a totally new career. You're a bit too young and not really ready for it yet'. I thought he was a silly old buffer. But he was quite right; you can easily get thrown off course because you get offered all sorts of things you don't really want to do and shouldn't do. You become easily flattered because you like this first taste of fame.

Why was it such a huge success?
It was about something which, until that time, had been treated with as much reverence as you would treat your confessor. People held medicine in great awe. There had been 'Dr Kildare' things in which 'young doctor saves lives in hospital'. In our film, people liked and identified with the funny situations they had seen happen or which had happened to themselves as patients, doctors or nurses. It had an enormously wide common appeal — much wider than we understood when we were making it. It was first shown in 1954 and now, in 1990, it is still being shown all around the world and is still producing revenue after thirty-seven years.

I recall a very touching scene with an actress called Maureen Pryor.
Yes, she was an exceptional actress. An ordinary little woman, she had this gift of instant emotion. She could say a word which didn't actually mean much, look at the camera and make you cry. She had enormous vulnerability, and was very special. We used her several times and she always delivered this sort of thing.

How would you compare it with the Ealing films at the start of the decade and with the 'Carry On' films at the other end of the decade?
It was less quaint and more realistic than the Ealing films which I adored, but it didn't have any sort of whimsy at all. You laugh because you are involved in and amused at the situations, rather than at big payoff gags. The 'Carry On' films, which my brother directed, were immensely funny farces constructed to have as many laughs as possible within their ninety minutes of screen time. They were not stories; they used comics, and were like seaside picture postcards or old variety turns. *Doctor in the House* was between the two, because it was a realistic picture which set a new trend in this sort of comedy and I'm very proud of it.

You were under contract to Rank, so how much control did you have over making them?
After *Doctor in the House* we had quite a lot of control. We had promised to make another 'Doctor' and, as long as the thing we wanted to make had a reasonable budget and was not too idiotic, they would let us do it. There was a hge, cosy operation which served you well if you served them well. I think Rank probably felt that Betty and I *had* served them well; we had three long-term contracts with them, and we liked it because the contracts gave us the same crew. We were allowed to have our own cameraman, art director, production designer, assistant director and production accountant — the five key people. They were on our payroll for the whole year every year, and that was ideal. We probably got a little less in fees through that arrangement, but we got a great deal of comfort and a very nice atmosphere. A long-term contract generally meant a certain number of pictures over so many years. If such an operation existed now, we would have a continuity of programming that would enable more people to get chances.

British films of the 50s are sometimes criticised for their preoccupation with wartime themes. Is this a fair criticism?
Yes, it is, and it's perfectly natural too. One of the reasons, though it sounds rather callous, is that there is no easier place to find drama — or comedy — than in a wartime situation. Also, most of the people involved had been much affected by the war. They were still living under wartime conditions several years after the war had finished, because of rationing and shortages, and it seemed that we all became slightly obsessed with war films. Well into the 50s, I made a war picture called

Above Us the Waves, which was made because William MacQuitty, who produced it, was very involved with the Navy and loved submariners. He had read a book by two young journalists about the sinking of the *Tirpitz* and thought it was very exciting. I thought it was, too, and I suppose there was an element of nostalgia about it even though I had been a soldier, not a sailor. So we made it.

There were some wonderful stories about the war around, and there still are. There was also *Appointment with Venus*, a comedy totally about war in which the main protagonist, apart from David Niven and Glynis Johns, was a cow. We actually had about twelve plain-coloured cows which we used to paint with this particular patch on the side. That was a sod because we shot the film mainly on location on Sark and Guernsey and every time it rained, which it did regularly, the colours would run! It was a difficult picture, but it was fun.

Another war film was *The Wind Cannot Read*, which I made in India. It was a wonderful book which David Lean had once been going to film, and he gave the script to Betty and me to read. We were about to go off to shoot *Campbell's Kingdom* on location, and Betty rang John Davis from London Airport. She told him what *The Wind Cannot Read* was about and the numbers involved. He very bravely told her that, unless he cabled her in Cortina to the contrary, we could make the picture in India. I think he agreed to it because he trusted David Lean's judgment that it was a splendid book. It was a real three-handkerchief picture, which I thoroughly enjoyed making, and Dirk was very good in it. In the late 50s, we made another war picture called *Conspiracy of Hearts*, in black-and-white. It was also a very moving, very different picture. It had mainly women in it, all playing nuns. It was very successful in America. Barney Balaban, the head of Paramount at that time, happened to be in London and came to the première. He loved the picture and, at the after-show party at the Dorchester, told John Davis that he wanted to buy it. Davis protested that none of his salespeople was there, but Barney insisted he wanted to buy it then and there, and paid the largest amount that Rank had ever received for a picture. You see, few Americans, other than servicemen, had seen anything of the war and America also has large Catholic and Jewish populations; so the prospect of Catholic nuns saving the lives of little Jewish children had a very large, inbuilt audience.

What of *No Love for Johnnie?*
We made that because we wanted to make it very much.

We all loved it – Betty, myself, Peter Finch. Peter got an award for it in Berlin. Although it was never a commercial success, didn't even pay for itself, it got great notices. The Rank Organisation threw a surprise party for Betty and me after it was finished, and Harold Wilson was there and said that he recognised a lot of things in the picture as being absolutely true. It very much reflected the politics of the day.

The film was very heavily censored because, at that time, people didn't believe that 'love in the afternoon' by an MP who should have been voting in the House was possible. It's happened rather a lot since!

Betty Box said she wished she'd chosen to make *A Tale of Two Cities* in colour.
Yes, and that was really my fault. I had seen a French picture called *Casque D'Or*, set in France at almost the same period. It looked so marvellous in black-and-white, it made a great impression on me. I argued that if we wanted to keep the flavour of Dickens' book, with a vague feeling of documentary about it, we ought to make it in black-and-white. We fought for that and I'm very sorry we won the battle. It would have been much more successful in colour, and would have had much more exposure on television. The Russians thought it was the definitive work on Dickens! It was one of Dirk's best pictures, I think. It was a well-cast picture; Cecil Parker, Stephen Murray, Athene Seyler, and Duncan Lamont was a terrific Defarge – it was full of people who knew how to play that sort of piece. Christopher Lee's straight performance as the Marquis was very good, very contained. There was also a marvellous girl, Marie Versini, in *A Tale of Two Cities*, the one who went to her death in the tumbril with Dirk. She had this quality of saying two lines, looking at the camera, and making you want to cry. The screenplay was written by T.E.B. Clarke who wrote most of the best Ealing pictures.

It wasn't all drama, though, on *A Tale of Two Cities*. One of the funniest experiences was when Dirk's manager, Tony Forwood, was snoozing in Dirk's new Rolls Royce in a side street whilst we were shooting. He was woken up by a loud bang, and came to Dirk in fear and trembling, saying, 'Dirk, something terrible has happened to the car and I'm afraid the door and the wing are irreparable. One of the tumbrils ran wild and it ran into us!' We had great trouble helping them to fill in their insurance claim. I mean, how do you say that your Rolls was damaged by a tumbril drawn by a white horse?!

Ann Todd

Keepers of Youth, These Charming People, The Ghost Train (1931), The Water Gypsies (1932), The Return of Bulldog Drummond (1934), Things to Come (1936), Action for Slander, The Squeaker (1937), South Riding (1938), Poison Pen (1939), Danny Boy, Ships With Wings (1941), Perfect Strangers, The Seventh Veil (1945), Gaiety George (1946), Daybreak, So Evil My Love, The Paradine Case (US) (1947), The Passionate Friends (1948), Madeleine (1949), The Sound Barrier (1952), The Green Scarf (1954), Town Without Pity (1957), The Taste of Fear (1961), Son of Captain Blood (1962), Thunder in Heaven* (1964), 90 Degrees in the Shade (1965), Thunder of the Gods* (1966), Thunder of the Kings* (1967), The Fiend (1971), The Human Factor (1979), The McGuffin (1985).

* Documentary (directed by Ann Todd).

Although she had made thirteen previous films, it was Ann Todd's role in *The Seventh Veil* that made her a household name. She played the suicidal Francesca, and she and James Mason (in the mid-40s, every woman's favourite brute), aided by a skilful script from producers Muriel and Sydney Box, made one of the most popular entertainments of the entire 40s. Ann Todd was, perhaps, best served by those roles in which her fragile blonde beauty seemed to be concealing passions and ambiguities at odds with the exquisite surface. Hence, she is remarkably effective as Ralph Richardson's demented wife in *South Riding*; as the missionary's widow caught up in a tangle of crime and newly-wakened sensuality in Lewis Allen's superb melodrama, *So Evil My Love*; and as the duplicitous *Madeleine* (one of three films directed by her then-husband David Lean). Her Hollywood experience with Hitchcock in *The Paradine Case* looms large in her recollections of her career and one sees why he was drawn to use her. She has directed, written and appeared in some very individual travel documentaries, and is the author of an autobiography entitled *The Eighth Veil*.

Interview date: June 1990.

Alexander Korda's *Things to Come* is one of the most ambitious British films of the 30s. What do you recall of it?

I don't remember very much about it because I was very young and didn't have a large part. I can remember having to be gassed. They tied me to a post and floated in a lot of smoke, which was intended to represent the attack. It was so real, and I was so nervous and overacting that I actually passed out. Korda said, 'Leave her there and keep filming'. My second husband Nigel [Tangye] got an award for it; he did an incredible job on the aviation sequences. When I saw it on TV, I thought it was a *wonderful* film and Raymond Massey was marvellous in it. Although the film was meant to be science fiction, it was an uncanny portent of what was to come. Korda was a marvellous man – not just a great name, but a great man as well. He was a wonderful teacher. He said to me, 'I don't want you to *act*. I want you to *be*',

which I had never heard said before.

How was the scene of riding the horse up the stairs done in *South Riding*?

I actually did do it. I don't ride, so it was very alarming. (I had more riding problems years later in *Madeleine* in a scene with Norman Wooland.) The noise of its hooves on the stairs frightened the horse even more than me. I played the demented wife by remembering Alex's words about 'being', instead of acting. There was something in *me* which Korda could just find, to draw out that performance. I was terribly disappointed and angry when Alex decided not to film *Lottie Dundas* with me in the part I'd played on the stage. He said I wasn't ready to play a murderess on the screen yet, and I said, 'I could kill you now!'

There was a long gap, while you were on the

213

stage, until Korda's *Perfect Strangers* in 1945. What was your experience of playing opposite Robert Donat?

I loved him. He suffered a lot from ill-health – he had to have screens all around him so that he wouldn't see anybody because of his nerves – but he was so sympathetic to work with. There was a real sense of hierarchy of stars then, and I was grateful to him – the studios were still rather awesome to me, though it helped to have Korda directing.

Georges Périnal photographed you superbly in *Perfect Strangers*.

I hadn't realised it was him on that film. He did photograph me beautifully, it's true, but it's really only a few

shots of me in nurse's uniform with Bob. I saw it last year and thought it looked so touched up and glossy.

Was *The Seventh Veil* the film which made you a top star?

Yes, it was the turning point of my life, as I say in my book [*The Eighth Veil*]. It had magic and it gave me magic. I don't remember 'acting' the part, but, of course, I fell in love with James [Mason], which helped. Today directors are the most important people involved, but in those days it was the stars who were important, and the way Sydney Box [producer] put us together was magical, the chemistry was there. It wasn't a startling script, but James and I played the looks between the words.

I went to the Royal College of Music to learn the Grieg

Ann Todd and James Mason in Compton Bennett's *The Seventh Veil*, 1945

Concerto and the Rachmaninov for the film, though not actually playing myself, of course. Herbert Lom was marvellous in it, too; I'm such an admirer of his. When I saw the film again last year at the British Film Institute, I was thrilled with it, and with me *in* it! People still remember me as Francesca, and that makes me happy. I did the part later on the stage, with Leo Genn, but it wasn't anything like as successful. I honestly think the success of *The Seventh Veil* came from our personalities and they *were* exciting; it's something you get from inside which you convey to an audience. The great directors know it. I remember Hitchcock telling me he didn't want me to rehearse: he just wanted what I could bring to it when I did it for the first time.

Your next film, *Gaiety George*, sounds a rather limp follow-up to your great success.

No, it wasn't. I was really quite pleased about that; I loved the character, for which I changed from being a tart at the beginning, wearing fishnet stockings as a 'Gaiety Girl', to eventually marrying into the aristocracy, as Lady Someone, aged fifty or sixty.

You made two striking melodramas in 1947, *Daybreak* and *So Evil My Love*.

Nigel [Tangye], my husband, wrote the theme song for *Daybreak*, which was set on a barge, I think. Eric Portman was in it, as my husband, but I don't recall much about it. I do remember Geraldine Fitzgerald as the alcoholic wife in *So Evil My Love*. She was *lovely* to work with, a great actress I thought. Ray Milland was very much the star! Hal Wallis, the producer, certainly had style; it's extremely important in films. I loved the beginning of *So Evil My Love*, when I was on the boat coming back to England; it always reminds me of Garbo at the end of *Queen Christina*.

Did you get the Hollywood offer to play Gregory Peck's wife in *The Paradine Case* on the basis of *The Seventh Veil*?

Oh, yes, it came very quickly after the first night. Hitchcock took me out to dinner and explained that I was to play the poor little girl whose husband had left her for another woman [Valli], but that he wanted me to be the most exciting person in the film. If he hadn't said that I would never have thought of playing it that way. I know people say that, for Hitch, actors were just part of the furniture but Grace Kelly, Ingrid Bergman and I loved him and loved working for him. He would say, 'Relax, girl, relax! You can't act if you're not relaxed!'

Your next two films were both directed by David Lean for Cineguild, *The Passionate Friends* and *Madeleine*. Where were they filmed?

They were mostly shot at Pinewood. I loved *Madeleine*; David was never happy about it, but I think he did it quite beautifully. It didn't seem to me to matter that people knew about the 'Not proven' verdict. Guy Green was the cameraman and he was marvellous. A good cameraman goes into *you*, and the part you're playing. If he sees you do something in rehearsal which brings a certain expression into your eyes, for instance, he will go to the director and say he's seen something which should be brought out, maybe a camera angle needs changing or something. He and the designer, John Bryan, worked *very* closely with David on *Madeleine*; they were round at the house every day for breakfast, talking and planning.

David liked to have every detail right under his thumb. He was the first director I'd worked with in this country to have that sort of presence, to be the master on his set. People ask me now whether it was difficult for me, as his wife, working with him, and I say, 'Of course it was. Having a genius around *is* difficult. Perhaps you haven't had one!'

He directed you in three films in a row, the third being *The Sound Barrier*. How do you feel about that film now?

I think it was marvellous. I was so proud and excited to see it shown at a National Film Theatre 'do' recently. David did one of the first sort of *cinéma vérité* things when he shot me in the cinema watching the film when my husband [Nigel Patrick] was killed. The cameras were all hidden and nobody realised that all the bright lights were actually film lights. I had to queue to get my ticket for the film and I got a message telling me to hurry because they were getting into trouble outside. I tried to push forward and a woman in the queue snapped, 'Wait your turn!' and knocked me in the stomach. I was wearing a 'pregnant' cage under my coat. The woman was alarmed and said, 'Oh, I'm so sorry – I've killed it!' I just had to say, 'No no, it's quite all right'. It was a film full of chilling moments, but there were a lot of very human bits too, when I would react as I thought a woman under strain would do, with lots of aggression. David liked to rehearse a lot, which Hitchcock of course didn't. I wouldn't say I like to get a lot of direction from a director, but I like the director to *know me*.

In 1954 you worked with a now largely forgotten

director, George More O'Ferrall, in *The Green Scarf*.

Oh, I loved him. We were students together at the Central School where he was studying direction. He didn't have a lot of strength, but he was a most sensitive director. I had been very ill before making *The Green Scarf* and someone told me afterwards that, before I came down from my dressing-room, George explained to everyone that, to help me get through, everything on the set had to be just so, very quiet. But I didn't really like the film very much. As I recall, I had to learn how deaf-and-dumb people speak for it.

Three years later you worked with Joseph Losey on *Town Without Pity*, his first English film under his own name, after he was black-listed in Hollywood for so-called unAmerican sympathies.

Yes, I enjoyed working with him very much, although a lot of people found him difficult. I don't think artistes bothered much about that black-listing stuff – except in Hollywood, of course. People would say, 'You worked for Joe Losey! Did you have a terrible time?' And I'd say, 'No, of course not'.

Town Without Pity was one of Alec McCowen's first films and almost certainly the first for Leo McKern. Joe Losey brought Leo to my house and told him to stand up and play a scene with me. It was very embarrassing for both of us; I've never had another director do that.

What do you remember of Seth Holt's *The Taste of Fear*? It was a genuinely scary thriller I thought.

I thought it was a terrible film. I didn't like my part and I found [Susan] Strasberg impossible to work with, all that 'Method' stuff. Insofar as it worked, it was due to the director, Seth Holt. The story was very silly, but he kept it going. He made it exciting so that you could forget that the body couldn't possibly be lifted out of the swimming pool and so on. It felt very stagy to do, though, and it was one of the few films I didn't like doing at all. However, it was very popular.

Do you have a favourite role in films?

I'd have to say *The Seventh Veil* – it has never left me and has never been allowed to. It made me a 'star', though that is a label I can't stand, and that status didn't give me any more freedom to pick and choose and to do parts I wanted.

Richard Todd

For Them That Trespass (1948), *The Hasty Heart, The Interrupted Journey* (1949), *Stage Fright, Portrait of Clare* (1950), *Flesh and Blood, Lightning Strikes Twice, The Story of Robin Hood and his Merrie Men* (1951), *24 Hours of a Woman's Life, The Venetian Bird, Elstree Story* (1952), *The Sword and the Rose, Rob Roy, the Highland Rogue* (1953), *The Bed* (1954), *A Man Called Peter, The Virgin Queen, The Dam Busters* (1955), *D-Day the 6th June* (1956), *Saint Joan, Yangtse Incident* (1957), *Chase a Crooked Shadow, The Naked Earth, Intent to Kill, Danger Within* (1958), *Never Let Go* (1960), *Don't Bother to Knock, The Long and the Short and the Tall, The Hellions* (1961), *The Boys, The Longest Day* (1962), *The Very Edge, Death Drums Along the River* (1963), *Coast of Skeletons* (1964), *Operation Crossbow, Battle of the Villa Fiorita* (1965), *The Love-Ins* (1967), *Subterfuge, The Last of the Long-Haired Boys* (1968), *Dorian Gray* (1970), *Asylum, The Aquarian* (1972), *No. 1 of the Secret Service, The Big Sleep* (1977), *Home Before Midnight* (1979), *House of the Long Shadows* (1983).

Richard Todd became a major British film star with his second film *The Hasty Heart*, and his performance as the stocky, touchy Scot remains one of those with which he is most closely associated. Hitchcock had the wit to use him as a killer in *Stage Fright*, though the rest of the 50s he was usually cast in heroic and/or romantic roles. Of these latter, perhaps the most notable were as Guy Gibson in *The Dam Busters*, one of the best of the decade's many war films, and as the Rev Peter Marshall in *A Man Called Peter*, made during his second spell in Hollywood. He brought a very convincing no-nonsense sincerity to both of these roles and, indeed, this sturdy believability – in or out of uniform – was his distinguishing feature. As one who values a well-prepared production, he particularly enjoyed his three costume romps for Disney – *Robin Hood*, *The Sword and the Rose* and *Rob Roy*. In recent years he has been much preoccupied with the stage, but he continues to bring authority to supporting roles in the occasional film.

Interview date: June 1991.

Suddenly, at thirty, you became a major British film star in *The Hasty Heart*, your second film. How did this happen?

I didn't want to go back into the theatre after being in the Army, but I agreed to do one play for Dundee Rep – and stayed eighteen months. Then Robert Lennard, my agent for a short time before the war, rang me to say that he had the ideal part for me and would I come to London to test for it. So I did a screen test for a film called *For Them That Trespass*, directed by Cavalcanti, and was given the leading role. As a result of this, I got a contract with Associated British Pictures [Corporation – ABPC], one of the two big production companies in Britain at that time. The contract was for seven years – peanuts to begin with, but I thought I was damn lucky to get a contract at all.

My first film didn't light any fires, but Cavalcanti taught me a great deal about techniques to overcome my faults and the rudiments of screen acting. On the last day of the film there was a reception at Elstree Studios for Jack Warner Jr and Vincent Sherman, who were in England to make *The Hasty Heart*. Sherman caught sight of me while he was talking to Robert Clark, the executive director of productions, and said I was just the kind of guy he wanted for the Scot in *The Hasty Heart*. Clark said I was one of their contract players, so Sherman said he wanted me to test. I did two scenes and a few days later I was called to Bob Lennard's office and told I had the part.

What was your experience of starring with Patricia Neal and the former President of the US?

They were wonderful. At that time they were both established and I was totally unknown, having done one film which hadn't even been screened yet. I did get the impression that Ronnie Reagan was sizing me up a bit at the beginning, but I think his misgivings faded when he saw that I could handle the part all right; he was extremely nice and helpful.

The film was all shot in the studio; most of the action takes place inside the hospital, the only exterior scenes being those of the sandy compound outside. It is also largely interior in that it is about Lachlan McLachlan coming to terms with other people. I had seen boys in the war in much the same state and knew what he was feeling. I got a great deal of direction from Vincent Sherman, who was most helpful. If you were doing a very emotional scene and you saw tears running down his face, you knew you were doing all right! The film was a huge popular success and it made me an international artiste straight away.

What were your views on the British star-building system?

There wasn't one really, not anything like they had in America. I was extremely lucky because I was, more or less, the white-haired boy at ABPC and they actually bought subjects for me and got behind me in terms of publicity. Then, when I went to do my first film in America, ABPC went to quite an expense to see that my new bride and I went in style. But I was lucky; that was not normal here.

In 1950, you worked for Hitchcock in _Stage Fright_ – was it a daring move for a newly established star to play the murderer?

I don't think so; it was a terrific surprise and a feather in my cap to have Hitchcock wanting me. It was my fifth film, I think, but only a couple of my earlier films had come out – _The Hasty Heart_ hadn't even been released then. That came out while we were shooting _Stage Fright_ and Hitchcock's attitude to me changed overnight!

Hitchcock was a strange man, and not a lot of help to his actors. He didn't rehearse you, he just gave his first assistant a diagram of what he wanted, and then went off to his office. Once we had rehearsed together and worked out our moves, he would come down to have a look, say if it was OK or not, and then shoot it. I think he took the view that you only hire people who know what they are doing. However, he said I had expressive eyes and spent a lot of time doing shots on me where only the eyes were lit, because they tell the story.

What was your experience of working with the legendary Marlene Dietrich?

Wonderful, we got on tremendously well together. She was a great professional. What a cast that was! Dietrich,

Jane Wyman, Michael Wilding, Sybil Thorndike, Alastair Sim, Kay Walsh, Joyce Grenfell – little parts, some of them, but brilliantly done.

You made _24 Hours of a Woman's Life_ for Victor Saville almost at the end of his career.

Yes, we shot a lot of that in Monte Carlo. It was very enjoyable to make, although I don't think it was a great picture. Saville was all right and Merle Oberon was another of those highly professional people. So was Anne Baxter, with whom I played in _Chase a Crooked Shadow_. I had to drive a sports car very fast round a mountain ledge in the south of Spain. It was pretty dicey, because the balance of the car had been changed considerably by having cameras bolted to it on scaffolding. I had a couple of really nasty moments driving it. It was very dangerous, but Anne never turned a hair. That's what I admired about her. She was a very intelligent actress.

What sorts of differences did you find between British and American directors and stars, either here or in Hollywood?

Everything in Hollywood was so well-geared and professional compared with the rather haphazard, happy-go-lucky way that things were done in England. At Elstree, the ABPC studios, the so-called star dressing rooms were very spartan and I once said to Robert Clark that visiting American stars would expect a good deal better than that. In America you had a whole bungalow to yourself – you were really pampered.

English productions were often good, but they were nothing like so organised as the American productions. The best-organised films I ever did here were for Disney – _Robin Hood_, _The Sword and the Rose_ and _Rob Roy_. For each of those, before we went into production, I (as the star), the director, producer, scriptwriter and cameraman all had conferences. As we went through each shot, a sketch artist would sketch exactly what each angle was to be, so that when the set designer started building the sets there was never an inch of wood or whatever wasted. I could look through my copies of the sketch artist's drawings for a particular scene and know exactly where I was to come into close-up, where I would be in a medium or a long shot. Not only were they extremely efficient, they were also extremely nice to work with. Walt himself wasn't too much in evidence during the making of the films, although he came over to visit us a number of times and became a great friend of mine.

Richard Todd and Ronald Reagan in Vincent Sherman's *The Hasty Heart*, 1949

You worked a number of times for Michael Anderson ...

I did *Yangtse Incident*, *The Dam Busters* and *Chase a Crooked Shadow* for him – all good films, and Michael was to me a supremely authoritative, quiet, collected director who knew exactly what he wanted and what he could get out of his actors. He only had to give me a little quiet guidance, and we worked together very well.

When I was first told that Michael was to direct *The Dam Busters*, I thought this was typical ABPC cheeseparing, instead of getting an expensive well-known director. Michael had made only small films before that, having previously been the best first assistant director in

the business. But I had dinner with him one night and was totally won over by him. He knew what he was doing and was a delight to work with.

The British cinema of the 50s seems to have been dominated by war films. Why do you think this was so?

America had cowboys and Indians and we didn't. The only action films that we made with any sort of reality were war films. I suppose there was also an element of nostalgia for 'our finest hour' as well.

I do think *The Dam Busters* is the best military war picture ever made. I never met Guy Gibson, but I got to know as much as I could about him. We spent about two years researching and preparing the picture and I spent a lot of time with his father, his widow and Micky Martin who served with him. I also spent time with Barnes Wallis [the inventor], who was a fascinating man. We got the technical details about the bomb itself from him, although some of that had to be cheated a bit because it was still secret. The crucial thing about the preparation was the model work on the dams because, if they didn't burst realistically, we wouldn't have a film. So all the model work was done first and, when that was OK'd, we started shooting the film. We had to have five Lancasters rebuilt for us as well.

There were terrible floods in the Ruhr Valley that year, so we sent a plane over and shot a lot of film there. Micky Anderson deliberately made it in black and white, for two reasons: one was that we could use a lot of stock shots in black-and-white of the original bombs being tested. Second was that he felt colour would prettify it too much and I think he was right. Erwin Hillier was the cameraman on it and it was very well photographed.

We had one RAF officer who was actually the station commander on the airfield at Scampton at that time, and he was with us as technical adviser. I also had with me an RAF flying instructor who sat in the fuselage with me and taught me the movements I should go through. The aircraft in the studio was mounted on a pedestal with a ball-and-socket mechanism that could be electrically activated, so that it banked, climbed and dived.

You made a good war film called *Danger Within* with a director called Don Chaffey.
Don was very workmanlike. It was a true story and a very

gripping picture. It was filmed on the Heath in Surrey, where they constructed a complete prison camp. The opening was inspirational on Don's part. It opened with a full-scale battle in the desert, stock shots taken from actual war footage; the titles rolled over this huge battle and, when they finished, the camera came in to a body lying in the sand, face down. You naturally think this is one of the casualties of the battle. The camera dwells on the body for a few moments and, suddenly, its right hand comes around and scratches its backside. Then the camera pulls away and you see it is just one of the prisoners-of-war snoozing in the compound. It was a wonderful shot.

Your last film of this period sounds rather bizarre — *Never Let Go* with Peter Sellers and Adam Faith.
Ah, yes, that was a good film. It also had Elizabeth Sellars and Carol White, who were very good. I loved doing it because it was a character part for me, playing a scruffy little salesman whose car had been stolen. Sellers played the head of the gang of crooks.

Which of your films are you particularly pleased with?
Certain films are much better than others, but, when you look back, you recall enjoying one because you had a good part in it, or because you made a lot of money out of it, because it was an exciting location, or because it brought a lot of kudos. In my memory, the outstanding films I've done are *The Hasty Heart*, *Robin Hood*, *Rob Roy*, *The Dam Busters*, *A Man Called Peter*, *Never Let Go*, *Chase a Crooked Shadow*, *Yangste Incident* and *The Virgin Queen*.

Conspirator (1949), *Trio*, *The Wooden Horse* (1950), *The Browning Version* (1951), *Hindle Wakes*, *It Started in Paradise*, *The Planter's Wife* (1952), *Mantrap*, *Street of Shadows*, *Counterspy*, *The Square Ring*, *The Genie* (1953), *Romeo and Juliet* (1954), *Footsteps in the Fog*, *Geordie* (1955), *Bhowani Junction* (1956), *The Barretts of Wimpole Street*, *The Seventh Sin*, *The Smallest Show on Earth* (1957), *Passionate Summer* (1958), *The Bridal Path* (1959), *Gorgo* (1961), *Two Living, One Dead*, *The Green Helmet*, *Invasion Quartet* (1961), *Born Free* (1965), (US) *Duel at Diablo* (1966), *The Lions are Free* (1967), *A Midsummer Night's Dream*, (1968), *Ring of Bright Water*, *An Elephant Called Slowly* (1970), *Boulevard du rhum (Rum Runner)* (1970), *The Belstone Fox* (1977).

The key films in Bill Travers' career are *Geordie* (1955) and *Born Free* (1965). *Geordie* established him as a popular British leading man, after a dozen small roles in the preceding five years. There is a strong element of wish-fulfilment, of the local-boy-makes-good, about its theme. This, together with Launder and Gilliat's good-natured screenplay, helped to make it a strong box-office favourite, both in Britain and America. As a result, Travers won starring roles in three MGM films – *Bhowani Junction*, *The Barretts of Wimpole Street* (made in England) and *The Seventh Sin*. After several bouts of trans-Atlantic work and a stint with the Royal Shakespeare Company, Travers and his wife, Virginia McKenna, made the hugely successful *Born Free*. This launched a career as a film-maker with a particular interest in the way that animals are treated in captivity (*Ring of Bright Water* also treats this theme), and provided him with another opportunity for the convincingly natural, good-humoured playing that was his forte.

Interview date: February 1991.

After war service and some theatre work, you had small roles in ten or eleven films between 1949-53. What do you recall of these?

I remember doing bits in *The Wooden Horse*, mainly vaulting over the bloody thing; then quite a nice part – Benvolio – in *Romeo and Juliet* for Castellani, a good director. That was a good step forward and I learned quite a lot doing it. I joined the company in Venice; they had lovely, specially woven clothes of the period and we used to dress up in these seventeenth-century clothes, then wander through the streets to make-up where they had wonderful Italian artists doing everyone's make-up. Then we would get into a gondola and go down the canals. The tourists would see us dressed in these beautiful clothes, on our way to the set, and would wave to us and we would carry the part off as best we could.

The turning point in your career seems to be 1955 with the title role in *Geordie*. How did you come by this?

I was about to take a part at Windsor Rep when I was offered a test for *Geordie*. I did nine tests altogether, some with people who were going to play the other parts, but I think Launder and Gilliat, who had scripted and sunk a lot of money into *Geordie*, had great difficulty in persuading the distributors that they could play an unknown in the title role. I had to train at Joe Bloom's Gym in Cambridge Circus, eat a lot of red meat, and do exercises to build up my muscles, so that I could actually throw the Scottish hammer and, hopefully, the Olympic hammer a reasonable distance. They wanted to make the thing as real as possible. As the pull of the Olympic hammer increased with each spin round, my arms grew if my chest didn't.

Why do you think the film was so popular?

I think Launder and Gilliat were good scriptwriters, producers and directors. They let you get on with it; they had great patience and, if you weren't happy with it, they let you have another shot. They listened to what you had to say and so were good from the actors' point of view. Also, they certainly knew how to write and edit. *Geordie* has a good theme – 'local boy makes good' sort of thing. It was a bit jingoistic about the Scottish but the Scottish people are very popular, particularly in America, and are spread out all over the world, and people liked to see a Scotsman doing well. I signed a personal contract with Launder and Gilliat on making the film.

Were your next three films – *Bhowani Junction*, *The Barretts of Wimpole Street* and *The Seventh Sin* – part of an MGM contract? Did you find differences in working for a Hollywood company?
I got an MGM contract after making *Bhowani Junction*. I made *Footsteps in the Fog* first, with Stewart Granger and Jean Simmons, which gave me a different kind of part to do and I guess that was important; it also got my name around, which was useful. I was interested to get the part in *Bhowani Junction* because the book had been written by my Brigade Major in the Chindits, John Masters, who wrote many best-sellers.

Also, being in the Gurkhas for some time, I could speak Gurkhali and of course Urdu; I had seen quite a lot of India in the six years I was in the East, and I knew how it was for the Anglo-Indians or Eurasians who were working on the railways. I have always had great admiration for Anglo-Indians: a lot of them were very brave indeed. So I knew a little about the character of Patrick, how vulnerable he was, and I could also do a fairly reasonable 'chi-chi' or Anglo-Indian accent. There was a lot of location work, all done near Lahore. George Cukor was a wonderful director, who really knew how to get people to act. He didn't look through a camera very much. Freddie Young, who did the lighting, got on with it while George was rehearsing.

There was all the difference in the world working for a Hollywood company. You were in with the 'big boys' instead of 'Uncle Frank and Uncle Sidney' as they were known. You had lots of 'Heads of Department' and you had to adapt to the treatment, to people photographing you all the time, and people talking about careers much more than what the part was like. *The Barretts of Wimpole Street* was a remake and occasionally the director [Sidney Franklin] would call me 'Freddie' (because Fredric March had played it before) and he really only wanted to repeat the earlier film. Jennifer Jones was OK, but she didn't like rehearsing and, since all my experience had been on the stage, I relied totally on rehearsing a scene before we played it.

Your other 1957 release, *The Smallest Show on Earth*, is a very British, rather Ealing-like film. Do you enjoy playing comedy?
That was Bill Rose's script; Frank Launder showed it to me and said he hardly had to rewrite anything at all. Rose was an American, yet he had a wonderful understanding of the British. *The Smallest Show on Earth* was a most enjoyable film to make. Going on the set with Peter Sellers (it was his first film) was magical – he had such a great sense of humour. Margaret Rutherford was quite wonderful to act with – I mean, you didn't know when she was acting or not. So was Bernard Miles. They were just great people to work with.

I did enjoy playing comedy, yes, it was fun, but it wasn't always that easy. We had quite a small budget for films in England and, because there was no guarantee they were going to be sold into the big markets of the world, we had to make them cheaply enough to recover the majority of their costs in this country. So there was quite a lot of pressure to get on with the job. I recall watching other people working and thinking, 'He's doing that, so what will I do next. Where will they cut in this next scene? How am I going to manage my props?'

Jennifer Jones and Bill Travers in Sidney Franklin's *The Barretts of Wimpole Street*, 1956

Dougie Slocombe, who lit *The Smallest Show on Earth*, was always lighting as we were rehearsing; he was a marvellous lighting cameraman. There wasn't really much wasted time, and that's how we 'got on'. Also the director cut as he directed; he wouldn't take a scene further than where he knew he was going to cut.

Were producers keen to promote you and your wife as a team in films like *Passionate Summer* directed by Rudolph Cartier, an important figure in British television?

I suppose producers thought that if they offered us parts together, we would be more keen to do it. Neither of us cared very much for *Passionate Summer*. Cartier was already an important person in television – that was how he got *Passionate Summer* – but I'm not sure that he translated well to the big screen. He did a lot of rehearsal, and, by this time, I'd begun to shed the idea of doing a tremendous amount of rehearsal. By then, I wanted to make things more natural and I found that Cartier was too bound by what had happened at rehearsal. I think the film needed something much more impressionistic than Cartier's direction. It needed to be made like a French film. I also think that it was as a result of that film that Ginny and I became less than favourites with the Rank Organisation.

Was *The Bridal Path* conceived as a follow-up to *Geordie*?

Frank Launder rang me up and said he'd got another film; he sent me the book and then I received the script. Yes, *Geordie* had made Launder and Gilliat quite a lot of money, so, I guess they saw *The Bridal Path* as a follow-up. I don't think it had quite the dimensions of *Geordie* and wasn't such a success, but it was always fun working with Launder and Gilliat. I liked them tremendously as people.

I remember driving around Scotland with Frank looking for locations. Sometimes we'd shoot a bit along the way; I had some of my kit in the back of the car, so, every now and then, I'd get into my gear and run up and down the mountains while they filmed me. We would do that if it was particularly beautiful, if the lighting was wonderful (as it often is in Scotland) and you just had to grab it while you could.

What light can you shed on *Two Living, One Dead*, one of the most 'missing' films of all time?

It was made by myself and Carl Moseby. The story had been suggested to me by Frank Launder. I read it and tried to get the film rights because I thought it would make an interesting film about what happened to people after the crime. I found out that Moseby, a Norwegian, had also tried to get an option. Someone engineered it so that we met his agent and we decided to go into it together. My wife and I were to play in it and we had several meetings. But in spite of the fact that Puffin Asquith was the director – a wonderful director – and Teddy Baird was the producer, it didn't work out. One of the problems was that Carl Moseby was unfortunately an alcoholic and desperately ill, and we were left with too many financial uncertainties.

How did you come to make *Born Free* in 1964-5, after a gap of several years away from films?

In 1962 when I was at Stratford, Tom McGowan (the original director of *Born Free*) told me about this property he had, called *Born Free*, although he hadn't got the money for it or got it set up. He was trying to find out if anyone would be daft enough to take on the part. So, after a play that I did in America folded, I got in touch with my agent to ask what had happened to *Born Free*. I was amazed to get a telegram back saying yes, they were going ahead and Carl Foreman was waiting to meet us when we got back.

We went to see Paul Radin and Sam Jaffe, the two producers, at the Mayfair Hotel in London. By that time we'd read the book. We thought it sounded like an amazing challenge although we didn't know how we would do it. Having said that, it is part of both Ginny's and my make-up to welcome a certain amount of risk or danger.

Born Free was directly responsible for my later work. Because of the experience of working with the lions, I then went on to make my first documentary on what happened to the *Born Free* lions. The film is called *The Lions Are Free*.

Sir Peter Ustinov

As actor, except where otherwise indicated:
Hullo Fame, *Mein Kampf*, *My Crimes*, *Let the People Sing* (dialogue dir) (1940), *One of Our Aircraft is Missing*, *The Goose Steps Out* (1942), *The Way Ahead* (+ co-scr), *Carnival* (co-scr) (1944), *School for Secrets* (dir, scr, co-prod), *Vice Versa* (+ dir, scr, co-prod) (1946), *Private Angelo* (+ co-dir, prod) (1949), *Odette* (1950), *Hotel Sahara*, *The Magic Box*, *Quo Vadis* (1951), *Beau Brummell*, *The Egyptian* (1954), *We're No Angels*, *The Wanderers*, *Lola Montes* (1955), *Les Espions*, *The Man Who Wagged His Tail* (1957), *Adventures of Mr Wonderbird* (voice only) (1959), *Spartacus*, *The Sundowners* (1960), *Romanoff and Juliet* (+ dir, prod, scr) (1961), *Billy Budd* (+ dir, sc-scr, co-prod) (1962), *John Goldfarb, Please Come Home*, *The Peaches** (narrator), *Topkapi* (1964), *Lady L* (dir, scr) (1965), *The Comedians*, *Blackbeard's Ghost* (1967), *Hot Millions* (1968), *Viva Max!* (1970), *Hammersmith is Out* (dir), *Big Mack and Poor Clare* (1972), *Robin Hood* (voice only) (1973), *One of Our Dinosaurs is Missing* (1975), *Logan's Run*, *Treasure of Matecumbe* (1976), *Double Murders*, *Taxi Mauve/Purple Taxi*, *The Last Remake of Beau Geste* (1977), *Death on the Nile*, *Tarka the Otter* (voice only) (1978), *Ashanti* (1979), *Charlie Chan and the Curse of the Dragon Queen* (1980), *The Great Muppet Caper* (1981), *Evil Under the Sun* (1982), *Memed My Hawk*, *Grendel, Grendel, Grendel* (voice only) (1983), *Appointment with Death* (1988).
* Documentary or short film.

Writer, producer, director, actor: Peter Ustinov has carried out all these functions in British films, as well as finding new audiences all over the world for his television performances, his plays and one-man stage shows, his novels and autobiography. But diversely talented as he is, it must be said that British cinema has never made the most of him. Indeed, both his Oscars were for American films, *Spartacus* and *Topkapi* and his Emmy for US Television. However, when barely twenty he was already giving notable character performances in such films as *One of Our Aircraft is Missing* and *The Way Ahead* (which he also co-authored) and he gives a lovely comic performance as the Protean inn-keeper in *Hotel Sahara*. The films he directed are an idiosyncratic bunch: in the 40s he made three off-beat comedies, *School for Secrets*, *Vice Versa* and *Private Angelo* (in which he also starred), full of sly humours; while his personal favourite is *Billy Budd*, a fine version of Herman Melville's novella. In recent years he has played a very engaging Poirot in several Agatha Christie films, establishing yet another hold on the popular imagination.

Interview date: August 1990.

Which do you generally find more satisfying: acting, producing, writing or directing?

I think acting is intrinsically easier than writing. It is a sort of tactical excitement; it does not give you the strategic pleasure of writing something that is accepted. I have never regarded myself as a professional director, in the sense of knowing how to deal with actors. I know what I want, but I do not have a very developed visual sense in the case of moving pictures. You always betray where you come from: anybody who sets out to be a film director must start somewhere else. He is either an assistant, or a writer, or a cutter. I suppose my path has been a more literary one and, therefore, in the last analysis, I trust a verbal imagination more than a visual one. So, I have never really thought of myself as a professional director who is waiting for material.

Billy Budd is probably my most successful and certainly my favourite film as a director, and it was extremely rigorous because they were asking me, 'Where are we going now?' They were asking me as the skipper as much as the director. Also, the visual imagination was automatically stunted by the narrow possibilities imposed by the fact that we were on a ship. I, therefore, feel that I probably have more to contribute as an actor because I am a type of which there are not a tremendous number about. I do not work terribly consistently because people have a conventional sense of casting. Poirot has been very helpful to me because it has found me a niche, but I would hate to spend the rest of my time doing nothing but Poirot.

Were you given leave from the Army to make *One of Our Aircraft is Missing*?
No, I wasn't in the Army then. I did that film in 1941. It was directed by Michael Powell, who was a very disturbing kind of director because he would stare at you and never say anything. I got to know him much better when he was very old and he had plans to do *The Tempest* as a film and wanted me to play Caliban. He was much more approachable then, and I suspect his earlier manner was a strange shyness and certainly [Emeric] Pressburger was more approachable. Powell, when young, was rather metallic and obscure, even up to a point cruel, which I don't think he was by nature. I thought that everything he said needed translation. I felt he didn't really understand actors well but, at the same time, he knew what he wanted. When he was young he was frightfully like a sarcastic schoolmaster, and I was still near enough to my own schooldays for that to worry me.

How did your collaboration with Eric Ambler work on *The Way Ahead*?
It began as a training film. We were all sent to Scotland and that's where we first met. Carol Reed applied for me and I joined him in Troon, in very strange circumstances. Carol had automatically been made a captain, Ambler was still a lieutenant and David Niven was a colonel; I was the only private there. We had a make-up man from Ealing who was a lieutenant, but he was well over sixty, a technical man with an almost sexual respect for pay parades; I had to go off with him in a truck to a disused hotel, in order to have a pay parade all by myself. He would go into a room while I waited outside; then he would shout, 'I'm ready now!', like children playing hide-and-seek, and I would go in, sign for my pay and take it out to the corridor. Then we would drive back together while he told me nostalgically about other pay parades in the south.

We were brought there to make a film describing in detail the technique of landing on enemy beaches by commandos. Then came Dieppe and it was such a shambles that the whole procedure had to be re-examined and we realised that whatever we did would be out of date by the time the film came out. So the whole project was abandoned and we were threatened with being returned to our own units.

I then had the idea, simply because I was closer to that situation than anyone else, that there should be a film shown to new recruits as they came into the Army to show that, however inhuman the Army seemed, it was still an organisation made up of human beings. So we did a forty-minute training film called *The New Lot*, based on the idea of a group of new recruits, who got to know each other while they learned the techniques of discipline and so on. Eventually they went to see a commercial film (a mock one) on their day off, in which Robert Donat, being extremely funny, led a charge in the 1914 war and was silhouetted on the skyline; and they all roared so much with laughter they were asked to leave the cinema. They realised how stupid that film was and that they were now different, they were trained.

From that forty-minute film, which was very highly approved of by the Army Council, Two Cities Films asked us to do a commercial film on the same basis, but on a much larger scale and starring David Niven. I was put on reserve for a while because, being still a private, I couldn't deal with generals, and I came out of the Army for about eight months and did *The Way Ahead*. We had the bright idea of putting at the end, instead of 'The End', 'The Beginning'. It came out on the day of the invasion of Normandy and was sensational. I was very upset at having to play a Moroccan, because they thought I didn't look English enough to play an Englishman, but at least I was out of the Army and able to travel to North Africa. Then I had to go back into the Army again, still as a private. The first thing that happened to me was that I was marched four miles to Dover Castle to see *The New Lot* – because I was a new recruit!

How, at twenty-five, did you come to be directing Ralph Richardson and Richard Attenborough in *School for Secrets*?
At twenty-five I thought they had left it rather late to ask me! *School for Secrets* was the idea of Del Giudice, a man who was a kind of Sancho Panza to J. Arthur Rank's Don Quixote. They didn't get on terribly well and I knew that he couldn't last, but at one time he was tremendously important. It was he who gave me that chance, although I did *School for Secrets*, which was a big success, for the Air Ministry really. They wanted to have something about radar which was on the same lines as *In Which We Serve* or *The Way Ahead*. I did all my research in uniform at RAF stations, often getting rooms which were reserved for visiting air marshals and having WAC corporals clean my shoes, and I was dressed as a private.

You mentioned the actors . . . I knew Dickie Attenborough very well because my first play had been done at the Arts Theatre just after he had made a great hit there in *Awake and Sing*. So we were great buddies at that time. Raymond Huntley had been in a play with my then-wife; he was a wonderful kind of sourpuss. He was also in *The New Lot*, playing a private and was very funny in it. I was always very fond of him. Ralph Richardson I was a little scared of. He was like a gigantic Pyrenean puppy who would put his paws on your shoulders and lick your face. I thought he was overdoing things while I was directing him but it turned out to be just him and was, as always, acceptable.

Were you under contract to Two Cities at this time?
The contract with Two Cities was verbal: we had an agreement with each other which was valid while Del Giudice lasted. He left following a terrible row. It's never gone on record but I remember that Rank was trying to do a deal with the Americans and it attracted enough American executives to awaken anybody's suspicion. I was sitting at a huge banquet given by Rank for these sleazy people at the Dorchester Hotel and, as Rank got up to speak, Frank Launder turned to me and said, 'Is this the face that lunched a thousand shits?'.

What do you think is the enduring appeal of your second film, *Vice Versa*, recently remade? Were

Peter Ustinov, Yvonne De Carlo and Mireille Perry in Ken Annakin's *Hotel Sahara*, 1951

you happy with the way your version turned out?
I am surprised at how well it has stood up. All I know is that when I watched it again recently, I couldn't remember, at one point, what came next, but I said to myself, 'If I were writing this today, the next line would be so-and-so', and strangely enough it was. My favourite author at the time was Linklater and it had his kind of quality, I thought. I was amazed at how convincing Anthony Newley was as someone with an old mind inside him; I thought he was rather better than Roger Livesey who somewhat overdid the infantile side. The business of the boy changing into the man without any apparent cuts involved a lot of split-screen stuff and we had to be very careful that everything matched.

What attracted you to the Linklater novel, *Private Angelo*?
I wanted to do a film absolutely in the countryside and, in that sense, I was ahead of everybody. I wanted to do an *affected* film, one without any incidental music; the music was all supplied by the village band from that particular Tuscan village, Trequanda, near Siena. It was all made on location. The British unions insisted we put a toilet there because of the low standard of local sanitary engineering. We built the toilet in the village, and it was unveiled by the priest who prayed to God to 'render our work fecund'. We used everything local except one or two English actors, including Marjorie Rhodes and James Robertson Justice. Maria Denis was a local girl we discovered; as far as I know she never filmed again.

Did Michael Anderson essentially direct you?
He's an old friend of mine and we've always got each other out of difficulties. I was in Michael Todd's office when [John] Farrow called to say that he couldn't do *Around the World in 80 Days*. This was really a conspiracy by the other film companies who did everything they could to bitch Michael Todd. I myself had a strange contract with 20th Century-Fox that pre-empted me from playing Detective Fixit in the film. Michael didn't know what to do, so I suggested that he try Micky Anderson and he ultimately did the film. Years later, I was having a kind of crisis and didn't know what I was going to do next, when Micky called up and asked me to play that old man in *Logan's Run*.

Your next two films offered you very solid character roles. What do you recall of working with Herbert Wilcox and Anna Neagle in *Odette*?
Herbert, with his inability to pronounce his 'r's', was a

very endearing character. He was like a guardian to her. I talked to her after he died and found her to have much more spirit than she displayed under his aegis, however good he was for her in other ways. I thought *Odette* was a good, functional film of the period, although I find it difficult to judge any film about the war because it always has the same kinds of biases in it. God knows, it's difficult today, but in those days it was damn near impossible because we had all got used to certain conditioned reflexes. At one point I even satirised the kind of scene that would happen between Dickie Attenborough and Jack Hawkins in a Naval film, where Jack would say 'That will be all, Bellamy', and Dickie would say 'Yes, thank you, sir'. Then he'd go to the door, turn, and say, 'And sir . . .', 'Yes?', 'Nothing, sir'.

In your next film, *Hotel Sahara*, you had the chance to work with a different approach to the problems of war.

Yes, that's what attracted me to it. I felt that war mystique needed a bit of debunking and ventilating. And that film gave me my one romantic triumph in films, in that I ended up with Yvonne De Carlo – apart from one other with Maggie Smith, but that was a more mature relationship! Yvonne had the reputation, through the press, of being the most beautiful woman in the world. She was a very simple girl who certainly didn't behave as if she were the most beautiful girl in the world. She was absolutely charming, very professional, and even rather giggly. She was very relaxed, and entered into the spirit of whatever was going on.

Why didn't you direct more films? The three you did direct in the 40s showed a quirky talent that British films could have used.

I'm never very much in vogue, I think that's the trouble. I felt the British film industry was barking up the wrong tree. They were trying to get advice from the Americans on how to break into the American market. This meant they got hold of some very third-rate American advisers to tell us how to do it, like how to develop mid-Atlantic accents so we could be understood. I opposed the tendency of trying to enter the American market with an amorphous, hybrid product. Then, for some reason, my career as an actor developed very quickly. I was asked to do *Quo Vadis* and suddenly there was no looking back in that line.

What do you recall of making spectacular films such as *Quo Vadis*, *The Egyptian* and *Spartacus* in America?

I think the Americans are the only people who can do ancient Roman films for the simple reason they are *like* the ancient Romans. If you go into the Chase National Bank to get a loan you are taken into a room with columns of gorgonzola and, in the middle of all this, the bank manager, his feet on the table, a furled flag and an eagle behind him, is saying, 'Why don't we go home and continue this conversation by the atrium and kick this idea around?'. It is the mixture of extreme relaxation, formality, and majesty, which Americans do terribly well.

Michael Curtiz really didn't know what he was talking about most of the time. With *The Egyptian*, I felt that I was on the set of a provincial company of *Aida* and the music hadn't arrived yet, so we were rehearsing the text! In fact, one day I came on the set and found him shooting on my stand-in by mistake.

Back in England you made *Beau Brummell*. Did you relish the role of the Prince Regent?

Yes, I rather enjoyed that role. It's a lovely period. Liz Taylor was very agreeable and Rosemary Harris, with whom I had a lot to do in the film, was excellent as Mrs Fitzherbert. The Royal Family was supposedly outraged by the film because it showed the Queen's great-great-grandfather trying to strangle her great-grandfather.

Were the 40s and 50s a key period in the British film industry?

Yes, but I would say this: the British film industry can never really be regarded as a consistent industry. It has a sudden blossoming of wonderful things that die again as the industry is absorbed by the Americans.

How's Chances?, *Get Your Man* (1934), *The Luck of the Irish*, *Smith's Wives* (1935), *All That Glitters*, *If I Were Rich*, *The Secret of Stamboul* (1936), *Keep Fit*, *The Last Adventurers* (1937), *I See Ice*, *Meet Mr Penny* (1938), *The Mind of Mr Reeder*, *All at Sea*, *Sons of the Sea*, *The Missing People*, *The Middle Watch*, *The Chinese Bungalow* (1939), *The Second Mrs Bush* (1940), *In Which We Serve* (1942), *This Happy Breed* (1944), *Vice Versa*, *The October Man* (1947), *Oliver Twist* (1948), *Last Holiday*, *Stage Fright*, *The Magnet* (1950), *The Magic Box*, *Encore* ('Winter Cruise') (1951), *Hunted*, *Meet Me Tonight* (1952), *Young Bess* (US), *Gilbert Harding Speaking of Murder* (1953), *The Rainbow Jacket*, *Lease of Life* (1954), *Cast a Dark Shadow* (1956), *Now and Forever* (1956), *The Horse's Mouth* (1958), *Tunes of Glory* (1960), *Greyfriars Bobby* (1961), *Lunch Hour* (1962), *80,000 Suspects*, *Dr Syn – Alias the Scarecrow* (1963), *Circus World* (US), *The Beauty Jungle*, *Bikini Paradise* (1964), *A Study in Terror*, *He Who Rides a Tiger* (1965), *The Witches* (1966), *A Taste of Excitement*, *Connecting Rooms* (1969), *The Virgin and the Gypsy*, *Scrooge* (1970), *The Ruling Class* (1971), *Night Crossing* (1982).

After a busy apprenticeship during the 30s, Kay Walsh twice co-starred with George Formby, as well as working with other now-forgotten comics. In 1942 she found real scope for her warmth and naturalness as an actress in *In Which We Serve*, for Noel Coward and David Lean. In the next Lean-Coward collaboration, *This Happy Breed*, she brought sympathetic understanding to the role of Queenie, the discontented daughter of the family who kicks over the traces. Though she greatly dislikes her performance as Nancy in *Oliver Twist* many have found it very affecting. Perhaps she moved too soon into character roles after that, but what a gallery of these she created – the sly housekeeper in Hitchcock's *Stage Fright*, the garrulous spinster in *Encore*, the frustrated vicar's wife in *Lease of Life*, and the shrewd and worldly Charlotte in *Cast a Dark Shadow*, to name but four. Wit, precision, and a capacity for making ordinariness significant were among her many strengths.

Interview date: June 1991.

You began as a dancer. Did you come from a theatrical background?

No, but I'd always danced. I can't remember a time when I didn't dance. My first memory of a public performance was when, aged three, I darted into Church Street, Chelsea and danced to a barrel organ.

Do you remember any of those 30s films with special affection or interest?

I remember all those 30s films with affection and fear. Affection because of the warm-hearted old pros Sandy Powell, Will Fyffe, Ernie Lotinga. Fear, because I broke out of the chorus at a time of appalling unemployment and presented myself as an actress. I had had no training and dreaded being rumbled.

Later in the 30s you made two films with George Formby, *Keep Fit* and *I See Ice*. Did you have experience of the formidable Mrs Formby?

The Formby films at Ealing were high-flying compared with the 'fit up' DIY quickies. But then Ealing Studio was a well established concern – Monty Banks, Gracie Fields, J.B. Priestley, Basil Dean, with his wife Victoria Hopper, brought comedies and classics to the screen with skill and first-class technicians. I particularly remember Jack Kitchin, a film editor, who simply made those Formby films move.

I didn't find Beryl Formby formidable. She and George had been a professional team for many years and I could understand that she felt rejected when these little blondes cavorted around her George and his ukulele. For me it was tough being under contract to Ealing for a year. I was happy when it came to an end, but Basil Dean persisted in thinking me talented. He had seen me in a play starring Victoria Hopper. He tested me and I was given a contract for a year – I was glad of the 'shoe leather'. My flatmate, David Lean, was still unemployed and we walked everywhere.

You did a lot of films during the 30s, did you have a good agent at this time?
No, I didn't have an agent. Agents are big business and I had nothing to sell. I'd spent desperate months, years knocking on doors; and they didn't always open.

Would you agree that the turning point in your career, the film that put you into the big time was *In Which We Serve*?
Yes, that film was a turning point, but it didn't put me, as you say 'into the big time'. I was never in the big time, and I don't remember ever wanting to *be* in the big time. I enjoyed working, just working.

What do you think of the way *In Which We Serve*

represented class distinctions in Britain at the time?
I don't agree that it represented class distinction in Britain in 1942. There were professional naval officers present to give technical advice to the actors, director and the producers, and they needed it. There were representatives from the upper deck and the lower deck, and that is the structure of the British navy. I can't imagine going to sea in a ship without it.

Your next film, *This Happy Breed*, in 1944, was again a Coward film. I thought your part was very significant for the way in which you are dissatisfied with being stuck in that class and wanting something more.
I never got over the wonder of working with Noel Coward. My part in *This Happy Breed* was a gift from him to me and to my then-husband David Lean. I played

John Mills and Kay Walsh in David Lean's *This Happy Breed*, 1944

Queenie Gibbons. The only difference between Queenie and me was that I would never have given in, would never have gone back home.

The credit on *Great Expectations* says 'written by David Lean, Ronald Neame, Anthony Havelock-Allan, with additional dialogue by Kay Walsh and Cecil McGivern'. How much can you remember about that?

I remember everything about *Great Expectations*, especially the loss of 'Trabb's Boy' – and many other jewels that had to go in order to fit standard film lengths. During my life with David Lean I had worked closely on scripts with him – the silent opening of *Oliver Twist*, the end of *Great Expectations* – and much besides. As an actress I was delighted to be given a writer's credit.

You didn't make another film appearance until 1947 when you did *Vice Versa* with Peter Ustinov. How do you remember that experience, playing an easy-going lady opposite Robert Livesey?

I went to the first day's rushes on *Vice Versa* and saw two wonderful wicked characters burst out on the screen – James Robertson Justice – his first film, and Anthony Newley, aged fifteen, another first. I telephoned David at Pinewood, where he was preparing *Oliver Twist* and doing dreadful things in the make-up room to Alfie Bass's face [to test him for the Dodger], and I said, 'I've got your Dodger'.

What do you recall of a film for Roy Baker called *The October Man*, playing the good-hearted Molly who gets murdered?

Another original face and voice burst forth in *The October Man* – Joan Greenwood, tiny Joan, we called her 'Half Pint', a true original.

I enjoyed Catherine Lacey's unpatronising performance as the landlady, too.

I could never believe that the silent woman I would pick up at 6 a.m. for our Denham call was the powerhouse of acting, Catherine Lacey. From a frivolous character in J.M. Barrie's *The Admirable Crichton*, to Schiller's *Mary Stuart*, to the agony of *The Trojan Women*, an actress to remember.

How much choice did you have about those many character parts in the 50s? I am (thinking particularly of the *Stage Fright* role, the very sympathetic housekeeper in Henry Cass's film *Last Holiday* with Alec Guinness, and the wonderful part in *Encore*.

Hitchcock gave me a good part in his not very good film *Stage Fright*. By now, I had met so many giants that I gave up thinking I was dreaming. Watching Marlene Dietrich tuck into the steak-and-kidney pudding in the canteen was something! By now, I had worked with some marvellous actors and the most lovable was Ted Ray with whom I did the 'Red Peppers' segment in *Meet Me Tonight*. I would have loved to have gone on the halls with him.

Directors I have enjoyed most are not always the best known – such as Don Sharp, a one-time actor and an Australian, I believe. Basil Dearden, Lewis Gilbert, Val Guest – these are directors who have made me feel, at the end of a difficult day, that I was not in the wrong box.

GOOGIE WITHERS:

The Girl in the Crowd, The Love Test (1934), *Windfall, Her Last Affaire, All at Sea, Dark World* (1935), *Crown vs Stevens, King of Hearts, She Knew What She Wanted, Accused, Crime Over London* (1936), *Pearls Bring Tears, Paradise for Two* (1937), *Paid in Error, If I Were Boss, Kate Plus Ten, Strange Boarders, Convict 99, The Lady Vanishes, You're the Doctor* (1938), *Murder in Soho, Trouble Brewing, The Gang's All Here, She Couldn't Say No* (1939), *Bulldog Sees It Through, Busman's Honeymoon* (1940), *Jeannie* (1941), *Back Room Boy, One of Our Aircraft is Missing, The Silver Fleet* (1942), *On Approval, They Came to a City* (1944), *Dead of Night, Pink String and Sealing Wax* (1945), *The Loves of Joanna Godden, It Always Rains on Sunday* (1947), *Miranda* (1948), *Once Upon a Dream, Traveller's Joy* (1949), *Night and the City* (1950), *White Corridors, The Magic Box* (1951), *Derby Day* (1952), *Devil on Horseback* (1954), *Port of Escape* (1956), *The Nickel Queen* (1971).

JOHN McCALLUM:

South West Pacific*, Joe Came Back*, A Son is Born, Australia is Like This* (1946), *Bush Christmas*, The Root of All Evil, The Loves of Joanna Godden, It Always Rains on Sunday* (1947), *The Calendar, Miranda* (1948), *A Boy, a Girl and a Bike, Traveller's Joy* (1949), *The Woman in Question* (1950), *Valley of the Eagles, The Magic Box, Lady Godiva Rides Again* (1951), *Derby Day, Trent's Last Case* (1952), *The Long Memory, Melba* (1953), *Devil on Horseback, Trouble in the Glen* (1954), *Port of Escape, Smiley* (1956). As Producer: *Three in Love* (1956), *They're a Weird Mob* (1966), *Nickel Queen* (+ dir) (1971), *Attack Force Z* (1978), *The Highest Honour* (1981).
* Commentary only.

There was nobody like Googie Withers in 40s British cinema. Throughout the 30s, she learnt her trade in 'quota quickies', several directed by Michael Powell who subsequently gave her her first big chances in *One of Our Aircraft is Missing* and *The Silver Fleet*. After holding her own against the formidable competition of Beatrice Lillie and Clive Brook in the delectable *On Approval*, she embarked on her great period with Ealing and this is where her individuality is most potently seen. Whether she is seducing Gordon Jackson in *Pink String and Sealing Wax* or proving a match for several men (including husband-to-be McCallum) in *The Loves of Joanna Godden* or jeopardising her marriage to help an ex-lover (McCallum again) in *It Always Rains on Sunday*, there is a marvellously confronting sensuality about her, a brazenness and authority that rivet the attention.

When John McCallum came to England in 1947, after brief experience of film-making in Australia, he quickly found himself in leading roles opposite Phyllis Calvert and Googie Withers. His best films are also the Ealing-made ones – *The Loves of Joanna Godden* and especially *It Always Rains on Sunday*. (The quality of Ealing and director Robert Hamer can be judged by comparing the latter with the McCallum-Withers episode in Herbert Wilcox's *Derby Day*: it is not that they perform less well, but that the whole enterprise lacks the Ealing point and rigour.) McCallum had other successes as a romantic leading man in *The Woman in Question* with Jean Kent, and in the entertaining satire *Lady Godiva Rides Again*.

Interview date: March 1990.

Miss Withers, during the 30s you were on stage seven times and made twenty-four films. Did this reflect your preference at the time?
My preference was for where the money and the work

were and, naturally, my agent [Picot Schooling] was pushing me like mad for films because you get great exposure from them. It was very good training for me. In those days they made 'quickie' films in three weeks. My first was an early Michael Powell film, called *The Girl in the Crowd*, and, however great a director Micky was, he was not a very easy man to work for. He used to say terrible things and upset people badly. I got on very well with him because I'm pretty tough – and was, even at that age. I can only say that he became a good friend of mine, because when Michael came up against someone he found he could not bully he respected them. I think he admired my acting talent; and he was the man who really started my career with *The Girl in the Crowd*, and *One of Our Aircraft Is Missing*.

He told me that he had a wonderful script and that, because I was half-Dutch and could speak Dutch, I would be perfect casting in the part. 'But', he said, 'the producers are terribly against you playing it because they say you have only played opposite comics like Will Hay'. They wouldn't take me seriously for the part, which had no comedy in it at all. I asked Micky if he thought I could do the part, and he said he was *quite* sure I could. He remembered me in *Her Last Affaire*, when I had to play a serious bit, realised I could play drama, and believed I would be very good in *One of Our Aircraft Is Missing*. I read the script and told him I would give anything to do it, because it would give me a jump into major films instead of little quickie comedies. So he persuaded the producers to let me do it.

I think that *One of Our Aircraft Is Missing* and *The Silver Fleet* were the two most 'understandable' films he made; they were true stories. Godfrey Tearle was one of the people who Michael was rude to, and Godfrey said nothing – he was *very* dignified, but I used to get very angry with Michael if he said anything I didn't like. He was very meticulous about what he wanted – from actors as well as everyone else. He used to *say* exactly what he wanted, but I sometimes wondered how much he knew about acting. Micky produced *The Silver Fleet*, but Vernon Sewell directed. Micky was there all the time; we saw all the rushes together, and it was Micky who decided what had to be re-taken.

I remember Ralph Richardson on that film – he was truly an adorable man, kind, funny and witty. He used to think up the most extraordinary things: for instance, in one scene, he had to say goodbye to me in the morning, knowing he would never see me again, but pretending that he would be home that evening; and he said 'I think it would be rather nice, Googie, if I brushed your hair'. I said, 'What!? I've just had my hair done and what on earth will I look like after ten takes, with you pulling it about?' 'Oh, just a thought', he said. The hairbrushing was in the film eventually.

One of your great strengths was that, on screen, you never looked like a stage actress.

That is probably because I had no proper theatre training except as a dancer. After I had made some films I started doing a play here and there. So probably I was bringing a film performance to the theatre, and just made it louder and funnier!

Did you feel you had a long apprenticeship throughout the 30s?

I've never really had to go after anything; I've just been offered things I've wanted to do. I didn't have any of that 30s studio grooming. Like many actresses, I did a film with George Formby at Ealing – *Trouble Brewing*. That was a saga because his wife, Beryl, was a terribly jealous woman and she used to organise every moment of his life. Apart from lines in the script, he wasn't allowed to speak to anybody, especially not a pretty young leading lady. And, of course, he always insisted on *having* pretty young leading ladies because it was good box-office. Beryl always sat on the set, and there was always the kiss at the end, to which Beryl, not the director, said 'Cut!', because the director might have let it go on two seconds longer! George was awfully clever, very funny. I learned technique from comics like him and Will Hay, who was wonderful but is pretty much forgotten these days. He was a very academic man, a comic by accident, I think.

No sooner had you established yourself as a star in the two Powell films, than you vanished for a year. Was this to do the Priestley play, *They Came to a City*?

Yes, for two years actually. I was thrilled to be asked to do it because I was known as a film star in those days and, when Binkie Beaumont (who ran H.M. Tennent) suggested me for the part, it was I suppose because I was a name. That was when I very nearly *changed* my name, because Binkie was horrified about putting my name up in lights. He tried to persuade me to change it before we opened in London. But, finally, I decided I couldn't bear to, told him I wouldn't, and pointed out that he had already signed the contract with me. He insisted nobody would be interested in someone called 'Googie' playing Lady Macbeth or whatever, and I pointed out that someone called Ginger Rogers was doing rather well despite her name. So, I did the play for two years and also did a film of it for Ealing. It was totally uncommercial. I don't know who Ealing imagined would be interested in it. *We* were all pleased because they were giving us a percentage of the profits but, of course, there were none!

How did you come to make *On Approval*?
A lot of funny things happened with that. We started off with Brian Desmond Hurst as director, but Clive Brook didn't see eye-to-eye with him at all. They had some awful rows. The film was finished and put on the shelf, then a few months later my agent told me that Clive was putting up his own money because he believed it would be a money-spinner and he wanted to cut a lot of it, redirect it and spend three weeks reshooting. I imagine he was responsible for that spoken prologue. So it was eventually released, got fabulous notices and went to America. Clive turned the film around and it was a great success. It was extraordinary casting; I mean, Bea Lillie was bizarre, she really was! She was hopeless to work *with* because she was too used to working on her own. She really was a marvellous performer, so funny, but she had to be a one-woman act.

I see the great period of your screen career as your time at Ealing. How was it as a place to work?
It was lovely – and they had the most wonderful directors. Charlie Frend, Charlie Crichton, Sandy Mackendrick. They were all such dear people and such fun. And Robert Hamer, if he had been alive today, would have wiped Micky Powell and all those other directors off the map. I did *Pink String and Sealing Wax*, *Dead of Night* and *It Always Rains on Sunday* with Robert. He threw his life away with drink. He was very sympathetic to work with; he knew what you wanted to do. He was not an actor but he understood actors, the way actors wanted to work, and he would give you your head and be patient. And that's what you want as an actress; you do it a few times, improving as you do so, and if a director is worth his salt he then knows where he can push you.

(John McCallum entered the room at this point in the conversation)

You came into British films around 1947. Was it a good time to be launching a career?
JMc: It was an extraordinary period. I was here [Australia] with Gladys Moncrieff in a musical comedy and they wanted me to go to New Zealand. I read in the paper, one day, that my old friend Trevor Howard had been an enormous success in a film called *Brief Encounter*, so I thought, 'If old Trevor can do this, why can't I? Better than going to New Zealand'. I'd had some small film

experience in Australia, so I packed my trunk and went to England. I had an agent in England from before the war, who suggested the part of a lawyer in *The Root of All Evil*. There was a shortage of actors then, and I got the part. The director, Brock Williams, asked me to test for a part in another film and I got the lead – I was staggered!

You worked with director Ralph Smart on *A Boy, a Girl and a Bike* in England. What do you remember of him?
JMc: I remember the film with affection and it had a lovely location in the Yorkshire Dales. A lot of the cast (Diana Dors, Honor Blackman, Barry Letts) were only in it for three or four days and there was a great pool of available talent then. Ralph became a good friend and he was a very funny man. He was fun to work with for a start; he didn't know much about acting, but he knew his camera. Of all the directors we have worked with, there are very few who are good with cameras *and* good with actors.

Is the cameraman almost as important as the director to an actor?
GW: It is for women. The first thing you ask is who's on the camera and who's lighting it.
JMc: Also, a lot of lighting cameramen actually direct the film, because many directors don't know much about camera. In fact, quite often a cameraman will go on to be a director. Mutz Greenbaum [a.k.a. Max Greene] used to say to Herbert Wilcox, 'You'd be better doing it this way, Herbert', and he would change the whole set-up. Greenbaum really directed most of Wilcox's films.

Did you feel you were being groomed as a leading man, given a star-building treatment?
JMc: Not really. They did that with young starlets in their Charm School (Diana Dors and Honor Blackman were in that) but they didn't say much to the men. You just went from one film to another; you were supposed to know your job. I think Rank Central Office did have some eye on promoting, and also, according to my contract, you could be farmed out for a profit. I made one or two outside films from which they got some money.
GW: We never came across J. Arthur Rank much. I don't think he cared for actors very much. He just put his money where he thought it would make the most for him. He had an interest in films, but he didn't have much interest in us. We were making money for him, but we never saw him.

John McCallum and Googie Withers in Robert Hamer's *It Always Rains on Sunday*, 1947

How do you compare the two studios you worked at in the 40s — Gainsborough and Ealing?

GW: Ealing was miles ahead of Gainsborough as a place to work. Gainsborough's Islington studios were abominable. To get there, you had to drive through slums. When you arrived, there was this awful old building and the dressing-rooms were dreadful. The make-up room was a box and the canteen food was uneatable. But Ealing was a little bit countrified, just off the Ealing Common — it was a house with gardens that had been made into studios.

JMc: It had a family atmosphere; if they liked you you were there forever. The directors were under contract so they were guaranteed a yearly salary — although it was a pittance. Michael [Balcon] paid them very little.

GW: He paid us *all* very little! But, at the same time, it was a fascinating place to go because there were some

extraordinarily clever people there. There was Robert Hamer, of course; and then there was Diana Morgan and Bobbie McDermott, her husband; [Monja] Danischewsky, Michael Relph, Sidney Cole, Charles Frend, Angus McPhail, and so on. They were extremely intelligent, very highbrow, and, at lunchtime in the canteen, they used to play the most extraordinary wordgames. And then there was always the evening at the pub over the way. They all went there and most of them got very, very drunk.

I had done five films there by then, so John and I were very 'in'. Mind you, there was something of the headmaster in Michael Balcon; we almost leapt to attention when he came in. He was a funny fellow, very sweet with us, but he was also a moralist — didn't like any hanky-panky, yet he had all these men around him getting terribly tight all over the place! I think he knew how

---

234

brilliant they were so he let them have their fun. Every single morning at 10.30 a.m. sharp he walked on to the set as the producer. Filming stopped, and we stood there while he watched a scene or two; we would all say 'Good morning, Michael', then he would go off again with a retinue of men behind him.

Your image in the 40s was extraordinary: nobody else was as bold, sensual and brazen as you were.

GW: I wasn't aware of it; something to do with my own personality, I suppose. I was very comfortable in *Pink String and Sealing Wax*; I loved those meaty parts. I didn't want, and never played, the 'genteel' parts, the English rose type. Maybe it has something to do with the fact that I'm not altogether English. My mother was a mixture of Dutch, French and German. It never occurred to me that I had that image, though.

Robert Hamer used to try very hard to get around the rule that you had to have one foot on the floor in a scene with a couple on a bed. Although in *It Always Rains on Sunday*, I was in bed with Edward Chapman (my husband in the film), reading the Sunday papers, we were almost fully dressed, with the covers pulled up. Sex was very understated in films, then, and your imagination took over, whereas now . . . I think it was *much* better when it was left to your imagination.

You were both in *It Always Rains on Sunday*. Were you very taken with that film then?

GW: It's always in retrospect that one sees how good they were. The thing that struck me then was that Bob said, 'I want to do this out in the streets where it all happens', so there was very little studio work. I think this was the first film to be made like that.

JMc: Because *It Always Rains on Sunday* is a group film, we didn't really know what was going on with the others – marvellous character actors who each contributed their own little stories. There were about four plots going on, but we didn't see them in the making. Bob was a perfectionist: he took five weeks to shoot that end sequence in the railway yard. We took awful risks – going under moving trains and running on top of them, things like that. The same lighting man, [Douglas] Slocombe, did all those films – *It Always Rains on Sunday*, *Pink String and Sealing Wax* and lots of other Ealing films of the period, and he has won an Oscar since. He didn't interfere in the direction as much as Max Greene did but, by God, he was good.

To jump a couple of years, what do you think of

***Derby Day*, in which you seemed to be doing a kind of watered-down re-run of *It Always Rains on Sunday*?**

GW: It was one of those fill-in things. John was under contract to Herbert Wilcox who thought it would be rather fun if I came along and played in the film with him. I don't think we were keen on it then, and I hate it when I see it now.

JMc: It was papered together compared with the other film and, of course, there is a vast difference between directors, between dear old Herbert and Robert Hamer! Herbert was a dear sweet man but . . .

GW: He used to break every day at 12 o'clock for a glass of champagne! I ask you!

JMc: He would do nothing in the mornings, just sort of work it out with Mutz [Max]; then came the champagne, and, by the end of the day, you had five minutes in the can and it was terrible stuff. But he was a showman: he had a nose for what subject to make. Also he was a very congenial man and could get immediately on side with the big American stars and persuade them to do things against their better judgment!

Rank was going downhill, not making many films, and Herbert kept going. He was a real terrier. Herbert was tied up with RKO and they eventually took him over. He set up his own independent production company, but went bust in the end.

He did two films with Orson Welles around this time. How directable was Welles?

JMc: Absolutely not. Orson took over entirely. At one point Herbert pointed to an empty sound stage, telling Orson to go over there and work out what he wanted to do while he, Wilcox, carried on without him. Welles had great presence and was wonderful in *Trent's Last Case*. For all that, he was a very selfish actor, and was very difficult for other actors to work with. I worked with him again on *Trouble in the Glen* and we got on very well, but he was one of those actors you act *against*, not with. I played Victor McLaglen's son and we were gypsies. We had a great time, but it was a dreadful film.

***Joanna Godden* was a charming film. Were you attracted to it at the time?**

GW: It was lovely, and we adored working on it. It was the most beautiful location, in the Romney Marshes, though unfortunately bad weather. But that meant we were there for three months instead of about three weeks. We were living in the most beautiful house, which belonged to a family who couldn't afford to keep it going; so they turned it into a sort of hotel taking twelve paying guests. They had, would you believe it, a cook and a butler called Neat and Tidy! It was an interesting film which pre-dated the feminist movement. Even now, when I am in that part of the world, elderly people often come up to me and say they were extras in the film. Once again Douglas Slocombe did the lighting on that – beautiful black-and-white photography. It was the only time I worked with Charles Frend, but we got on terribly well. He didn't spend much time with actors on their performances. He had been an editor, I believe, before he turned to directing.

You did that batch of three comedies at Gainsborough including *Miranda*, *Traveller's Joy* and *Once Upon a Dream*. Had the studio changed much now that Sydney Box was running it?
GW: No, it hadn't changed much.
JMc: Sydney became a good friend of ours. He was very fair, full of ideas and brought a lot of properties with him. He had a great success with *The Seventh Veil*. He did a lot of work with Ralph Smart; they used to do radio scripts together.
GW: Sydney's sister, Betty Box, produced *Miranda*. And *Once Upon a Dream* was quite extraordinary because Ralph Thomas was auditioned by *me*. Sydney told me he wanted Ralph to direct it but that, first, I was to do a scene with him and, if I liked him, they would give him the job! Since then, of course, he has become a very well-known director. When we went to work at Pinewood there wasn't really a head there. They were studios that were let out to various companies who worked there. Earl St. John was there in charge of the studios, but no one was really there as head.

I want to ask about a Pinewood film, *White Corridors*.
I adored that. I was determined to look as if I could hold a stethoscope and take someone's pulse, as if I was a surgeon. I went into Richmond Hospital every day for a month to watch people at work; I was taught how to give

injections, watched operations, and that sort of thing. We had a surgeon on the set with us the whole time, to make quite sure that what we did was correct. The film was largely made in the studio but we did do some work at Richmond Hospital, mainly exteriors.

Your nearest brush with Hollywood was making *Night and the City* for Fox. I'd have expected you to be drawn to the *films noirs* being made then.
The reason I didn't go to Hollywood was that I was married with a child in England. I liked working with Richard Widmark and with Jules Dassin, who was an amazing director. We worked all through the night in the slums in this film. Dassin was very good with actors but, of course, the original version was slashed and he wrote me long letters full of four-letter words about the censors who had cut so much of the film.

Gene Tierney was a very nice girl – poor thing later became seriously ill. There was none of that 'big-American-stars' act with her or Widmark. In the film, I was married to Francis L. Sullivan, and that was rather an unpleasant experience, principally because I'm a bit squeamish and he was very fat, and also sweated a lot. I had to put my arms around him and cuddle his head. He was an unhealthy man and all that sort of thing rather revolted me, but he was so dear that one could never let him know how one felt. Most of the men who played those Soho parts were the real thing; they had been picked out by Jules and were ponces, racketeers, very dangerous men most of them – but they just loved being in the film!

Did you feel that British films were running out of steam in the 50s?
JMc: Yes, they were. Rank had pulled out; they were losing money and weren't making many films – down from one hundred or so a year to about fifty or sixty.
GW: And people were either going to America or into television, or back to the theatre as we did. We simply found the theatre more congenial and we wanted to come back to Australia.

Sir John Woolf

As producer, with brother James Woolf, for Romulus or Remus Productions:
Pandora and the Flying Dutchman (1951), *The African Queen* (1952), *Moulin Rouge, Innocents in Paris, Beat the Devil* (1953), *Carrington, VC, The Good Die Young* (1954), *The Bespoke Overcoat, I Am a Camera* (1955), *Dry Rot, Sailor Beware!, Three Men in a Boat* (1956), *The Story of Esther Costello* (1957), *The Silent Enemy, Room at the Top* (1958), *Term of Trial, The L-Shaped Room* (1962), *Life at the Top* (1965).

As producer, alone:
Oliver! (1968), *Day of the Jackal* (1973), *The Odessa File* (1974).

It is always more difficult to obtain accurate credits for, and information about, producers than it is for directors or stars, perhaps because the producer's function is less clear-cut. It is even more difficult when the producers' names are subsumed in a production company's name as the Woolf brothers' names were in Romulus and, later, Remus Films. The Woolf brothers' distinctive contribution was to produce films genuinely international in appeal, but films which also brought credit to the British film industry. While they also made smaller, more parochially British films such as *Sailor Beware!*, their name – or that of Romulus – was really made with their first three Anglo-American productions, especially *The African Queen*, and with *Room at the Top*, the film which ushered in a new realist strain in British cinema.

Interview date: June 1990.

How did Romulus Films begin?

When I returned from the war at the end of 1945 I went back as joint managing director of General Film Distributors which had become a subsidiary of the Rank Organisation. I didn't enjoy being a small cog in a large wheel, so, in 1948, with my brother's help, I started Romulus Films (a production company) and Independent Film Distributors, financing a programme of British films. Independent started by putting up 70 per cent of the cost of a number of films, most of which weren't very successful. In fact, I started off as badly as my father [C.M. Woolf] had with General Film Distributors. My brother and I then decided to go into production ourselves, and that's how Romulus started.

I sent my brother to America at the time of the Un-American Activities Committee, when a number of directors and artistes wanted to leave America because they were being questioned by McCarthy and co. He went to California to look for interesting proposals to bring to England. The first one he found was *Pandora and the Flying Dutchman*, which was to be directed by Albert Lewin who was having trouble with the Un-American Activities Committee. He used to be a director for MGM which was going to make *Pandora*, but MGM cancelled it because of the political problems. So we brought Lewin to England to make the film with James Mason and Ava Gardner. That's what started us off with Anglo-American productions because British films were then very parochial – the best were the Ealing films and even they didn't sell in America.

Pandora wasn't all that successful, although it eventually covered its costs. It was a rather turgid film, but we didn't have much experience as film producers then. Lewin was actually the producer but it was made through Romulus Films and to that extent we were in charge of production. It was too long and I couldn't get Lewin to agree to cut it, but, in many ways, it was a brilliant film. For instance, that night bull-fighting scene was superbly shot and the opening shot, through the bell, had a very poetic quality. It was shot at Tossa del Mar, on the coast near Barcelona.

What was your experience of working with John Huston?

The book, *The African Queen*, was owned by Warner Brothers who had bought it for Bette Davis. At the time we became interested in it, John Huston thought he was going to be able to get Humphrey Bogart and Katharine Hepburn. Sam Spiegel was involved in it but his company didn't have the finance, so we undertook the finance, other than the American contribution. We signed Bogart, Hepburn, Huston and Spiegel, and Huston made the film magnificently, reliably, in time and under budget.

As far as I was concerned it was a very harmonious production, but Spiegel and Huston fell out because Sam was always short of money. When the unit was in Africa at the beginning of the film, Sam was supposed to have paid Huston and Bogart out of the American budget, but the money hadn't arrived and I think Huston got very fed up. In the end I had to give the guarantee of completion to the American bankers (Heller and Company) myself. So I took a huge risk with *The African Queen*, but fortunately it was an enormous success. Alexander Korda, who had been an old friend of my father's, warned me against a film 'about two old people going up and down a river in Africa, with a director whose last film was a disaster'. If it had failed, it would probably have been the end of Romulus, but it was the only film we ever made, apart from *Room at the Top*, which didn't get one single adverse criticism. Bogart won his one-and-only Oscar for his magnificent performance, and Hepburn was also nominated.

After he finished *The African Queen*, Huston didn't particularly want to go back to America and naturally we wanted to keep him in England. We had just read *Moulin Rouge*, by Pierre LaMure, and thought it would be a wonderful follow-up to *The African Queen*. I gave it to Huston to read, but he didn't want to do it. We nagged him until, eventually, he asked who we envisaged as Toulouse-Lautrec. We told him we thought Jose Ferrer would be perfect. Huston said that if we could get Ferrer he would think about it again. Ferrer loved the idea, so then Huston agreed to do the picture. The rest of the cast was gathered from all over. We were friendly with Zsa Zsa Gabor and she very much wanted to play the part of Jeanne Avril. Her singing was, of course, dubbed.

The film was not all plain sailing. We were shooting it in Technicolour, through gauzes and smoke to get that hazy effect, and after a month the Technicolour people met Huston, Ossie Morris, our cameraman, and me and said it was a disgrace, not the sort of thing they wanted

to put their name to. Elliott Elisofon was advising Huston and Morris on the use of colour because, in those days, Technicolour was very chocolate-boxy. It was a big international success, though it didn't get as good reviews as *The African Queen*. It won seven nominations and three Oscars, including colour photography!

What drew you to *Beat the Devil*?

Huston still wanted to stay in England and gave me a book called *Beat The Devil*, written by an Irishman named Claude Coburn. I didn't like it but John said he'd directed *Moulin Rouge* at my insistence, and in return I should back his judgment on *Beat the Devil* – it would be another *Maltese Falcon*. So I interested an Italian friend of mine, Robert Haggiag, in making the film as an Anglo-Italian production and it had a wonderful cast – Humphrey Bogart, Jennifer Jones, Robert Morley, Peter Lorre and Gina Lollobrigida – but it never had a proper script. It was being rewritten every day as we were shooting. It taught me a lesson and I never did that again. It was quite an amusing film and has, in fact, become a cult film in America. But at the time it was a disaster and, as Executive Producer, I was rather ashamed of it.

Just after that period, by which time we were well established, we were going to make *I Am a Camera*. The director, Henry Cornelius, and producer, Monja Danischewsky, wanted to do it on location in Berlin, rightly, because it was based on Christopher Isherwood's Berlin stories. At that time there was a freeze and we couldn't get any currency for overseas location work, so I went to see Alex Korda who was very pleased with the success of *Moulin Rouge*. He had a German film distribution company and I had given him *Moulin Rouge* to distribute there. I thought he would provide us with the Deutschmarks we needed. He had left British Lion by that time, and I had visions of him sitting in his office with nothing to do, being delighted to be back in association with us. Instead, when I walked in to his offices, he had with him Laurence Olivier, Carol Reed, David Lean, and his brother Zoltan Korda. I asked what he was doing and he said he was making four films – one with each of them!

By the time I left him I had forgotten all about having gone there to get marks to make *I Am a Camera* in Berlin. Instead, I found I was his partner and had put up half the money for his four films – more money than I had available! It was not far short of £1m which, in 1953, was a very considerable sum. However, Lloyds Bank backed my judgment as they always had done. The films were *Richard III*, *Summer Madness*, *A Kid for Two*

Lawrence Harvey in *Room at the Top*, 1958

Farthings, and *Storm Over the Nile*. Fortunately, all four films were successful.

You then made several smaller, more 'English' films . . .

There were two or three comedies, *Sailor Beware!* which was a big success, and *Dry Rot*. I had seen the play, *Sailor Beware!*, at the Connaught Theatre in Worthing with a marvellous funny actress, Peggy Mount, who of course also starred in the film. We then made *Innocents in Paris*, with a very good cast (Margaret Rutherford, Alastair Sim, Larry Harvey, and Claire Bloom). I remember flying over to Paris with the cast and Margaret Rutherford was sitting next to me. She saw the Eiffel Tower through the window and, with all her chins wobbling said, 'Oooh, lattice work!'.

Then there was *Three Men in a Boat* which we made at Henley – disastrous location, it never stopped raining. It was a funny film, but it wasn't successful except in England, and in Paris where it ran for nine months on the Champs Elysees.

Room at the Top *was a change of pace after these films . . .*

It was the first film on which my brother and I put our own names as producers. I was watching *Panorama* on television and Woodrow Wyatt was interviewing a group of housewives in Bradford about a book that their local librarian had written. It was called *Room at the Top* and the librarian was, of course, John Braine. They made the book sound quite sensational. I told my brother about it and we got hold of the galleys from the publishers. It obviously had two marvellous parts: for Laurence Harvey and Heather Sears, whom we had used in *The Story of Esther Costello*, and who were both under contract to us.

We acquired the film rights the next day for, I think,

£5,000. Jack Clayton, our Production Executive, who had always wanted to direct, had made a success of directing a short film I had given him, *The Bespoke Overcoat* (Oscar for Best Short Film), so we offered him *Room at the Top* to direct, having already cast it with Larry Harvey and Simone Signoret. (We'd tried to get Vivien Leigh, but she wasn't free.) Simone was marvellous and won an Oscar; Larry was also nominated.

At the time, did *Room at the Top* seem to be a breakthrough for British cinema?

I don't know if we realised that when we were making it, but we had turned the film over to the censor and it came back with a red slip – which meant they were turning it down. The only certificate they would give it was an 'X' certificate which had just replaced the 'H' (for Horror) certificate. So I rushed over to see Arthur Watkins and said I couldn't possibly accept an 'X' certificate; the Rank Organisation had announced they wouldn't play any 'X' films, so it would be a disaster. But Watkins said it was exactly the film they wanted to establish the 'X' certificate, and that it was a brilliant film.

So, we decided to try it out on an audience and had to find somewhere where 'X' certificate films were shown. We chose the Bruce Grove Cinema in Tottenham because they were showing *Dracula* and *Frankenstein*, two 'H' films which had become 'X' films. The audience booed at the showing and poor Jack Clayton was in tears, this being his first feature film. The audience, however, was annoyed that they had come to see *Frankenstein* and been fobbed off with social realism. Rank wouldn't play 'X' films; ABC wouldn't touch it unless they could see what happened after it opened. So I opened it at the Plaza, in central London, and it got rave reviews. On the strength of these, ABC agreed to book it. We had had nothing like those reviews since *The African Queen*, and the film was a great success all over the world.

Title Changes

The Admirable Crichton (UK)
Paradise Lagoon (US)

Albert R.N.
Break for Freedom

The Amorous Prawn
The Playgirl and the War Minister

Appointment with Venus
Island Rescue

Atlantic Ferry
Sons of the Sea

Background
Edge of Divorce

Barnacle Bill
All at Sea

The Battle of the River Plate
Pursuit of the Graf Spee

Beat Girl
Wild for Kicks

Before I Wake
Shadow of Fear

Beyond This Place
Web of Evidence/PO Box

Blind Date
Chance Meeting

Brighton Rock
Young Scarface

Britannia Mews
The Forbidden Street

The Card
The Promoter

Carleton-Browne of the F.O.
Man in a Cocked Hat

Carrington V.C.
Court Martial

Cone of Silence
Trouble in the Sky

Conflict of Wings
Fuss Over Feathers

Contraband
Blackout

Cottage to Let
Bombsight Stolen

Danger Within
Breakout

Dear Octopus
The Randolph Family

The Demi-Paradise
Adventure for Two

Derby Day
Four Against Fate

The Drum
Drums

English Without Tears
Her Man Gilbey

Fanny by Gaslight
Man of Evil

The First of the Few
Spitfire

The Foreman Went to France
Somewhere in France

49th Parallel
The Invaders

Freedom Radio
A Voice in the Night

Gaiety George
Showtime

Geordie
Wee Geordie

The Gift Horse	*Light up the Sky*
Glory at Sea	Skywatch
Gone to Earth	*Lilacs in the Spring*
The Wild Heart	Let's Make Up
Grand National Night	*London Belongs to Me*
Wicked Wife	Dulcimer Street
The Guinea Pig	*London Town*
The Outsider	My Heart Goes Crazy
The Happy Family	*The Long, the Short and the Tall*
Mr Lord Says No	Jungle Fighters
The High Bright Sun	*Love Story*
McGuire Go Home	A Lady Surrenders
Highly Dangerous	*The Man Who Watched Trains Go By*
Time Running Out	Paris Express
Hot Enough for June	*The Man Within*
Agent 8 3/4	The Smugglers
House of Secrets	*Mandy*
Triple Deception	The Crash of Silence
Hunted	*Manuela*
The Stranger in Between	Stowaway Girl
I See a Dark Stranger	*A Matter of Life and Death*
The Adventuress	Stairway to Heaven
Ice Cold in Alex	*Men of Two World*
Desert Attack	Witch Doctor
Ill Met by Moonlight	*The Million Pound Note*
Night Ambush	Man with a Million
The Kidnappers	*Morning Departure*
The Little Kidnappers	Operation Disaster
Knave of Hearts	*My Teenage Daughter*
Lover Boy	Teenage Bad Girl
The Late Edwina Black	*The Net*
Obsessed	Project M7
Life for Ruth	*Night of the Eagle*
Walk in the Shadow	Burn Witch Burn

Nor the Moon by Night
Elephant Gun

Northwest Frontier
Flame over India

Odd Man Out
Gang War

Once a Jolly Swagman
Maniacs on Wheels

The Passionate Friends
One Woman's Story

The Passionate Stranger
A Novel Affair

Perfect Strangers
Vacation from Marriage

Pimpernel Smith
Mister V

The Planter's Wife
Outpost in Malaya

Q Planes
Clouds over Europe

Quatermass and the Pit
Five Million Years to Earth

The Quatermass Experiment
The Creeping Unknown

Quatermass II
Enemy from Space

The Rake's Progress
Notorious Gentleman

Rockets Galore
Mad Little Island

The Romantic Age
Naughty Arlette

Rough Shoot
Shoot First

Sailor Beware!
Panic in the Parlor

Saraband for Dead Lovers
Saraband

Sea of Sand
Desert Patrol

Seagulls over Sorrento
Crest of the Wave

The Seekers
Land of Fury

The Ship That Died of Shame
P.T. Raiders

The Shop at Sly Corner
The Code of Scotland Yard

Singlehanded
Sailor of the King

The Small Back Room
Hour of Glory

The Smallest Show on Earth
Big Time Operators

The Small Voice
Hideout

The Sound Barrier
Breaking the Sound Barrier

South of Algiers
The Golden Mask

The Spy in Black
U-Boat 29

The Story of Esther Costello
The Golden Virgin

Street Corner
Both Sides of the Law

Summer of the Seventeenth Doll
Season of Passion

Taste of Fear Scream of Fear	*Went the Day Well?* 48 Hours
Tom Brown's Schooldays Adventures at Rugby	*Where No Vultures Fly* Ivory Hunter
Top Secret Mr Potts Goes to Moscow	*Whisky Galore* Tight Little Island
A Town Like Alice The Rape of Malaya	*White Cradle Inn* High Fury
Trottie True The Gay Lady	*Who Goes There?* The Passionate Sentry
Tudor Rose Nine Days a Queen	*The Woman in Question* Five Angles on Murder
Twenty Four Hours in a Woman's Life Affair in Monte Carlo	*The Woman with No Name* Her Panelled Door
Uncle Silas The Inheritance	*Yangtse Incident* Battle Hell
The Way Ahead Immortal Battalion	*Yield to the Night* Blonde Sinner
The Way to the Stars Johnny in the Clouds	*The Young Lovers* Chance Meeting

Green, Janet 29, 69, 96, 191
Green Man, The 60
Green Scarf, The 216
Greene, Graham 6, 8, 15, 34, 35, 112, 129
Greene, Max (Mutz Greenbaum) 32-3, 196, 197, 207, 233, 235
Greengage Summer, The 98
Greenwood, Joan 21, 124, 125, 193, 230
Greenwood, Walter 11
Gregson, John 16, 23, 88, 185, 200, 201
Gregson, Richard 67, 69, 86
Grenfell, Joyce 200, 218
Grierson, John 63, 95, 135, 138, 155
Griffiths, Hugh 4, 57
Guest, Val 105-8, 205, 230
Guinea Pig, The 13, 15, 16, 31, 34, 166-7
Guinness, Sir Alec 12, 66, 109-12, 118, 124-5, 126, 135, 137, 161, 168, 173, 174, 176, 177, 178, 185, 230
Gynt, Greta 23, 176
Gypsy and the Gentleman, The 186

Haffenden, Elizabeth 52, 103, 147
Haggiag, Robert 238
Hakim, André 178
Half a Sixpence 2
Halfway House 191
Ham, Harry 144
Hamer, Robert 57-8, 61, 111, 124, 135, 181, 231, 233, 234, 235
Hamilton, Guy 84, 85, 113-15
Hamlet (1969) 134
Hammond, Kay 117, 145, 175
Hanbury, Victor 30, 80
Hands of the Ripper 46
Hanley, Jimmy 26, 42, 198
Happy Ever After 62
Happy Family, The 40, 42
Happy-Go-Lovely 134
Happy is the Bride 32, 55
Hardwicke, Sir Cedric 168, 187, 188
Hare, Robertson 62, 188
Harris, Rosemary 227
Harris, Vernon 96
Harrison, Kathleen 6, 7, 90, 166, 199
Harrison, Rex 91, 103, 112, 117, 196
Harvey, Frank 32
Harvey, Laurence 43, 70, 77, 108, 133, 206, 240
Hasty Heart, The 217, 218, 219, 220
Hatter's Castle 151

Havelock-Allan, Sir Anthony 116-19, 124, 125-7, 175, 230
Hawkins, Jack 8, 20, 53, 85, 114, 193, 202, 227
Hay, Will 105, 232
Hayter, James 7
Hayworth, Rita 106
Headline 81
Heart of the Matter, The 129
Heavens Above 58
Hell Below Zero 84
Hell Drivers 160, 162
Hell is a City 105, 108
Hell is Sold Out 160, 161
Heller, Otto 115
Hellman, Marcel 92
Hello London 46
Helter Skelter 209
Henie, Sonja 46
Henrey, Bobby 45
Henry V (1945) 9, 10, 59-60, 125
Henson, Gladys 9, 45
Hepburn, Audrey 75
Hepburn, Katharine 180, 181, 238
Her Last Affaire 232
Herlie, Eileen 146, 200
Hicks, Sir Seymour 35
Hide and Seek 58
High Tide at Noon 70, 156
High Treason 32, 87
Highly Dangerous 19
Hiller, Dame Wendy 54, 91, 120-3, 174
Hillier, Erwin 220
Hinds, Anthony 107
Hinton, Mary 6
Hird, Thora 11, 42, 53
History of Mr Polly, The 169, 172
Hitchcock, Alfred 198, 213, 215, 217, 218, 228
Hobson, Valerie 22, 78, 104, 110, 116, 119, 124-7, 172, 177
Hobson's Choice 133, 169, 173
Holden, William 26
Holiday Camp 5, 6, 199
Holloway, Stanley 88, 117, 132
Holt, Seth 216
Home and Away 90
Homolka, Oscar 184
Hopper, Victoria 228
Hordern, Sir Michael 128-30
Horse's Mouth, The 174, 176, 178
Hostile Witness 133

Miles, Lord (Bernard) 32, 34, 35, 87, 142, 165, 166-8, 170, 175
Miles, Vera 114
Milland, Ray 101, 133
Millar, Sir Ronald 56
Miller, Mandy 53
Million Pound Note, The 3, 177
Millions Like Us 135, 136
Mills, Sir John 19, 21, 29, 104, 110, 112, 115, 126, 158, 168, 169-73, 174, 188, 229
Mills, Juliet 24
Mind Benders, The 193
Mine Own Executioner 79, 113
Minnelli, Vincente 178
Minney, R.J. 98
Miranda 6, 38, 210, 236
Mirror Crack'd, The 201
Miss London Ltd 147
Miss Pilgrim's Progress 106
Mitchell, Yvonne 206
Mix Me a Person 203
Moby Dick 168
Modesty Blaise 69
Mogambo 203
Montgomery, Douglass 141, 142
Moonfleet 104
Moonraker, The 205, 206-7
Moore, Kieron 23, 79
More, Kenneth 17, 39, 76, 94, 97, 98, 185, 201, 204, 210
Morgan, Diana 234
Morley, Annabel 123
Morley, Robert 8, 27, 39, 238
Morning Departure 18, 19, 61, 173
Morris, Oswald 238
Moseby, Carl 223
Moulin Rouge 238
Mount, Peggy 240
Mr Drake's Duck 106
Mr Emmanuel 91, 93
Mr Perrin and Mr Traill 80, 82, 99, 100, 101, 131, 133, 154
Mullen, Barbara 22, 91, 92
Murder in Reverse 198
Murdoch, Richard 51
Murray, Stephen 188, 212
My Brother Jonathan 74, 75-6, 79, 91, 93
My Brother's Keeper 60
My Gal Sal 106
My Teenage Daughter 205

Mycroft, Walter 188

Naismith, Laurence 21
Narizzano, Silvio 181
Neagle, Anna 3, 188, 205, 206, 226-7
Neal, Patricia 217
Neame, Ronald 84, 109, 118, 119, 121, 125, 134, 137, 173, 174-9, 230
Neff, Hildegarde 43
Negulesco, Jean 113
Net, The 160, 185
Never Let Go 220
New Lot, The 154, 225, 226
Newley, Anthony 226, 230
Newman, Nanette 86
Newman, Paul 29
Newton, Robert 121, 122, 151, 183, 184
Next of Kin, The 188, 189
Nicholson, Nora 3, 159
Nicholas Nickleby 168, 190
Night and the City 236
Night Boat to Dublin 183, 184
Night Invader 80
Night Mail 138
Night to Remember, A 18, 19, 20, 21
Nine Men 135, 139
Niven, David 212, 225
No Love for Johnnie 36, 39, 212
No Time for Tears 205, 206
No Trees in the Street 205
Nolbandov, Sergio 64
Nor the Moon by Night 5, 7, 8
Nordern, Christine 79, 197
North-by-Northwest 58
Nose Has It, The 106

Oberon, Merle 142, 218
O'Bryen, Bill 200
O'Connor, Una 2
October Man, The 18, 19, 21, 173, 230
Odd Man Out 44
Odette 206, 226-7
O'Ferrall, George More 216
Oh! What a Lovely War 22
Oliver, Anthony 106
Oliver Twist (1948) 109, 110-11, 116, 119, 176, 228, 230
Olivier, Lord (Laurence) 9, 10, 12, 59-60, 88, 98, 125, 143, 238
On Approval 233